SCRUTINY

A Quarterly Review

I

1932–33

CAMBRIDGE

AT THE UNIVERSITY PRESS

1963

PUBLISHED BY
THE SYNDICS OF THE CAMBRIDGE UNIVERSITY PRESS

Bentley House, 200 Euston Road, London, N.W.1
American Branch: 32 East 57th Street, New York 22, N.Y.
West African Office: P.O. Box 33, Ibadan, Nigeria

First issued quarterly at Cambridge 1932–53
Reissued in 20 volumes, with index 1963

Printed in the United States of America

Vol. 1. No. 1   MAY, 1932

SCRUTINY

A Quarterly Review

Edited by

L. C. KNIGHTS and DONALD CULVER.

CONTENTS

SCRUTINY : A MANIFESTO

THE first number of a review is not, of course, an ideal place in which to discuss the best Method of Conducting a Critical Journal. To do so provides openings for irony, and caution would suggest that we creep into print meekly. But such a course is impossible; the age is illiterate with periodicals and no ordinary reasons will excuse an addition to the swarm. Policy, as well as honesty, demands that if we imagine ourselves to have a valid reason for existence, we should state it.

The general dissolution of standards is a commonplace. Many profess to believe (though fewer seem to care) that the end of Western civilization is in sight. But perhaps even the Spenglerian formula, in its deterministic nonchalance, represents an emotional as much as an intellectual reaction; and if optimism is naïve, fatalism is not necessarily an intelligent attitude. Intelligence has an active function.

Those who are aware of the situation will be concerned to cultivate awareness, and will be actively concerned for standards. A review is necessary that combines criticism of literature with criticism of extra-literary activities. We take it as axiomatic that concern for standards of living implies concern for standards in the arts.

At this point we remind ourselves of the recent history of critical journalism. In England during the last two decades no serious critical journal has been able to survive in the form in which it was conceived; and how many have been able to survive in any form? *The Calendar of Letters,* which deserved the whole-hearted support of the educated, lasted less than three years. And more recently the *Nation,* itself the grave of the *Athenæum,* has suffered a euphemistic extinction. There are survivors, but they have for the most part steadily lowered their level of appeal. There is no need to describe the more blatant signs—gossiping essays, inferior criticism, competitions and crossword puzzles. In America there is the *Hound and Horn, The Symposium,* and the *New*

Republic, all of which remind us that America is not inhabited solely by Babbitts. The *New Republic* in particular combines literary criticism with sensitive attention to modern affairs. But these papers have no English counterparts, and the ordinary man receives far less help from the better-class journals and the critics than, in a civilized community, he has a right to expect.[1]

* * *

The reader will have gathered by now that *Scrutiny* is not to be a purely literary review. But what exactly, he may wonder, is meant by that hint of a generous interest in ' modern affairs ' at large? There are politics, for instance. Well, a devotion to them at the party level, is, no doubt, somewhere necessary. But something else is necessary—and prior : a play of the free intelligence upon the underlying issues. This is to desiderate a cultivated historical sense, a familiarity with the ' anthropological ' approach to contemporary civilization exemplified by *Middletown,* and a catholic apprehension of the humane values. When we say that the political ambition of *Scrutiny* is indicated here, we incur criticism from two sides : to the effect that our ambition is amusing, and that we are too remote from practice to interest anyone really alive to the plight of the world. As for the former criticism, a glance round at current journalism suggests that at any rate to be too ambitious will be something of a novel fault. As for the latter, the impotence of the practical mind to do anything essential in practice is being so thoroughly demonstrated that the retort needs no pressing.

Scrutiny, then, will be seriously preoccupied with the movement of modern civilization. And if we add that it will direct itself especially upon educational matters the reader will realize

---

[1] There is of course *The Criterion,* of which it is difficult to speak without respect. It is still the most serious as it is the most intelligent of our journals. But its high price, a certain tendency to substitute solemnity for seriousness, and, during the last two years, a narrowing of its interests, prevent it from influencing more than a small proportion of the reading public. It is necessary, but not the *unum necessarium.*

that there may, after all, be a fairly close approach to practice.

*   *   *

Where literary criticism is concerned we can be immediately practical and political. The first duty is to publish good criticism judiciously directed. And inseparable from this is a conscious critical policy, if anything is to be effected in the present state of culture. For to-day there are anti-highbrow publics and ' modernist ' publics, but there is no public of Common Readers with whom the critic can rejoice to concur. He cannot leave his standards to look after themselves. When Mr. Eliot's *Ash-Wednesday* appeared it received one intelligent review, in an American paper.[1] Mr. Empson's *Seven Types of Ambiguity* apparently caused nothing but bewilderment in the minds of nearly all its reviewers. On the other hand *Jew Süss* received a noisy welcome in the Press (' Everybody who respects himself has read it ' said Mr. Arnold Bennett); and *Dusty Answer* was said to ' reveal new possibilities for literature.' There is no need to multiply examples. They can be found in almost any number of the *Times Literary Supplement* (where at one time it was possible to find criticism), in the columns of the Sunday papers and elsewhere.

And when criticism defaults the loss is not merely the reader's. Of late years important works of art have appeared, serious books of criticism have been written, but their reception has been such as to discourage further production on the part of their creators, if not to make creation impossible; for in spite of the romantic conception of the poet as a bird (preferably a skylark) singing to please himself in glorious isolation, the artist does depend in large measure on the prevailing standard of taste. On occasions he may be able to ignore his age and its demands, but in the past the relation between artist and patron (the person or persons for whom he writes, builds, carves, etc.) has been of great importance in determining the use of talent. There is no reason to suppose that it will be otherwise in the future.

*   *   *

It goes without saying that for the majority neither the present

---

[1] By Allen Tate in the *Hound and Horn*.

drift of civilization nor the plight of the arts is a matter for much concern. It is true there are many who are interested in one or the other without seeing any connexion between them; but it is only a small minority for whom the arts are something more than a luxury product, who believe, in fact, that they are ' the storehouse of recorded values ' and, in consequence, that there is a necessary relationship between the quality of the individual's response to art and his general fitness for a humane existence. The trouble is not that such persons form a minority, but that they are scattered and unorganised. Every year, for instance, intelligent young men and women go down from the Universities and are swallowed by secondary and public schools. Their interests wilt in the atmosphere of the school common room, and isolation makes their efforts to keep themselves informed of ' the best that is known and thought in the world ' unnecessarily depressing and difficult. Others besides schoolmasters are in the same position. *Scrutiny* has been founded on the assumption that a magazine in which such men and women can exchange and refine their ideas, and which provides a focus of intellectual interests, will perform a service attempted by no other paper.

* * *

It would perhaps be wisest not to define the programme of *Scrutiny* too narrowly until intentions can be judged by performance. But if the case which we have outlined above is to be something more than a gesture of dissatisfaction, it is necessary that we should at least indicate the policy which we intend to follow.

Scrutiny will print critical articles on literature and the arts and on various significant aspects of contemporary life. In both these departments of criticism, analysis and interpretation will be with a view to judgment—from a standpoint which will have been made clear when one or two numbers have been published.

Besides essays in literary criticism, a few carefully selected books will be reviewed each quarter, of the sort that is so frequently passed over by the newspaper supplements and the monthly magazines, or inadequately treated. Occasionally there will be reviews of books which have appeared in the past and which have suffered an unjust disregard; and it may seem profitable to analyse certain popular successes. In each case consistent standards of criticism will be applied.

A pervasive interest of the magazine will find expression in disinterested surveys of some departments of modern life in an attempt to increase understanding of the way in which civilization is developing. In the collection of material it is hoped to secure the co-operation of readers who are in a favourable position for observation.

Related to this kind of analysis are the articles which we have planned on various aspects of education—the teaching of English in schools and universities, the training of teachers, and similar subjects. Traditional methods of education are being subjected at present to fairly rigorous criticism and a certain amount of overhauling; criticism which sees educational problems as part of the larger problem of general culture is, however, still necessary. To say that the life of a country is determined by its educational ideals is a commonplace; but it is a commonplace that is passively accepted more often than it is acted upon.

Scrutiny will also publish original compositions. Since, however, more people are able to write good criticism than good verse or short stories, we commit ourselves to no large or constant proportion of creative work.

In conclusion, we wish to make it clear that active co-operation from readers is invited. All contributions will be carefully considered, in order to make current the best of that kind of criticism which is now so often confined to isolated groups and private discussion. We have long been told that *les clercs* have betrayed their function. It would be more true to say that their voice cannot be heard above the confused noises made by the self-appointed sponsors of civilization. We do not know how long this will be so. Meanwhile the attempt is worth making to provide a focus of ideas and a centre of resistance for those who accept the case presented in this manifesto.

*   *   *

We have a critical policy. This does not mean that all articles printed in *Scrutiny* will be identical in outlook. In particular, the points of view of articles with immediate practical bearings may differ considerably from each other, and they will not necessarily coincide with editorial opinion. For instance, the reader need not draw from the essay on Public Schools any conclusions regarding our own attitude to them. We shall publish articles which—whether we agree with them entirely or not—are of intrinsic importance, which help to clear up current confusions and suggest a new approach to standards.

*   *   *

In the choice of paper, type and general format the editors have attempted to combine a minimum of expense with a maximum of reading matter. It remains for those who think that a review such as this is worth their support to guarantee their subscriptions to the editors, and (in place of the usual advertising, which we cannot afford) to make it known to others who may be interested.

A subscription form will be found inside the back cover.

No payment is made for contributions.

All communications should be addressed to: The Editors, 13, Leys Road, Cambridge, England.

A NOTE ON NOSTALGIA

ALL one can gather from the present day use of the word 'nostalgia' in criticism is that it confers on the user a kind of aloof superiority. 'Somewhat nostalgic,' says J. B. Trend of an article he reviewed in *The Criterion* last January, and a few pages further on another critic brings the same charge against Middleton Murry. E. Miller, the psycho-pathologist, makes a most sweeping generalisation on the relation between nostalgia and some forms of art: ' In so far as poetry in its lyrical manifestation is the nostalgic cry of the mind expressing its attitude towards nature, experience, and the inner self, it is *par excellence* the voice of the schizothymic temperament. . . This nostalgic background of all lyric art. . . ' [*Types of Mind and Body*, p. 100]. The word invariably conveys the same tone of slightly pitying disparagement, but what it implies beyond this vague attitude of the critic is seldom clear. Generally, of course, it is no more than a conveniently non-committal derogatory label. But even when the theme is developed a little no very precise meaning appears, although the potency of the word becomes impressive. Waldo Frank shows what can be done with it: ' The nostalgia of T. S. Eliot and Berlin (Irving Berlin, the songwriter) is feeble; it is the refrain, dissolved in our world of early nineteenth-century romantics (Musset and Nerval— Schubert and Robert Franz) ' [*The Re-discovery of America*, p. 131.] With nostalgia neither defined nor evaluated, utterances like this remain safely beyond the range of discussion.

Simple homesickness appears to be typically an aspect of social life. True, the ' home ' one yearns for comprises the whole familiar framework—objects and institutions as well as people— within which one lives and in dealing with which one possesses established habits and sentiments. (It was inevitable that Proust should record the experience: *Place Names* the second section of *Within a Budding Grove* has this for one of its explicit themes). Nevertheless, out of the whole framework, people are missed most.

And it seems probable that the comfort of familiar furniture and routine is only a substitute for, or a suggestion of, the sense of security given by membership of an adequate social group. It may be that a ' herd instinct ' has to be assumed to explain the fact that social life gives this satisfaction, but the assumption is questionable. All that seems indisputable is the obvious fact : that we do put high value upon the sharing and sanctioning by others of our interests, attitudes, and sentiments.

But the notion of ' others ' and the group in this sense needs to be examined. Being bound to other people by having any interest in common with them constitutes group membership of a sort. An explorer living with a primitive tribe and sharing their interest in food-seeking, means of shelter and what-not, is in some degree a member of the group. Nevertheless he is much more a member of his civilized group at home, for that group shares not only his primitive impulses but some at least of his more highly developed ways of behaving and feeling. To be fully adequate a group must not only offer fellowship in the everyday concern for simple comfort, physical and emotional; it must also be able to appraise the finer achievement of its members. Not that a genius must surround himself with equals before he can feel comfortable; simply that he and his group should recognise that his most advanced work is at least rooted in socially sanctioned evaluations. Loyalty to the group and satisfaction from it must both be incomplete for people whose deepest concerns appear to be unrelated to those of the group. And in everyday life the fundamental need for social backing is obscured by the necessity for constantly ignoring the standards of the group with which one happens to dwell, but of which one is not wholeheartedly a member. It is the frustrated desire for an adequate group that lies behind typically nostralgic writing.

Synge's *Aran Islands* illustrates the point admirably. Synge periodically fled from ' civilization ' to the primitive Aran islanders, seeing in their manners something more congenial to his own attitudes. Certainly they jarred on him less than did civilized people, but naturally they could give him no positive fellowship in his complex interests. He would have liked to think that their manner of living was the everyday manifestation of a rather highly developed culture, of what he calls ' the real spirit of the island. '

' Yet it is only in the intonation of a few sentences or some old fragment of melody that I catch the real spirit of the island, for in general the men sit together and talk with endless iteration of the tides and fish, and the price of kelp in Connemara.' He had abandoned one inadequate group for another, and he could find full fellowship in neither. His indictment of the civilized group after his return to the mainland is bitterly nostalgic. ' I have come out of an hotel full of tourists and commercial travellers, to stroll along the edge of Galway Bay, and look out in the direction of the islands. The sort of yearning I feel towards those lonely rocks is indescribably acute. This town that is usually so full of wild human interest, seems in my present mood a tawdry medley of all that is crudest in modern life. The nullity of the rich and the squalor of the poor give me the same pang of wondering disgust; yet the islands are fading already and I can hardly realise that the smell of the seaweed and the drone of the Atlantic are still moving round them.' His relief on taking flight is pathetic : ' It gave me a moment of exquisite satisfaction to find myself moving away from civilization in this crude canvas canoe that has served primitive races since man first went on the sea.' And his slight puzzled disappointment after sojourning with the primitive group points clearly to the social implication of his recurrent nostalgia : ' In some ways these men and women seem strangely far away from me. They have the same emotions that I have, and the animals have; yet I cannot talk to them when there is much to say, more than to the dog that whines beside me in a mountain fog. There is hardly an hour I am with them that I do not feel the shock of some inconceivable idea, and then again the shock of some vague emotion that is familiar to them and to me. On some days I feel this island as a perfect home and resting place; on other days I feel that I am a waif among the people. I can feel more with them than they can with me, and while I wander among them they like me sometimes, and laugh at me sometimes, yet never know what I am doing.'

Thomas Mann confirms the view that nostalgia is one outcome of incomplete membership of any social group when he describes lifelong nostalgia as the lot of Tonio Kröger, ' a *bourgeois* who strayed off into art, a bohemian who feels nostalgic yearnings for respectability, an artist with a bad conscience.'

It is obviously impossible to state in general terms the causes underlying a writer's failure to satisfy his social needs. Each case would need separate analysis. Certainly there is no universal circumstance that renders nostalgia inevitable. The contemporary flank-rubbing herd that highly-developed people can form at any one period is naturally small, but it has the advantage of a tradition extraordinarily rich and accessible compared with that of the main community.[1] And though the flank-rubbing herd is a necessity, yet the recorded feelings and attitudes of people no longer living are remarkably effective in sanctioning and confirming one's own ways of living. However, it conceals a complication to speak as if the group simply sanctioned, or failed to sanction, the individual's way of living. It demands of him some degree of submissiveness. Sanction can have no meaning without the admission that social disapproval would have been equally significant. The individual need not submit to any person or accept any formulated canon, but he must acknowledge that other people's experience is relevant to his own. From that there follows inevitably the progressive modification of his personality as he deepens his understanding of contemporary attitudes, and still more of tradition. That part of him that he considers unique grows smaller and smaller (and at the same time more and more significant) the more fully he comes to see his own experience in the light of other people's.

You tell me I am wrong.
Who are you, who is anybody to tell me I am wrong?
I am not wrong.

That was a typical attitude of D. H. Lawrence, so Richard Aldington suggests. It is an attitude that everyone who matters in the least must hold in reserve, for it represents the only way in which the conservatism of the group can be overcome, the only way in which changes can be made in contemporary life, and tradition extended. But with Lawrence it was a more or less permanent attitude. He seems to have wanted sanction, and nothing but sanction, for the whole of his personality, and so, inevitably, he cut himself off from the possibility of group life.

---

[1] The relation between the cultural tradition and different sections of the contemporary group deserves to be examined rather fully.

The yearning for a group remained. It showed itself in him, as it did in a less significant way in Synge, as a desperate experimenting with primitive peoples. Naturally none of the experiments gave him what he wanted. An air of fantasia marks those parts of *The Plumed Serpent* that describes the general, social re-creation of the religion; an air that is absent from the treatment of the individual characters' experiences. His need of a group is always present; he was never self-sufficient. He seems to have been one of those men who cannot add to a tradition without first wrecking it—who cannot co-operate. It is typical of such men to believe that the mass of humanity or the mass of a people would come to support their particular valuations if only it could be freed from some artificial overlay. Gordon Craig's writings present the same picture of rebellion with nostalgia, and it is this state, perhaps, that underlies his belief in the possibility of a ' people's theatre ' (if he still believes in it).

These are crude simplifications, however, and the evaluation of nostalgia in writing demands the most delicate perception of a writer's attitude to his experience. It can be said in general that complete absence of nostalgia in a modern writer is suspect, suggesting complacent fellowship with the main commercial group, or seclusion with an academic group, or life among the cliques, or too little questioning and testing of the tradition. But permanent, unresolved nostalgia is a failure too. In most cases, probably, it can be traced to a failure of discrimination in resisting social coercion. It is presumably impossible to achieve the knife-edge balancing between humility and servility, the insight to judge one's judges, that would be ideal in one's relation to a social group; and the temptation to reject everything, cliques, conventions, and tradition, baby and bath, is unfortunately strongest for the most vigorous personalities.

Another kind of writing, altogether distinct from that considered already, might seem to invite the description ' nostalgic,' for one thing because it frequently expresses the writer's longing for his home. The following poem which I quote from memory is an instance (it is attributed to Rudolph Valentino):

> All of them gift-books,
> But plainly I see
> Not one of them holds

The gift for me.
I want a book
That will lazily roam
Down the dear pathway
To folks back home.

Lawrence's poem *Piano* is another example at a different level. This kind of writing reveals no craving for the social sanctioning of the writer's adult and complex ways of living. It seems more closely related to the impulse to abandon these for a time and regress to a simpler level of life, at which one's needs were slight and their complete satisfaction comparatively easy. Every advance to more complex integrations of behaviour involves, of course, effort, and the tendency is always present to throw up the sponge and take things easily—to regress to the earlier and simpler organisations of impulses. J. T. MacCurdy points out that the welcoming of death as a rest and a sleep is one expression of the tendency: the underlying impulse is not to go forward to meet death, but to go back to a state of freedom from effort, a state which has been approximated to only in pre-natal life. ' If reality is difficult to endure, and if acute consciousness is developmentally connected with the recognition of external reality, and if contact with the environment is essentially a function of consciousness. . . then a most natural regression would appear with a dissolution of consciousness associated with some expression of return to the earlier type of existence. One would expect the latter to be formulated as ideas of death and, in fact, this is a universal phenomenon. Suicide is common, death is frequently portrayed as a release from life. . .' [*Problems in Dynamic Psychology* p. 158—159]. So Chaucer makes his old man, weary of living, say:

' And on the ground, which is my modres gate,
I knokke with my staf, both erly and late,
And seye, " leve moder, leet me in!
Lo, how I vanish, flesh, and blood, and skin!
Allas! when shul my bones been at reste? . . . " '

A clear example of verse expressing regressive impulses is provided by Edward Shanks in *The Grey Land* :

There was a man who loved a wood so well,
Each separate tree, each flower, each climbing weed,

That at the last he thither went to dwell
And mix himself with all those quiet things.
Then gradually left him thought and deed
And dead were all his soul's imaginings.
    So day by day,
All his own being gently flowed away
    And left him mixed indeed
    With flower and climbing weed,
With them in summer green, in autumn grey.
So the grey country calls me till I go
And make surrender of myself again;
The misty hill, the leaden stream below
Are waiting to receive me when I will.
And if my stubborn heart and hands complain
A slow wind moves upon the misty hill
And whispers to me here of peace and rest,
Of union with stone and grass and tree,
Where being sleeps and is not curst or blest,
Where hands can never feel and eyes not see,
    Where life and death alike are grey,
In this grey land that sucks my life away.

The underlying regressive tendency in this verse comes out clearly
in contrast with the following by T. S. Eliot:

Because I cannot drink
There, where trees flower, and springs flow, for there is
    nothing again

        .   .   .

Because I cannot hope to turn again

Consequently I rejoice, having to construct something
    Upon which to rejoice.

Rupert Brooke's poem *Retrospect* offers an example of regressive
verse in which the ' mother ' references are very prominent:

        O mother quiet, breasts of peace,
        Where love itself would faint and cease!
        O infinite deep I never knew,
        I would come back, come back to you,

Find you as a pool unstirred,
Kneel down by you, and never a word,
Lay my head, and nothing said,
In your hands, ungarlanded;
And a long watch you would keep;
And I should sleep, and I should sleep!

The fact of experiencing the tendency towards regression means nothing. It is the final attitude towards the experience that has to be evaluated, and in literature this attitude may be suggested only very subtly by means of the total context. In *The Grey Land* and in *Piano* the writer's attitude is clear. Shanks obviously finds a tranquil pleasure in the thought of throwing up the sponge. In Lawrence's poem the impulse seems to have been equally strong and is certainly expressed more forcefully, but the attitude is different. Lawrence is adult, stating the overwhelming strength of the impulse but reporting resistance to it and implying that resistance is better than yielding:

In spite of myself the insidious mastery of song
Betrays me back. . . . .
     The glamour
Of childish days is upon me, my manhood is cast
Down in the flood of remembrance, I weep like a child for
     the past.

There are of course several connecting links between regression and nostalgia. One is the likelihood that regressive tendencies will be especially strong in people who have found no adequate social group and tend to be nostalgic. Another is the fact that the longing for some remoter period than the present may unite both tendencies; regressive because the ideal period seems to have been free from difficulties that have to be met in the present, and nostalgic because the difficulties of the present are seldom unrelated to the difficulty of living with an uncongenial group.

The critical usefulness of an evaluation of nostalgia must rest on the possibility of detecting the feeling in a writer, and, here, unfortunately, definition and analysis are not much help. Everything depends on the reader's sensitiveness. One can say, however, that the word ought not to be used unless the quality of feeling to be described is recognisably similar to the common experience of homesickness: the feeling of distress for no localised, isolated cause, together with a feeling that one's environment is strange, and vaguely wrong and unacceptable. There is hardly a trace of this feeling—and it seems curious at first that there should not be—in Thomas Hardy's poems. Grief, regret, disappointment, remorse, are all to be found there, in their most poignant forms, but they have been felt only in situations in which they are generally recognised to be appropriate: the grief is for someone dead, the regret for neglected opportunities of living. There is no suggestion that Hardy was aware of isolation. The suspicion is unavoidable that his freedom from nostalgia implies too great a readiness to conform without question to the accepted canons of art and behaviour, and in line with this suspicion are the absence of significant technical innovations in his writing, and the fact (reported by Robert Graves) that he regarded *Marmion* as an indisputable standard in poetry. The account of his life by Mrs. Hardy reinforces the impression that he was never aware of isolation. One may quote in particular a letter he wrote to Alfred Noyes, severe, and full of surprise that such a man as Alfred Noyes should misinterpret his philosophy. ' It seems strange that I should have to remind a man of letters of what, I should have supposed, he would have known as well as I—of the very elementary rule of criticism that a writer's works should be judged as a whole, and not from picked passages that contradict them as a whole—.' Further in the letter he says, ' But it has always been my misfortune to presuppose a too intelligent reading public . . . " What a fool one must have been to write for such a public! " is the inevitable reflection at the end of one's life ' [*The Later Years of Thomas Hardy*, pp. 216-217]. This naïve exasperation at the end of his life strongly suggests that he somehow failed to see the impossibility of any genuine community between himself and the general public. His avoidance of public attention does not contradict this conclusion: he was still accepting a recognised niche in the public mind—that reserved for ' the secluded author '—just as Sir Basil Zaharoff and Mr. Montague Norman fit perfectly into the classificatory system of the public they shun.

No pervasive tendency to nostalgia is to be found in T. S. Eliot's poems, but its absence here obviously demands a different explanation. There can be no doubt of Mr. Eliot's awareness of the limitations of the group he lives amongst: *Triumphal March,* and *The Journey of the Magi* express clearly an attitude that is evident enough in most of his work.

> We returned to our places, these kingdoms,
> But no longer at ease here, in the old dispensation,
> With an alien people clutching their gods.

But the feeling of nostalgia is not pervasive, because the predicament it results from has been faced consciously and understood :

> I have heard the key
> Turn in the door once and turn once only
> We think of the key, each in his prison
> Thinking of the key, each confirms a prison
> Only at nightfall, aethereal rumours
> Revive for a moment a broken Coriolanus

His realisation of the inadequacy and misfortune of the ' independent ' man seems to underlie Mr. Eliot's insistence on the importance of a tradition and of the Church.

In Edward Thomas's poetry the feeling of nostalgia is pervasive.

> Never a word was spoken, not a thought
> Was thought, of what the look meant with the word
> ' Home ' as we walked and watched the sunset blurred.
> And then to me the word, only the word,
> ' Homesick,' as it were playfully occurred :
> No more.

> If I should ever more admit
> Than the mere word I could not endure it
> For a day longer: this captivity
> Must somehow come to an end, else I should be
> Another man, as often now I seem,
> Or this life be only an evil dream.

Occasionally, its social origin is suggested, as in a poem where he speaks of being ' born into this solitude,' and describes himself listening to the rain,

> . . . thus in sympathy
> Helpless among the living and the dead,
> Like a cold water among broken reeds

In most of the poems there is no recognition of any underlying social cause for his feeling. Yet the quality of the melancholy so often suggests nostalgia that it is hard not to suppose that the unadmitted craving for an adequate social group lay behind his most characteristic moods. Even when he describes his unhappiness as the inevitable outcome of his temperament there are social overtones still to be heard:

> Over all sorts of weather, men, and times,
> Aspens must shake their leaves and men may hear
> But need not listen, more than to my rhymes.
>
> Whatever wind blows, while they and I have leaves
> We cannot other than an aspen be
> That ceaselessly, unreasonably grieves,
> Or so men think who like a different tree.

It is symptomatic too that his happier and more satisfying moments are often associated with an escape from other people, as though normally he never felt free from the pressure of a social group with which he could make no satisfying contact.

> Once the name I gave to hours
> Like this was melancholy, when
> It was not happiness and powers
> Coming like exiles home again,
> And weaknesses quitting their bowers,
> Smiled and enjoyed, far off from men,
> Moments of everlastingness.

The same feature is evident in the poem, springing from a different mood that begins:

> Early one morning in May I set out,
> And nobody knew I was about.
> I'm bound away for ever,
> Away somewhere, away for ever.

It would be a mistake to complain because Edward Thomas refused to account for his moods and label them. But it is a defect that, through a failure to probe his unhappiness, he implied that its causes were remoter, less tangible and more inevitable than in fact they were. He seems to do this, for instance, in a characteristic poem called *Home*. The poem almost certainly springs from nostalgic feelings, but Edward Thomas gives them a much larger significance, larger than they deserve.

> Not the end: but there's nothing more.
> Sweet Summer and Winter rude
> I have loved, and friendship and love,
> The crowd and solitude:

> But I know them: I weary not;
> But all that they mean I know.
> I would go back again home
> Now. Yet how should I go?

One may even detect, what Thomas rarely betrays, the nostalgic's lack of genuine humility: ' all that they mean I know.' But he goes on to confess, not to nostalgia, but to the much more overwhelming doubt whether any life, once known, could satisfy him. It is well to remember that these, after all, are criticisms of what might have been only one phase of Edward Thomas's poetry. *The Other* (perhaps his most interesting poem) shows signs of a much more precise probing of experience that he usually attempted, and it is possible that he would have developed this kind of work. But of his existing body of poetry one may say that, though he does not avow it, there are signs everywhere of the predicament encountered by those who are isolated without being self-sufficient.

D. W. HARDING.

'THE LITERARY MIND'

M R. MAX EASTMAN, in the book[1] that bears the title at the head of this essay, presents an interesting case. It is of himself that I am thinking. For, while the case he propounds about ' the literary mind ' is too naïve and muddled in its complacent philistinism to be seriously discussed, he does indeed witness most impressively to the decay of literary culture. His book may be recommended as a representative document. He is ' intellectual and a poet,' he tells us. Yet he can point to the almost complete disappearance of serious critical journals in the last few decades as evidence that we have improved. They have disappeared, he thinks, because Science has put out of date the literary culture they represented. We know nowadays where to go for ' verified statements,' and those who contend that literature matters vitally to civilization ' are fighting for the right of literary men to talk loosely and yet be taken seriously in a scientific age.'

Now ' literary men '—moralizing dons, Humanists and others—have indeed been guilty of a great deal of ' loose talk.' But the critic who proposes to discuss a ' classical movement ' led by ' Allen Tate, Ezra Pound, T. S. Eliot, Ivor Winters, Edith Sitwell, Robert Graves, Laura Riding ' convicts himself of a looseness that dimisses him with the loosest. Anyone who offers such a list must be pronounced not to know what he is talking about. Mr. Eastman simply cannot see the difference in intellectual status between Mr. Eliot and Miss Sitwell, except that he finds Miss Sitwell more discussible. In poetry he positively prefers her. *Ash-Wednesday* he refers to as an ' oily puddle of emotional noises,' but ' Edith Sitwell is, in my opinion, the most gifted of the modernist poets.' The late Arnold Bennett, it will be remembered, had a like preference. The reason is simple : it is that Miss Sitwell is simple, and offers her admirers, with ' modernist ' garnishings, what they expect to find in poetry— sentimental reveries, reminiscences of childhood, and so on. For

---

[1]*The Literary Mind*. Max Eastman [Scribners. 10/6d.]

criticism she does not exist, either as a poet or a critic.

But no suspicion of his total incapacity troubles the assurance with which Mr. Eastman puts ' humane letters ' in their place. ' Modernist ' poetry is unintelligible, he explains, because ' Science has withdrawn intellect from literature,' and has left the poet nothing more serious to do than to engineer, as a defensive bluff, a ' revolt against meaningful language.' This innocent self-exposure, this complacent illiteracy, if it were merely amusing, would not be worth dwelling on. But what public can one count on to find it amusing? If one says that it is as absurd to defend as to attack ' modernist ' poetry—that there is no ' modernist ' poetry, but only two or three modern poets—what public will recognise a platitude? Mr. Eastman is an American, but here in England Mr. Eliot's poetry is explained over the wireless by Mr. Harold Nicolson, and our most intelligent weekly is, where literary criticism is concerned, a stronghold of anti-highbrow prejudice.

Mr. Eastman is right, though the case that he enforces is not what he intended: the tradition of literary culture is dead, or nearly so. If it was Science that killed it, it was not in the way that Mr. Eastman explains, but by being the engine of the social changes that have virtually broken continuity. The standards that, maintained in a living tradition, constituted a surer taste than any individual as such can pretend to, have gone with the tradition; there is now no centre and no authority, so that Mr. Eastman, Mr. Nicolson, Mr. Priestley or Mr. Walpole can assume authority without being in the eyes of the world ridiculous.

Mr. Eastman of course does not grieve over the loss, one of its manifestations being that he cannot realize it. For what I have spoken of as the literary tradition was more than literary, and it dissolution has bearings outside the field of mere adornment and amenity. To start with a limited and immediately pertinent one: what, as exhibited in *The Literary Mind,* is wrong with Mr. Eastman's *intelligence?*—That he is deficient in taste and sensibility is plain. My present point is that these deficiencies are associated with others of a kind that he could, perhaps, be brought to recognize. By a little analysis it should be possible to bring home to him that he is deficient on the side of intelligence. He maintains an air of incisiveness and intellectual rigour, but his writing is both loose (to use his own term) and blunt. Not only does he use such key words as ' experience,' ' interpretation ' and ' meaning ' with an uncritical looseness, but, apart from (or rather accentuated in) localizable confusions and fallacies, there is a pervasive debility, a lack of tension, outline and edge in his thinking. The point might be made by saying that he has none of that sensitiveness of intelligence without which all aparent vigour of thought is illusory. And when such a phrase as ' sensitiveness of intelligence ' suggests itself it begins to appear that the relation between ' intelligence ' and ' sensibility ' is not the simple distinction that is readily assumed.

In fact, Mr. Eastman's defect of sensibility is a defect of intelligence. This becomes plain if we say that he lacks fineness of perception, though there is a great deal more to be said. What we diagnose in expression, as inadequacy in the use of words, goes back to an inadequacy behind the words, an inadequacy of experience; a failure of something that should have pressed upon them and controlled them to sharp significance. Mr. Eastman does not offer himself, at any rate in *The Literary Mind,* as a poet, and so it is not required of him that his prose should evoke the concrete particulars of immediate experience. But his undertaking is such that without a fine sensibility, without a discriminating awareness, and without an ability to discern and fix differences of quality and degree, he is without his essential data. A certain fidelity to concrete particulars *is* required of him. And it may be hazarded of all thinking, however abstract, that is likely to interest those of us who are pre-occupied with the problems of living, that the criticism of it concerns its fidelity to concrete particulars, and the quality of these. No easy distinction between intelligence and sensibility comes to hand here. Of a good prose, in so far as it is abstract and general, it may be said that its virtues are a matter of the negative presence of the concrete and particular; it is not merely absence, but exclusion, an exclusion felt as a pressure. Exclusion implies a firm and subtle grasp; to exclude, the writer must have experienced, perceived and realized. Mr. Eliot is a major poet, and Mr. Eliot's prose is among the most finely and purely prosaic ever written; it is the efficient instrument of a fine critical intelligence.

The psychologist (if he bothered) might comment that to

attempt to pass off such terms as ' intelligence ' and "sensibility ' in this way, without analysis and definition, is an amusingly innocent and impotent procedure. The reader I have in mind may, while agreeing that my use of the terms is plain enough for my purpose, comment that a truism could be enunciated with less fuss. I hope in this essay to show why I think the point worth insisting on, and worth developing at this non-technical level, in spite of the risks.

To begin with, let the reader I have supposed recall the reception that any serious attempt to apply critical intelligence to poetry almost universally meets with. If the critic is complimented on being intelligent, it is commonly with the implication that he would be a better critic if he were less so : ' intelligent ' becomes, by an imperceptible transition, 'too intellectual.' The appreciation of poetry, we are told, is a matter of ' feeling ' or ' insight,' not of ' willed intellectual effort.' A related judgment is that the ' Cambridge School ' (whatever that may be) conceives poetry too much as a ' deliberate intellectual criticism of life.' I am not denying that certain wrong approaches to poetry may fairly be described as too intellectual (to err in such ways is to err by not being intelligent enough). My point is that any serious attempt to apply intelligence to poetry has to face prejudice against the ' intellectual ' approach.

The reception of Mr. Empson's *Seven Types of Ambiguity* [Chatto and Windus, 7/6d.] illustrated this. Reviewers who nerved themselves to tackle the book (it was shamefully neglected) commonly paid tribute to the author's remarkable intelligence, but contrived to suggest that it was employed, at the best, in an arduous and interesting, but gratuitous, form of exercise which had little bearing upon ' appreciation '; for those of us who are no good at mathematics and science, it would be hinted, there is still a field, requiring no cerebral tension, where we need not feel inferior. Now I will not deny that Mr. Empson's zest has sometimes kept him going too long and too ingeniously in the pursuit of ambiguities; but for the most part his analysis is simply the appropriate, critical, and very unusually efficient application of intelligence to poetry. Partly it is a matter of noting and registering with conscious attention what was implicit in our response. But also (and this is the report of everyone with whom I have discussed the book) Mr. Empson convicts us again and again of having missed something essential in the passages we thought we knew—of having failed to respond properly. It was an illusion that, though we might not be given to ' intellectual ' analysis, we were, as persons of taste, able to ' appreciate.' And was the deficiency in our response one of sensibility or intelligence?

' Intelligence ' is the word that, with my eye upon Mr. Max Eastman, I want at the moment to stress. Mr. Empson's book serves to bring home how largely and in what ways literary criticism is a matter of intelligence. The bearings of this conclusion upon Mr. Eastman's case are well brought out by this admirable passage from Mr. Ezra Pound's perverse but fruitfully provocative pamphlet *How to Read* [Desmond Harmsworth, 2/-] :

' Has literature a function in the state, in the aggregation of humans, in the republic, in the *res publica* . . . ? It has.

' . . . It has to do with the clarity and vigour of " any and every " thought and opinion. It has to do with maintaining the very cleanliness of the tools, the health of the very matter of thought itself. Save in the rare and limited instances of invention in the plastic arts, or in mathematics, the individual cannot think and communicate his thought, the governor and legislator cannot act effectively or frame his laws, without words, and the solidity and validity of these words is in the care of the damned and despised *literati*. When their work goes rotten—by that I do not mean when they express indecorous thoughts—but when their very medium, the very essence of their work, the application of word to thing goes rotten, i.e., becomes slushy and inexact, or excessive or bloated, the whole machinery of social and of individual thought and order goes to pot.'

This is well said. Literary criticism has a correspondingly high function, and literary study, so far from producing the ' literary mind ' conceived by Mr. Eastman, should be the best possible training for intelligence—for free, unspecialized, general intelligence, which there has never at any time been enough of, and which we are peculiarly in need of to-day. This is not to say that literary criticism should not be specialized, in the sense that its practice should be controlled by a strict conception of its special nature and methods. Indeed, the more one realizes its importance in the education of general intelligence, the more is one concerned for strictness of conception and practice.

But to demand such strictness in any field is to invite the charge of dogmatic intolerance and narrowness. It will not, for instance, do to refer as matter of commonplace to the almost complete absence of profitable Shakespeare criticism after two centuries of what must, for want of another word, be called critical activity. It may be said that, as a rule, the more respectable the critic the more deplorable the result: if, of the the academics, Bradley is the best, he is the worst. How long has Hamlet been down from Wittenberg? How many children had Lady Macbeth? Those *Appendices* of Bradley's are, perhaps, now commonly thought odd, and if they don't bring home the preposterousness of his approach (which is the orthodox), argument hardly will. There may sometimes be uses for the detective, psychological, moral, philosophical or acrostical approaches, but they are not literary criticism, and unless controlled by literary criticism they are vicious. Of course, where Shakespeare is concerned, literary criticism needs its auxiliaries[1], but it is still the essential approach; yet, though we have the auxiliaries, their *raison d'être* (for want of which they themselves are usually defective) hardly exists. The critical approach to a Shakespeare play will not consider it as primarily a pattern of characters (or persons), with their ' psychologies,' in action and interaction, but will remember that *we* form these by abstraction from Shakespeare's words—that he didn't create persons, but put words together—and it will apply this principle or truism in a strenuous critical method. This does not mean that the critic will not have to consider character, action and moral questions, but that his concern with these will be a relevant one and so profitable. Bradley's is, as a rule, more or less subtly irrelevant, and has little to do with the appreciation of Shakespeare. His method is not intelligent enough, and, to reverse my earlier stress, the defect of intelligence is a default on the part of sensibility; a failure to keep closely enough in touch with responses to particular arrangements of words.

---

[1] I find that Miss M. C. Bradbrook deals admirably with the issues raised here in her *Elizabethan Stage Conditions* [Cambridge University Press, 5/-].

The need for a strict conception of literary criticism and for a rigorous discipline in practice will perhaps be assented to as obvious where Shakespeare is concerned. Something that may be called in a respectable sense the ' literary mind '—a mind with a special literary training—is obviously in place here. It is equally so, if less obviously, in dealing with certain writers, poets or prose-artists, who are not pure artists, but invite the discussion of doctrine or ideas as such; by intelligence, that is, apart from sensibility, or apart, at any rate, from the trained sensibility of the literary critic. Wordsworth is an instance. He invites us to discuss his ' philosophy.' It is disastrous to accept. Or rather, the only profitable approach to the ' philosophy ' is by way of strict literary criticism. Arnold's word is perhaps even more apt than he intended; the philosophy is an illusion. It simply does not exist to be discussed as such. If you find anything to discuss, to a great extent you put it there yourself. ' To a great extent ' is a necessary concession: that Wordsworth *had* ideas is not an illusion. But the only way to fix anything for discussion in the shifting verbosities of his abstract ' thinking ' is to start from the concrete and never to lose touch with it. What is successful as poetry is obviously 'there'; its abstractable implications, or those encouraged by a general knowledge of Wordsworth, may be coaxed out as far as seems discreet into the Wordsworthian philosophic fog and the poetry made the solid nucleus for such organisation in terms of ' thought ' as seems worth attempting. But we ought never to forget that Wordsworth matters as a ' thinker ' only (if at all) because he is a poet.

The same rule and the consequent procedure apply to D. H. Lawrence, and in his case, perhaps, it will be more readily perceived that there is reason for insisting on them. For Lawrence's ' thought ' bears upon issues that are urgent to us and have been much in debate. He was a ' prophet,' but it is only because he was an artist of genius that his prophecy matters. But for that genius he would have demanded no more attention as a thinker than the mob of anthroposophists, Keyserlings, and hierophants of psycho-mythopœia. His gift lay, not in thinking, but in experiencing, and in fixing and evoking in words the feelings and perceptions that seemed to him most significant. Lawrence's commentary on experience, his doctrine, must be approached· by way of the concrete, the successful art; criticism of the doctrine cannot be separated from judgments concerning literary success or failure; discussion, to be intelligent, must be controlled by the critical sensibility. There is no other way of maintaining relevance, of fixing anything in Lawrence for examination, of ensuring that discussion or elucidation shall not be merely a matter of using Lawrence as an opportunity to expound something of one's own. I had insisted on this approach by literary criticism in an essay on Lawrence and so was gratified as well as depressed when Mr. Middleton Murry confirmed me. For, in writing *Son of Woman,* he was so interested in the doctrine and so convinced that he understood it and Lawrence that he did not trouble to apply such a discipline as I have contended for. And *Son of Woman* is another book about Mr. Middleton Murry. As such it is interesting. But it has the appearance of being a book about Lawrence and in so far as it passes for such it is vicious. However, perhaps the pervasive tone and the constant implication that Mr. Murry has the key and the measure—the Absolute—in his pocket, give warning enough to all but the simple-minded. But the book remains an apt illustration for my argument, and not the less so because when Mr. Murry does make judgments of literary criticism he shows himself, for one who has been so fine a critic, almost incredibly defective in sensibility. He says, for instance, of *The Plumed Serpent :* ' It is Lawrence's greatest work of " art." ' Now to the critical sensibility *The Plumed Serpent* is notable among Lawrence's novels for betraying by a certain strain, a falsity, a forced tone (capable of analysis), that Lawrence does not really feel what he wants to feel, that he does not believe what he is trying to believe. Here was an opportunity to open an indubitably relevant critique, which might in due course have pointed out, among other things, that the terrible monotony of *The Plumed Serpent* (this is not to deny the marks of genius in it) is a comment on Lawrence's prophecy. But whatever Mr. Murry's intelligence may have been doing, it was not a critic's sensibility he chose to employ here; and the defect of sensibility shows as a defect of intelligence.

It should now be plain that the ' literary mind '—the intelligence trained as it can be only in the study of literature— has work to do outside the field of literary ' appreciation.' Why, for instance, has the debate about ' Humanism ' been so depressing? The issues it handles belong to a realm where it is extremely difficult to do anything at all—to say anything that advances discussion; for the handling, intelligence of the kind indicated is an essential qualification. Its absence, the defect of sensibility, is manifested in the debile abstraction of that prose with which we are all too familiar. There may be no gross fallacies; but without a sustained, tense and living relation with the concrete, with the particulars of experience, the intellectual respectability and the erudition are barren. Many Humanists (and anti-Humanists) seem incapable of particular experience at all. D. H. Lawrence had a genius for it, and his importance as a ' thinker ' is that he could command the concrete by creative art. One does not criticize Humanists (or anti-Humanists) for lacking this gift. Their undertaking is not creative; but it does nevertheless demand a discriminating capacity for experience, and an ability to keep in close touch with the concrete by means of the critical intelligence. So it was a damning comment on Professor Irving Babbitt and his associates when, in a manifesto published in *The New Republic,* they were challenged to produce their record with regard to contemporary letters : it is, of course, one of complacent obtuseness.

We have in England erudite and laborious essayists who invite the same kind of comment. Mr. McEachran, for instance, is distinguished, not only by his comparative modesty of tone and his brevity, but also by the frankness with which he exhibits something like a complete lack of interest in literature, music and art. That he knows nothing of music he explicitly does not consider a disqualification, for he argues that it is better to be unmusical [see *The Civilized Man* pp. 132 ff.]. The plastic arts he does suppose himself to be interested in; but how complete an illusion this is may be gathered from his finding it possible to argue (the extraction does him no injustice) that ' because a civilized man is higher than a savage, a statue portraying him is a greater thing than a statue of a savage, however beautifully executed, and this because a civilized man is higher than a savage ' [*The Civilized Man* p. 117]. As for his degree of literary education, it is fairly suggested by the way in which he argues from *Faust :* ' The task of the second part, which from the point of view of poetry is inferior to it on the whole, was to fill out some of these defects [of the first part, which doesn't suit Mr. McEachran's argument at all] : to present Goethe's outlook as not finally diverse from the one we have said to be human ' [*The Civilized Man* p. 70]. The assumption that poetical inferiority has no bearing on the argument is characteristic of the type of thought : an abstract ' outlook ' that in its loose generality can be attributed to Goethe is all the writer is interested in. Here we have localized for inspection the pervasive weakness that makes such books as *The Civilized Man*, however erudite and careful, so barren and impotent.

Mr. Lawrence Hyde is a critic of Humanism, but his book, *The Prospects of Humanism*, exhibits the same weakness. He appears to be entirely without critical sensibility. He finds that, in the sphere of literature, ' there is a never-ending stream of biography, criticism, and fiction, all incredibly interesting and readable, all artistically produced, all written with a clearness, a vivacity, a subtle provocativeness, which makes them almost irresistible to any person of imagination and taste ' [*The Prospects of Humanism* p. 126]. He speaks of ' the remarkable amount of distinguished and sincere work which is appearing at the present time. The standard of execution is incredibly high; every month there appear a whole row of books, each of which represents the best which the talented author has in him (or her; particularly her) ' [*The Prospects of Humanism* p. 155]. This innocence is so amiable that one would rather not have had to point out how completely it damns Mr. Hyde as a thinker. It is not unrelated to the quality that enables him to discuss the ' thought ' of Mr. J. C. Powys seriously.

Then there is Mr. Montgomery Belgion, who is not amiable, but as ' a steady contributor ' to *The Criterion* (see April issue), insists on some notice. His function in the commonwealth, he feels, is to expose current confusions and fallacies by rigorous intellectual analysis; and it would not be difficult to expose Mr. Belgion's confusions and fallacies by the method he affects. But few sensitive readers of *The Human Parrot* will bother to do that; it is so plain that Mr. Belgion's is not a sensitive intelligence. He does not hazard himself much in the field of literary judgment, but he leaves no room for doubt about the quality of his critical sensibility. For all his air of nice precision his tools are soft and blunt.

I have already referred to the relation between Mr. Eliot's poetic gift and the quality of intelligence exhibited in his literary criticism. It is in place to note that the distinction of his intelligence appears as plainly when he applies it to general questions. Whether one agrees with him or not, it is impossible not to see that he is in a very different class from Professor Irving Babbitt and Messrs. McEachran, Hyde and Belgion: he really does something with his words.

But up to now I have narrowed the issue too much. To return to Mr. Max Eastman: in the deficiencies that we have discussed he does not, we see, stand alone; but in his attitude to Science he is, at this date, remarkable. Few scientists would make the claims for it that he does. He believes with implicit faith that it will settle all our problems for us. In short, he lives still in the age of H. G. Wells. ' And nobody,' he says scornfully, ' is going to consult humane letters about the mortal problems of our industrial civilization; he is going to consult sociology and economics.' But sociology and economics, if they are to be sciences, can give no adequate answer to the questions that are waived by that phrase, ' the standard of living,' as the economists use it. Our problems cannot be settled without reference to the ends of life, without decisions as to what kind of life is desirable, and it is an elementary fallacy to suppose that such decisions can be left to Science. But ' humane letters,' though they may have no authority in the province of ' certified facts,' have a good deal of authority in the question of what, in the long run, humanity its likely to find a satisfactory way of life. One way of indicating the deficiency as prophets of Mr. Bernard Shaw, Lord Russell and Mr. H. G. Wells (Mr. Eliot's disrespect towards them shocks Mr. Eastman) is to say that they have missed, or are incapable of, the education that can be got through ' humane letters.'

What I have in mind is no mere training of the individual sensibility such as, for the not incapable, a course of practical criticism could provide. Indeed, the problem cannot be adequately thought of as one of the ' culture ' of individuals. No doubt if Mr. Wells could read Shakespeare and had some knowledge of Dante his sense of value would be finer. But a concern for ' culture ' in that sense is inadequate to the issues. It is to the culture that transcends the individual as the language he

inherits transcends him that we come back; to the culture that
has decayed with tradition. The standards maintained in such a
tradition, I remarked near the beginning of this essay, constitute
a surer taste than any individual can pretend to. And it is not
merely a matter of literary taste. The culture in question, which is
not, indeed, identical with literary tradition but which will hardly
survive it, is a sense of relative value and a memory—such wisdom
as constitutes the residuum of the general experience. It lives
only in individuals, but individuals can live without it; and where
they are without it they do not know what they miss. And the
world, troubled as it is, is unaware of what is gone. So nearly
complete is the gap in cultural consciousness that to-day those
who win attention by their disinterested concern for the future of
the race are mostly of the type of Mr. Wells. Mr. A. L. Rowse's
Politics and the Younger Generation is representative. Though it
mentions most of the names that are current to-day as having
' culture ' value, it betrays an essential illiteracy; the author, that
is, in so far as reading means ability to approach literature, shows
that he cannot read. And to this illiteracy relates, in the ways
suggested, the blurred muddle of the writing, a certain unnecessary
grossness of manners and a disabling impercipience where the
problems of the ' standard of living ' are concerned.

To revive or replace a decayed tradition is a desperate
undertaking; the attempt may seem futile. But perhaps some
readers of *Scrutiny* will agree that no social or political movement
unrelated to such an attempt could engage one's faith and energy.
The more immediate conclusions would seem to bear upon
education. No one aware of the problem will entertain easy hopes,
for, inevitably, the machinery of education works in with the
process of the modern world; and in the absence of standards,
how can we start a reverse process? Something in the nature of
luck is needed; the luck, let us say, that provides a centre of
stimulus and a focus of energy at some university. All that falls
under the head of ' English ' there becomes, then, in spite of
Mr. H. G. Wells, of supreme importance.

Unhappily, the connotations of the term ' academic ' are of
ill augury: the concern for ' tradition ' that I have in mind will
not be that commonly associated with formal education. Everything must start from and be related to the training of sensibility,

that kind of training in which Mr. Richards has been a pioneer. Then with some hope the study of literary history—of periods, developments and relations—may be directed to producing a real grasp of the idea of living tradition. Sensibility and the idea of tradition—both concerns are essential. The latter is inseparable from the former; otherwise we have the academic sterility, the Humanist manipulation of the barren idea, the inability to conceive tradition as a matter of organic life. And no one could propose to foster the idea of living tradition by a study of literature that should ignore the present. It is when we come to the present that a serious interest in literature becomes inevitably something more; and a serious attempt of the kind under discussion would associate education in ' English ' with the study of the background of literature, its cultural and sociological conditions and bearings, present and past, of cultural history and so on.

As for the schools, it seems a particularly vicious waste that intelligent men should have to enter teaching as a *pis aller,* with little hope but to become spiritless tenders of the machine. That, for those who teach English, there is, or might be, a function commanding enthusiasm I have implied above. For the training of sensibility should begin at school, and would command in both teacher and pupils a deeper interest than Verity's notes. And a good deal might be done to cultivate a critical awareness of contemporary civilization. Many who have to make their living by the machine will smile sadly or cynically at these suggestions. And yet there are some opportunities. Even now, without the impulsion and support that I have desiderated and without good books, men are contriving to do valuable work on these lines.

An essay on the ' literary mind ' has developed, significantly (if I have not divagated), into this. The reader may smile at my portentousness. I do not, at any rate, suppose myself to have suggested a complete programme for the regeneration of mankind. My essay is an answer to the challenge represented by Mr. Eastman's book. As one devoted to the study and teaching of literature I have asked myself: why do I think this devotion, in an age of ' crises,' a worthy one? My answer, if not modest, is as honest and as serious as I can make it.

F. R. LEAVIS.

NOTES ON THE STYLE OF MRS. WOOLF

I N reading any of the later novels of Mrs. Woolf, a curious and persistent trick of style obtrudes itself on the attention.

' But for women, I thought, looking at the empty shelves, these difficulties are infinitely more formidable. . . '[1]

' The mind is certainly a very mysterious organ, I reflected, drawing in my head from the window, about which practically nothing is known. . . '[2]

' There is a coherence in things, a stability: something, she meant, is immune from change and shines out (she glanced at the window with its ripple of reflected light). Here, she felt, putting down the spoon, here was the still space that lies about the heart of things. . . '[3]

The first two passages are ratiocinative, the last a description of a mood. Yet the little asides serve the same purpose in all three: by stressing time and place, they deflate the statement: the affirmation is given a relative value only: neither the reader nor the writer is implicated: they are not trapped into any admissions, or required to endorse anything in more than a qualified way. The effect has been described by T. E. Hulme:

' The classical poet never forgets the finiteness, the limit of man. . . If you say an extravagant thing, there is always the impression of yourself standing outside it and not quite believing it.'

Mrs. Woolf refuses to be pinned down in this way, and consequently she is debarred from a narrative technique, since this implies a schema of values, or even from the direct presentation of powerful feelings or major situations. In *Mrs. Dalloway* the most powerful feelings depend on more powerful feelings long past: the old

---

[1]*Room of One's Own*, p. 79. [2]Ibid, p. 146. [3]*To the Lighthouse*, p. 164.

relationships between Clarissa, Peter, and Sally Seaton, the war experiences of Septimus Warren Smith. They are reflected, indirect, ' the reward of having cared for people. . . '[1] In *To the Lighthouse* the feelings are peripheral: they are minor manifestations of powerful forces: as for instance when Mrs. Ramsay reassures her husband on the terrace. The success of the book is due to the fact that the reader accepts the implication of the major forces behind the small situations. But even then the real nature of the subject is cloaked by Mrs. Woolf's method of description through a kind of metaphor which has a highly abstracting effect.

Whenever the direct presentation of powerful feelings or major situations is inescapable, Mrs. Woolf takes refuge in an embarrassing kind of nervous irony (as in the bracketed passages in *To the Lighthouse,* part two).

' This violent kind of disillusionment is usually to be expected of young men in the prime of life, sound in wind and limb, who will later become fathers of families and directors of banks.'[2]

' Here a girl for sale: there an old woman with only matches to offer.'[3]

' A shell exploded. Twenty or thirty young men were blown up in France, among them Andrew Ramsay, whose death, mercifully, was instantaneous.'[4]

That ' mercifully ' at least might have been spared.

For Doris Kilman and Charles Tansley (who are parallel figures) Mrs. Woolf reserves her heaviest satire. Miss Kilman's feelings for Elizabeth or Tansley's sensations at the dinner party are analysed with a brutality that is faintly discomforting. They are both devoid of the social sense, scholars who have developed the intelligence at the expense of the arts of living.

The heroines on the contrary live by their social sense: they are peculiarly sensitive to tone and atmosphere: they are in fact artists in the social medium, with other people's temperaments and moods as their materials. Mrs. Ramsay is the complement of Lily Briscoe, ' Mrs. Ramsay, saying *Life stand still here :* Mrs. Ramsay making of the moment something permanent (as in

---

[1]*Mrs. Dalloway,* p. 13.   [2]*Jacob's Room,* p. 247.   [3]Ibid, p. 132.
[4]*To The Lighthouse,* p. 207.

another sphere Lily herself tried to make of the moment something permanent). . . In the midst of chaos there was shape: this eternal passing and flowing was struck into stability. *Life stand still here*, Mrs. Ramsay said.'[1]

It is the arresting of a single ' moment,' a significant spot in the temporal sequence that is Art for Mrs. Ramsay and Mrs. Woolf. In *The Spot on the Wall*, Mrs. Woolf describes her technique, which is essentially static. A single moment is isolated and forms a unit for the sensibility to work on. The difficulty lies in relating the various moments. Intensity is the only criterion of a detached experience and there is a consequent tendency for everything to be equally intense in Mrs. Woolf's works. Everything receives the same slightly strained attention: the effect is not unlike that of tempera painting, where there is exquisite delicacy of colour, but no light and shade. (The connection of this with the refusal to assent to a statement absolutely is too obvious to need any stressing).

Mrs. Woolf's difficulties have always been structural. In *Jacob's Room* she hardly attempted a solution: in *Mrs. Dalloway* she began the rigid telescoping of the time sequence which was developed in *To the Lighthouse*. A series of echoes and cross references form the real framework of the book; they are of the kind Joyce had used in *Ulysses*, but there is nothing to correspond to the more bony support which in *Ulysses* is provided by the structure of the episodes. The precarious stability of *To the Lighthouse* dissolved into the muddle of *Orlando* (in any case a *jeu d'esprit*), and the futile counterpointing of *The Waves*.

Mrs. Woolf's books seem to be built up in a mosaic from the ' moments ': scenes, descriptions, odd names recur from time to time. Here is a typical case:

' Already the convolvulus moth was spinning over the flowers. Orange and purple, nasturtium and cherry pie, were washed into the twilight but the tobacco plant and the passion flower over which the great moths spun were white as china.'[2]

' How she loved the grey white moths spinning in and out, over the cherry pie, over the evening primroses.'[3]

Moll Pratt the flowerseller and the Reverend Edward Whittaker,

---

[1]Ibid, p. 249. [2]*Jacob's Room*, p. 90. [3]*Mrs. Dalloway*, p. 22.

figures who appear for a moment only, are in *Jacob's Room* and *Mrs. Dalloway;* and the Dalloways themselves are of course from *The Voyage Out.*

This kind of thing developed into the subtler correspondence between parts one and three of *To the Lighthouse,* as for instance, Cam's recollections of the stag's head.[1]

The significant moments, the units of Mrs. Woolf's style are either delicate records of the external scene, expressed in epigrammatic metaphor usually (' The whole platefuls of blue sea,' ' The dragon-fly paused and then shot its blue stitch further through the air ') or the presentation of a mood such as Mrs. Ramsay's reverie on the terrace.[2] These moods are hardly ever dramatic, i.e., bound by the limitations of the character who experiences them. The personality of Mrs. Ramsay on the terrace or of Mrs. Dalloway in her drawing room does not matter : neither their individuality nor the plot is of any relevance. The mood is in fact an isolated piece of pure recording, of a more complex kind but not essentially different from the epigrammatic metaphor. It is less an emotion than a sensation that is presented : the feeling is further depersonalized by Mrs. Woolf's use of metaphor : for instance in the description of Mr. Ramsay appealing to his wife.[3]

These two elements of Mrs. Woolf's style, the observation of the external world and the description of moods, are separated out in her last book, *The Waves.* The interchapters describe the movements of sun and tides (the sea is for Mrs. Woolf a symbol of the eternal and indifferent natural forces)[4] : this movement forms a kind of parallel to the development of the lives of the characters. But the effect of a page or two of epigrammatic metaphor is very fatiguing : the myopic observation, the lack of variations in the tension impose a strain on the reader. Sometimes phrase-making conquers accuracy : ' the lark peeled his clear ring of song and dropped it through the silent air ' suggests the long call of a blackbird, but hardly the trills and twitters of the lark.

In the main portion of the book, there are no solid characters, no clearly defined situations and no structure of feelings : merely sensation in the void. Without any connections of a vital sort

---

[1]*To the Lighthouse,* pp. 177 and 313. [2]Ibid, p. 29-30. [3]Ibid, p. 61.
[4]*Mrs. Dalloway,* p. 61; *To the Lighthouse,* p. 30.

between them, with no plot in the Aristotelian sense, the sensations are not interesting. Emotions are reduced to a description of their physical accompaniments: the attention is wholly peripheral. This for example is the equivalent of the experience of being in love:

' Then there is the being drawn out, eviscerated, spun like a spider's web, twisted in agony round a thorn: then a thunder clap of complete indifference: the light blown out: then the return of measureless inexpressable joy: certain fields seemed to glow green for ever.'[1]

There had been hints of this danger even in the earlier works: ' how could one express in words these emotions of the body? To want and not to have, sent up all her body a hardness, a hollowness, a strain.'[2] Physical sensations, which are immediately present, and have no relations to any schema of values, are all that Mrs. Woolf dares to assume in her readers.

All attempt to order and select has gone. 'There is nothing that one can fish up with a spoon, nothing that one can call an event. . . How impossible to order them rightly, to detach one separately or give the effect of the whole. . . Nevertheless, life is pleasant, life is tolerable. Monday is followed by Tuesday, then comes Wednesday.'[3]

Mrs. Woolf never, as is so frequently asserted, attempts to reproduce the process of thinking. Such generalized activity does not interest her: moreover, thinking implies a thesis which one is ready to defend. Mr. Ramsay, who is a philosopher, ' thinks ' with the most helpless particularity: the progress of human thought is symbolised for him by an alphabet, just as for Lily Briscoe, a large kitchen table stands for the mental pursuits of Mr. Ramsay himself. Their mental atmospheres are indistinguishable: and in both cases, the mood is not one of thought but of reverie.

The heroines are astonishingly ingenuous. Their tact and sensitiveness are preserved in a kind of intellectual vacuum. Mrs. Dalloway ' muddled Armenians and Turks: and to this day, ask her what the Equator was and she did not know.'[4] Mrs. Ramsay ponders ' A square root? What was that? Her sons knew. She

---

[1]*The Waves*, p. 274. [2]*To the Lighthouse*, pp. 274-5. [3]*The Waves*, pp. 280-2. Cf. *Monday or Tuesday*, her first attack on the problem of the time sequence. [4]*Mrs. Dalloway*, p. 185.

leant on them : on cubes and square roots : that was what they
were talking about. . . and the French system of land tenure. . .
She let it uphold her, this admirable fabric of the masculine
intelligence.'[1] Compare the dependence of Mrs. Flanders and even
of Lady Bruton.

The camouflage in *A Room of One's Own* serves the same
purpose as this nervous particularising : it prevents Mrs. Woolf
from committing the indelicacy of putting a case or the possibility
of her being accused of waving any kind of banner. The arguments
are clearly serious and personal and yet they are dramatised and
surrounded with all sorts of disguises to avoid an appearance of
argument.

The shrinking of the heroines is too conscious as the playfulness of *A Room of One's Own* is too laboured. To demand
' thinking ' from Mrs. Woolf is clearly illegitimate : but such a
deliberate repudiation of it and such a smoke screen of feminine
charm is surely to be deprecated. Mrs. Woolf has preserved her
extraordinary fineness and delicacy of perception at the cost of
some cerebral etiolation.

M. C. Bradbrook.

---

[1] *To the Lighthouse,* p. 164.

ON A GRAVE OF
THE   DROWNED

They whittle their life-stick who go
Down to the threshing jaws. Goodbye
To the smutty lamp, goodbyes are hoarse,
Disused. ' Draw the last pint! ' There in the
Oil-black bay the muttering nets, a gale
Blowing against the wet finger. Gull once a
W pencilled against the gray, now
Dismantled, maimed and set upon by friends:
Beaten off by bloody beaks, crunched feathers
Strike the shale ledges, wearily take
The backward, forward of the foam.

These went the watery bridge to know
Or numb, insurgent; on thole-pins spent
The dizzy creak of racked sinews and
Stalled with a thew-thrust, whipcord taut,
Jarring alarms that throbbed at ear
Passing bells of singing drowsiness.
Then glaucous eyes crammed full.

Above that mounded tale of many,
Disintegrated one, a beacon autumn tree
Irradiated from within swirls
Outward in eddies of russet light.

RONALD BOTTRALL.

THE POLITICAL BACKGROUND

S CRUTINY, I understand, is not primarily a political journal. It will not discuss party politics, nor the detailed methods of social or political reforms. But it will consider the broader political issues; and there it is surely right. For, in that larger sense, these determine everybody's life. When, therefore, I was asked to contribute an article to this first number, I thought I could not do better than say a few words about the political outlook, as it appears after the four years of war and the fourteen of what can hardly be called peace.

Peace and war, I will say to begin with, is still the main and dominant issue affecting everybody, whether they realise it or no, in the most intimate and personal way. For if another big war breaks out, as it might do almost at any moment, every young man of military age will be conscripted, and probably every woman too, and everyone not of military age will be expected to devote themselves to work bearing directly upon the war. The French have actually worked out a complete scheme on these lines, and quite possibly the English have too.

Now, thought it is only fourteen years after the close of the Great War, the danger of another is more obvious, and perhaps greater, than it was in 1914. Already indeed war has been waging in the Far East; and, though there is a temporary lull, there is no sign or probability of permanent peace. Nor is there any evidence that there is a real and genuine revolt against war in what is loosely called public opinion. The pacifists—too few to begin with—are divided among themselves on the great question of sanctions; and their influence suffers accordingly. Another minority, much more powerful than they, for it includes the officers of the army, navy and air force as well as a considerable body of laymen, is sceptical about the possibility, and even the desirability, of getting rid of war; while the mass of people is simply inattentive and indifferent. To illustrate the state of mind in this country, I will recall to your minds that, while Lord Cecil was doing his best at Geneva to stop the Far Eastern War, the Government at home was sanctioning the export of arms to extend and increase it; and this course of procedure was clearly approved by the bulk of public opinion. The same thing, of course, was going on, with the same frank cynicism, in France and in the United States, and no doubt in other countries. This one fact, to those who can reflect, throws a flood of light on the real character both of governments and of public opinion.

In England, nevertheless, there is, I should say, no active desire for war, merely the confused muddling which invariably leads to it. But it is very different on the continent of Europe. In Fascist Italy, the whole population, from the age of five upwards, is being militarised from top to bottom. Germany, driven to desperation by the treatment meted out to her during the last ten years, with an unemployed population of some seven million male adults, with a standard of life so low as to be hardly better than starvation, with the middle class practically destroyed and with an intellectual proletariat of something like a hundred thousand— Germany is in a state of desperation which is reflected in the enormous minority of Nazis and Communists at the recent presidential election and their successes in Prussia and other states. And the followers of Hitler, it must be remembered, have no constructive policy at all. They are a despairing mob, ready for any adventure, to whatever catastrophes it may lead. Then there is Bolshevist Russia, which, though it is the only state that stands for complete disarmament, is also convinced both of the necessity and the desirability of world revolution, and is devoting much of its energy to fostering that, all over the world, wherever it sees an opportunity, while China is quite likely to go Bolshevist in despair at its treatment by the League and the Powers—in which case, the Eastern War may easily be imported into the West.

This is a picture, not I think exaggerated, of the real condition of the world. What, if anything, is youth going to do about it? I cannot answer that question. I can only distinguish certain alternatives. There is, first, the view that it is no use to attack war directly, since it is the consequence of a whole complex of sentiments, passions, political and social conditions, and only a slow process of education and transformation can conjure it. That would be a view sound enough, if we had indefinite time to play about in. But, in view of the really imminent danger of war, we cannot afford to wait a hundred, or fifty, or twenty, or even ten years. A single war on the modern scale, with its necessary consequence, another bad peace, might very likely finish our civilization, either by a swift and therefore more merciful death, or by a slow and agonising consumption. Youth cannot afford to leave the problem of war alone and concentrate on other issues, in the hope that war will eliminate itself.

But if action is to be immediate, it can only take place through the activities, on the one hand, of the League of Nations, on the other, of the great Powers. I am not one of the many who hate or despise the League of Nations, but I recognise, as everyone else does, that it is very weak just because it is not supported anywhere by the bulk of public opinion. We are thrown back, therefore, on the great Powers; and that is a rather desperate recourse. At this moment the Disarmament Conference is meeting at Geneva, and disarmament is the crux of the whole matter. It is not only that the bigger the armaments the greater the danger to peace, though that is a self-evident proposition, and one which, for that very reason, those who desire war are eager to discredit. But also the failure of the Conference would mean the frank resumption of that anarchy of competitive armaments which led up to the war of 1914, and will lead as infallibly, and probably more rapidly, to another war—that will be indefinitely more destructive than the last. I need not dwell on these facts, which are perfectly well-known, to anyone who will take the trouble to learn, whether he be a militarist or a pacifist.

At the moment, therefore, the Disarmament Conference is the balance on which war and peace are being weighed; and two opposing attitudes confront one another. The British and Americans, acting apparently in harmony, are urging the abolition of certain types of weapon; while the French, pursuing consistently the policy they have adopted from the beginning, are insisting on an international force to be directed against an aggressor. This is the dilemma which has held up disarmament for the last ten years, and will hold it up again, unless it is somehow circumvented. We English are apt to think that we are plainly right on this issue, and the French plainly wrong. I do not agree. So long as we refuse any guarantee that we will assist the League to deal with an aggressor, so long the French, and by consequence all other states, will rely only on their own forces. What we ought to have done, I suggest, when M. Tardieu made his proposals, is this. We should have said to the French: ' Certainly! We are all for sanctions. But on condition that national forces be reduced to a mere police to preserve international order.' If the French, as we are apt to suppose, are merely bluffing, that would at least call their bluff. The British attitude in my opinion is, and always has been, mistaken. Nor is it really because we are more pacific than other nations that we refuse to commit ourselves to sanctions. It is because we want to keep a free hand, to go to war when we like and abstain when we like. That is the attitude of military and naval authorities, here and everywhere else; and the reason why we have never been able to move a step towards disarmament is that admiralties and war-offices are opposed to it, and governments and public opinion follow them like a lot of sheep, though the only place they can lead to is the steep place that plunges down into a sea of blood. You young men may or may not agree with this view, but you ought at least to have a view; for, if you are indifferent, you will pay the price of indifference with your lives.

The other great question to which you cannot afford to be indifferent is that of property. More young men, I suppose, than ever before, even in the better-to-do classes, are in a precarious economic situation; and in the 'working' class we have, in England alone, between two and three millions unemployed. And here it will be worth while for you to consider whether really, under the present economic system, there is any chance that the number of unemployed will ever be reduced, whether it must not, on the contrary, be continually and indefinitely increased. Anyone who wants new light on that subject should read a book by Alec Henderson, called *The Economic Consequences of Power Production,* and see if he knows the answer to it. But, putting aside that possibly questionable view, we have, even so, between two and three millions unemployed in England, seven millions in Germany;

even in France a number which begins to alarm that comparatively prosperous nation and a similar position in Italy; while, portent of portents, in the United States, hitherto regarded as the El Dorado of capitalism, more millions than can be computed are not merely out of work but starving, with the consequent imminence of a hunger revolution on a scale as yet unprecedented in history. That, surely, is enough to give anyone pause who may be inclined to suppose that our economic system is satisfactory.

If next one turns to the treatment of this problem by those who govern the world, and who belong, practically everywhere, to the capitalist classes, what have these governments done to deal with unemployment? Their one idea has been economy, and economy means, of necessity, the greatest sacrifices and hardships imposed on those who can least afford them. They have failed to see, or have preferred to ignore, the plain fact, that increased taxation, and consequent reduction of incomes, means fewer purchases, and therefore is injuring with one hand the industry it is endeavouring to help with the other. That the governments should perceive, what all intelligent economists now begin to assert, that it is spending not saving that is really wanted, would be expecting too much of them, but younger men it will seem, under the instruction of Mr. Keynes, are beginning to understand that point. All this, and much more, must be said from the merely domestic point of view. And when we turn from domestic to international issues the outlook is even worse. Every country is endeavouring to sell as much as it can and buy as little, with the result that international trade is gradually petering out, throttled by tariffs and currency restrictions. This is how Sir Arthur Salter in his recent book *Recovery* describes the position; and Sir Arthur is our best authority, and by no means a pessimist:—

' The defects of the capitalist system have been increasingly robbing it of its benefits. They are now threatening its existence. A period of depression and crisis is one in which its great merit, the expansion of productive capacity under the stimulus of competitive gain, seems wasted; and its main defect, an increasing inability to utilise productive capacity fully and to distribute what it produces tolerably, is seen at its worst. And, in the mood of desperation caused by impoverishment and unemployment, the challenge of another system becomes more formidable. No one can expect that even if we now get through without disaster, we can long avoid social disintegration and revolution on the widest scale if we have only a prospect of recurring depressions, perhaps of increasing violence.'

On the other hand, and here is the paradox, all this is only one side of the picture. Looked at from another angle, it changes to its own opposite; for, in this world which is in danger of perishing by its own incapacity, the production of wealth is continually increasing. The same science that is preparing, on the one hand, to destroy the world by war, is also furnishing the means to make it rich beyond the dreams of avarice, so that we are perishing in the midst of a plethora of abundance. Listen once more to Sir Arthur Salter summing up the facts: In 1925, he tells us, only seven years after the Great War with its immeasurable wastes and losses, world production had increased to 18% above the level of 1913; and by 1929 not only the world as a whole, but belligerent Europe had a substantially higher level of prosperity and average standard of living than in 1913. Figures, of course, being averages, are always deceptive, and in this world of increasing wealth the Chinese have been starving by millions. The fact, nevertheless, is that science has put within our hands, if we would but stretch them out to take it, all that we could possibly need in the way of material wealth. Why then do we not take advantage of our opportunities? The answer is because of our national passions, our class antagonisms, the lack of intelligence in our leaders of industry, and the general ignorance and indifference of our populations.

But now turn and look at another great fact. In one country and one only, Bolshevist Russia, the first attempt in history is being made, on a vast scale, to reconstruct society on the basis of the principle: ' He that will not work, neither shall he eat.' I need not elaborate the obvious qualifications which are necessary to convert that epigram into a political truth for the modern world. The term ' work,' of course, requires definition, and the exceptions, such as children, the sick and the old, require recognition. But the principle is sound, and I would suggest to the young that that too is a matter of the first importance to all of them, and not merely to those who are politically minded. What is wrong with Bolshevist Russia is not its goal, but its method, which is that of violence and dictatorship by a minority. Those evils, it is true, were forced upon Russia by the greater evil of the Czardom, and by the desperate efforts of the old régime, supported by this country, to overthrow the Revolution by force. That however, does not destroy and should not conceal, the significance of the Bolshevist Revolution. For Russia, in spite of agonies, cruelties and follies is blazing the path for the world. The economic system she is determined to establish is the right one; it is the means which she has been compelled to adopt that are wrong. The western world might, if it would, reach the same goal by a process less bloody and destructive. But for that we shall need the conviction and the work of the young.

I have selected as my theme these two issues, of war and capitalism, because they are plainly the great issues of our time, and because they must effect, directly and radically, every one whether a politician or no. They are no longer now what they might well have seemed when I was young, "academic." They stand here at the door, like Fates. Destruction or Salvation, and that not in some dim future but to-day or to-morrow, that is what politics, as I understand the matter, really means. Nor does politics exclude science, literature, art. Science in fact is a great political engine, working for good or for evil as it is directed by those who control society; and even if literature and art are held (wrongly I think) to be independent of all other interests, yet artists and writers are not. We really are, whether we like it or not, all members of one another, and that membership is one of the things *Scrutiny* can hardly avoid scrutinising.

G. Lowes Dickinson.

THE DEVELOPMENT OF
THE PUBLIC SCHOOL

I N the year 1500 the Italian *Relation of England* comments adversely upon the hardness of heart shown by the English in their treatment of their children, whom they used to send away, gentle and simple, to other families during what we should now call the school age, receiving other children in exchange; this practice they defended upon the grounds that it taught the children better manners. It is perhaps not fantastic to consider this belief as the root of our Public School system; certainly if we were to talk merely of instruction in class rooms there would be no reason to choose between boarding and day-schools, and if we attach to the word " manners " its former extensive meaning, we should find that the modern parent answers much as his predecessor did.

It is not my purpose in this essay to discuss the fascinating story of the remarkable growth of the Public Schools in the course of the 19th century; elsewhere in Europe the Renaissance foundations were overwhelmed by the tide of State Education, but in England they were re-edified with the result that to-day they stand as the one really powerful bulwark against bureaucratic instruction; this is a very important result, for educational progress is always made by local adaptation, by trial and experiment, by the creative work of individuals dealing with individual problems; it cannot be standardised. The achievement of this unique independence was largely the result of creating certain mechanisms by which the schools produced a type satisfactory to the Victorian middle classes; most of the institutions that are thought to be characteristic of the Public School, the Chapel, the Prefects, Compulsory Games, the O.T.C., for instance, are such 19th century mechanisms; and this is important, for the double problem of a boarding school is to make the school a satisfactory society to live in, and to relate this microcosm to Society in general. The problems of the microcosm itself alter little except in so far as the expedients used to solve them must be adapted to the changing Society, both as its changes effect the ideas and emotions of boys entering the school and as they affect the world they will have to live in.

Some of these changes appear in the expedients just mentioned; life in a Public School a century ago was chaotic, brutish, and violent, and Arnold used against it all the full fervour of his eschatological oratory—' The spirit of Elijah ' he said ' must ever precede the spirit of Christ '—and the full force of his mediaeval baronage, his prefects; later, after Darwinism had spread, we heard less of the Chapel as the centre of school life, more of the cricket-pavilion and of the excellent (pagan) tag ' Mens sana '; and later yet the O.T.C. appears as the adaptation for pre-war nationalism. In short, these means to producing a disciplined life varied as the idea of social duty varied, but their efficacy in each case depends upon the general views of Society. The Chapel played a very different part for the children of an age in which Mr. Gladstone classified people as ' Oncers ' or ' Twicers ' according to the number of their Sunday attendances at Church from that it can ever play for those whose parents usually attend no regular form of service at all; Mr. Gladstone had no need to classify any such. The O.T.C. had a different meaning in the period anticipating the War from any that it can have in a war-weary world. And, to take a different aspect of the problem, the value to a boy of prefectship in a chaotic and unruly school was very different from what it is in a civilised and orderly one; any feudal barony may become a mere privileged noblesse without function.

Yet the problems are basically always the same; it is the function of the school to be a half-way house between the home of one's parents and the home of one's own; to bridge the gap between sonship and parenthood, dependence and independence. The natural forces at work in the adolescent are invariable too, and the real meaning of the word " adult " remains permanent.

Regarding the schools for a moment as societies in themselves one sees in them a steady process of civilisation comparable to that which has occurred in the Middle Class itself; the change is from a Dickensian melodrama to Galsworthian comedy, and it has accompanied a change in social status, too, for just as the apothecary from whom Major Pendennis blushed to admit descent may now be Sir Horatio Bolus, Bart., or even Lord Bolus of Probe, so the little Grammar School has become the great Public School; and just as the aristocracy, headed by the Monarchy, became respectable, so the great Public School became bourgeois. With this general process of assimilation there has been a rapprochement of boys and masters that is, in its post war acceleration, the most important recent feature of Public School life.

Perhaps the most significant thing about this essay is that it has arrived so far without mentioning questions of curriculum; the important part of a Public School is its life, in which the boarder must contain all his emotions and feelings by the mere force of circumstance; he cannot, like the dayboy, regard his school life as a clerk regards his office life, as something extra to his real life at home. The comparison will serve to illuminate the difference of problems between the two sorts of school; Mr. Jones, the clerk, may be an excellent man, but to the office he is merely part of the mechanism for some specific purpose, his class-efficiency; the boarding school has to consider Jones as a whole, as a cell in an organism, and the curriculum is no more than a part of life in the school, and is governed by the living conditions. In practice the curricula of the two sorts of school differ little, but the importance attached to them differs considerably; in the Public Schools Latin is more generally taught; but in general the other secondary schools have drawn so much from the example of the Public Schools (as witness the spread of athleticism and institutions of various kinds) that in discussing curriculum the remarks are of general application; to point them at the Public School is nevertheless reasonable, for the Public School can initiate reforms if it will.

If the last century has established social order in the room of social chaos it has done the opposite to the curriculum. Arnold's dogmatic theology was in accord with the clear-cut and coherent classical world to which he limited the studies of the school, and the whole conception, however narrowed, had purpose and vital principle; his garden was formal, if you like, but it was decently arranged, and its false perspectives were harmoniously related; our modern curriculum lacks both unity of purpose and the vitality that springs from it; it is the *hortus siccus* of a collectionnaire, and as fair a museum specimen of it as anyone could require may be seen in the School Certificate, an examination that the Public Schools have, most regrettably, accepted—most regrettably, for here is just such an instrument as an increasingly bureaucratic and banausic system of education finds apt to its purpose, the standardisation of thought.

Nothing is easier than to cram boys through the different subjects of the School Certificate with an entire disregard of the educational values of each subject. This is hardly the fault of the examiners in the first place nor of the subjects of examination; it is partly inherent in the mere idea of a generally applicable examination to comprehend several academic subjects. The real villains of the piece are the headmasters who allow " Certificate forms " to exist, well knowing (for they are not fools) that the blandest assurances that results are not measured by certificates will not prevent the master responsible for the form from judging his own efficiency in that way, and who, knowing this to be so, take the certificate form as the standard up to which junior forms work and into which new intelligent boys are drafted. A cramming form may be a necessity, in view of the pathetic belief of the business world in such certificates; but it is criminal to make it the model for the rest. It should exist naked and ashamed on a bad eminence beside the main stream.

Sentimental traditionalism, however, has retained the form master, who was an excellent institution while the restricted range of the curriculum allowed him to take his boys in most subjects, but who is now largely a myth; if the school is organised in this way the tendency is to range forms above and below the School Certificate as x-1, x-2, and so on. Of course, if boys are rated in each subject purely on their ability in that subject they can take the Certificate with a short intensive course in the set books as soon as their different subjects come up to that level. This prevents the far too common absurdity of finding a boy whose ability in two subjects is spoiled by keeping him down in a low form because of his weakness in others; on the other hand it necessitates some authority other than the old form master to watch over the boy's general development. Before considering this question of organisation it will be as well to collate the different problems so far stated.

We are endeavouring to bridge the gap between childhood and parenthood, dependence and independence, irresponsibility and responsibility; certain mechanisms, the Chapel and the Prefectorial body, and their descendants, the compulsory games and the O.T.C., designed to adapt the boy to Society through his social life in the School, have lost force and application; on the other hand the School microcosm has been civilised, and the relations between boys and masters of the post-war generation are friendly to a degree hitherto unknown. The curriculum has lost unity of purpose in widening its field of application, and dogmatism has moved from the Chapel to the Laboratory.

The first obvious necessity is to find a unifying principle that shall relate life and learning, and there can only be one. This is to seek the truth; Arnold stated his truth; the Renaissance sought it in the past; Socrates and Jesus sought it in the minds and hearts of their fellows; but no living educational force can come to birth without passion for the truth, and it is precisely the absence of this passion that has sterilised our educational system as a whole, and has degraded our scholars to the level of performing animals and our teachers to ringmasters and sheep-tamers. A passion for accuracy produces only pedants.

There is really only one subject in education and that is life itself, and there is only one object of education, to live abundantly. But this splendid and exalted conception, this religion, that has inspired and united every creative movement of thought, has been fribbled away in one or another form of Pharisaism. The chair of my master has become of more importance than French thought and feeling, and good form has replaced goodness. The materials worked upon are treated as so much cloth that may be cut this way or that, à la mode, to conceal our nakedness or ignorance, so that the scholar is lapped in so many mufflers and shawls again the cold breath of reality on his heart, his solar plexus, and his genitals, and in that grotesque robe he cuts a fair enough figure; the sheep are not fed, but wrapped about to hide their leanness.

Yet the circumstances of Public School life are such as to make an education based on truth and the love of truth the most obvious in the world. Can any adult reader cast his mind back and recreate for himself the emotions, half realised, dimly apprehended in a hundred impulses, the anxious sense of personal achievement and growing force, that came upon him in puberty, the most intimate revolution and revelation that he was ever to experience? How great was his desire for reassurance, for the certainty that he was only as other men were, and how deep his longing for atonement with humanity; and in that uncertainty of a half-seen visionary future, how naturally he retreated from the newly significant, newly dangerous other sex into the herd of his fellows! It is upon this emotion that our system plays, reinforcing its anxieties by our fumbling evasions and embarrassed silences, though to the boy the two new adventures, his new self and his new school, will be inextricably linked, so that failure to solve the problems of the one will be linked with failure in the other. It is at that stage that we present him, too, to a herd so large that he may well shrink back in the fear that he can never win his way through anything so large. To such a boy the problem of entering the herd remains a permanent problem, for it cannot be solved by a regression to the methods of the nursery. Yet it is our first duty to bring him out of the family into the herd, and our second to bring him through the herd to individuality.

The most comprehensive solution would seem to be to group new boys in gangs of half a dozen or so, each to work during the first term almost entirely with its House Master, a system that would necessitate careful arrangement of entries; this first term would be devoted to the adaptation of the boy to school life, and to introducing him to the conception that education consists in living and in the study of life; this is open to different approaches, and naturally each master would have to be given considerable latitude in his handling of the problem. He would endeavour to ascertain where the boys' abilities and weaknesses lay so that he could draft him at the second term into the appropriate set for each subject that he was to study, but above all he would need to establish confidence in his own honesty, courage, and understanding, for it would be his duty to give the boy confidence in facing his own difficulties, backed by the knowledge that he would secure assistance when he needed it. It is quite obvious that this is no job for the average man in the schools to-day; it is well known, and reflected in the common derision of schoolmasters in such phrases as ' Those who can, do, those who can't, teach,' that a high percentage of school-masters are merely men who suffer from an inferiority-sense that forbids their competing with their fellows and urges them subconsciously to increase their stature by the master's dais and gown even when competing with children. Such an inferiority sense is commonly linked with a fantastic guilt-sense attached to sexual matters quite without relation to any responsible acts in the past or present, and based on childish experiences. It is worse than useless for such men, whose inferiority-sense may urge them to great industry and whose hunger for power may masquerade as a very plausible sympathy, to deal with the problems of adolescence until they have solved their own; they will only project their own fantasies into their pupils. Ideally, no doubt, such masters as we require should have proved their freedom by life in other spheres than school before appointment; at least they must have been brought to face their own characters; further, they must of course have a good range of subjects.

The House Master will of course continue to supervise his boys' progress after the first term, and he will also share with the Headmaster in what I will call the educational, as opposed to the academic part of the curriculum; for this part the boys would be grouped by psychological age, and it would be constructed to develop along the natural lines to accord with the needs of those ages. Thus in the earliest stages, in the first term and for some time later, competition would be between gangs rather than between individuals, so that the boy can find his individuality through his common activities; if he does not do this he lacks the confidence to compete alone except through childish vanity, or, if it is preferred, out of over-compensation for an inferiority sense. It can hardly be stressed too strongly that most boys who wish to stress their individuality at this age are over-compensating; their claim to be free of the herd arises from fear that it will destroy a fantasy picture of themselves in which they are unique as one can only be in the eyes of one's mother; they are tied to their mothers, and hence their cry for freedom and sympathy, for it is the slave who talks of liberty, the free man is not aware of it. Certain sorts of work are peculiarly suited to group handling, and specially those which require contributions from different subjects; naturally they want thinking out, but half a dozen men of intelligence and with clear ideas of their purpose could find plenty of material to employ several branches of the curriculum together, with full use of local advantages for historical matter, etc. Again, the intense preoccupation of the adolescent with the physical would be used; naturally boys, whose minds are very concrete, rate growth chiefly in physical terms, and growth is their main business in life; if you ask small boys what they mean by the phrase the " average man " the most common feature of their answers is that they give figures for height and weight. At present the most characteristic thing about our approach to science is that we begin by Inorganic Chemistry. A better approach would be by Biology, and an even better by Physiology, for the boy is absorbed in the problem of his own bodily growth; Biology seems to have been chosen by some because of its sexual value, which no doubt is great, but I think that a healthier approach would be more general, for most boys are as interested in their stomachs and their muscles as in anything sexual; to put it crudely, they like to see the works, and probably this would be a more direct and simple approach to the whole question of life, bearing too on general questions of health, than any other.

The later developments from this firm basis of self-realisation to the more abstract and ethical need hardly be sketched; from the " works " of the body to its " communications " in the nervous system and so to the whole question of thought and feeling is an obvious transference. From the gang to the gang-leader is equally so, and thence to a wider view of the whole question of conduct considered impersonally. Moreover, in this method of development we should merely be copying the story of racial development, and we have ready to hand in the institutions, religions, and people of the past ample material to suggest subject matter for use as illustration or inspiration. Nor need it be supposed that all this will seem extraordinary to the boy when he encounters it; he comes at an age when he is ripe for change and adventure, for widening horizons, and he expects his Public School to be different from his prep. school; he feels that he is, and in fact he is, a new person. That is why the first term is of such paramount importance, for he will either advance joyfully to assault the unknown or he will retreat from it; and he has two unknowns, his new self and his new environment, failure to deal with either of which will lead to failure with the other. So the work of the first term is to relate the two to the idea of successful growth. How often this is not done is shown by any anthology of Public School verse, in which one will find a preponderance of compensatory fantasy, whether of the rebel or the martyr pose. Such attitudes are not creative, for they are self-regarding; they do not spring from the impartial direction of the whole integrated man towards any object, but are the symbols of inward strife.

Throughout the object must be to show the boy that he is seeking the truth, and that his teachers do not fear the truth. In this a very big part will be played by the handling of his written English, which must come to be viewed as an expression of himself; if the boy writes a story he is in some way or another its hero; it cannot but be part of him; and in this way he soon gives an indication of his mentality and psyche; but there is more that can be done, apart from this, for nothing could be more significant than such things as failure to distinguish between " if " and " but," " I want " and " I will," when they are real habits of mind, and nothing could be more significant than the different pictures that boys will attach to such phrases as " power," " enterprise " and the like, all of which are things easily prepared for and observed in handling the general question of writing. This is all work for the first term, during which the master is in close enough contact to relate these observed traits to action; it can all be done very easily and naturally once the master is not scared of facing facts, when the boy will be ready enough to be absolutely frank and to be himself; of course the master's difficulty will be to see where the roots of a trouble lie at first, but he will find that the boy's mind has a directness that takes him there very quickly, and it is not difficult to show him how false associations between ideas and emotions lead to courses of action, or how his expression of ideas depends on his attitude to life in general, and how that attitude rests on his earlier life. This, he can feel, is truth in a real form, and one that means growth and progress; it relates thought to life, and when it is attached to the rest of the curriculum, as it obviously can be—witness the whole question of languages—there can be no question that the curriculum will appear in a new light. The advantages of such personal matters being touched by the routine of the first term is obvious; if you endeavoured to reassociate the ideas and emotions of only those who had obvious inferiority complexes, many as they are, the particularisation would only feed the complex. With the whole matter handled in the course of routine there is hardly any need to make use of psychological terms that can only be perplexing, and the adjustments can take place without the boy's realising that anything has happened.

Presumably there are those who fear that any handling of the truth leads to licentiousness; it is a view revealing a pitiful lack of faith in the eager spirit of youth that makes any such professor quite unworthy of the opportunity to wreck it. It is a belief that might have had more substance until masters and boys lived on such friendly terms as they do now, and it must be realised that the consequence of a first term that brought a boy so closely into contact with his house master would be a much closer relation than now exists; moreover we should have eliminated the master whose power complexes take the form of a dominating sympathy. In such a society the idea of gross and extensive licence is merely ludicrous. There is more substance in the criticism that the organisation would present difficulties, but they are by no means insuperable, and it is rather the value of finding a unifying principle than the local application that matters. To those who object that the early stages of the process are entirely self-regarding, it is necessary to reply that the boy of fourteen is not capable of being more obsessed than he is with the new problems of his own growth, which are really the first things to make him think seriously, for they are problems demanding a private moral code as opposed to the childish acceptance of what he is told to do; the prohibitions and stimuli of childhood relate to overt acts, but the new world of the adolescent has to be lived alone, and it is the school's job to assist him to do this; unless it succeeds he is certainly no person to have children of his own, for he will merely marry a mother-substitute and will be unable to inspire his own children with the virile confidence of independence.

No doubt these ideas will meet with little favour in the scholastic profession, for whose earnestness, complexes or no complexes, one has respect. That cannot be helped. There is not a lack of young men who think roughly on these lines. Perhaps the bitterest pill to the preachers will be the statement that egocentricity is right for the boy of fourteen, and that he must grow to altruism; Arnold, at least, realised the fact, for though he held out the ultimate ideal of the Christian gentleman he taught from pre-Christian history and ethics; you cannot be a gentleman until you are a man.

The chief weakness of our system as a whole is that it does not so much help as retard growth; it relates social prestige to physique, and its athletic ideal is not of permanent value, for nothing is worse than the athlete run to seed through absence of the strenuous activities of his school-days; it sets a premium upon compensation for the inferiority complex by encouraging academic success as a compensation for lack of self-respect. Such compensatory successes give us the scholars who flee reality; our presentation of learning is of an abstract and unreal world, flight to which is an obvious escape from what is felt to be real, but unpleasant—it may be an organ-inferiority, or it may have more intellectual roots and be described merely as a sense of inadequacy.

The errand-boy of seventeen who left school at fourteen is a better man than the undergraduate of twenty; he has been forced by circumstances to face the realities of his own nature and to realise what the specific functions of manhood are. Our conservatory tends to conserve childishness; for those who are fortunate enough to be nursed into the world the kill or cure process is not necessary, but we must admit the coarseness of adolescence with its Elizabethan vigour and fertility if we are to toughen the moral fibres and gain strength of character; refinement is a process applied to crude and coarse materials. The first step is to eliminate the mother-fixated schoolmaster; the second is to work out the possibilities of each individual school so that its life shall be a progressive revelation of the art of living, in which the intellect shall play its part as the frank servant of truth, and the curriculum show the way to a fuller life. Such a system cannot be built on negations or evasions; it must be affirmative, positive, and relatable to emotional and mental experience.

Genius, the creative mind, does not consist in abnormality of nature; the creative mind is centred as others are, but has a more comprehensive radius; what others apprehend dimly as touching the edge of their consciousness emotionally, the genius comprehends and can integrate with the rest of himself. Hence the universality of genius, by contrast to the particularity of the false individuality that is over-compensation—in which category much commonly called poetic must fall. Such apparently individual views are only unique in the eccentricity of their author; they state no more than any man knows, but distort it, and their interest is pathological.

Wholeness, by contrast with sickness, integrity by contrast with duplicity, are processes of perfection, that is, of growth; they cannot be acquired as personal properties, but must be cultivated. And this is not merely a matter of rational comprehension, for to believe in the truth of anything we must perceive it emotionally, especially if it concerns our own natures. It is not only foolish to set a reasoned system of prohibitions against unrelated emotional urges, it sets up a conflict between heart and head that leads to duplicity, and to the abandonment of thought for sensuality on the one hand, or the endeavour to live in the head alone on the other, that is unstable and untrue, that does not express the whole man as an individual, but lets first this side, then that seize control; this is the instability of the child, and it lacks the concentration of purpose required for any serious adult life.

I have purposely refrained from discussing the later applications of the main principle, partly because to go into the details would necessarily be lengthy, partly because any such endeavour to sketch a detailed system could only have local interest; it seems to be obvious that the applications of the principle must vary with conditions of staff, academic curriculum, and environment. This is particularly true of the phase towards the end of the school age when the boy emerges from his homosexuality and becomes heterosexual. But to embark upon this or the many other aspects of our problem would lead to interminable discussion, and they must be left to the reader's imagination; the first phase is the really important one. I shall be content if I have urged anyone to question the soundness of any system of education that does not consciously seek the truth and that does not satisfy its pupils that it does so : that question granted as legitimate and justifiable, I do not see what we can do but follow the natural lines of the boy's questioning spirit and seek to attach our curriculum to his real interests. He will work hard enough at the most tedious labours that have a discoverable purpose.

From time to time social forces make educational revolutions inevitable, as when Arnold seized his opportunity and in his moral reformation of the Public School produced the moral reformers that the Middle Class, coming to power, needed for its reformation of society; this was the opportunity created by the fall of the ancien régime and the Industrial Revolution. A comparable change has occurred since the War shattered the Edwardian society. The class from which the Public Schools are recruited is no longer really a middle class as the disappearance of Liberalism testifies; it has gained economic security and a place with the rulers, and with this has come the possibility of independence, which is the virtue of aristocracy; the specifically bourgeois virtues of complaisance, safety, the golden mean, are not really adequate to the children of more emancipated parents, nor are they adequate to the part those children should play later as enlightened citizens; a stronger, freer-minded aristocracy is needed, and unless the Public School creates it it will deservedly die of atrophy, for it must justify the social privileges gained in the past by present function. The alternative is the complete subordination of our educational system to bureaucratic control, with all that is implied by mass-production and the exaltation of certificates and diplomas to be pursued most successfully by those compensating for inadequacy to any real test of virtue.

That virtue is the real object which justifies this expensive form of education is a truism; it cannot be conferred by the guinea stamp of the most famous school, but must be mined for in the clay of the pupil himself, and the implement must be his own mind and spirit as tempered by his earlier life. It is for us to examine the weapon, and to hearten the digger; it cannot be done without calling a spade a spade.

MARTIN CRUSOE.

RELEASE

I have ransacked drawer and cupboard
To find the instrument I put away:
Memories hang upon its stops—I am afraid
The notes I waken will betray
Old testaments I sealed and signed. I fear
The winding stair of fugue will lead me to
Those places where the mind impels a stay:
To windows where the blinds are drawn,
Not without caution to be raised again.
I would prevent emotions in the brain,
Once vital, fading to an undertone
Whose dull recurrence wears the sense's edge,
As thunder rumoured on a sultry day.
And there are chords I shun lest they recall
Things which the mind would rivet to:
Some wallflowers on a crumbling wall,
And their soft smell. And to the inner sense
I would deny the rhythmic swing and fall
Of waves that gather in a Summer bay.
And to the hidden mouth the blown salt spray,
Felt as a boat steers to the deeper sea.

In contradiction, it is best to bind
The sense for freedom; not to give much scope
To retrogression, lest the biassed mind
Turn inward on itself. The mill-wheels grind
The life-charged grain to whitest flour.
I would not have life whittled to an hour
Of sifted essence, and all memories creep
Round one small orbit, while the visual power
Becomes not means to gain, but keep.
Better to leave all legacy behind,
Than sign acceptance in the terms of sleep.

C. H. PEACOCK.

THE ART-FORM OF DEMOCRACY?

IT was not until after the War that the cinema began to be seriously considered as a means of artistic expression. Only a few people saw any æsthetic possibilities in the early American and French two-reel comedies, tragedies and dramas. It was left to the serious Germans to elevate this new popular entertainment to the level of ' art.' *The Cabinet of Doctor Caligari,* made in 1919, was the first film to interest intelligent people in any large numbers in the potentialities of this new and crude medium.

This was thirteeen years ago. Since then the cinema has made vast technical strides, and produced a number of remarkable personalities. In 1928 the industry was beginning to discover its technical limitations and possibilities; it stood on the threshold of its own methods. The Russian proletarian cinema, notably under Eisenstein and Pudovkin, had carried it forward to a state of technical perfection. Then a hundred per cent. talking, singing and dancing monstrosity turned the whole industry topsy-turvy, and it found itself almost where it had begun.

From this blow, it has in four crowded years rallied with an encouraging speed; the additional techniques of sound are being assimilated with a gratifying success by a few accomplished technicians. The principles of sound technique are beginning, in actual films as opposed to theory, to outline themselves, if faintly as yet.

But sound, even if it has increased the potentialities of the cinema, has also made it doubly potent as an anaesthetic: the personifications of the day-dreams of shop-girl and bank-clerk are more thrillingly ' real ' when one can hear as well as see them, and a whole new galaxy has arisen to replace those unfortunates whose voices were too destructive of illusion.

But how is the fastidious minority to regard this curious and intricate phenomenon, the cinema? Certainly it is impossible to disregard it sociologically. It is equally impossible to follow the advanced critics and talk of Eisenstein and Pudovkin as second Shakespeares and Leonardos. Occasionally a film is shown that is stimulating, but more often than not the ' good ' turns out to be merely unpopular, ' incomprehensible,' ' highbrow,' or forbidden public showing. (Even Chaplin's latest film is, as far as I can gather from casual conversation with a varied collection of people, ' a lot of rot.') But the great popular successes, such as *Ben Hur* and *Disraeli,* are to most intelligent people a source of embarassment. The cinema is the art-form of ' democracy ' (the inverted commas are to admit that it might equally be called the art-form of capitalism).

We should, most of us, I imagine, like to see such films as (to take a representative handful) *Ben Hur, Our Dancing Daughters, Cuban Love Song, The Big Parade, Secrets of a Secretary,* banished from the screen, not by the action of a censor, but by lack of public support. But it would be unreasonable to hope for a cinema beyond the intelligence of the general public. The Russian films, Chaplin, and René Clair represent the highest level of the popular cinema, and it is a level sufficiently high to give us excuse for optimism. They may all be appreciated for quite wrong reasons, but that they are appreciated at all is hopeful, and a public which supports *City Lights, Le Million,* and *A Nous La Liberté* will perhaps soon demand a generally higher level than they have been given up to date.

The cinema is unlikely ever to reach the level of the best literature (for reasons which I have explained elsewhere), and will never satisfy the most exacting demands of the minority. It must always remain to some extent popular and democratic, and on a lower level than its contemporary art-forms. In any case the ' popular ' work of Clair or Chaplin is truer cinema and a finer synthesis of experience than the ' advanced ' work of Bunuel or Dulac. Popularity does not necessarily (though it does almost more often than not) mean mediocrity.

With these reservations, then, we may say that a number of films are produced each year which justify an interest in the technical aspect of the cinema, and a smaller number of films that justify one's belief that the cinema is an art-medium out of which serious and successful records of human experience have already emerged, and out of which in the future something finer will come.

We may divide the entire output of the international cinema into two very broad sections, though each is capable of numerous sub-divisions. The first, comprising the vast majority of films, contains those which appear, have their short life, and vanish; the second, of more particular interest, contains films which represent technical innovations of importance or are for various other reasons capable of exciting the intelligent person's interest, and on rare occasions can be recognised as the attempt of a serious artist to express himself.

Two films have recently been shown in England which will enable me to illustrate and bring home some of my points in a necessarily brief space.

*　　*　　*

Five Star Final is an attack on tabloid journalism. Technically it is much like other American films—it is only inside the newspaper office that the film is at all considerable—crude, competent and second-rate, in short, a good typical example of our democratic art-form.

But it attacks journalism; that is in itself notable. Anything critical emerging from Hollywood is an achievement, and an exposure of so huge a vested interest as journalism through a medium as like journalism as the cinema is positively miraculous. Of course it only exposes the cruder and more obvious vices that journalism is subject to. (Thus, the ' respectable ' Press can hail it as ' the film of the year '; a real exposure of popular journalism would be much less complacently received, or disposed of by that most effective weapon—disregard). The film could be commercially produced and receive the Press publicity which alone made it a commercial proposition, only because it deals with the material and less insidious kind of ' corruption.' The Press, we all feel, needs attacking in a different way; but if (assuming it capable) the cinema attempted this, the film would be incomprehensible to the great majority. It would reach only those who need no enlightenment, and would serve no useful purpose.

We find ourselves therefore in the paradoxical position of having to assert that a film because it is crude and superficial is ' good ' which, if it had been more sensitively and intelligently handled, would have had its efficacy destroyed. The cinema can hope to transcend this dilemma not by withdrawing to æsthetic sophistication but only by appealing, as the best directors have in fact appealed, at a number of response-levels. (The essence of Chaplin will always elude the bulk of his audiences). So Shakespeare and the more notable Elizabethan dramatists solved the same kind of problem.

The most *Five Star Final* can hope to do is to sow suspicions of the popular Press (if the audience doesn't reflect : ' This is perhaps true of American journalism but not of English.') This no doubt will make in a sense for sweetness and light; and so much—and little more—may be claimed for a film so highly rated as *Kameradschaft*. And this function begins to look important when we reflect that the Press has, by its more attractive lay-out and its literary gossip, its snappy articles and serial stories, all immediately assimilable, ' superseded ' for the great majority all but the crudest books and all printed criticism outside its own pages. But all this has nothing to do with art.

* * *

Westfront 1918 is of a very different quality from *Five Star Final*. It is the best of the numerous war films (and probably the last). Again we have the situation outlined in the previous paragraph. A public opinion hostile to war could have been created and fixed by the multitudinous war novels—if they had been read by the masses. But, ' unpleasant ' and requiring the imaginative co-operation of the reader, they scarcely reached the public whose immunity against stampeding can alone secure us from war. The thrilling ' reality ' of the cinema which generally subserves a narcotic effect has in *Westfront* an opposite function. Most war-films set out (more or less openly) to arouse the bellicose instinct of the man in the street and provide romantic glorification of war (*Hell's Angels*) and of nationalism (*The Big Parade, Verdun, Tell England,* etc.) The exceptions are unfortunately those (e.g. *The End of St. Petersburg*) which are the least widely shown. Pabst has employed the peculiar capacities of his medium to create a complete illusion of the battle-field, and cannot be accused of any of the vices just described. Yet, accomplished as is the ' art ' of this most remarkable of the West European directors, we must not allow the ambiguity of the term, ' art,' to confuse our sense of values. No film yet produced can justify the serious critical approach demanded (for instance) by a good novel or poem. This needs saying firmly, since the cult of 'Cinema' by intellectuals, English, French and American, shows how insidious may be the forms of *la trahison des clercs*. Thus we find in the *Hound and Horn* a solemn appreciation of Mickey Mouse and the animated cartoon vulgarities.

It remains for Mr. Delisle Burns or someone else with Faith in Democracy to retort by reminding us that *Quem quaeritis* led to *Lear*.

WILLIAM HUNTER.

COMMENTS AND REVIEWS

' SELECTED LIST OF SPRING BOOKS.'

Under this head the *New Statesman and Nation* (Spring Book Supplement, March 12th, 1932) prints a pathetic little note: ' These lists make no attempt to be exhaustive. No one who has not attempted the task can imagine how invidious a business it is to read so many catalogues, and try to choose those books which are important in themselves, and likely to have a particular appeal to one's readers.' The selected list which follows contains 618 titles, of which 148 are ' fiction.' Under such a spate it is clear that something different from the traditional methods of reviewing must be adopted if readers are not to waste their time sorting out the tenth rate for themselves. It is only possible to know whether a reviewer's praise or blame has any meaning if the journal for which he writes has ascertainable standards of criticism. It is interesting to speculate how many good reviews have been prejudiced in the mind of the discerning reader because of the non-critical matter with which they were surrounded.

THE STATE OF REVIEWING

Mr. R. Ellis Roberts contributed to *The New Statesman and Nation* for March 26th, 1932, *An Open Letter to Frank Swinnerton.* Mr. Swinnerton had been complaining about the state of reviewing. Coterie? exclaims Mr. Roberts with ingenuous surprise: ' I became literary editor of the *New Statesman* at the beginning of 1930, and honestly I can only just understand what you mean by the sentences I have quoted.' Whatever Mr. Swinnerton may have meant, Mr. Roberts in his reply gives away the essential case. Answering the suggestion that reviewing has deteriorated: ' Are you sure that the *News Chronicle,* to name only one, is so much inferior? I seem to have read criticisms, there, not only by Robert Lynd, but by E. M. Forster, Rose Macaulay, E. E. Kellett,

D. C. Somervell, H. C. Wylde, Sylvia Lynd, Phillip Guedalla, Winifred Holtby, and Charles Williams.' Mr. Roberts assumes, with justice or otherwise, that Mr. Swinnerton, and, certainly with justice, that the majority of readers of the *New Statesman,* will be impressed by this list. What more need be said about the state of reviewing? Mr. E. M. Forster we know as a distinguished novelist; but of the rest, of how many can anything be said except that they are authorities like Mr. Roberts? And yet Mr. Roberts can safely refer to them as authorities like himself. Here we have the top level in contemporary critical journalism. They and their friends control the more intelligent weeklies. Coterie or no coterie, they exhibit the kind of solidarity innocently exemplified by Mr. Roberts' letter. They are no doubt without personal malice (most of them). But towards anything that, explicitly or implicitly, challenges their standards or their competence they inevitably exhibit something that looks like malice (solidarity, of course, makes it something else : they stand for Good Taste, Good Sense and Right Reason).

Mr. Robert Lynd, perhaps the most eminent of them, is, to do him justice, so sure of his judicial authority that he can generally command good humour. Here we have him, ten years ago, on *The Sacred Wood :* ' Mr. Eliot fails as a critic, because he brings us neither light nor delight. But this does not mean that he will always fail. He has some of the qualities that go to the making of a critic. . . . '

It was Mr. Lynd who anticipated Mr. J. B. Priestley's discovery of a modern Donne in Mr. J. C. Squire : ' Like Donne, he is largely self-occupied, examining the horrors of his own soul, overloaded at times with thought, an intellect at odds with the spirit. . . . '

But his taste is catholic, or rather, democratic, in its range, and his activity untiring. In the *Observer* for April 3rd we read : ' Mr. Robert Lynd has edited for Harraps a new omnibus volume called *Great Love Stories of All Nations.* Mr. Lynd, like Elia, is an immortal disinfectant. Nothing false or septic can endure his neighbourhood. We can be certain, then, that nothing he has decided to include will be unworthy. . . . '

THE B.B.C. QUESTIONNAIRE caused some strange reactions. We do not altogether agree with Sir William Beveridge's methods, but the kind of opposition encountered is significant. Under the heading ' The B.B.C. Wants to Know About You and Your Wife ' (January 28th, 1932) the *Daily Mail* made merry, after its fashion, with the whole idea. Those who wish for evidence about the interests concerned in remaining ignorant about ourselves may turn to the articles in the *Daily Mail* about this date, where the questions are proclaimed as ' impertinent inquiries into the private affairs ' of the British people. There are savage tribes, we remember, who so regard questions concerning their names or those of their relations. Surveys are dangerous. ' The unusually heavy rains which happened to follow the English survey of the Nicobar Islands in the winter of 1886-1887 were imputed by the alarmed natives to the wrath of the spirits at the theodolites, dumpy-levellers, and other strange instruments which had been set up in many of their favourite haunts; and some of them proposed to soothe the anger of the spirits by sacrificing a pig.'— *Taboo and the Perils of the Soul*, p. 231.

A MIDDLEMAN OF IDEAS

THE NEMESIS OF AMERICAN BUSINESS (Allen and Unwin, 7/6d.).

THE TRAGEDY OF WASTE (Macmillan $1.50).

MEN AND MACHINES (Jonathan Cape, 1929, 12/6d.).

MEXICO (The Bodley Head, 1932, 12/6d.).

The work of Stuart Chase, even his name, is scarcely known in England. The kind of awareness he represents is significantly absent from the contemporary intelligence on this side of the Atlantic. This does not mean that our culture is healthier; it is merely that our educated class is more complacent and blind.

The books by Stuart Chase, listed above, are devoted to answering questions raised by the work of economists, statisticians, sociologists, industrial experts, and the drift of the modern world generally, questions which, in our innocence (if Mr. Wells is our spokesman), we have scarcely thought of asking over here. In *Men and Machines,* for example, there is an examination of the history of the machine in world civilization and a carefully substantiated discussion of its place in the modern community. All the available evidence is summarised that bears upon such basic questions as:

How far are we ' slaves ' to machinery?

What exactly are the effects (if any) of different kinds of machine-tending on the worker?

Is the efficiency of machine work greater than that of hand work?

Has machinery (and the complicated apparatus of living it has brought with it) produced a more satisfactory life for the individual?

What are the disadvantages and dangers of a machine civilization?

How can the machine be used to produce the maximum human happiness?

The author has no cultural axe to grind—he is inclined to all-round scepticism and would frankly like the showing to turn out in favour of the machine civilization for which he makes out so instructive a profit-and-loss account—but he suppresses nothing, he colours nothing, and he is never less than penetrating and racily informative. At his best he exhibits the kind of percipience the absence of which renders futile such undertakings as *The Work, Wealth and Happiness of Mankind;* he is explicitly dealing with the practical issues raised by the use of the machine—' I am not so much concerned with the character of a shipping clerk with a line of wise cracks and a Chevrolet as I am about his ignorance of the environment which furnishes him food and shelter '—but his method, subtler, defter and less pretentious than Mr. Wells's, obliges him to penetrate behind the imposing façade of Progress and note the drastic changes in work habits and play habits effected in the last generation, to observe ' the aesthetic account against the machine,' and the outward evidences of a breach of cultural continuity :

' Compare the Hoe printing press—that diabolic modern marvel—with the primitive hand press of Caxton. Merciful Heaven, what a gain! Then compare its flimsy, fading output with the sturdy folios which have come down the centuries. Merciful Heaven, what a loss! Here is a Foudrinier machine with perfect co-ordination, turning out five miles of paper in one spasm, at a speed greater than a man can walk. What is the function of this triumph of engineering? '' To produce the worst paper that has ever been made, or that it is possible to make '' . . . . With the decline of handicraft in certain fields, a standard by which the factory article can be judged no longer exists. . . . The more he (the householder) reads, the more illiterate he becomes. . . . He stands goggle-eyed before a thousand advertising campaigns pulling him in as many directions. The sense of quality, durability, value, which was strong in his less lettered grandfather, has well-nigh evaporated from his more lettered self.'

Such conclusions are not present to disturb the reader of *The Work, Wealth and Happiness of Mankind;* they do not come within Mr. Wells's ken, for one thing because he is not, in all his 825 pages, near enough to the facts at any point. The Wellsian display of vast stores of information is merely display; in *Men and Machines* there is evident a sharp, disinterested intelligence at work on data with which it is at home, selecting the significant from the trivial. Mr. Chase, far from surrendering to the dazzling achievements of industrialism, is anxious to bring home to us

its great dangers—' mechanised warfare, technological tenuousness, and the mounting drain upon natural resources.' He
discusses the terrifying complexity of the physical organization
of the modern city, with its complete absence of ' a central
intelligence to nurse it through a nervous breakdown.' ' All
previous cultures,' he points out, ' have got along with hardly
any central nervous system at all; they could only be destroyed
village by village. . . . Our connection with the realities of our
environment is far more tenuous than was ever the case in
Imperial Rome.' And he speculates what adequate insurance
against a metropolitan calamity would entail; he recommends, in
default of a distributed population, ' special educational courses
for the entire population. . . . a sort of general civic
mobilization.'[1]

It is impossible in a brief review to do justice to any one
of Mr. Chase's exciting books, and I should prefer in any case
to discuss him as a phenomenon. The scientist who, after
surveying *The Work, Wealth and Happiness of Mankind* can
conclude coolly : ' We are all cluttered up with progress,' is
evidently not of Mr. Wells's kind and stands, one may hope, for
the new order. It is not that any strikingly new data is advanced
in his books, but that he conveys the specialists' conclusions to the
layman. He is in short a first-class educational publicist. Take
for instance *Mexico,* his latest book, where he makes use of two
famous sociological surveys, *Tepoztlan* (made in 1930 of a large
Mexican village forming part of a small economic region with a
handicraft culture) and *Middletown* (the type-city of the Middle-
West), in addition to six-months' first-hand study on the spot. Here
we really have a very detailed and yet a fascinatingly interesting
comparison between two opposite ways of living, and the effect
of Tepoztlan's contact with Middletown is duly charted. The
value of such a middleman of ideas in our present state of
ignorance and muddle is inestimable. The work of specialists is
apt to be unassimilable by the general reader (*Middletown* alone
runs to 550 large pages) yet the ordinary cultured man demands
and requires to be kept in touch.

---

[1]Another aspect of ' technological tenuousness ' is suggested by
Malaparte's *La Technique du Coup d'Etat* (translated Paris, 1931).

Qualified and trustworthy middlemen are rare. Mr. Chase is an American, and whom have we in England to serve this function? The obvious criticism of our scientific publicists is that they are not educated in the important sense, and in this respect the younger generation shows little signs of improvement. Professor Julian Huxley is not so obviously crude as his collaborator, Mr. H. G. Wells, but what else is there to be said for him? *Africa View* contains nothing to give a single jolt to the *Punch*-reading public. Literary-philosophic middlemen in this country are apt to be distinctly bogus (*The Criterion* harbours not a few), and while in France they are both livelier and more authentic, they are also, as Frenchmen, faced by a situation so much less complex that they are of little use to us. In one field we have the shining exception of Sir Norman Angell, to whom we pay no attention—his best book, *The Press and the Organization of Society*, has long been out of print.

Why have we no Stuart Chase over here? I can best suggest the answer by referring to another of his activities—Consumers' Research, Ltd., which has built laboratories where a disinterested band of specialists employs every kind of test to every kind of commodity and issues frequent bulletins on competing brands of goods, informing members of their findings. These findings are not merely material. The bulletins contain also articles exposing the arts of modern advertising and high-pressure salesmanship, designed to promote ' sales resistance.' No doubt a civilization is in a bad way when it has to educate its citizens into not being at the mercy of its industrial system. But it is in a worse when it lacks even the recognition of its need. This is perhaps the measure of the difference between the U.S.A. and Great Britain: further along the road we are travelling, they have produced a conscious counter-movement. The services of such a movement need extending: we require instruction how to resist not merely that powerful combination, Big Business plus copywriter, but also the more sinister allies of Big Business—the newspaper, the magazine, the film, the best-seller, even more subtle enemies of national decency and spiritual fineness than the advertiser is of our pockets and our health. Again, *The New Republic* exerts itself to perform these offices as no cis-Atlantic periodical, and yet a conscious recognition of purpose other than political would do much to remedy the anæmic futility of our critical weeklies. England will have to produce a few assorted middlemen of Stuart Chase calibre—say, as a start, an economist, a sociologist, a handful of scientists and some University teachers in the Humanities, as well as some one in a strategic position in the journalistic field—before our attitude to the cultural situation can be said to be a wholesome one.

What is to prevent it? Well, it is not altogether unreasonable to assert the existence of a spirit hostile to such activities in the only class in England that could sponsor them. The spirit, of course, which considers it bad form to take such issues seriously. The genteel tradition of the academic world, from which the educated middle-class takes its tone, has no place for Mr. Chase. It would cut him instinctively, beautifully unaware that the chief excuse for an academic order is that it should produce an intellectual climate in which sensitive curiosity and intelligence can flourish.

Q. D. Leavis.

HOW HIGH IS THE HIGHER EDUCATION?

Dr. Abraham Flexner's *Universities*,[1] an expansion of his Rhodes Lectures given in 1928, enjoyed a scandalous success among the professors in America. He had revealed, it is true, follies and hypocrisies in university administration in the States which members of the teaching profession were acutely aware of, though quite helpless to amend. But the circumstantial directness of his attack was heartening if its revelations were not altogether novel. The presidents and trustees whose shoddy educational ideals he justly questioned have not made public confession in a white gown, though the chief evil-doer, in Dr. Flexner's eyes, President Butler of Columbia, made a covert rejoiner while seeming to talk about something else. The American Press was bewildered. They perhaps mistook Dr. Flexner for a disciple of Mencken,

---

[1] *UNIVERSITIES : AMERICAN, ENGLISH AND GERMAN.* Abraham Flexner (Oxford, 16/-).

and the reporters never know where to have Mencken. In the turmoil of the moment when state legislatures are cutting the universities off with a dollar and private institutions are boarding up their shiny new buildings, the book has been quickly forgotten.

I have no idea how it made its way in England. I imagine that a frank and informed exposition of the defects of the universities of Oxford, Cambridge and London by an American administrator would not be received by the reviewers with unconfined enthusiasm. Very few English university men, as far as I can discover, have ever had it in their hands.

It is regrettable that indifference in England and gunshyness in America have deprived Dr. Flexner of the controversy his book should have produced. Valuable as it is for its documentation and the relentless impartiality of its judgments, it is a dangerous book, dangerous not only because its doctrine is decidedly open to question but because it seems at first glance to demand our complete assent.

Dr. Flexner listened with delight in his youth to the surge and thunder of the seminars at Johns Hopkins, the most German of American universities. He has built a solid bridge across the chaos of American medical education, and as the influential officer of a great educational foundation he has helped to burn out of American universities the bunkum he so hilariously describes. These admirable qualifications for writing such a book have, however, given a curious bias to his understanding of the whole business of learning and teaching. In spite of his zeal to be fair to what must be called, I suppose, the humanities, he has little idea of the traditional ' goods ' of humanistic study. His idea of a university must seem to many an idea which is not universally applicable. The attempt to force it everywhere would certainly destroy a particular quality in English and American life which is properly regarded as valuable and necessary.

Universities exist, Dr. Flexner believes, to search for truth. ' The university professor has an entirely objective responsibility to learning, to his subject, and not a psychological or parental responsibility to his students.' The end-all of university training is the development of the student's ability to ' attack a piece of research.' The intensive study of phenomena under the most favourable conditions is the university's most important function.

No sweeter or more significant words, he believes, were ever uttered by man than Jacques Loeb's immortal ' I am a student of problems.' These words suggest Dr. Flexner's ideal: a vast army of God's spies with its non-coms. and its field-marshals. The graduate seminar recruits and trains and passes on the new subalterns to the research institutes, the officers' mess of this scientific army.

We are familiar with the creed of the scientist and we have no desire to prevent him from using it for family prayers in the laboratory. In America certainly and in some English colleges it might with benefit be a more prominent article of faith. But is it true, as Dr. Flexner says with a sweeping gesture, that the university has no responsibilty to the individual?[1] To him the humanities are to be encouraged because new discoveries yet to be made in them may lead to new evaluations. He would not admit that the end of such study is the transformation of the individual himself, by the heightening of his perceptions and the quickening of his ability to penetrate the consciousness of men and the temper of periods both near him and remote from him in time. The scientist is not concerned with the result to himself of the work he does. He cannot understand the selfishness of the humanist who prefers the particular truth which he has discovered to be most harmonious with himself to the average truth which may possess enough general sanction to be called an hypothesis or a law. Loeb's vision of the world as a pleasant succession of problems to be mowed down one after the other is a queer paradise to offer a poet. And are the poets to be sent to special trade schools—those technical schools which Dr. Flexner offers as consolation to men who are not spartan enough to sell all their aesthetic goods and devote themselves to the search for truth? Was Virgil a 'problem ' to Petrarch and was Petrarch a ' problem ' to Chaucer?

The lunatic modern world, Dr. Flexner insists, needs specialists and has no money to waste in training at the universities men who are content with half-knowledge. No one wishes to contradict him. We are learning in America that congressmen whose only qualification for office is a degree of expertness at hitting the

---

[1]He begs the question when he writes *parental* responsibility.

spittoon at forty paces take very little interest in a balanced budget. Mr. Hoover's autocratically appointed commissions might more safely be entrusted with the country's welfare. But the supply of trained intelligence available in England and America does not depend on the official exclusiveness of the university seminars in these countries. No system can create intelligence and there is no economy in supplying forty seminars where there are only ten first-rate minds to use them.

Are the colleges to be emptied of the others who, though they are by no means geniuses, wish to associate themselves with the most advanced thought of their time and intend to make what practical use of it in their lives they can? One might suppose—since the prow of modern democracy is pointed toward communism—that as many men as have a remote chance of taking the longitude of our present position ought to be allowed to listen to the best navigators.

WILLARD THORP.

BIOLOGY AND MR. HUXLEY

BRAVE NEW WORLD by Aldous Huxley (Chatto and Windus, 7/6d.).

' Utopias ' writes Prof. Berdiaev, in a passage which Mr. Huxley chooses for his motto ' appear to be much more realisable than we used to think. We are finding ourselves face to face with a far more awful question, how can we avoid their actualisation? For they can be made actual. Life is marching towards them. And perhaps a new period is beginning, a period when intelligent men will be wondering how they can avoid these utopias, and return to a society non-utopian, less perfect, but more free.' Mr. Huxley's book is indeed a brilliant commentary on this dismally true remark. It is as if a number of passages from Mr. Bertrand Russell's recent book *The Scientific Outlook* had burst into flower, and had rearranged themselves in patches of shining colour like man-eating orchids in a tropical forest. Paul planted, Apollos watered, but who gave the increase in this case, we may well ask, for a more diabolical picture of society (as some would say) can never have been painted.

Mr. Huxley's theme, embellished though it is by every artifice of that ingenuity of which he is master, is primarily dual, one of its aspects being the power of autocratic dictatorship, and the other, the possibilities of this power when given the resources of a really advanced biological engineering. The book opens with a long description of a human embryo factory, where the eggs emitted by carefully tended ovaries, are brought up in the way they should go by mass-production methods on an endless conveyor belt moving very slowly until at last the infants are ' decanted ' one by one into a highly civilised world. The methods of education by continual suggestion and all the possibilities of conditional reflexes are brilliantly described, and we are shown a world where art and religion no longer exist, but in which an *absolutely* stable form of society has been achieved, firstly, by sorting out the eggs into groups of known inherited characteristics and then setting each group, when adult, to do the work for which it is fitted, and secondly by allowing ' unlimited copulation ' (sterile, of course) and unlimited sexual gratification of every kind. Here Mr. Huxley, whether consciously or not, has incorporated the views of many psychologists, e.g. Dr. Money Kyrle. In an extremely interesting paper[1] Dr. Kyrle has suggested that social discontent, which has always been the driving force in social change, is a manifestation of the Œdipus complexes of the members of society, and cannot be removed by economic means. With decrease of sexual taboos, these psychologists suggest, there would be a decrease of frustration and hence of that aggression which finds its outlet in religion, socialism, or more violent forms of demand for social change. This doctrine is indeed an extremely plausible one, and provides an answer to the question of what the ' born ' reformer is to do when the ideal communist state, for instance, has been brought into being. Supposing that we have what we regard as an ideal state, how shall we ensure its continuance? Only, says Dr. Kyrle, by removing the sexual taboos which make the ' born ' reformer. Accordingly, Mr. Huxley shows us the state of affairs when the attack on post- and pre-marital, and pre-pubertal taboos has long succeeded. The erotic play of children is encouraged, universal sexual relations are the rule, and indeed any sign of the beginning

[1] R. M. Kyrle *A Psychologist's Utopia* (Psyche, 1931. Pp. 48).

of a more deep and lasting affection is rebuked and stamped out, as being anti-social.

But Mr. Huxley, of course, sees so clearly what the psychologists do not see, that such a world must give up not only war, but also spiritual conflicts of any kind, not only superstition, but also religion, not only literary criticism but also great creative art of whatever kind, not only economic chaos, but also all the beauty of the old traditional things, not only the hard and ugly parts of ethics, but the tender and beautiful parts too. And it may well be that only biologists and philosophers will really appreciate the full force of Mr. Huxley's remarkable book. For of course in the world at large, those persons, and there will be many, who do not approve of his 'utopia,' will say, we can't believe all this, the biology is all wrong, it couldn't happen. Unfortunately, what gives the biologist a sardonic smile as he reads it, is the fact that *the biology is perfectly right,* and Mr. Huxley has included nothing in his book but what might be regarded as legitimate extrapolations from knowledge and power that we already have. Successful experiments are even now being made in the cultivation of embryos of small mammals in vitro, and one of the most horrible of Mr. Huxley's predictions, the production of numerous low-grade workers of precisely identical genetic constitution from one egg, is perfectly possible. Armadillos, parasitic insects, and even sea-urchins, if treated in the right way, do it now, and it is only a matter of time before it will be done with mammalian eggs. Many of us admit that as we walk along the street we dislike nine faces out of ten, but suppose that one of the nine were repeated sixty times. Of course, the inhabitants of Mr. Huxley's utopia were used to it.

And it is just the same in the philosophical realm. We see already among us the tendencies which only require reasonable extrapolation to lead to Brave New World. Publicism, represented in its academic form by Mr. Wittgenstein and Prof. Schlick, and in its more popular form by Prof. Hogben and Mr. Sewell, urges that the concept of reality must be replaced by the concept of communicability. Now it is only in science that perfect communicability is attainable, and in other words, all that we can profitably say is, in the last resort, scientific propositions clarified by mathematical logic. To the realm of the Unspeakable, therefore, belong Ethics, Religion, Art, Artistic Criticism, and many other things. This point of view has a certain attraction and possesses, or can be made to possess, considerable plausibility, but in the end it has the effect of driving out Reason from the private incommunicable worlds of non-scientific experience. We are left with science as the only substratum for Reason, but what is worse, Philosophy or Metaphysics too is relegated to the realm of the Unspeakable, so that Science, which began as a special form of Philosophy, and which only retains its intellectually beneficial character if it retains its status as a special form of Philosophy, becomes nothing more nor less than the Mythology accompanying a Technique. And what will happen to the world in consequence is seen with perfect clearness both by Mr. Aldous Huxley and by Mr. Bertrand Russell. ' The scientific society in its pure form ' says Mr. Russell ' is incompatible with the pursuit of truth, with love, with art, with spontaneous delight, with every ideal that men have hitherto cherished, save only possibly ascetic renunciation. It is not knowledge that is the source of these dangers. Knowledge is good and ignorance is evil; to this principle the lover of the world can admit no exception. Nor is it power in and for itself that is the source of danger. What is dangerous is power wielded for the sake of power, not power wielded for the sake of genuine good.'

Such considerations, of course, do not solve the problem, they only convince us that a problem exists. But Mr. Huxley's orchid-garden is itself an exemplification of the contention that knowledge is always good, for had it not been for his imaginative power, we should not have seen so clearly what lies at the far end of certain inviting paths. To his convincing searchlight, humanity (it is not too much to say) will always owe great debt, and it must be our part to get his book read by any of our friends who suppose that science alone can be the saviour of the world.

JOSEPH NEEDHAM.

'BABBITT BUYS THE WORLD'

THE WORK, WEALTH AND HAPPINESS OF MANKIND.
H. G. Wells (Heinemann. 10/6d.).

' Few people ' notes Mr. Wells on page 199, ' can be trusted
to cut and arrange their own toe-nails well.' He is describing,
with the detail that this extract suggests, the particular advance
of civilization represented by the beautician's parlour. ' Museums
are littered with the rouge cups, trays, manicure sets, mirrors and
pots for greases and messes, of the pretty ladies of Sumeria,
Egypt and Babylonia, and thence right down to our own times;
but never can the organization of human adornment have reached
the immensity and subtlety shown by these American figures.'
No, there may be archness, but there is no irony in Mr. Wells's
account of the up-to-date ritual. ' But, you will say, this is a
very exceptional woman, and indeed this is a superfluous section
to insert in a survey of world economics! ' Wrong! Before long,
Mr. Wells implies, many more hundreds of millions a year will
be spent on these things, and in a Utopia not very remote (if we
will listen to Mr. Wells) *every* woman will enjoy the advantages
of rouging, face-lifting, massage, pedicure, manicure, greases
and messes even more scientific. This fairly represents the essential
triviality of a large part of *The Work, Wealth and Happiness of
Mankind.*

And yet Mr. Wells's directing idea—' the re-orientation of
loyalties through a realisation of the essential unity of our
species '—is not trivial. To this he has devoted his life with a
noble disinterestedness. So I reminded myself when, having first
thought of replying to the editors of *Scrutiny* that Mr. Wells is, at
this date, not worth reviewing, I started on this his latest book.
We may find it hard to like or respect him, but he is doing work
that needs doing and that at the moment seems terribly urgent.
Yet we must also remind ourselves that the more his kind of
influence seems likely to prevail (and the process of civilization
works with it) the more urgent is drastic criticism. If he belongs
to the past it is only in the sense that it has long been impossible
to discuss him seriously except as a case, a type, a portent. As
such, he matters. More and more the disinterested power in the

world seems likely to be Wellsian. Mr. J. M. Keynes hailed *The World of William Clissold* as a distinguished and important book. So the essential points are perhaps worth making once again.

Mr. Wells energizes tirelessly on behalf of a ' world-machine, planned and efficient, protecting and expanding human life. . . . ' And, if there is not a speedy approximation to such a machine the un-Wellsian preoccupations of some of us will, it is plain, soon cease to trouble us or the world. But once the machine is smoothly running, what then? What is this ' expanding,' this ' richer,' life, what are these infinite ' possibilities,' that Mr. Wells promises us, or rather, the species? Roger Bacon knew (according to Mr. Wells) that if men would listen to him, ' Vision and power would reward them. Steamship, aeroplane and automobile, he saw them all, and many other things.' Steamship, aeroplane and automobile, and many other things, have already rewarded us. Does ' expanding life ' mean more and more ' vision and power ' of this kind? Mr. Wells notoriously thinks it the duty of the civilized man to own or use the latest products of civilization, and I knew a French friend of his who thought this sense of duty vulgar. But it is plain that what Mr. Wells says of Edison might be adapted to himself: to him ' the delights offered by the luxury trades must have seemed extraordinarily stupid.' He has found fulfilment in his life's work. He can find his Utopia satisfactory because he has found his actual life satisfactory.

But there are some of us to whom the satisfactions of Edison and Mr. Wells, when offered as ultimate ends, seem insufficient. And Mr. Wells is not unaware of this perversity of human nature. He even devotes the twelfth, and last, volume of his ideal World Encyclopædia to ' beauty.' ' In it aesthetic criticism would pursue its wild, incalculable, unstandardized career, mystically distributing praise and blame. . . . The artist in his studio, the composer in his music room and all the multitude who invent and write down their inventions, have hardly figured in our world panorama, and even now we can give them but a passing sentence or two. They are an efflorescence, a lovely and purifying efflorescence on life.'—In this essay on the Happiness of Mankind, we can give them but a passing sentence or two. Mr. Wells, of course, believes that if we look after the machinery, they will look after themselves. But the perverse among us persist in urging that looking after the machinery should mean seeing that it works to desired ends, and that a world that gives no more attention to the ' lovely efflorescence ' than Mr. Wells does is likely not to know what it desires; the efficiency of the machinery becomes the ultimate value, and this seems to us to mean something very different from expanding and richer human life.

Mr. Wells, however, is not interested in this kind of question. And it is for this reason that his book, for all its wealth of information, has a total effect of triviality : the energy that made it seem to the author worth writing is indistinguishable from a schoolboy immaturity of mind. Mr. Wells is praised for his interest in the world, but he is not interested enough. ' The story of New Zealand is particularly illuminating,' he notes. It is : I know someone who is enquiring why New Zealand has developed nothing in the nature of a distinctive literature. But Mr. Wells's notion of an educated man is one to whom such questions wouldn't be worth troubling about.

Yet inadvertently (he is not an athletic thinker) he admits their importance—and unwittingly passes judgment on himself. ' One peculiar value of the '' Five Towns '' novels of Mr. Arnold Bennett lies in the clear, convincing, intimate, and yet almost unpremeditated way in which he shows the industrialized peasant mentality of the employing class in a typical industrialized region, The Black Country, waking up to art and refinement, to ampler personality and new ideas '—The Wellsian man *will* wake up to ' art ' and ' refinement ' and ' ampler personality ' and it will be in Mr. Arnold Bennett's way—a way that, we know, ended in the Imperial Palace Hotel. In spite of Edison's asceticism the inventor, the researcher, the man who gets things done, will seek his guerdon of the ' luxury trades.' And perhaps even Mr. Wells does not find his work and his Vision quite self-sufficing. Perhaps his interest in beauty-culture is significant. And it is perhaps permissible to suggest that specialized sexual charm counts for more in his scheme of things than a mature mind could think worthy; Mr. Wells will not blush.

But he might, perhaps, blush if one pointed out the falsities of his book in matters of fact. Take, for instance, his naïve account of beauticianry: he pays here, as the articles on the Beauty Racket published recently in the *New Republic* might bring home to him, involuntary tribute to the power of advertising that he acclaims elsewhere. Again, he has swallowed with completely uncritical innocence the official Ford legend. Let him read *The Tragedy of Henry Ford* by Jonathan Norton Leonard (G. P. Putnam's Sons, $3). This book is just out, but so much was already common knowledge that Mr. Wells cannot be acquitted of complicity—he was not an unwilling gull. This may seem a severe verdict. But read him on the ' ultra-scholastic education ' that the ' citizen ' gets from newspapers, radio, cinema, and so on (pp. 745ff.) : ' On the whole, it is sound stuff he gets.' I know that Mr. Wells's criteria are not mine; but even by his own what he lets out elsewhere is enough to brand his complacency as something worse.

We can respect him as we cannot respect Arnold Bennett, but it is significant that, for all his disinterestedness, he is not safe from the Arnold Bennett corruption.

F. R. LEAVIS.

MANY PSYCHOLOGIES

PSYCHOLOGIES OF 1930. Edited by Carl Murchison (Clark University Press. London : Humphrey Milford. 1930. Pp. xx-498. 36/-).

THE MIND AND ITS BODY. Charles Fox. (Kegan Paul. 1931. Pp. xii-316. 10/6).

THE NERVOUS TEMPERAMENT. Millais Culpin and May Smith (H.M. Stationery Office. 1930. Pp. iv-52. 1/-).

Psychologies of 1930 would, if it were generally read, help to correct two mistaken attitudes towards psychology. Sharp divisions of opinion on technical questions, endless difficulties in interpreting experimental results, age-old dilemmas of theory to be faced—all these are exhibited here, and ought to give check to the people who think cheerfully that it's only a matter of time before psychology has everything straightened out. It possibly is only a matter of time, but such a long time that none of us need feel cheerful about it. On the other hand those who regard ' psychologies ' as being nothing but undisciplined speculation by psychopathologists or extreme behaviourists will find such points of view as these put into perspective among definitely technical problems. Twenty-four well-known psychologists have contributed to the volume, most of them concerned with expounding and vindicating their own views. There is a preponderance of American writers, but the German and Russian workers are fairly well represented and the rest of Europe not overlooked. Apart from its value as a survey of contemporary psychological controversy, however, the book is worth possessing for several of the individual essays. G. S. Brett and John Dewey, for instance, have made distinguished contributions which are only semi-partisan in character and possess permanent value.

In *The Mind and Its Body* Mr. Fox vigorously makes hay of some of the untested assumptions that orthodox psychology harbours and allows to become fixed in popular opinion. He is aided by such recent work as Lashley's, which seems to upset most of the current working hypotheses about learning, without putting anything simple and definite in their place. It is his excellent summary of such work as this, and his indication of what it implies for psychological theory, which constitute the chief value of his book. His constructive work is much less convincing. For one thing the book is too brief for the amount of ground it covers, and Mr. Fox's vigorous and confident statement of his heterodox views on technical questions (for instance on instinct and fatigue) must for many people be seriously misleading. Had they been given the more detailed and laborious statement they needed we should have had several books instead of one, and none of them so stimulating as this.

The Nervous Temperament, a brief report from the Industrial Health Research Board, comes as a relief from ' psychologies.' It describes the diagnosis of psychoneurotic conditions among industrial workers and provides evidence of the extremely wide incidence of these troubles. In this report, as in all psychological work, the difficulty (completely ignored by popularisers) of getting simple tests and clear-cut statistical results is very apparent. Yet the work is convincing. The methods of diagnosis are noticeably sensible. The authors imply no theory of the ultimate causation of the neuroses, and they avoid the dangerous question of normality and the identification (too often implied by psychologists) of the abnormal with the subnormal. One need not commit oneself to belief in some hypothetical ' normality ' in order to agree that what they call ' symptoms ' are certainly undesirable. In short the work shows what can be done in psychology without dubious assumptions or presumptuous cultural implications.

The three books go to show how far psychology is from being a unified science, how inappropriate it is as a weapon for attacking philosophical views that you object to (it will be just as useful to your opponent), and how valuable some of its conceptions and methods may be as tools for dealing with specific problems.

D.W.H.

FELO DE SE?

WHAT WOULD BE THE CHARACTER OF A NEW WAR? An Enquiry of the Inter-Parliamentary Union (P. S. King, 16/- net).

THE DRAGON'S TEETH by Major-General J. F. C. Fuller (Constable, 10/- net).

THEY THAT TAKE THE SWORD by Esmé Wingfield-Stratford (Routledge, 12/6d. net).

THE UNSEEN ASSASSINS by Norman Angell (Hamish Hamilton, 7/6d. net).

We may as well be frank. The chances of our organising permanent peace before the next war comes are now practically *nil*. The Disarmament Conference will have disarmed nobody. Not one armed power that has sent a delegation, with the exception of Soviet Russia, has shown any serious desire to initiate disarmament on a general scale. The League of Nations, not through the inability of its officials but because of the dishonourable cowardice of the world's leading statesmen, has conspicuously failed to stop a war waged by one member state upon another, and there can no longer be any pretence that it affords the slightest protection to a state that is the victim of aggression. The movement that sprang from the suffering of the last war to establish peace has broken down. It is too easy to be cynical, and too useless: one can but inquire why this breakdown has occurred and find out whether anything not quite useless may yet be done.

First, we might as well be clear what War, if we are to have it, will now be like; and for this the Inter-Parliamentary Union's Enquiry is an invaluable piece of work. An expert here and there may disagree with a particular point some other expert has made, but the general picture drawn by these scientists and technical writers is one that (unless we refuse to look) we cannot but accept. The ratio of our destructive powers to the vulnerability of modern civilization has increased so rapidly that another war on the scale of the last one would loose powers big enough to smash the whole structure that has made civilized life as we know it possible in the west.

Many informed and sensitive people have realised the danger and have written suggesting ways of escape. But few of them have had anything adequate to say. Either, like General Fuller, they have possessed some interesting technical information but have failed to grasp the general problem in anything like a lucid way, or they have evaded that general problem by running off on some hobby horse of their own. Dr. Wingfield-Stratford and Mr. Norman Angell have at least avoided these dangers. The former has written the first book which this reviewer has seen which provides a serious historical philosophy to inform the movement for peace. It is not a work of ' propaganda ' but a commentary on history by a free intelligence moved by great events. Dr. Wingfield-Stratford does not over-simplify: he shows War as a function of civil expansion in the past, and its interworkings, both positive and negative, with the progress civilisation has made. His analysis reveals the unreality of the historical fictions which are now the justifications of wars in the popular mind. Norman Angell's book is largely based on one useful conception: that what has changed the direction of human activities in a forward direction has often been, not the erudition of scholars nor the weight of institutions, but the discovery and acceptance by the people of some quite simple idea. Witchcraft trials ended, not because of books written about witchcraft nor because of pressure from above, but because for various reasons the whole idea came to seem cruel and absurd. The progress made in public health in the last century has been possible because the public has grasped the idea that disease can be spread by micro-organisms and has taken preventive action based on this idea. The new political idea that must be propagated is simply this: that it is foolish to expect world peace while there is world anarchy in the economic and political relations of the different states. As so often before, Norman Angell puts his case with such lucidity that one wonders that even statesmen should fail to see his point.

It is clear that a development in human society is possible only when there is both machinery to implement it and an acceptance of the psychological assumptions without which the machinery cannot work. At the moment we have for the organisation of peace certain machinery which, though inadequate, is in advance of the state of mind of those by whom it is to be used. The right thing to do is to attack ruthlessly the pre-peace assumptions (such as the inviolable sovereignty of nations) which still generally prevail, and to displace those statesmen (however well-meaning) whose actions and inactions are based upon assumptions that must lead to another world-war. There is no very great hope of success, yet surely only those can fail to make an effort who are untroubled by the ironical thought that Man may well be extinguished through lack of adaptability to an environment he has created for himself. H. L. ELVIN.

NEW BEARINGS IN ENGLISH POETRY by F. R. Leavis. (Chatto and Windus, Pp. 214. 6/-).

It is the distinction of this book that it consistently treats poetry as one of the major products of normal human activity, and the making of poetry as being at least as responsible an occupation as, say, scientific research. In fact the quality of the book may be indicated by saying that an intelligent scientist (if he were free from conventional preconceptions about literature) could read it without getting exasperated and without a sense of

lacking initiation. It is only those for whom poetry is a cult
with initiates, or an archaic pursuit surviving as a pastime, like
archery, who will complain that the book is esoteric. They will
be puzzled by the constant implication that a poet's ' magnificent
qualities of intelligence and character ' are the concern of a critic
of his poems. They will be irritated by the assertation that there
are in the present age ' no serious standards current, no live
tradition of poetry, and no public capable of informed and serious
interest.'

As a consequence of his point of view much of Mr. Leavis's
criticism of poetry becomes, in a certain limited sense, a criticism
of the poet's personality. Not that he is a moralist or
psychopathologist *manqué*. He sets out to confine himself ' as
strictly as possible to literary criticism, and to remember that
poetry is made of words.' Yet he makes it clear, for instance in
condemning the bulk of Ezra Pound's poetry, that his only deep
interest is in words that communicate valuable attitudes towards
experience. ' The possible interest in verse form so distinguishable
from interesting communication seems extremely limited.' He is
constantly engaged in appraising the poet's state of mind, of
which any one poem may be only a partial indication. He says
of De la Mare's later poems, for example, ' the poignancy turns
into a duller, heavier desolation. . . the unwholesomeness of the
fantasy habit is, implicitly and explicitly, admitted. It is as if
the disastrous consequences of drug addiction were being
recognised. Life seems now not tragic but flat and empty.' He
reminds himself, in discussing *Ash Wednesday,* that ' the sequence
is poetry, and highly formal poetry.' But he proceeds: ' Yet it
is impossible not to see in it a process of self-scrutiny, of self
exploration. . . The poetry. . . is a striving after a spiritual state
based upon a reality elusive and yet ultimate.' This concern with
the spiritual state that poetry reflects involves no prying biography
and no irrelevant probing for the poet's ' underlying experience.'
He quotes T. S. Eliot's saying: ' the more perfect the artist, the
more completely separate in him will be the man who suffers and
the mind which creates.' But he recognises that there must, nevertheless, be one individual who is responsible for the state of being
out of which the poems have come. And this belief that the poet
is morally accountable for what he writes lies behind the critical

position that Mr. Leavis has taken up and consolidated in *New Bearings*.

No one is more aware than Mr. Leavis of the dangers of this critical approach, and of the necessity for remembering ' that poetry is made of words.' A discussion of many contemparary poems is bound to be, as he remarks of one, ' a delicate business, incurring danger both of crudity and impertinence.' But the danger only shows the need in the critic for fine insight and complete seriousness. And these qualities Mr. Leavis undoubtedly possesses.

Though *New Bearings* contains some excellent exegesis and detailed criticism of poems by T. S. Eliot, Gerard Manley Hopkins, and Ezra Pound, Mr. Leavis's main concern with separate poems is to relate them to the rest of the poet's work; just as, in turn, the whole of the poet's work is related to the state of culture in which it was produced. His argument is, in brief, that poetry in the nineteenth century became established in a tradition of remoteness from other human activities, not merely from industrialism, but also from pursuits demanding fine intelligence, such as research and speculation· in science. He then proceeds to an admirable summary of ' The Situation at the End of the War,' a chapter distinguished by extremely skilful compression and generalisation combined with scrupulous care for exceptions from the general statement. The study of W. B. Yeats is an outstanding example of this capacity for making comprehensive statement without distorting or neglecting any of the facts.

Having demonstrated the unsatisfactory state of poetry at the end of the war (and, implicitly, of most of it still) Mr. Leavis looks for a way out. He looks for an attitude to poetry that will allow it to become not merely the poet's comment on his life but an integral part of his life and growth. He looks too for a way of using language which will make this attitude effective. This use of poetry and this technique he finds in the work of three poets: in T. S. Eliot's poems pre-eminently, in Ezra Pound's *Mauberley,* and in Gerard Manley Hopkins' poems. These three poets he studies in detail, and fully establishes his claim that they are to be considered as giving, in their various ways, new bearings in English poetry.

Mr. Leavis ends his book with a brief examination of the

work of two young poets—W. Empson and Ronald Bottrall—whom
he regards as being in the tradition of poetry re-opened and
extended by T. S. Eliot. Bottrall's work he classes confidently
with Eliot's *Waste Land,* finding not merely similarities of outlook,
but also (what is more important for the validity of the comparison)
significant differences and originality in Bottrall's poems. Here one
may feel inclined to question his conviction. It is difficult to
believe that Bottrall's extra buoyancy and ' positive energy ' were
not well within Eliot's spiritual compass, but that Eliot saw their
limitations and so had to make a less direct approach to assurance.
It may be, as Mr. Leavis suggests, a representative difference
between the generations; but it seems possible that it is a difference
between greater insight and less. The question can be answered
only by Bottrall's future work.

It testifies to the healthiness of Mr. Leavis's critical standpoint
that one can question his detailed opinions and yet wholeheartedly
accept his main contentions. It means that he has brought to his
task not merely keen sensitivity and personal taste, but sufficient
intelligence and power of generalisation to approach a genuine
discipline of criticism.

D. W. Harding.

*THE LONDON BOOK OF ENGLISH PROSE, Selected and
Ordered by Herbert Read and Bonamy Dobrée (Eyre and
Spottiswood, 7/6d.).*

The London Book of English Prose marks the end of the
purple patch anthology. This is significant, for the type of mind
which rejoices in the more highly coloured passages of prose is
the type which seeks in poetry merely a particular kind of
emotional stimulus, which is satisfied with the immediate thrill,
and is uncritical of the way in which the effect is produced. Its
possessors are the last adherents of the magical attitude towards
words, and their criticism resembles incantation rather than
reasoned statement. Fortunately Messrs. Herbert Read and
Bonamy Dobrée are free from this kind of romanticism; for them
prose is an instrument which may serve the humblest as weil as

the most exalted purposes, and their aim is ' to provide material for investigating how far the instrument differs according to the use to which it is put.' The result is that *The London Book* is one of which the intelligent reader can make good use, not perhaps, as the editors suggest, as ' an instruction in the art of writing good prose,' but as a means of increasing his power as a reader, as a storehouse of material which can be used for testing and discriminating between the different responses to many kinds of prose.

On the other hand, no scheme of classification such as is attempted here can be entirely satisfactory. ' *Le style, c'est de sentir, de voir, de penser, et rien de plus,*' and as there are as many ways of feeling, seeing and thinking as there are authors and moods, each passage is in a sense unique, and the attempt to herd over three hundred examples into twenty-one categories is bound to be unsuccessful. The editors admit that their grouping has perforce been somewhat arbitrary, since ' few examples can be found which are single in their aim ' (though they curiously suggest that ' the best specimens are those in which the motives are least mixed,' which is not true unless one adopts a very naïve definition of ' motive '). Nevertheless it is possible to devise categories based on the different ways in which the mind works which would better serve the editors' declared purpose. Consider, for example, the difference in tone and intention between the extracts from Defoe, Swift and Conrad (all from the sub-section ' Story Telling '); the contrasted attitudes to their subjects of Gilbert White and Cobbett (' Autobiography and Journals '); the difference in poise between Dorothy Osborne and Pope (' Letters '), and it is immediately apparent that the psychological foundations are not properly laid. ' History,' ' Letters,' ' Politics,' 'Drama,' etc., are categories imposed from without, not necessarily corresponding to different tones, intentions and modes of feeling within the individual passages, and not necessarily implying any important similarity between the various exhibits collected under the single head. Psychology as well as sensibility is necessary for anyone who undertakes to edit an anthology.

L. C. KNIGHTS.

PHILOSOPHY OF THE SCIENCES by F. R. Tennant (Cambridge, 6/-).

Dr. Tennant is one of those philosophers who are engaged in discovering how many of our beliefs can possibly be doubted, and how far the doubtful ones can be eliminated without leaving our experience entirely meaningless. In the present work he brings the weapons of analytic and genetic psychology to lean on the task of discrediting as many of these beliefs as he considers dispensable. The only fundamental principle which he does not permit himself to doubt, and which he therefore refrains from examining by his method, is that any belief which enables us to make verifiable predictions gives us some sort of knowledge— possibly imperfect—about reality. All others, after a rather summary trial, are found wanting and rejected. The author points out that this is the criterion of truth actually employed by the sciences, and discusses the use made of it in various branches of so-called knowledge. History and natural theology, which accept it, are ranked by him as sciences, but dogmatic theology, which does not, is dismissed.

The book contains some penetrating criticisms both of rationalist philosophies and of the more extravagant speculations of modern mathematical physicists. There is little doubt that Dr. Tennant overrates the importance of genetic psychology as an instrument of philosophy, but his book can be recommended nevertheless as a lucid and readable exposition of a method of approach which is becoming increasingly fashionable nowadays, and is undoubtedly yielding some valuable results.

J. L. RUSSELL.

BOOKS RECEIVED

We have found it necessary to hold some of the reviews intended for the first number until the second, in which it is hoped our full reviewing policy will be apparent. Mention of a book under this head does not preclude a full review later.

MEMOIRS OF OTHER FRONTS: An Anonymous Novel. *(Putnam, 7/6d.).*

VARIETY OF WAYS, by Bonamy Dobrée. Oxford *(Humphrey Milford, 5/-).*

BYRON AND THE NEED OF FATALITY, by Charles *du Bos, translated by Ethel Colburn Mayne (Putnam, 10/6d.).*

THE CRISIS AND THE CONSTITUTION: 1931 *AND AFTER, by Harold J. Laski (Hogarth Press, 1/6d.).*

McTAGGART : A Memoir by G. Lowes Dickinson *(Cambridge University Press, 6/-).*

PLATO AND HIS DIALOGUES, by G. Lowes Dickinson *(Allen and Unwin, 6/-).*

CHAUCER, by G. K. Chesterton *(Faber and Faber, 12/6d.).*

SCEPTICISM AND CONSTRUCTION : BRADLEY'S SCEPTI-CAL PRINCIPLE AS THE BASIS OF CONSTRUCTIVE PHILOSOPHY, by Charles A. Campbell *(Allen and Unwin, 12/6d.).*

THE THEORY OF LEGISLATION, by Jeremy Bentham, *edited with introduction and notes by C. K. Ogden (Kegan Paul, 15/-).*

THE SOCIAL LIFE OF APES AND MONKEYS, by S. *Zuckerman (Kegan Paul, 15/-).*

DEVIL'S TOR, a novel by David Lindsay *(Putnam, 7/6d.).*

DEVIL TAKE THE HINDMOST : A YEAR OF THE SLUMP, by Edmund Wilson *(Scribner's, 10/6d.).*

NOTES ON CONTRIBUTORS

M. C. BRADBROOK is at present working on Elizabethan dramatic conventions. She has recently published an essay on *Elizabethan Stage Conditions : A Study of their place in the Interpretation of Shakespeare's Plays.*

RONALD BOTTRALL is the author of *The Loosening, and Other Poems*, published at Cambridge by the Minority Press.

' MARTIN CRUSOE ' is a house master at a well known public school.

G. LOWES DICKINSON'S most recent books are *McTaggart : A Memoir* and *Plato and His Dialogues.*

H. L. ELVIN is a fellow of Trinity Hall, Cambridge.

D. W. HARDING is researching on rhythm at the British Institute of Industrial Psychology.

WILLIAM HUNTER published an essay on T. F. Powys with the Minority Press. He is at present writing a book on the cinema.

L. C. KNIGHTS is researching on the background of comedy in the Jacobean period.

F. R. LEAVIS is the author of *New Bearings in English Poetry*, and *Mass Civilization and Minority Culture.*

Q. D. LEAVIS has recently published *Fiction and the Reading Public.*

JOSEPH NEEDHAM is, of course, *The Sceptical Biologist.* His latest book is *The Great Amphibium.*

C. H. PEACOCK is an undergraduate at Cambridge.

WILLARD THORP is an Associate Professor of English at Princeton University.

SCRUTINY is published by the Editors, 13 Leys Road, Cambridge, and printed by S. G. Marshall & Son, Round Church Street, Cambridge, Eng.

Vol. I. No. 2.   September, 1932

SCRUTINY

A Quarterly Review

Edited by

L. C. KNIGHTS and DONALD CULVER.

CONTENTS

'ENLIGHTENED' EDUCATION

A Discussion of
The Young Child and Cultural Problems.

IT would be perhaps useful to begin by making a rough classification of educationalists. My reasons for so doing will be
apparent later; at present we shall know thereby more clearly
whom we are discussing. I generalise, therefore, four ' classes ':

a. Those who are *seriously* and intelligently concerned with
cultural or psychological problems—a very small minority.

b. The ' enlightened ' parents and teachers of the ' New
Era ' or ' New Ideals Fellowship '—Froebel and Montessori
teachers, craftwork experts, etc.

c. Those who accept as right and healthy the conventional
education of the prep. schools and public schools. To these class
b are chiefly anathema; class *a* either ignored or classed with
Communism, so-called obscene novels and much else as dangerous
and unhealthy.

d. Those to whom education means instruction; not being
concerned with moral or cultural problems at all, they do not
concern us in this essay.

Class *c,* also, I don't feel it is necessary to discuss in much
detail. Their prejudices are often enough and rightly attacked,
but they are too obviously a stumbling block to trouble the
personal discrimination, if not the eventual existence, of the
intelligent. It is rather the subtler danger presented by the
'enlightened' educationalists that I feel to call for present analysis,
more particularly in the face of the somewhat careless and complacent approval given to them by admittedly intelligent people.

One number of the *New Era* will give anyone the necessary
pass-words of ' enlightened ' education. The child is taught to
' express ' itself through composition, through handwork, through
' freedom '; to learn by the ' play-way,' by individual work and
attention; usually, to absorb by example and otherwise an ideal
of collective service. To me, forewarned, it seems that the very
humanistic idealism of these ' pass-words ' ought to be a danger-
signal clear enough to make us suspect, at least :

(i) That the educationalists who use them have probably very little idea of what they are really doing.

(ii) Concurrently, that what they think they are doing bears small relation to cultural reality.

That these suspicions are well-founded I fully believe. To substantiate them it is obviously impossible to review *New Era* education in one lump; this must be done gradually. It does not however seem unfair to educators such as Froebel and Decroly to see as a constant background and type the work of Dr. Montessori, who would seem, moreover, the hardest to attack in face of her undoubted ability and the almost fanatical conviction of her followers.

Montessori sets out, in her own words, to produce ' the civilised child.'[1] What this means we shall see. She was intelligent enough to realise that the educator, especially the ' infant ' educator, must deal not only with the child's intellect but more constantly with his practical abilities. Her system evolved on practical lines. The children were taught to distinguish, to match, colours, sounds, tactile feelings, scents. They were taught economy (and ' beauty ') of movement—how to carry a chair, to strew rose-petals, to wash up, even to scratch gracefully and without unnecessary movement. I am certain that she was right in supposing that most children enjoyed the sense of mastery this gave them, as their play was taken up into the business of being educated.

The didactic apparatus followed. By long practice the children were able to ' feel ' and ' see ' their letters and their numbers— at their own trained speeds they began to get a mastery over the environment supplied to them by adult life. They began to concentrate on this achievement.

That was enough. Had Montessori been a genius she might have stopped there. But she did not. The moment the children began to concentrate she might have seen that too much of the child's energy was in danger of being absorbed into an artificial world.[2] She had not told the child to concentrate, but she was

---

[1]From a student's notebook. [2]The *utilization* of every atom of (the child's) natural energy ' Dr. Theodate L. Smith, *The Montessori System.*

leading it on—giving it just as much as it could manage and no more, till more and more of the child was being taken up into the business. Above all, she was suggesting that the child ought to be busy.

(To say that Montessori leaves a child free from suggestion is nonsense. The whole atmosphere of a Montessori classroom suggests an ideal of ' being busy,' and Dr. Montessori herself is not above direct suggestion of the crudest and most dangerous sort. I know of only one intelligent educationalist who could put the equivalent of *Mi volete bene?* on a school blackboard, and he would do it only to provoke an outburst of ' No's.')

Perhaps, even then, the life outside the classroom might have diluted to a mutual advantage the influence within it, but not so completely as would be possible in a ' Class *c* ' school. There the classroom interests a child so little that he can hardly form his standards from within it. He forgets or reacts. But with the coming of the Montessori, or otherwise ' enlightened ' boarding school practically the whole of a child's energy is organised educationally. The handwork specialist comes into her own. The child is set to create. He weaves, plays organised games, makes pots, models the moon (peccavi!), dances, does sums by the Montessori apparatus, above all is ' interested ' all the time. It is hard to realise, perhaps, the complete artificiality or the pervasiveness of a world in which everyone is ' interested ' or producing something the whole time, unless one works in it. Laying aside its effects on the children, the cultural conception behind it is badly distorted.[1]

Psychologically it may be due to sublimation on the part of unmarried women teachers, or to any other cause; culturally, the fact remains : it is the educationalists' conception of culture that is wrong. Without being unduly cynical, we need not be surprised. Culture is becoming more and more the concern of the few—there are too many ' enlightened ' schools. The parents or teachers who believe in the artificial educational world of constant creative activity, stimulation, ' intelligent interest,' idealism itself are those who aesthetically contribute to the conceptions of ' beauty ' of

---

[1] It would be worth while to investigate the culture of a decade that produced Ford and Montessori. Their likenesses seem to me more essential than their differences.

' style '; who appreciate the precious and reminiscent in literature—
a fact reflected too often in the handwork, art and music of these
schools, which retain all these misconceptions. (This is particularly
the fault of P.N.E.U. schools, if one is to judge from their publications.) It does not indeed need much knowledge of actual
conditions to sustantiate the suspicion that what the educationalist
thinks he is doing bears little relation to cultural reality.

What seems to me more important is our first suspicion—that
the ' enlightened ' educationalists have very little idea of what
they are really doing. This may concern the educationalist more
directly than the man with critical standards in view, but he cannot
afford to neglect it.

I will begin with a concrete, though perhaps particularized
example. I was at school at a somewhat conventional prep.
school, where boys from 9 - 13 were allowed three afternoons free
a week—Tuesdays and Thursdays, 2 - 4.30, Sundays 1.30 - 5. I
certainly cannot remember any boy abusing, except trivially, this
free-time. They went for walks, played cards or billiards, stuck
in stamps, did anything or everything. Where I am now teaching,
at an ' advanced ' school, we dare not leave the children an hour
alone.[1] If we do so, they destroy something, or fight. The children
are constantly (not only in their play) restless and listless at the
same time, and this with few exceptions (invariably at present
children born abroad and caught late into the system). The cause
as I see it is two-fold:

(i) They have in reality as much or more against which to
react than in a strict school—a constant moral or idealistic suggestion, probably not directly realized.

(ii) They are ' played out ' nervously or emotionally; consequently have less nervous power to react. So much energy
has been taken up into their work that they are in a highly
' nervous ' (i.e. devitalised) condition.

The two may appear contradictory—perhaps I may say that
my use of the word ' energy ' is suspect. Of course it needs

---

[1] A child in a prep. school is left much more ' alone ' than in an
advanced school. He may be subject to strict laws, but supervision
out of school hours remains mercifully inadequate.

' energy ' of a sort to be destructive—a physically exhausted person cannot be violent. I have found it necessary to use the term to denote what I might otherwise call the ' cultural potential,' that is, the nervous and emotional ' fund ' of the child. The assumption of the existence of some such basic vitality seems to me necessary. I would refer the reader for a parallel to the philosophy of Lao Tze (*The Secret of the Golden Flower,* trans. Wilhelm, notes by Jung). The point in question is the ' outward flowing ' and ' backward flowing ' methods : the contention that too much creative action leaves the ' soul ' wasted, so that at death it becomes ' kuei,' a daemon or unsubstantial ghost.

I have taken perhaps an extreme example. It happens to be one that concerns me at present. Essentially however I think my case to be fair—that the ' enlightened ' education of to-day is producing children brought up in a world of false values, and that in absorbing his energies to this end his teachers are ' expressing ' him rather than letting him express himself. The same objection exists in relation to any method carried far enough of 'interesting' a child—teaching by the ' play-way,' etcetera. It arises from a failure to understand amongst much else the meaning of play : above all, to say that the children are expressing themselves in doing four hours a day of handwork (if we count model-making for didactive purposes as handwork) is not true—unless we care to be pedantically honest about ' express.'

It is perhaps worth while, when a conclusion is reached, to reset it in different terms. I do not for a moment pretend that Montessori's work is valueless : I argue it to be insufficient to tackle cultural problems, dangerous because it has arrogated to itself control of a child's cultural and emotional existence. The cultural ideal of the enlightened educationalist is that of the 'escape' poet (*cf.* the world of Morris' *News from Nowhere*); this means a denial not only of the actual world but of the emotions connected with it. (It is something of a shock to realise that an ' enlightened ' sex education is often the result of a refusal to recognize the importance or indeed existence of sexual impulses in children.) The cultural problem re-sets itself to the educator as an emotional one. That this is possible should be clear by inference to any reader of D. H. Lawrence, where the emotional problem is seen to be indissoluble from the artistic.

I very much doubt the possibility or the wisdom of a direct cultural education.[1] Despite Montessori, children are not civilized beings. The responsibility for culture lies, as far as educators are concerned, with those who are trying to deal intelligently with the problem of clarifying and organising the emotions.

The majority of so-called psychologists or psycho-analysts must be ruled out. They are wholly uncritical[2] towards their own conclusions, they deal largely with definite neuroses that need little subtlety in analysis. For most of these Adler, Freud or Jung has prescribed a rule of thumb. It is as easy, it must be remembered, to be derivative in psychology as it is in poetry—and just as ineffectual. That is why I have italicized the word ' serious ' in my initial classification—those *seriously* concerned with cultural or psychological problems.

It is not my place here to discuss in detail the work of the two men who seem to me to fulfil in some measure this requirement— Homer Lane and A. S. Neill. Lane dealt largely with delinquent children, and Neill has also dealt with these. Also he writes badly, so that it is difficult for the public to realise the subtlety or the significance of his work. I do not for a moment suggest that Neill's work is in any way a solution of the cultural problem, nor that it is not largely remedial. But it is difficult to see from whom else the education of the next twenty years shall derive if culture is to remain a reality. Certainly, and this is my main theme, it has little chance by way of ' enlightened ' methods.

ALAN KEITH-LUCAS.

---

[1]This was being done however with some success, but under exceptionally favourable circumstances, by J. N. Wales at Dartington Hall two or three years ago. The school is now in other hands. [2]To trace a neurosis to a single incident is often considered sufficient, whereas it does not need much perspicacity to realise that the exaggerated importance of this incident can only be due to an emotional state already existent.

THE CHINESE RENAISSANCE

THERE are not many parallels to be drawn between China's Renaissance and our own. In one obvious respect the two are sheer opposites: China is not now restoring contact with a past phase of her tradition, she is deliberately breaking away from it. Here, for example, is a description of the attitude taken up towards Confucius, Mencius, and their followers by the creator of the Chinese Revolution, Dr. Sun Yat Sen (died 1925), whose portrait now looks down on every school room or University Auditorium and whose influence still dominates the political ideology of China.

' He was not in the habit of picking up the doctrine of any great author for discussion. Perhaps their power over him was mainly negative, in affording a ground for his attack on the existing social order, although he showed a great respect for these thinkers of his native land. His work was to overthrow the then existing Government, and he found no support from the philosophers whose views had been adopted to support a regime that he intended to overthrow. To popularise the work of revolution he needed to have an intellectual basis. It is evident that this new intellectual basis of his must go contrariwise to the old. As we know, he was a revolutionist in thought as well as in action.'[1]

Two points which appear clearly in this extract must be kept in sight if what is happening is to be understood. The intellectual movement in Modern China is primarily a consequence of the political movement. The traditional Chinese outlook is being remade—not because it was felt to be unsatisfactory in *itself* but because it plainly put China at a disadvantage in

---

[1] *The History of the Kuomintang,* by T. C. Woo.

the world-struggle. In itself, it is probably—to those brought up in it—the most satisfying that has been developed in the world. Its historic stability is almost a proof of this, but to the new generation it has already ceased to be satisfying. The second point to which my quotation witnesses is the extraordinary candour with which the pragmatism of the movement is confessed. A Western reader considering the last few sentences may have a queer sense that the unwritten rules which govern decency in our dealings with philosophical principles are broken. The intellectual game known as The Pursuit of Truth is being given away. If he feels this he will be tasting one of the fundamental differences between the Chinese and the Western traditions.

Pragmatism, the doctrine that ideas are tools to be judged by the work they do, we have of course in the West—but with us it is a fairly modern opinion, a result of reflection and a result still treated in most European schools of philosophy as a heresy to be refuted. Chinese philosophy, in its main stream at least, seems to have been very little concerned with the Problem of Truth ' as such.' Reflection has not exercised itself on the question ' What do we mean when we say that a statement is true? ' The place of the problem has been taken by an assumption, so initial as to be unformulated, that what is true is what had better be accepted. (Perhaps this is why the Western philosophy which has hitherto had most influence and been most helpful in China is John Dewey's Instrumentalism). The purposes of Chinese philosophy have been different from ours, and therefore the problems and the forms of argument and the structure of ideas have been different. The methods of comparing, defining, analysing and uniting notions, which we know in the West as Logic (whose physical application is Science) gained no permanent footing in the Chinese tradition. They developed instead another kind of subtlety, to which we are not ready yet to give the right kind of attention.

Naturally such a difference as this makes the translation of Western ideas into Chinese terms, and the introduction of Western methods into Chinese practice, an extraordinarily difficult undertaking. And the difficulty is immensely increased by the linguistic obstacle. The Chinese Classical language (only acquired fully by those who have been through an elaborate education which is already becoming rare) is, through its aptness for its own purposes, a most embarrassing medium for Western thinking. Often an impossible medium, in fact. The first great translator, Yen Fu, who gave China versions of Huxley's *Evolution and Ethics,* Spencer's *Sociology,* Mill's *Logic* and *On Liberty,* Jevon's *Elementary Lessons in Logic,*[1] Montesquieu's *l'Esprit des Lois,* and Adam Smith's *Wealth of Nations,* used a modified form of Classical Chinese, going back to the earliest language available, because, as he says, ' refined theories are better explained in the language before the Ch'in and Han Dynasties than in the literary language of to-day, which has a tendency to adapt the meaning to a certain stereotyped phraseology.' But this device is, I think, generally regarded to-day as inadequate.

The alternative is to use the colloquial, the new literary language of China, the *pei hua* whose relation to the classical language, *wen li,* is always so mysterious to us in the West. Perhaps we can come nearest to understanding the relation by comparing *wen li* to the language of the Authorised Version of the Bible and *pei hua* to our current spoken idiom. Always remembering that each word in *wen li* is essentially a *character,* which cannot be spelt out but must be known, a character whose sound is by itself not a sufficient clue to its meaning, since the same sound will belong to many characters. *Pei hua* on the other

---

[1]Yen Fu's choice of Mill and Jevons shows that the Chinese were quick to recognise the importance to them of our logic. And Hu Shih—the chief guiding spirit of modern intellectual China—chose for his Doctoral Thesis at Columbia *The Development of the Logical Method in Ancient China,* a work whose aim was to find in Ancient Chinese thought a stock with which Western logical method could be organically linked. His *History of Chinese Philosophy* (in Chinese), which followed, was received with an enthusiasm that showed how widely the problem was felt. The first volume sold 16,000 copies in the course of two years. Since then the critical work, to which many have contributed, on the early texts has made this age remarkable even in the annals of Chinese scholarship. But two strains of such diverse conditioning as Chinese and Western thought are not easy to unite.

hand is essentially a spoken language, though it is written also in characters a large part of which are the same as those used in *wen li*. As a language it has a more explicit articulation, a syntax more nearly equivalent to Western languages and a much greater facility in borrowing alien forms.

These considerations and the overwhelming advantage that the colloquial is spoken and read by millions, while *wen li* is known only to thousands and will soon be known only to hundreds, have made the creation of a *pei hua* colloquial literature the great effort of the last decade. In fact the phrase, ' the Chinese Renaissance,' is closely associated with this undertaking.

The pioneers in this movement have often compared it with the transformations that occurred in Western languages with Dante, Chaucer and Luther. But we should realise that the task for Chinese is more difficult and needs more conscious direction. The history of their vernacular literature is interesting. There had been great vernacular novels *(The Dream of the Red Chamber)* in the eighteenth century, enormously influential romances *(The Three Kingdoms)* earlier, and some colloquial verse. But these were frowned upon officially by scholarship, placed outside the pale of literature. So long as the Examination System with its stress upon a very rigid type of literary composition remained the only gate to influence, this could hardly be otherwise. In 1776, for example, the eminent critic Yao Nai enumerates thirteen types of literature (Essays, Forewords and Appendices, Memorials to the Emperor, Letters, Farewells, Decrees from the Emperor, Biographies, Epitaphs, Epigrams, Verses, Funeral eulogies, and Histories). Novels and drama are not mentioned. The Examination System went in 1904. Already by 1916 the creation of a vernacular literature had been urged—among others by Hu Shih[1]—but the real impetus to the movement came only in 1919 with a political incident.

---

[1]Hu Shih needs to be mentioned in connection with nearly every aspect of the Chinese Renaissance. His eight ' nots ' became the formula of the new vernacular style. Three of these read as follows:—*Not* to avoid vulgar words and expressions; *not* to use classical allusions; *not* to use hackneyed literary expressions without real emotion behind them. It is to be wished that our own

Modern China is very largely a students' creation—which should win it a special sympathy in the Universities of the world. In the peace settlement of 1919, the Japanese through the secret treaties with England and France which were their price for naval assistance, had gained at Versailles the former German settlement of Tsingtau. The news, reaching Peking, stirred the students of the Peking National University to an organised attack upon the pro-Japanese Ministry in power. When the betrayers fled all China applauded the students. A moment came of intense national consciousness and of angry criticism for the weaknesses of the old tradition. And with it the movement to create a new instrument for the national spirit in a vernacular literature triumphed. By next year a Dictionary of National Phonetics had been launched and *pei hua* was officially adopted in the primary schools as the National Language. A tendency— to look backwards instead of forwards—twenty one hundred years old had been reversed.

In the excitement of the new awakening, a crop of journals, political, literary, philosophic, came out. The best known was the monthly, *The New Youth,* which in the past had advocated radical reforms and had been the organ of the *pei hua* movement. It now became intimately associated with the Peking National University which, under a great Chancellor, took its place as China's premier University. The monthly had, as its editors and contributors, an extraordinarily able group of university lecturers. Another magazine, coming from the student body of the university, bore the significant title *The Renaissance*—its Chinese name, literally translated, means *The New Tide.* These journals did much to encourage vernacular poetry and the introduction of Western Literature into the vernacular.

With the use of *pei hua* the technique of translation changed. Formerly a translator, to command respect, had to be before

---

renaissance had had an equally influential and sagacious mentor in its early days. Later when vernacular poetry seemed slow in starting Hu Shih gallantly stepped into the breach with a volume of ' Experiments.' To-day he is directing a corps of translators whose programme includes a complete Shakespeare and the whole of Gibbon.

everything a master of the classical style. The famous Lin Shu is the outstanding example. Unacquainted himself with Western Literature or with any foreign language, he yet translated more than a hundred novels from several languages. An assistant sitting at his elbow would give him a rough version which he would render into classical Chinese. With a well matched pair of workers the method might have its advantages. Lin Shu's versions were often uncannily successful, capturing the spirit of the original much better than mere literal renderings. But he was often misled, sometimes far afield, by the incompetence of his assistants and his own literary exigencies. So Rider Haggard and Conan Doyle came to be placed by his prefaces among the best representatives of Western letters. But now clear and literal translation became a chief aim—partly as a means of testing and exhibiting the power of colloquial. Chou Tso-Jen, a professor of Western Literature in the Peking National University shows the change clearly. Formerly an able translator in the classical style, he gave up the Lin Shu tradition and carried literalism so far that his translations are sometimes unintelligible to the Chinese without previous knowledge of the language of the original. And not only the style but the matters translated changed significantly. In place of Lin Shu's *La Dame aux Camelias* and *Uncle Tom's Cabin,* came Tolstoy, Dostoevsky, Ibsen, Strindberg, Hans Anderson, and took the new generation by storm.

Meanwhile creative writing struck out in new paths also. Before long an important writer of short stories, Lu Shün, had appeared. His *True Story of Ah Q* (translated into English and available until the Commercial Press was bombed in Shanghai this year) treats the lowest, most helpless, type of coolie with a bitter unsentimental discernment that we could do with in modern English writing. He has Russian influences behind him—an influence that has not been very happy, so far, with us.

In recent years, the movement—no longer called the Renaissance—has taken a new direction. A section of the educated youth of China, less numerous perhaps than important, is now Communist in general outlook, and a group of ' proletarian ' writers has appeared. Lu Shün, at first an opponent, has become its most important adherent. It is said that he was first moved to help in creating a vernacular literature through seeing in Japan a motion-picture of a Chinese, caught in the Russo-Japanese War, about to be beheaded. These writers, though they differ in the degree of explicitness of their propaganda, show a tendency which is sufficiently indicated in their title. Some undertook translations—Bukharin's *Historical Materialism* has four or five versions in Chinese. But since Russian is a language known to few at present, the usual way was *via* Japanese, with the natural defects of second-hand renderings. Great numbers of Chinese, until recently, went to Japan for their advanced studies. These translations, being more propagandist than literary in their purpose, are often slovenly. Few English writings are available, so Upton Sinclair became an idol. Most of his books have been translated— *The Jungle* exists in several translations—and a critical biography was compiled before he himself published his *Candid Memories*. Some of the group have written novels and short stories. Some turned critics to wage word-battles with the ' bourgeois ' authors and the literary ' gentlemen of leisure '—chiefly with the *Crescent Moon* group, contributors to the Shanghai periodical of that name, among whom Hu Shih and the late Hsu Tze-mou are the best-known writers. There is irony in the fact that the man who condemned *wen li* as the language of the aristocracy, the cultured few, should now be reproached for his aristocratic tone and bourgeois ideology. Time, once it moves, moves fast in the immovable East.

Among these ' proletarian ' authors is the gifted Kuo Moh Ju who was earlier the translator of Goethe. *The Sorrows of Werther* (in vernacular and said ' to read like German rather than Chinese ') went to ten editions in its first year. We shall not understand the vogue which extreme romanticism has at present in China unless we realise that the feelings which thus expand have been drastically shut down all through Chinese cultural history. The shock with which our Western love literature strikes the Chinese student has to be seen to be believed. In his tradition, sex and sentiment have been sharply separated— at least so far as official literature goes. Sentiment and the tender expansive emotions belong with friendship. Sex is an affair of appetite, pleasure, practical and family considerations and intrigue, and as such it has not been a literary interest. Hence

the importance of the old vernacular subterranean novel literature
(The Dream of the Red Chamber). Hence too the official ban
upon it as undignified, childish, debilitating or decadent.

This difference in the position of romantic passion in the
orthodox codes of China and the Modern West is typical of the
second chief barrier between us. The inner arrangement, the
social standing and the incidence of the feelings is not the same
in the two traditions. Much that has delighted us, and been
approved as delightful, merely shocks them. Or *has* shocked them,
rather, for they are coming to meet us very rapidly. The areas
chosen by our cynicism and theirs have been different. This is
partly, no doubt, a difference between social conventions, a matter
of details in the order of the virtues. Tess Durbeyfield, for example
(in spite of a general liking for Hardy), often strikes them as a
bad woman, deserving the punishment she gets, for she is plainly
an unfilial daughter. (After all she seems to have appeared to
many of her own generation over here in an equally unfavourable
light.) But the difference may go deeper than this. Not only
may similar feelings, for them and for us, be elicited by very
dissimilar situations, but the very make-up of the more complex
feelings is perhaps different. Their tradition seems to have combined the ingredients of certain sentiments otherwise than with
us and *vice versa*. Of this the chief instance would be Love.
The blendings of tenderness, protective feeling, affection, sympathy, worship, religious satisfaction, truth-seeking . . . . with
sexual desire in various degrees of sublimation, which are
expressed for us by poets as different as Dante and Shelley, have
never I believe been formed in China—or, at the least, have
never been given any comparable expression.

If so, the wave of influence, chiefly from our English Romantic poets,—Keats, Shelley and Byron—which is now foaming
magnificently through the youth of China must be counted as the
greatest of these poets' triumphs. It may well prove that passionate love is, with logical method, the best gift of the West to
China. Naturally the adventures of these new passions have
been varied. They are not yet altogether at home in these new
bosoms. As our history shows, the conditions under which they
can be healthful are delicate and instable. In China, at present,
they run easily to Wertherism. Or alternatively, the passion,

finding no nourishing social roots, turns into decadence. Ernest Dowson is a surprisingly important poet to many Chinese eyes. Proust also, and Katherine Mansfield have marked vogues, which seem to have more than fashion behind them. Tagore, for example, thanks partly to a visit he paid to China, but still more to the ease with which he could be imitated, had for a time a fashionable success which soon departed.

Naturally, the content of our poetry rather than its form has most influence. But a number of poets have succeeded in carrying our forms over into Chinese already. The obstacles seem less formidable than we should expect. I have listened to *Jabberwocky* in Chinese without any doubt as to its metrical identity. But the perpetrator of this *tour de force*, Y. R. Chao, a chief creator of the National Phonetic Transcription, is a linguistic wizard. He was the first man in the world to teach himself (with the aid of C. K. Odgen's reversed gramophone records) to talk backwards.

I pick out from among the poets of the New China, one whose connection with Cambridge gives him a special interest for us. Hsu Tze-mou's death last year in an airplane accident in Shantung was a loss to China (and we have to learn that this now means to the world also) which it is hard to accept. He came to Cambridge in 1921. Mr. Lowes Dickinson met him in London, where he was studying political science, and persuaded him to try King's. His impressions of Cambridge—as a place where you lay on the grass in the ' Backs ' while wise men came to talk to you and insensibly you became a poet—have given us an almost magical standing with many Chinese students. At Cambridge he experimented widely in translation. I remember him bursting in upon me very early one morning with the brisk exclamation ' Last night I translated Biographia Literaria! ' Returning to China he taught for some years in Peking and then in Shanghai, coming back in the Spring of 1931 to Peking as China Foundation Professor of English Literature at the National University. His return, with Hu Shih, seemed to restore Peking to its place as the chief centre of the new Culture. I remember the electrical effect of his appearance, straight off the train, upon a philosophical luncheon which had been going rather quietly. Everybody became at once twice as alive.

In Cambridge (he had adopted in America the 'foreign name' C. Hamilton Hsu, for the convenience of Western acquaintances) he looked gaunt and worn. In China his face had filled out. He seemed younger (he was thirty-five) and with his remarkable pallor he was arrestingly good-looking. Energy and spirit showed in every movement. It was not hard to understand that he had become a figure in Chinese literature not without some resemblances to Byron. I have at hand only one translation from his poetry, which I owe to Li An-che, who tells me that it does not show him at his best or at his most characteristic.

> In a rickshaw, in deep night, I am on my way home—a
>   ragged old man drags with great effort
>   Not a single star in the sky
>   Not a single light on the road
>   The little flame of the rickshaw's lamp
>   Faces the dust of the road—
>   Bump to the left, bump to the right,
>   Trudges the rickshaw-puller.

> ' Rickshaw-puller, I say, How can this road be so dark? '
> ' Quite so, Sir. This road is indeed dark! '
> He pulls, pulls on, passing a street, passing a gate,
>   Around a corner, around a corner, all the same darkness
>   Not a single star in the sky
>   Not a single light on the road
>   The little flame of the rickshaw's lamp
>   Is darkened with the dust on the road—
>   Bump to the left, bump to the right,
>   Trudges the rickshaw-puller.

> ' Rickshaw-puller, I say, how can this road be so quiet? '
> ' Quite so, Sir. This road is indeed quiet! '
> He pulls—closely along a wall, as long as the Great Wall[1]—

---

[1] Translator's note: This was probably the wall of the Royal City. As the Wall is torn down now, a contemporary poem has become a historical allusion. So quick are the changes of Peking.

Passing a moat he turns into an endless, deserted, dark
  space.
  Not a single star in the sky
  Not a single light on the road
  The little flame of the rickshaw's lamp
  Waggles in the dust of the road—
  Bump to the left, bump to the right,
  Trudges the rickshaw-puller.

' Rickshaw-puller, I say, why is there nobody about on
  this road? '
' Really there is, Sir, only you can hardly see them! '
The marrow of my bones suddenly shivers with chill
Are those blue-wrapped things ghosts or men?
Sobbing and laughing seem to be heard
Oh, after all there are tombs all over the space!
  Not a single star in the sky
  Not a single light on the road
  The little flame of the rickshaw's lamp
  Twists in the dust on the road—
  Bump to the left, bump to the right,
  Trudges the rickshaw-puller.

' Ric-rickshaw-puller, I say! How can this trip be so long? '
' Really, Sir? This trip is indeed long! '
' But—you drag me back home—haven't you been astray? '
' Hardly know, sir! Who knows whether or not we have
  been astray? '

In a rickshaw, in deep night I am on my way home,
A group of unrecognizable ragged spirits drags with great
  effort;—
  Not a single star in the sky
  Not a single light on the road
  Only the little flame of the rickshaw's lamp
  Curls in the dust on the road—
  Bump to the left, bump to the right,
  Trudges the rickshaw-puller.

Perhaps Pouskin's *troika* had something to do with this: perhaps too, it is only a Western reader who would make it as symbolic a vision of China's present as this comparison suggests. But it is proper that we should realise here that, however successfully the Chinese are rising to their new destiny, to them the struggle must often seem nightmare-like, heartbreaking and almost hopeless. From us—from the preoccupied, still too shortsighted, West—they have hitherto had little enough understanding or co-operation. We have not yet realised that the quality of the world-life that our children are to inherit depends quite as much upon the character of the new China as upon any other one factor we can think of. If we were wiser we would make incomparably greater efforts to see that the values we most believe in came to the Chinese as freely and by as good channels as we could devise. An enlightened policy would offer them, for example, a First Class young Shakespeare expert to relieve their translators of some of the philological burden. It would give to the wandering Chinese scholars the special care which their enormously important work deserves. It would deliberately collaborate with them in their task of assimilating what is best in Western culture and reshaping it to suit their needs as a part of the future world order. Only those who have had the opportunity of working with Chinese students know how great their powers and how needlessly entangling and frustrating their difficulties are. A new age is being created in this wedding of East and West. Those to whom history gives some faith in humanity will envy the Chinese the richness of the joint heritage which will be theirs.

I. A. RICHARDS.

THE NEW BENTHAM

JEREMY Bentham died on June 6th, 1832. According to his wish, his body was preserved for the obscure purposes of science; but his ideas, quickly forgotten by his unappreciative countrymen, enjoyed a merely oblique, though extensive, survival in the views of the few men whom he influenced directly and in certain reforms and tendencies towards reform in the legal system of England. What was mortal survived; what was immortal was buried and forgotten. But now, one hundred years later, though there is no suggestion that this grotesque skeleton were better underground, there is more than one suggestion that what was so thoughtlessly buried might be unearthed. Indeed, this business of exhumation has already begun. It remains to be seen, however, whether what comes to the surface is merely a corpse—a spiritual corpse to be set beside the still unburied skeleton—or a regenerate Bentham, a man with a new life and a new meaning. Nobody gets out of his grave exactly as he was put in, but unless there is some phœnix quality in the mind of Bentham, unless he was buried alive by his contemporaries, mere exhumation will do neither him nor us any good. My business is, then, to consider this attempt to rehabilitate Jeremy Bentham, to consider the skill with which it is being performed, and to consider whether the result is something alive and with a meaning for present consciousness, or just one more of these embalmed corpses with too many of which the world is already cumbered.

But first let us consider for a moment the Bentham who was buried, the old, unregenerate Bentham. At his death, to those who did not know him and to many who did, Bentham was, I suppose, little more than a figure of fun; an eccentric old gentleman who wrote much and published little. But to his intimates, to the ' School ' which in later years he gathered round himself, he was a master, ' the great critical thinker of his age and country.' And by many others he was recognised as a figure of importance in the history of their time. Moreover, among those who have

left us their thoughts on the subject, there seems to have been
a considerable agreement with regard to the character of his genius.
By his friends he was known as a man of acute feeling; an affectionate man, extraordinarily sensitive to the pleasure and pain of
others, ' passionately fond of flowers ' and with a peculiar
sympathy for animals. He was a man overflowing with benevo-
lence towards the human race; the hero of Fénelon come to life.
Further, it was recognised that, as far as his intellectual activity
was concerned, ' the field of practical abuses ' was his field. His
genius, as he says himself, was for legislation. Bentham ' combined
what had not yet been done, the spirit of the Philanthropic with
that of the Practical. He did not declaim about abuses; he went
at once to their root; he did not idly penetrate the sophistries
of Corruption; he smote Corruption herself. He was the very
Theseus of legislative reform—he not only pierced the Labyrinth—
he destroyed the Monster.' And the great benefit which he
conferred upon his age and country lay in ' the example which
he set of treating law as no peculiar mystery, but a simple piece
of practical business, wherein means were to be adapted to ends,
as in any other of the arts of life.' He was ' the man who
found Jurisprudence a gibberish and left it a science.' And he
achieved this end because he combined with a considerable knowledge of English law a considerable contempt for its
precedents, its prejudices and its irrationality. But Bentham was
not, for his contemporaries, merely a reformer of the law and of
jurisprudence; he was ' the great critical thinker of his age and
country ' : and the lesson of his life was ' to show that speculative
philosophy, which to the superficial appears a thing so remote
from the business of life and the outward interests of men, is in
reality the thing on earth which most influences them.' Bentham
not only reformed the law so that (as Dicey says) ' the history
of legal reform in England in the nineteenth century is the story
of the shadow cast by one man, Bentham,' but he ' introduced
for the first time precision of thought into moral and political
philosophy.' And finally, according to the view which has been
repeated by every writer on Bentham since Mill's astonishing
essay appeared in 1838, ' it was not his *opinions* but
his *method,* that constituted the novelty and the value
of what he did.' Bentham founded not a doctrine but a method;

the ' method of detail,' ' of testing wholes by separating them
into their parts,' the method of ' exhaustive classification.' He
was primarily and predominantly a master of detailed analysis,
the inventor of a method of thought destined to revolutionize
every department of intellectual interest.

But the defects, no less than the merits, of Bentham's genius
were recognised by his contemporaries. Mill, who at the age of
fifteen ' embraced Benthamism as a religion,' later conceived
some doubts about the competence of his master's philosophy
to explain all things in heaven and earth. And particularly,
Bentham's genius appeared to suffer from the fact that his life
was ' secluded in a peculiar degree, by circumstances and
character, from the business and intercourse of the world.' In
English philosophy it had become (and to some extent still
remains) a tradition to separate experience from reflection, and
Mill saw Bentham as a master of reflection whose experience was
peculiarly and fatally restricted. ' He had neither internal
experience, nor external; the quiet, even tenor of his life, and his
healthiness of mind, conspired to exclude him from both.' And
consequently ' he was not a great philosopher, but he was a
great reformer in philosophy.' And besides this defect, others
saw in Bentham a man who ' did not appear to have entered very
deeply into the metaphysical grounds of his opinions,' a superficial thinker, a man ' who enumerates, classifies the facts, but
does not account for them,' a man whose thinking stops short of
the satisfaction of thought. It is true that to Mill Bentham was
a man who ' always knew his own premises.' But on this point
Mill seems to have been misled by Bentham's contempt for
established authorities, particularly the acknowledged authorities
of Jurisprudence, into thinking that his master was ' critical ' in
a more profound sense. A hundred men are contemptuous of all
the obvious and established authorities for one man who really
begins to think for himself, for one who is an independent thinker;
and Bentham certainly was not that one.

This, then, is the old Bentham, the traditional Bentham to
whom all the old books (including the eleven volumes of the
' Collected Works ') introduce us. Other writers during the
last thirty years have extended the picture. Some, like Leslie
Stephen and M. Halévy, have shown us the connection between

Bentham and his predecessors and contemporaries; others, like Professor Phillipson and Mr. Atkinson have given us a more detailed view of some special aspect of Bentham's work. But, in the main, what they have had to say has not seriously modified, though it has considerably extended, the story told by Mill and other of Bentham's contemporaries. But the new, regenerate Bentham, revealed to us in half-a-dozen recently published books, appears to differ radically from the old. We are given a new view of Bentham's life and character, and we are given a new view of the range and significance of his ideas. The real Bentham, we are told, did not live the restricted life of the legendary Bentham; and the real Bentham was a man of a far more universal genius than his contemporaries ever supposed. It is, however, impossible here to discuss this rehabilitation in all its aspects, and I have chosen instead to consider it as it is attempted in the work of two writers: Mr. C. W. Everett, of Columbia University, who besides editing one of Bentham's hitherto unpublished works, has given us a new view of the life and character of Bentham[1]; and Mr. C. K. Ogden, who has given us a new view of Bentham's ideas.[2]

A new biography may be new because it is based upon new discoveries or because it ventures upon a new interpretation of material already well-known. And it may be said at once that the novelty of Mr. Everett's work on the early life of Bentham depends in the main (though not entirely) upon certain discoveries he has made during the last three years while examining the voluminous collection of Bentham MSS. in the British Museum and in University College, London. He has undertaken, on the strength of these discoveries, to refute biographically the traditional view (derived from Mill) that Bentham was incomplete ' as a representative of universal human nature,' and to show us a Bentham less cut-off from the world, less untouched by hope and fear, desire and disappointment, than the old Bentham appeared to

---

[1]C. W. Everett. *Bentham's Comments on the Commentaries,* edited with an Introduction (Oxford, 1928, 15/-). *The Education of Jeremy Bentham* (Columbia University Press, Humphrey Milford, 1931, 15/6d.). [2]C. K. Ogden, *Bentham's Theory of Legislation,* with an Introduction and Notes (Kegan Paul, 1931, 12/6d.).

be. Not one of Bentham's English school, he remarks, had known
him before the age of sixty; and this incomplete acquaintance
with the early life and fortunes of their master led them to mis-
conceive his character, to think him less experienced than he
actually was. His early love for Mary Dunkly was unknown to
them, they were imperfectly acquainted with his strained relations
with his father, and his intimate and affectionate relations with
his younger brother Samuel. They knew only a Bentham
passionately devoted to the reform of the law : they were ignorant
of Bentham the lover, the man of the world, the man of moods,
of gaiety and melancholy, the man who had a disappointment
to forget, and the man who had difficult questions of personal
conduct to answer. And Mr. Everett has been able to show us
this new Bentham directly and vividly in the hitherto unpublished
letters to his brother Samuel. Henceforward, whatever defects may
be found in Bentham's philosophy, it is no longer possible to
account for them by referring to the ' secluded ' character of his
life.

But this fresh account of Bentham's early life does not stop
there, with a mere amplification of our knowledge of the facts,
it ventures upon a new interpretation of the old material, the
biographical material to be found in the last two volumes of
Bentham's collected works. This interpretation is sometimes a
little uncertain and indefinite, but so far as it goes it is admirably
performed. We are given a picture of Bentham's early life and
activities less encumbered than is usually the case with the detail
of his later theories, his ethical, legal and political opinions. Indeed,
this is perhaps the first biography of Bentham written by a man
whose interest lies in biography rather than in law or philosophy;
and from this, I think, it derives its great merits. The book is
short, boldly conceived, simply planned and executed in a manner
at once thorough and unpretentious. As a biography its only
defect is, I think, a tendency to over-simplification : certain events
in Bentham's life are ,singled out and made to appear more
' decisive ' than is the case in any man's life. Bentham's attendance at Blackstone's lectures, his friendship with Lord Shelburn,
his meeting with Dumont at Lansdowne House—these no doubt
were important events, but too much can be made of them as
absolute ' turning-points.' In this, and in some other matters,

Mr. Everett seems to me to have been insufficiently critical, to have relied too much upon the appearance of things. And this relatively uncritical attitude has resulted in a partial failure to formulate clearly and unambiguously, and to place in the foreground, the real point of the biography. And it has resulted also, I think, in an actual misunderstanding of certain aspects of Bentham's genius. For what, in effect, we are shown is not a Bentham who is a mere reformer of the law, a speculative thinker, a man whose work looks forward into the nineteenth century, an early democrat, but Bentham the *philosophe,* the creature of the eighteenth century, the native of France rather than of England, the companion in thought of Helvetius, Diderot, Voltaire and d'Alembert, the last of the believers in Benevolent Despotism. And, when this view is grasped firmly, when its implications are fully appreciated, not only is a new Bentham revealed, but the two ' major problems ' of Bentham's life (which Mr. Everett states but solves only perfunctorily) are at once resolved;—Why was Bentham's genius recognised more fully on the Continent, in North and South America and in Russia, than in England? And why did Bentham write so much and publish so little? Indeed, they disappear as problems because they become what we should expect, and not what puzzles us.

Now, the character of the *philosophe* is both peculiar and interesting; and, taken as a whole, it is so foreign to the English character that it does not surprise us that Bentham was so little regarded in his own country and so greatly respected outside it, wherever this *philosophe* civilization had developed and established itself. There are, I suppose, three prime elements in this character, and all were highly developed in Bentham. First, an age of *philosophisme* implies a peculiar confidence in knowledge, indiscriminate knowledge; it implies an hydroptic thirst for information about the present world, its composition and its laws, and about human nature, its needs and desires. The *philosophe* believes in knowledge in a way which we find difficult to understand—we who have long ago lost this confidence. And he can exist only when there is a certain rude copiousness about the supply of knowledge which permits no suggestion of a limit. His is an inventive, ingenious, mildly perplexed and easily satisfied mind; there is vitality but no discrimination. All knowledge appears equally significant; and there is so much to be learned that there is neither time nor inclination to stay and learn anything profoundly. One thing leads to another before it has itself been exhausted; and when every suggestion is followed, it is impossible to follow one suggestion far. It is true that the world of knowledge, after a visitation of *philosophisme,* somewhat resembles a September orchard after a plague of wasps, but to the *philosophe* himself his life appears an endless intellectual adventure; he is entirely ignorant of the senseless depredation his lack of discrimination involves, and he is unconscious of his vulgarity. And, if he is fortunate, the disenchantment which, it would seem, must overtake such a way of living, can be avoided.

But secondly, besides this belief in encyclopædic knowledge, the *philosophe* is remarkable for his general credulity. He does does not know what it is to be perplexed; he only knows what it is to be ignorant. And he is protected from the dilemmas of doubt by a tough hide of self-confidence. Appearing to doubt everything and to be engaged upon the construction of a new world from the bottom up, he is really the most credulous of men. There is plenty of audacity and some courage in his thought, but little freedom and no candour. He does not, it is true, begin from the same place and with the same prejudices as his less enlightened contemporaries, nevertheless he begins with a whole miscellany of presuppositions which he has neither the time, the inclination nor the ability to examine. There is, in short, little or nothing in common between the *philosophe* and the philosopher. For the *philosophe* the world is divided between those who agree with him and ' fools '; ' science ' is contrasted with superstition, and superstition is identified with whatever is established, generally believed or merely felt.

And thirdly, besides his thirst for knowledge and his naïve cast of mind, the *philosophe* is a rationalist, in the restricted sense that he believes that what is made is better than what merely grows, that neatness is better than profusion and vitality. The genius of the *philosophe* is a genius for rationalization, for *making* life and the business of life rational rather than for *seeing* the reason for it, for inculcating precise order, no matter at what expense, rather than for apprehending the existence of a subtle order in what appears to be chaotic.

There is, of course, much that is admirable in this type of mind; but it will be seen at once that its justification lies solely in the present appreciation of life and the world which it achieves, and not in any contribution to knowledge it has to offer to later generations. If it gives no present enjoyment to those who possess it, it is idle to look for other achievements. It can make no serious contribution to our store of knowledge; it denies the traditions of the past and attempts to fasten no new traditions on the future. What was important to the eighteenth century *philosophes* was not what they learned or discovered, not the knowledge they acquired, but merely the sense of life which the pursuit of knowledge engendered. And what is important to us is not the discoveries they made—these, for the most part, were negligible— but the general view of life by means of which they succeeded in making themselves at home in the world. The *philosophes* were the initiators of innumerable practical reforms, but in no direction did they achieve any real extension of knowledge; their minds were replete with half-conceived ideas. *Philosophisme,* that is, is a backwater so far as the main stream of European scholarship, philosophy and scientific research is concerned. The character of Voltaire's biblical criticism, for example, is entirely misconceived if it is considered as an attempt to make a serious contribution to the historical study of the Bible.

Now, the view I wish to suggest is that Bentham was, in all respects, a typical eighteenth century *philosophe,* and that for this reason his reputation was greater on the Continent than in England. And for this view Mr. Everett supplies much of the evidence we require. First, Bentham was moved by this peculiar, indiscriminate activity which belongs to *philosophisme,* and which accounts for his having completed so little of what he began. ' I am still persuaded, my dear Bentham,' writes George Wilson in 1787, ' that you have for some years been thowing away your time. . . . Your history, since I have known you, has been to be always running from a good scheme to a better. In the meantime, life passes away and nothing is completed.' Chemistry, the law, education, engineering, prison reform, psychology, economics—these were a few of the interests which served to supply material for his ' unnatural, unexampled appetite for innovation.' Never for a moment was his mind occupied with one thing to the exclusion of all others. And it is not surprising that, ' for the sake of expedition,' Bentham should desire ' 5 or 6 pupils who were initiated in my principles to whom I could give as many parts of my plan to execute under my eyes.' In his undergraduate days at Oxford the study of chemistry had much engaged Bentham's attention; and along with chemistry, of course, went astronomy. But for Bentham, as for more than one of his brother *philosophes* on the Continent, the science which appeared more important than any other was the science of government, for by means of this the whole human race was to be rescued from superstition. To create a science of politics, to apply the scientific method to the field of law, to unite law and science, to discover some means for measuring accurately political satisfactions—these were his ambitions. And in pursuit of this end, two things appeared to Bentham's *philosophe* mind to be necessary: first, a clean start; secondly, a code, something made, organized and definite, as distinct from what had merely grown. The clean start he found, or he imagined, in Russia; though of course he did not stay there long enough to achieve anything significant. Russia was virgin soil for the legislator; it appeared to be in the condition which the eighteenth century *philosophes* believed the human mind to be at birth, a *tabula rasa*. And secondly, the organization and rationalization of law implied in a code was what engaged Bentham's attention more nearly to the exclusion of other interests throughout the whole of his life. It was natural for a *philosophe* to hate the English common law and to be suspicious of judge-made law, for in both there is an element of uncertainty; on account of both English law can never be an artistic whole. But, in his contempt of the first, Bentham seems to have forgotten that law must change, that law is an expression of what is and not of what ought to be; he forgot, in short, what all the benevolent despots forgot. And his suspicion of the second was based upon a misconceived theory of knowledge. He appears to have believed that thought is always and expressly dominated by the circumstances of its generation, that there can be no thought independent of the psychological situation. The whole of every judgment, he believed, depends upon the psychical state of the individual who judges and derives from this its truth or falsehood. Such an opinion involves, of course, at once universal scepticism and self-contradiction; but Bentham was aware of neither of these implications. And in this matter, as in many others, he would have been on safer ground had he maintained his opinion as a mere prejudice instead of attempting to establish it as a principle. It is all very well to see Bentham's influence everywhere in the legislation of the nineteenth century, but when we consider how extreme his views about English law actually were, what must be noticed is, not the number of his isolated suggestions which have been put into practice, but the total rejection which his fundamental principles have suffered.

My view is, then, that the value of Mr. Everett's biography lies in what it suggests rather than in any specific interpretation of Bentham's life and mind which it offers. It suggests a Bentham different from the old, traditional Bentham, who was created by the liberal writers of the nineteenth century. In it Bentham is seen to belong to his century—the eighteenth century—and his environment. We are shown a living Bentham, a complete man, and not the mere thinker with which we have so long been obliged to content ourselves. And it remains to be seen whether, when this study is carried into Bentham's later life, yet another Bentham will appear. But, thus far, whatever his democratic sympathies, whatever specific modernity some of his suggestions show, what we have is Bentham the *philosophe*. And I venture to think that he remained a *philosophe* to the end.

It is now time to turn from this, to the other side of the attempt to rehabilitate Bentham; from Mr. Everett to Mr. Ogden. This new edition of the *Theory of Legislation* is a reprint, with a few verbal alterations, of Hildreth's translation (originally published in 1864) of parts of the three volumes prepared by Dumont from Bentham's half-French and half-English manuscripts and published in Paris in 1802 under the title of *Traités de législation Civile et Pénale, etc.* Hildreth's was not the first translation; an earlier was published in 1830. And it is not the most recent; Mr. C. M. Atkinson prepared a fresh, and on the whole better, translation with notes which was published in 1914. Setting aside, however the need for this reprint, what are important for us now are Mr. Ogden's *Introduction* and his *Notes*. For it is in these that the attempt is made to give a new range and significance to Bentham's ideas.

The *Introduction* is divided into three parts. First there is a discussion of Bentham's genius and ideas generally, secondly a few pages on the *Theory of Legislation* itself, and thirdly, some consideration of the relations of Bentham and Dumont. And something of interest has been found to say on all these topics. I shall deal, however, only with the first. Nobody denies Bentham's importance in the history of English law and legislation and it would be difficult to exaggerate that importance; and the discussion of the Bentham-Dumont relationship is in the main of merely historical and biographical interest. What is important for us is the thesis which Mr. Ogden undertakes to defend in the first part. ' It is that Bentham's merits, in spite of his great and deserved influence on the nineteenth century, are only now coming to be fully realized; that with every decade after the centenary of his death (1932) the significance of his achievement will become more obvious; and that fifty years from to-day he will stand out as one of the greatest figures in European thought, along with Réamur, Leibnitz, Newton Malthus and Helmholtz. . . .

' The grounds for the view that the full recognition of Bentham's work is still to come are as follows:

1. His theory of Language and Linguistic Fictions.

2. His contribution to the problem of an International Language.

3. His insight into the Psychology of Value, in conformity with the most recent tendency of Criticism.

4. His proposals for the Codification of nearly every legal system in the world, and particularly the Constitutions of South America.

5. His services to International Law.

6. His work on the Foundations of Humanitarianism and Public Health.'

Now, it cannot be denied that this estimate of Bentham's genius and importance creates a considerable revolution in the current view. And the question for us is, how far can it be maintained?

With regard to Mr. Ogden's thesis, three general observations may be made. First, he somewhat naïvely remarks that ' of course any estimate of Bentham must depend to a large extent upon our interests and our general approach.' Thus, if we are interested in what interested Bentham, he will be important; if not, not. And since Mr. Ogden is most interested in the theory of language, this is the most important aspect of Bentham's work. Secondly, the criterion of importance which Mr. Ogden suggests is this: wherever in a writer who died a hundred years ago any ideas (however random, disconnected and undeveloped) appear which ' anticipate the modern view ' of the matter, that writer is important. What makes a long-dead writer important are ' the echoes of modernity which reverberate through the fabric of his system.' And, whatever we may think of this criterion, since Bentham was a *philosophe,* a man with an inventive mind, a man of innumerable ' ideas ' none of which he worked out fully, it is not difficult, if we adopt it, to represent him as ' a giant in the history of English thought.' Indeed, if these are our 'interests,' and this our ' general approach,' Bentham will have few competitors for the place of first importance; though if what we are after is modernity, I should have thought that, so far from being modern, at least one half of the grounds which are advanced to substantiate this claim on behalf of Bentham belong to the last century. And thirdly, Mr. Ogden everywhere asserts Bentham's importance, provides us with numerous quotations from present-day writers who also assert his importance, but nowhere is this importance actually shown and brought home to us. We are promised much, a bold thesis is proposed, but little or nothing is fulfilled.

The view is, then, that Bentham's chief interest lay, not in ' the law as it ought to be ' (as Bentham himself seems to have thought) but in Orthology; and that his importance in the history of thought lies in his contribution, not to legal reform, but to the ' science of symbolism.' In this field Bentham was ' a century ahead of his times,' and he omitted to publish his writings on this subject merely because ' he had little hope of being understood.' But it must be said at once that considerably more and better evidence than Mr. Ogden offers us must be produced before this view can be established. That Bentham had this interest has always been known, and it was an interest he had in common with many of his contemporary *philosophes;* but unless we are to consult merely our own interests as the criterion of what is important and of what interested Bentham most, there seems no reason at all for not believing that the established view of Bentham as primarily interested in the law and as performing his most important services in that field, is not merely established but also true.

The notion of an International Language from which the irrationalities and complexities (and subtleties) of all existing languages should have been removed, is one which would naturally appeal to the *philosophe*. Whatever has merely grown is for that reason abhorrent to him. And it does not surprise us to find Bentham engaged, for a while, with this notion. But whether, on this account, he is to be considered ' one of the greatest figures in European thought ' appears to me doubtful, if not ridiculous.

And again, with regard to Bentham's psychology, all he has to offer us is one or two half-formulated doctrines developed for the purpose of jurisprudence. And the fact that there is to be found in Bentham's works a ' remarkable anticipation of the modern account of appetency ' will scarcely persuade us that he was a great psychologist. When we consider the state of flux in which the science of psychology is at the present time, the fact that in Bentham there are to be found, disconnected and undeveloped, some of the ideas which for one school of psychologists appear, for the moment, true, cannot be considered very significant or important. And, in any case, although Mr. Ogden loudly announces Bentham the great innovator in psychology, no evidence is produced to show that such a Bentham exists outside his eager imagination.

Bentham's services to International Law are neither extensive nor striking; and Mr. Ogden says nothing to alter this view. Indeed when we consider what Bentham might have done, having regard to the state in which international law then was and to the real character of Bentham's genius we are surprised that what he has to say is so commonplace and devoid of significance. Of the whole of Bentham's *Principles of International Law* (a very brief work), only the last part, *A Plan for an Universal Peace* (which has nothing to do with international law itself), is of the least interest to-day. No amount of rehabilitation will make Bentham rank as one of the great publicists of international law. And what has Mr. Ogden to say to the contrary? Merely that ' the very term *international* was his own creation.'

But first, if it were, it would constitute no very staggering contribution; and secondly, does he suppose that Bentham had never heard of *jus inter gentes*? We shall be hearing next that Bentham is the greatest English theologian, on the strength of a couple of Voltarian anti-religious tracts.

Mr. Ogden's *Notes* are designed, for the most part, neither to elucidate Bentham's meaning, nor (like the notes in Mr. Atkinson's edition of the *Theory of Legislation*) to elucidate points of law and legal history, but to drive home the thesis of the *Introduction*, that is, ' to provide the student with references to the more important recent literature of the subject, partly in relation to psychology.' Thus, his first note is on the Principle of Utility, and the question proposed is, ' To what extent has the intervening century illuminated or invalidated (Bentham's) main position? ' But the writer of the note seems unaware of the magnitude of the question he undertakes to dispose of in half a page, and unaware also of the destructive criticism of the last century which the utilitarian moral theory has not managed to survive. He is satisfied with a reference to Sidgwick and to Dr. Broad and the remark that ' there the matter rests '—which, of course, it does not. Other notes approach Bentham's most casual remarks with a pathetic seriousness, as if everything he wrote were full of ' echoes of modernity.' When Bentham, with a charming eighteenth century carelessness, observes that ' the occupations of a savage after he has supplied himself with physical necessaries, the only ones he knows, are soon described,' the note directs us to the latest works on anthropology for ' the modern treatment of these subjects.' Some of these *Notes*, however, are more relevant, and the most useful are those which refer us to other passages in Bentham's works and those which elucidate some historical question.

In short, this attempt to represent Bentham as a greater Orthographist than psychologist, and as a more significant figure in both of these fields than in the field of law and jurisprudence, must be considered to have failed. It has failed because there is no evidence to support it and because it rests upon a false criterion of significance and upon the mere predilections of the writer who makes it. Bentham was an ingenious man, and if we look hard enough we shall certainly find in his works some 'remarkable anticipations' of fairly modern views. But what of it? Does that make him a giant? A thinker like Bentham does not trouble to discriminate or confine himself; he skims the cream. He is not listened to in his own day because he is ahead of his time; but, when it is all over, he has nothing to hand on to his successors save a few random suggestions and a few inventions more ingenious than sound. And this, I think, is the character of Bentham's genius whenever it applied itself outside the law.

Bentham as a thinker belonged essentially to the eighteenth century, and this fact has been obscured by writers on Bentham because they are determined to direct their attention away from what Bentham actually thought and the eighteenth century presuppositions of his thought, towards the so-called after-effects or consequences of his thought. What has practical consequence is, almost always, the idea itself severed from the grounds and reasons which lie in the mind of the thinker, the mere *obiter dictum*. Cremation, contraception, co-education, this or that reform of the law, may be advocated for a hundred different reasons, and what is influential is, usually, the bare advocacy of the view. But when we come to consider what a man actually thought, it is not these bare ideas which are important, but the grounds and reasons for them which he believed to be cogent, the *ratio decidendi*. And in the case of Bentham, these grounds and reasons were all typical of eighteenth century thought, and nearly all fallacious. For Bentham, so far from having thought out his first principles, had never given them a moment's consideration. He had studied closely the work of Locke, Hume, Condillac and Helvetius. And while he was a thinker rather than a reader when it came to dealing with the law, he remained always a reader and not a thinker with regard to the philosophical first principles which lay behind. No man with so little interest in or aptitude for philosophy has ever taken so large a place in the history of philosophy as Bentham. It is safe to say that, so far as philosophy is concerned, there is nothing in the whole of Bentham's works which is original either in conception or exposition: both his ideas and the words and phrases in which he expresses them are derived almost entirely from the half-dozen philosophical writers whom he had studied. The principle of pleasure and pain comes from Helvetius, sympathy and antipathy from Hume, utility from any one of a dozen writers; his theory of knowledge is derived entirely from Locke and Hume; and wherever he ventures beyond what others had already thought out—as for example in his formulation of the principle of utility—he becomes at once confused and self-contradictory. Utilitarianism as Bentham left it is nothing more than a chaos of precise ideas. No man was ever more at the mercy of traditional doctrines in philosophy than Bentham. He belongs in these matters to the eighteenth century, and is an example of that not uncommon character in England—a man revolutionary in almost all practical matters, but dependent, unoriginal and cluttered up with prejudice in matters of speculation.

The principle of utility performed wonders in the reform of the law, or rather wonders were performed in its name, but this was possible only because the inherent fallacies which lie at the root of this principle were unappreciated or neglected. The principle, for the purpose of reform, was a mere *obiter dictum;* its *ratio decidendi* was ignored or forgotten. But if we wish to discover Bentham's quality as a thinker, we shall turn from these *obiter dicta* to their *rationes decidendi*, and we shall find these, for the most part, pointing us back into the eighteenth century, and moreover disfigured with the most naïve blunders.

And when we turn from his doctrines to his method, we find something admirably suited to Bentham's schemes for reforming the law, but (as a serious contribution to thought) something so naïve and childish that it is difficult to understand how it could ever have been selected as the finest product of the genius of any man who achieved so much as Bentham achieved in the way of practical reform. Bentham's method is based, of course, upon his view that ' in the whole human race, considered at all periods of its history, the knowledge of particulars has preceded that of generals.' But it is not the mere fact that Bentham was the simplest and most unconstrained nominalist in the history of English thought which is fatal to his reputation as a philosopher, but the fact that he assumed nominalism to be the only possible theory of knowledge, and was neither interested nor troubled to think about the matter.[1] His method is based throughout upon

---

[1] On this point Mr. Ogden has a characteristically wild remark. ' That such a man,' he says ' should be content to hand over

presuppositions which he had never so much as considered. Analysis and synthesis, data and generalization, materials and conclusions, the bricks and the building—this was Bentham's crude and unconsidered conception of the character of knowledge. Thought, for him, as for most of the English philosophers at that time, was merely decaying sensation; and what could not be explained otherwise could always be accounted for by the principle of Association.

It appears, then, that Mill's estimate of Bentham's genius is, with certain reservations, more accurate than the view with which we are now presented. Mr. Everett has certainly proved to us that Bentham's life and character were somewhat different from what we had been led to suppose; thanks to him we are now in possession of a fuller knowledge of both than was at the disposal of Mill or any of the intimates of Bentham during his later years. But so far as the interpretation of his mind and genius goes, we have little advantage over Mill. And if it now appears that Mill was wrong in believing that this ' method ' of Bentham's was so original and so significant, that he was wrong in thinking that Bentham's utilitarianism was good enough as a theory of law, though not sufficiently comprehensive as a theory

---

his most profound and considered achievements without comment to posterity, is merely evidence that he had little hope of being understood by anyone who had lived but one contemporary life. Even fifty years later, we find Vaihinger delaying the publication of his work *The Philosophy of As-If* till 1911, on the ground that such an extension of nominalism would be ridiculed in official circles.' In the first place, there is no proof that Bentham delayed publication for the same reason as Vaihinger—that is mere conjecture. Secondly, it is stupid conjecture when we consider the extreme carelessness of Bentham with regard to the publication of any of his works : with Bentham it was not a policy so much as negligence. And thirdly, whereas when Vaihinger was writing the predominant fashion in philosophy was Idealism and a man might well wonder whether a nominalist theory would get a hearing, in Bentham's day in England nominalism was a fashion, a prejudice, a universal assumption. Bentham's nominalism so far from being revolutionary was merely insipid conventionalism.

of morals, his *Essay* on Bentham still remains the best short account of the work and genius of his master. Bentham is a great and important figure in the history of English law, but there appears to me no doubt at all that if we follow the direction in which Mr. Ogden points, and look in Bentham for a man whose main interest and most important work was in Orthology, psychology, logic and philosophy, rather than in ' the law as it ought to be ' and in jurisprudence, we shall end with an entirely false view of Bentham's genius.

Bentham's life and work abound in remarkable contrasts: a man without any real interest in speculative thought for its own sake, and yet a ' hermit '; a man who shrank from the world, the practice of the law and the compromises of politics, and yet one whose beneficial influence was felt entirely in these practical matters; a man who by force, cunning and ridicule killed many of the fallacies which dominated legal and political theory, yet one whose arguments were, in most cases, misconceived, and whose own thought was riddled with the most naïve fallacies; a man who spent his life talking about first principles, but who never once got beyond a consideration of what is secondary and dependent. The lesson of his life is not, as Mill thought, to show how speculative philosophy enters into and influences practical life, but to show that what in speculation is always the most influential in practical life is something half-thought out, something hazy, indefinite and confused. It is not the philosopher, the victim of thought, who influences our practical conduct of life, but the philosophaster, the *philosophe*. The significance of Bentham as a reformer of the law and as the first English writer on jurisprudence of any importance, is immense. But as a philosopher, as a thinker, he is negligible. ' It is the fashion of youth,' wrote Hegel, ' to dash about in abstractions: but the man who has learnt to know life steers clear of the abstract '' either-or,'' and adheres to the concrete.' And Bentham (says Mill) was ' a boy to the end.'

MICHAEL OAKESHOTT.

WHAT'S WRONG WITH CRITICISM ?

A REPRESENTATIVE set[1] of books of contemporary criticism is at any rate an occasion for the inquiry proposed above. That literary criticism is not in a healthy state we all— readers of *Scrutiny*, or those, at least, in sympathy with the under- taking—assume; the undertaking explicitly affirms it. But perhaps we assume a consensus too easily: it is of the essence of the plight that the plight can be questioned. As of taste, so of criticism; we must expect to be assured with Olympian dispassionateness that it always has been in a bad state and always will be. Such dis- passionateness is probably invincible. Yet that the argument should be found impressive represents one of the most desperate of the conditions that we have to deal with, and the challenge to cogency of statement should sometimes be taken up.

No one is going to assert that criticism was ever in a satis- factory state. Just what, then, is peculiarly, and so desperately, wrong to-day? Why all this fuss?

One may start, paradoxically, by asserting that this age will be remarkable in literary history for its achievement in criticism. The histories of literary criticism contain a great many names, but how many critics are there who have made any difference to one— improved one's apparatus, one's equipment, one's efficiency as a reader? At least two of them are of our time: Mr. Eliot and Mr. Richards; it is a very large proportion indeed of the total. Mr. Richards has immensely improved the instruments of analysis, and has consolidated and made generally accessible the contribution of Coleridge. Mr. Eliot has not only refined the conception and

---

[1]*Poetry and the Criticism of Life*, H. W. Garrod. *Variety of Ways*, Bonamy Dobrée (Oxford, 5/-). *Criticism*, Desmond MacCarthy (Putnam, 7/6d.).

the methods of criticism; he has put into currency decisive re-organizing and re-orientating ideas and valuations. The stimulus of these two very dissimilar forces has already made itself felt, and there is no reason to suppose that Mr. Empson's book will prove to be the only important critical work produced by their juniors.

But all this does not affect the conviction expressed in the second sentence of this essay. That this is so one might attempt to enforce by adducing Professor Garrod's *Poetry and the Criticism of Life*. Professor Garrod says of Coleridge : ' The appeal of his poetry is strong with me; and the appeal of the man. But just those qualities which make a critic he seems to me to lack.' And that disposes of Coleridge. It will be readily and rightly guessed that just those qualities which make a critic are what the rest of the book shows Professor Garrod to lack : yet it was respectfully reviewed by respected authority. But evidence of this kind is not to be seriously urged. There is long-established precedent for Professor Garrod and his reception, and his book does not really raise the important issues.

Nor does Mr. Bonamy Dobrée's *Variety of Ways*. One might set it over against Professor Garrod's book as showing that academic criticism is not necessarily unprofitable. Mr. Dobrée is not merely elegant, and such scholarly essays as his on Congreve perform a function, though his treatment of rhythm and style— indeed of all he handles—would have been more profitable if his scholarship and taste had been served by a better analytic equipment. But this is not the debate intended in the question, ' What's wrong with criticism? '; we cannot start from this text.

It is the third book, Mr. Desmond MacCarthy's, that really raises the issues. For Mr. MacCarthy is not a professor of poetry or a scholar or a specialist, but a professional critic, a journalist; in him criticism undertakes its essential function of keeping an educated body of taste and opinion alive to the age, of testing, nourishing and refining the currency of contemporary culture. And that there is still in some sense somewhere something like an educated body of taste and opinion the intelligence and limitations of Mr. MacCarthy's *Criticism* together show. For nowhere does it give evidence of any subtlety of first-hand judg-ment. In all the testing cases—in dealing with Donne and David

Garnett, for instance—he is conventional and superficial. D. H. Lawrence he compares with Carlyle and T. S. Eliot with Browning, leaving the stress on the likeness; no one intelligently interested in either could have done that. Mr. MacCarthy, then, is not an original critic; he is the journalist-middleman of cultivated talk.

On this estimate he does at any rate testify to the existence of a certain cultivated *milieu* where there is an active interest in literature. But his significance for this inquiry lies in his distinction—for he is distinguished, if not quite in the way his reputation intends. In the serious pursuit of his function he enjoys something like a lonely eminence. Who else is there? In a healthy state we should have at least twenty journalist-critics of his quality, whereas if we look round we can see only the *confrérie* of the weeklies and the Sunday papers. The distinction so indicated, moreover, is one that the bulk of his readers cannot be counted on to appreciate to the full. Who, if not they, form the *élite* that follows the reviewing in ' our more elegant weeklies ' (for the reviewing here, whatever may be the case with the accompaniment to the Sunday advertising, does appear to be taken seriously by such educated class as we have)?

Here, then, we have come to what is radically wrong with criticism. The public that makes any show of interest in literature is only a small minority, and though there may be behind Mr. MacCarthy a circle actively and intelligently interested, it is a tiny minority of a minority, which, for all the effect it has as representing generally operative standards, might as well not exist. And where there is no nucleus of an educated public representing such standards the function of criticism has fallen into abeyance, and no amount of improvement in the apparatus and technique will restore it. It becomes impossible even to get the plight recognized. My argument, for instance, (I lapse appropriately into the first person), will, except to those who find it obvious, seem for the most part an arbitrary tissue of arrogant dogmatisms.

It is more than the function of criticism that has fallen into abeyance. To those who take a serious interest in literature it must often seem as if their interest were curiously irrelevant to the modern world; curiously, because a serious interest in literature starts from the present and assumes that literature matters, in the first place at any rate, as the consciousness of the age. If a literary tradition does not keep itself alive here, in the present, not merely in new creation, but as a pervasive influence upon feeling, thought and standards of living (it is time we challenged the economist's use of this phrase), then it must be pronounced to be dying or dead. Indeed, it seems hardly likely that, when this kind of influence becomes negligible, creation will long persist. In any case, a consciousness maintained by an insulated minority and without effect upon the powers that rule the world has lost its function. And this describes well enough the existing state of affairs. To put it in more particular terms, no one interested in poetry can suppose that if all the serious poets now writing died within the year the newspapers would register any noticeable shock. The world is not interested; and this lack of interest must seem to those concerned about culture more frightening than hostility.

The world, it will be retorted, has something else to be interested in; those who see the desperate need for action, political and other, can have no concern to spare for the state of poetry and literary criticism. The need for political action few will be inclined to deny. But it seems pertinent to inquire the worth of political action or theory that is not directed towards realizing some idea of satisfactory living. I do not assert that traditional culture and literary tradition are identical, but their relation is such that those who are aware of it will not expect one to survive without the other; and it would seem romantic to expect that an adequate idea will issue out of amnesia—out of a divorce from the relevant experience of the race.

For some, of course, the problem is simple; inherited art and culture are bourgeois and must be replaced. Upon this philosophy I can hardly hope to make an impression, but I can hope, for most who are likely to read me, to have made clear the nature of my concern about the death of the literary tradition and the state of criticism—that is not a concern for the prestige of a minority as such.

The phrase ' minority culture ' appears to have gained currency. What does not appear to be equally current is the realization that a genuine concern for ' minority culture ' cannot be satisfaction with it. The more one cares about the values it preserves, the more clearly one realizes the function it represents, the less likely is one to be drawn towards the pleasures of Pharisaism.

There are, of course, the pleasures of pessimism, and they have no doubt been suspected of complicity in my assertion about the newspapers and the hypothetical death of all our poets. But the assertion was critically sober, and the stress judicial. For, as a matter of fact, the decay of the literary tradition is less conclusively manifested in the grosser absurdities of, say, the *Observer* (which after all are notorious) than in the more respectable absurdities of our most respected anthologies, with their scores of modern poets—Professor Lascelles Abercrombie recently presented a drove of forty. These anthologies are not, among Mr. MacCarthy's public (let us say), a byword for fatuity; they exhibit fairly the state of contemporary taste. The standards that, maintained in a living tradition, should have made them impossible have vanished, for the tradition has vanished, and the conventional respect for poetry of the cultivated remains, in general, purely conventional, uninformed by tradition—' traditional,' that is, in the bad sense.

Poetry, then, though it may still be examined on at school, has ceased to matter; it is taken, if at all, on authority. Where, on the other hand, the world takes interest, authority—the authority vested in tradition—has disappeared, as was foreseen by the late Sir Edmund Gosse forty years ago:

' One danger which I have long foreseen from the spread of democratic sentiment is that of the traditions of literary taste, the canons of literature, being reversed with success by a popular vote. Up to the present time, in all parts of the world, the masses of uneducated or semi-educated persons, who form the vast majority of the race, have been content to acknowledge their traditional supremacy. Of late there have seemed to me to be certain signs, especially in America, of a revolt of the mob against our literary masters. . . . If literature is to be judged by a plebiscite and if the plebs recognizes its powers, it will certainly by degrees cease to support reputations which give it no pleasure and which it cannot comprehend. The revolution against taste, once begun, will land us in irreparable chaos.'[1]

---

[1] *What is a Great Poet?* (1889), in *Questions at Issue.*

Skimming through *The Life and Letters of Sir Edmund Gosse* one cannot help reflecting that he himself was a portent. He had, it appears, no qualification for authority except a belief in his right to it. This was sublime : ' You are a poet of a high order,' we find him writing to Mr. J. C. Squire, 'and a mind in curiously close sympathy with me. I feel myself singularly in tune with you. I understand exactly what you say. It is so rare. . . . You will make a great name !' (And there are elsewhere in the book appreciations of Mr. Squire that deserve to become anthology-pieces). His inability to see what is in front of him is sometimes almost incredible : he cultivates André Gide and finds Mr. E. M. Forster's *Howard's End,* that most maidenly, most transparently innocent, of books, ' sensational, dirty, and affected.' His critical incapacity, sometimes comic, was always complete. And yet his success was complete too; he imposed himself and became an institution, the embodiment of critical authority. It looks as if the absence of standards that I have been deploring is no new thing. Nevertheless there is an important difference between the age of Edmund Gosse and the age of Arnold Bennett. The standards in Gosse's time may not have been generally operative among the ' cultivated,' but respect for them was. Nothing else can explain his ascendency : he stood for the taste and learning that, being above the general level, made it possible for the common man to hope to improve himself. But a tradition that allows itself to be embodied in a Gosse is obviously in danger.

Civilization advanced. The triumph of ' democratic sentiment ' that Gosse foresaw was brought about by forces that he does not appear to have noticed. Mass-production, standardization, levelling-down—these three terms convey succinctly, what has happened. Machine-technique has produced change in the ways of life at such a rate that there has been something like a breach of continuity; sanctions have decayed; and, in any case, the standards of mass-production (for mass-production conditions now govern the supply of literature) are not those of tradition. Instead of conventional respect for traditional standards we have the term ' high-brow '; indeed, such remains of critical standards as a desperate and scattered minority may now fight for can hardly be called traditional, for the tradition has dissolved : the centre—

Arnold's ' centre of intelligent and urbane spirit,' which, in spite
of his plaints, we can see by comparison to have existed in his
day—has vanished. Instead we have the Book Society, Ltd.,
recommending ' worth-while ' books with the psychological
resources of modern publicity, one of the most valuable of which
is the term ' high-brow.'

It is, then, vain to hope that standards will somehow re-
establish themselves in the higgling of the market; the machinery
of civilization works unceasingly to obliterate the very memory of
them. What then can be done? In despair one toys with desperate
recourses : would it be of any use, before it is too late and oblivion
sets in, to try to focus what remains of tradition in a ' central
authority representing higher culture and sound judgment '—to
try whether an organ can be found, capable of the function
that Arnold assigned to academies ? ' Such an effort,'
Arnold reminds us, ' to set up a recognised authority, imposing
on us a high standard in matters of intellect and taste, has many
enemies in human nature.' These enemies are now, to a degree
that Arnold can hardly have foreseen, invested with power and
conscious of virtue. Yet there are friends too—the need for such
a standard is also in human nature—and perhaps the extremity
of the case will rally them to the effort.

And then one remembers Sir Edmund Gosse : there we have
the kind of mind that gets into academies. There is also the
academic mind of the more respectable order represented by
Professor Lascelles Abercrombie. Professor Abercrombie, writing
on Literary Criticism in a recent *Outline of Modern Knowledge*
(a production symptomatic of the times), devoted a third of his
space to Aristotle and a proportionate amount to Longinus, and
in his bibliography mentioned at least one bad and several insignificant books, but neither Mr. Richards nor Mr. Eliot. Still, the
article is scholarly, and there might be something to be said for
this kind of academic mind if only it could be brought into touch
with what is alive.

Someone may by now have remembered that there is a Royal
Society of Literature in being. Founded by George IV, it is
already venerable : might not something be done to establish a
recognized ' centre of intelligent and urbane spirit ' here? The
Society is not notorious; no one, except its members, seems to

know much about it. Readers of the *Times Literary Supplement*, however, will remember to have seen at intervals long and respectful reviews of certain volumes called *Essays by Divers Hands*. The hands are those of Fellows of the Royal Society of Literature.

If one hunts down the books in a library one has to brace oneself before dipping, they look so dull. Yet they do contain light reading. For instance, one may have the luck to take down the volume (1923) in which Mr. Alfred Noyes discourses on *Some Characteristics of Contemporary Literature* : ' In the current number of the *Quarterly Review* there is a review—an exceedingly able review—of a recently published novel, which, I say without hesitation, and without the slightest fear that anyone here who has seen it will disagree with me, is the foulest that ever found its way into print.' After the moralist the literary critic : ' The technical quality of the writing is beneath contempt.' Mr. Joyce is not even original; in realistic audacity he was forestalled by Tennyson in *Locksley Hall*. (Of *In Memoriam*, by the way, we are told : ' It is probably the greatest elegy in any language, not because this or that authority says so, but demonstrably.') We are not, then, surprised to find that Mr. Noyes stands for tradition, and does not mince his words : ' All over the English-speaking world this hunt '—represented, we gather, by Mr. Joyce and Mr. Eliot—' for an easier way in technique has been accompanied by a lowering of the standards in every direction. This quality of the thought and the emotion has been incredibly cheapened, and the absence of any fixed and central principles has led to an appalling lack of discrimination. Literary judgments in many cases have become purely arbitrary.' And Mr. Noyes indicates his fellow-Paladins : ' . . . The desire to break the continuity of our tradition has been fought by Mr. Edmund Gosse with the weapon of an irony as delicate as that of Anatole France. Critics of a later generation like Mr. Clutton Brock, Mr. J. C. Squire, Mr. Robert Lynd have also steadily sought to maintain a just balance between the old and the new.'

Mr. Squire and Mr. Lynd, a defender of tradition in any serious sense would have to point out, have been among the most subtle and successful democratizers of standards. And it is comment enough on the academic conception of tradition—which is, of course,

what Mr. Noyes stands for—to point to the company it keeps. In
the Royal Society of Literature there is, for instance, Dean Inge,
in whom, no doubt, in spite of the differing communions, Mr.
Noyes finds a kindred spirit. Dean Inge, too, stands to the defence
of technique against literary Bolshevism. He prescribes (1922)
classical metres for English poetry: ' We want laws, or we shall
lose all beauty of form.' On the other hand we remember, hardly
with surprise, that Dean Inge has contributed his share to the
advance of civilization—not without due recognition, we may
hope: ' I cannot be too grateful for the generosity of the *Evening
Standard, . . . '* as he says in *More Lay Thoughts of a Dean.* He
has asserted authority in multifarious provinces, and maintained
standards, particularly in the matter of Christian gentility: ' He
was no gentleman,' he says of Donne, ' and a very equivocal
Christian. I have a rooted distrust of men of letters who, like
Donne, Huysmans, and the African novelist, Apuleius, wallow in
garbage for many years, and then suddenly '' get religion.'' '

     To-day journalism solicits us everywhere, and the academic
conception of tradition, clearly, does not save its champions from
wallowing. There are, of course, in the Royal Society of Literature more respectable representatives of the academic mind than
Dean Inge, and the aristocratic tradition is also represented. So,
since we are also told that it is the policy of the Society ' to focus
its prestige ' by ' adding to itself under a rigorous system of
election a majority of the most distinguished writers of the time,'
we can still be interested. We look anxiously to see who these
writers are. Mr. Laurence Binyon is one, we must suppose. Mr.
de la Mare is also of the Society. However, he cancels out against
Mr. John Drinkwater, who is also there: any ' recognised
authority ' hoping to impose on us ' a high standard in matters
of intellect and taste ' must combat the confusion that lumps Mr.
de la Mare and Mr. Drinkwater together as ' Georgian poets.'
Mr. G. K. Chesterton is also a member, which, perhaps, may pass
without comment one way or the other. But when we come to
Mr. Hugh Walpole and Miss Clemence Dane we know that the
worst is true and the hope was foolish. For Mr. Walpole and Miss
Dane are two-fifths of the Book Society Ltd. (or, to be strict, of
the Selection Committee) and Miss Dane wrote a book on ' the
traditive novel ' called *Tradition and Hugh Walpole.*

There are other Fellows. There is Miss V. Sackville West, for instance, who, addressing the Society on *Some Tendencies of Modern English Poetry* (1927) contends that ' free verse ' is a ' more civilized form ' than the other kinds. But this can hardly tend to make Mr. Eliot feel more at home in the Society (for we find him to our astonishment a Fellow). Nor can his presence in such company tend to reverse our conclusion as to the influence of the Society on standards.

The Royal Society of Literature, we must conclude, has no function, unless the incidental one of hall-marking the kind of literature standardized by the Book Society, Ltd.

The English Association, which in our search for a likely organ we turn to next, can, on the other hand make out a very strong case for its existence. Its province is education, and its function, in brief, to organize throughout the country such interest in English literature as will admit of organization. But, in the absence of any serious current standards or any ' central authority representing higher culture and sound judgment,' what can it do, we ask, to supply the lack, or to resist the triumphant enemy? And we note with misgiving in the Bulletins of the Association the prominence of certain familiar names, the interlocking with the Royal Society of Literature. But we are not in a hurry to generalize, or to cast up the account, though we get many disquieting glimpses both of the educational work in the country at large and of proceedings at the top of the hierarchy. What Mr. Alfred Noyes is reported as saying to various branches might be adapted and applied to lectures and addresses sponsored by the Association: ' It was perfectly obvious, he said, that many people who wrote about poetry didn't know what they were writing about.' There are lectures on Mr. Walpole's and Mr. Priestley's novels, and even on Mr. Priestley's schooldays. And the healthy-minded dislike of intelligence voiced by Colonel John Buchan does come to have the effect of a corporate spirit: ' Again,' he says, championing the Victorians in an address called *The Novel and the Fairy Tale* (July, 1931), ' they were not clever people, like those who decry them, and in this they were akin to the ordinary man, who is nearly as suspicious of mere cleverness as Mr. Baldwin.' Still, some compromise, perhaps, there must be, and if culture is to enjoy the support of Good-Fellowship it must pay the price; the Good-Fellow ticket is inevitably the anti-highbrow.

But after a glance through the current Bulletin (December, 1931) one's suspicion that the price may leave nothing worth keeping becomes something more than a suspicion. For Professor Oliver Elton, elected President for 1932, speaking at the Annual Dinner of the Association, with the Archbishop of Canterbury in the chair, is reported as having concluded : ' At any rate, whether we are saints or whether we are not saints, we shall all be the better for doing two things, reading the novels of Mr. Hugh Walpole and being members and supporters of the English Association.' Dr. Elton was not speaking without precedent : the *entente* between the English Association and the Book Society had already been well advertised. At the Annual Dinner a year before, Mr. Hugh Walpole, Chairman of Committee (succeeding Mr. J. C. Squire), had said with reference to Mr. J. B. Priestley (once of the Book Society) ' This is the point that I wish to make; that he has, particularly by a recent book of his which we all know, given a new dignity to the position of the " best seller." It is, I believe, a best seller, and it deserves to be. To call it a classic would be, of course, premature and perhaps exaggerated, but I think to say that it is a work of very high literary excellence and that it will live is not going too far.' Mr. Priestley, unfortunately, wasn't present to make the graceful reply, but the President of Magdalen, another fifth of the Selection Committee of the Book Society, Ltd., was, so that Mr. Walpole's ' eminence in letters and enthusiasm for literature ' did not go unsignalized.

Is it necessary to inquire further? Looking over the reports of educational work in the country generally we can no longer doubt that it is largely a matter of propagating, and endorsing with the authority and prestige of the Association, the standards of the Book Society. If anyone still hesitates to concur, there is the field of poetry to consider, where, unhappily, we are left no excuse for suspending judgment. For the English Association is responsible for the anthology, very widely used in schools, called *Poems of To-day*, the two volumes of which (as I have heard indignant teachers who have to use it lament) contain between them hardly half-a-dozen good poems. The importance of *Poems of To-day* to the finances of the Association is referred to at most Annual General Meetings. At the Annual Dinner, 1926, Mr. Baldwin, as President-elect, said: ' We are solvent, we are considerably on the right side; but that is because we have been living on the earnings of *Poems of To-day*. We hope to follow it up with equally profitable publications.'—A concise statement of the position : there can be no pleasure in dwelling on the irony.

The worst suspicions aroused by the Royal Society of Literature, then, have been confirmed. There is nothing for it but to conclude that, in the absence of current standards maintained by the authority of tradition, official machinery can only gear in with the mechanism of standardization and levelling-down—can, at the best, only endorse Book Society values. The L.N.E.R. advertizes that it ' brings you to Priestley's England.' The English Association is helping to bring us all to the Book Society's England.

It is then, without extravagant hopes that we turn to the British Broadcasting Corporation, the new organ of culture of which so much is expected. It has been taking its function with admirable seriousness. Last winter's set of talks entitled *This Changing World* was a laudable attempt at educating the public to cope with the modern environment. And good educational work the B.B.C. has, in some sense, undoubtedly done. But how little it can be expected to reverse the process we have been contemplating, to educate in the sense of promulgating standards that would make the Walpole-Priestley *régime* appear what it is, Mr. Harold Nicolson's notorious talks on *The New Spirit in Literature* should have been sufficient to establish.

Mr. Nicolson's talks were notorious because of the disapproving comment they provoked, and its sequel. They were not notorious for their extravagant absurdity, their vulgarity and their sciolism; the objectors did not point out that Mr. Nicolson had obviously not the first qualification for the undertaking upon which he had embarked with such assurance. However, it might be urged that the mere undertaking was something; it was at least a challenge to Book Society values. That it was so Mr. Nicolson took pains to deny, and we have here the most significant aspect of the whole affair.

' I have,' he assured his listeners, ' a great respect for Mr. Hugh Walpole, who in more than one way has rendered valuable service to literature.'—(Mr. Nicolson was perhaps thinking of the Book Society and the English Association.)—' I admire his character and I have often admired his books.' The assurance was as explicit as possible. ' I have no doubt whatsoever regarding the literary integrity of Mr. Walpole and Mr. Priestley. And I like their smiles. I might even go further. I might admit that writers such as these two stand in a more direct relation to the continuity of British letters than do any of the authors whom I shall discuss in this series. I am perfectly prepared to believe that they represent a " better " school of writing than do my own poor neurotics.' (*Listener,* Nov. 4, 1931). So it is not, all things considered, surprising that Mr. Nicolson should go on to ask : ' What, then, is the gulf that separates Mr. Walpole and me in literary matters? '

What indeed? And we might still have asked, even if Mr. Nicolson had re-iterated disagreement instead of agreement. For debate at Mr. Walpole's level could have no place in a serious discussion of modern literature, and there could be no serious discussion of modern literature that should not be an implicit condemnation of Mr. Walpole and Mr. Priestley. Mr. Nicolson, in fact, even if he had been qualified to explain Mr. Eliot and Mr. Joyce and Mrs. Woolf, would have been better employed explaining how Mr. Walpole and Mr. Priestley are, ' in more than one way,' *not* rendering valuable services to literature.

This, of course, he could not have been allowed to do had he so desired. And that is really the final comment on the kind of undertaking he took part in. A serious experiment in cultural education would have to start by doing what is and must remain forbidden.—There *are* authorities that may not be challenged, but none of the kind we are looking for. And there can be none.

As for Mr. Nicolson's embarrassing performance over the wireless, we should remind ourselves that he wrote in *Some People* a book of a certain distinction and that his *Tennyson* and his *Swinburne* are not negligible. These books are the work of a cultivated man of some talent, and his case is the more interesting, and the more illustrative of the times. These are the times in which the acquiring of taste and discrimination and ' sensitiveness of intelligence, is probaby harder than ever before in the history of civilization. The *Listener,* in which Mr. Nicolson's talks were printed, reminds us—none the less for the good quality of much of its contents—of his real excuse. In the environment it represents, the tropical profusion of topics and vocabularies and the absence of a cultural grammar and syntax, what chance had he?

Such an environment does not favour ' sensitiveness of intelligence,' which, as Arnold tells us, produces ' deference to a standard higher than one's own habitual standard.' And where is such a standard to be found? So a man may discuss ' matters of taste and intellect ' with the best people, and never be troubled even by the ghost of authority. And, now himself authority, so far from being able to induce ' sensitiveness of intelligence ' in his listeners, he is himself demoralized, and can tell them seriously that the ' modernists ' (conforming to progressive evolution, and interpreting man's unconquerable mind) preach : ' Sex is a form of food; do not starve it, yet do not guzzle ' (*Listener,* Nov. 25).

With no standards above, inherent in a living tradition that gives them authority, education can be only a matter of so much more machinery, geared to the general machine of civilization. I could produce the familiar evidence from the field of democratic adult education (lectures on Walpole and Priestley, etc.), but there has been much devoted work, and here, in any case, I would rather not risk being thought to take pleasure in irony.

Standards above, invested with effective authority—were there ever any? Were things ever much different? That such questions can be asked (as they commonly are) brings home the completeness of the change. There is no room here even to hint at the kind of evidence that can be marshalled. I can only reply that before the last century, in, say, Johnson's time, it never occurred to anyone to question that there were, in all things, standards above the level of the ordinary man. That this was so, and the advantage the ordinary man derived, might be brought home by a study (one is in fact being written) of the memoirs and autobiographies, which exist in considerable numbers, of persons of the humblest origin who raised themselves to intellectual distinction and culture. Johnson's own appeal to the ' common reader,' which is sometimes invoked in support of the democratic principle in criticism, has (odd that I should have to say it!) an opposite force. It testifies how far Johnson was from suspecting that there could ever be a state of affairs like that existing now. He could rejoice to concur with the ' common reader ' because taste was then in the keeping of the educated who, sharing a homogeneous culture, maintained in tradition a surer taste than any that is merely individual can be, and he could not have imagined such an authority being seriously challenged. To-day, as the Editors of *Scrutiny* pointed out in their first editorial, there is no such common reader.

And yet there are some (most readers of *Scrutiny*, let us say) to whom the substance of this essay is commonplace, otherwise it would not have been worth writing: where there are some to whom it is commonplace there are some to whom the commonplace has not come home in all its force. This is to suggest that full recognition from those capable of it is worth striving for; and that implies more. It is certainly not to suggest any simple prescription. For if what Matthew Arnold, pondering the Literary Influence of Academies, said seventy years ago might still be said, it would be with a very different accent:

‘ It is not that there do not exist in England, as in France, a number of people perfectly well able to discern what is good, in these things, from what is bad; but they are isolated, they form no powerful body of opinion, they are not strong enough to set a standard. . . . Ignorance and charlatanism. . . are always trying to pass off their wares as excellent, and to cry down criticism as the voice of an insignificant, over-fastidious minority; they easily persuade the multitude that this is so when the minority is scattered about as it is here. . . . ’

F. R. LEAVIS.

EAGLES AND TRUMPETS
FOR THE MIDDLE CLASSES

THERE is an interesting exception to the rule that in contemporary civilisation the poets are allowed a place of but little importance. No doubt, in general, they are sufficiently ignored. Even if (as is sometimes claimed for them) they express our life at its point of most conscious intensity, they are rarely disturbed in the privacy of their self-expression. And so far as any direct influence is concerned they are clearly less important in the community than their historical or mythical predecessors, the bards, the skalds and the prophets. These spoke with the voice both of God and of the People. Our modern poets normally make claim to no such authority. Yet there is one kind of national emergency in which even they have their moments. This comes usually during a reversion to a state of primitive excitement like that which gave the legendary bards their distinction, and it comes most often when a war is waged with some rival community.

When a modern nation goes to war, it experiences, during the early stages of the struggle, a species of folk-ecstasy, and it then feels a distinct need for some bard, prophet or poet laureate who will associate its new fury with the ancient heroics. This is the opportunity of the ' poet.' (I use the word, not to suggest any literary merit, but to denote a generally acknowledged office). If the poet experiences the new feeling at about the same level as his fellows and can express it with technical skill, he may suddenly find himself possessed of unexpected influence. This is especially true of modern wars, since these are won, more than ever before, not by the skill of the actual combatants, but by the preservation of the *morale* of the whole nation. It is in forming and maintaining this *morale* that the poet once more finds a national function. It may be interesting to look, from the social rather than the literary point of view, at the play of this tendency during the last hundred years or so of our history.

There has always been patriotic poetry, and even in the realms of autocrats it has been difficult to win wars without the generation of popular enthusiasm. But is it fanciful to discover a general difference between the patriotic rhetoric of earlier forms of society and that of democracy? Compare, for instance, the patriotic rhetoric of Shakespeare with that of the nineteenth century. The former is good swinging jingoism, expressed imaginatively; little more than a spirited poetic rendering of the well-known fact that one Englishman is as good as three Frenchmen. It may lend itself to super-patriots, but it is at least not apologetic: it is bombastic, but not priggish. But since the rise to economic and political dominance of the middle classes, there has been something over-moralised about our patriotism. Even Mr. Kipling, who passed with our fathers as so blatant an Imperialist, wrote *The Recessional,* a piece which would have been quite incomprehensible to the buccaneering Elizabethans, though now to a whole generation it has seemed the most edifying combination of patriotism and piety. If this is true even of what might be called Tory nationalism, how much more true is it of those nineteenth century nationalist movements that claimed to be Liberal. The whole complex of thought about popular nationalism between 1800 and 1920 was incurably idealistic.

During the nineteenth century the waging of wars became overlaid with an unhealthy self-righteousness everywhere redolent of a nation of shopkeepers getting special terms from the Deity. (Compare *Westward Ho!* with any genuine expression of the Elizabethan spirit). Feudalism, with its chivalry and its robber barons, had gone down before a society of mass production and respectable middle-class principles. But when wars were seen to be more than ever necessary, it was the poets who supplied the *bourgeoisie* with the eagles and the trumpets.

The new nationalist movements coincided, not accidentally, with the rise of ' Romanticism ' in the literatures of Europe. In the cult of the national soul there was something essentially Romantic, and the re-discovery of national pasts was one of the distinctive features of the new literatures. Typical Englishmen of the preceding century, though they had upheld the virtues of the patriot, had tempered their zeal with something broad and

Roman, and they were vigilant to discover the impostor under the guise of the too enthusiastic patriot (everybody knows Dr. Johnson's dictum on the subject). But to the young Wordsworth to be a ' patriot ' was essentially to be an enthusiast and a revolutionary. He himself found in the French Revolution that spirit of liberal patriotism which he tried later to instil into his own countrymen.

In England the forces of Romanticism and of idealised Nationalism frequently converged during the nineteenth century. In the period of something over a hundred years that is behind us we have had two really first-class wars, that against Napoleon and that against Germany, with between them the very nearly first-class war in the Crimea. In each of these the forces of national idealism found their poet, Wordsworth in the Napoleonic War, Tennyson in the Crimean War and Rupert Brooke in the War of 1914-1918. Wordsworth was perhaps least accepted as ' official,' but although he was still an unorthodox poet he felt himself to be speaking for the nation, and the welcome given to his patriotic sonnets by critics who disliked his other work shows that he did so. Tennyson, of course, was the Poet Laureate. And Brooke spoke for ' Youth ' and was admittedly representative. Each expressed for reading people the conviction that the war was no trivial or self-seeking quarrel, but a great crusade for Honour and Liberty. What they wrote, perhaps, does not read so happily now. Nevertheless it is not unreservedly bad poetry, and in spite of its incomplete integrity, one can feel something of noble sentiment in it. It is interesting to see how easily the loftiest of professions has lent itself to that which the Chinese (before the day of their Christian generals) considered the most degrading.

I.

It will be recalled that as a young man Wordsworth had been in revolutionary France and had propagated the new principles with ardour on his return to England. But, confronted with the disappointing development of the Revolution, and increasingly realising how uncongenial the life of a doctrinaire would be to him, he had withdrawn into himself. He made a severe break with his former mode of life, except in so far as a

campaign for the democratisation of poetry afforded him some
compensation for the abandonment of his enthusiasms.　　But
before he sank into the comparative quiescence of his later years
there was one more convulsion that stirred him deeply.　This
was the war with Napoleon. Under the stress of his public
excitement Wordsworth forgot that he was a Solitary and spoke
once more as a patriot.

He spoke not only with strong personal conviction, but with
an apparent immediacy of inspiration that was not always his
when he peered into the lives of dalesmen and peasants with
whom, despite his assertions to the contrary, he was rarely in
genuine and unselfconscious unison.　His voice at first may have
been a single one, but he felt rightly that it was the voice of
growing numbers of people in England and in the newly
awakening Europe.　The war was against the France that had
emerged from the Revolution, but Wordsworth's spirit in
supporting it was very like that which had moved him when he
had been a French ' patriot.'　For a time after the declaration
of war he had naturally been perplexed and at first had even
wished success to his country's opponents.　But as the Revolution
merged into the Napoleonic adventure and France, no longer a
liberalising influence, became an aggressive tyranny, Wordsworth
saw with relief that his own country was on the side of the angels.
It was indeed very ill-fitted for divine service, but Wordsworth
hoped that if the call were sounded clearly enough there was a
real chance that its spirit might be purified and its actions made
glorious for the future of freedom.

This was the mood at least in which his campaign opened,
soon after the resumption of fighting following the peace of
Amiens.　He by no means shirked criticism of his own country,
but rather admitted it, endeavouring at the same time to breathe
into his countrymen a more courageous and liberty-loving spirit.
The evils of the Napoleonic system were in any case greater than
the deficiencies of his own people.　One may say with emphasis
that Wordsworth did understand this importance of a nation's
moral attitude to its own actions.　He wanted his countrymen to
feel what France had felt when she was ' standing on
the top of golden hours and human nature seeming born again.'
He had said then (and time had proved him right) that hired

invading armies could never defeat a people with such a sense of purpose. He looked for every sign of such a spirit now, not only among the English, but in Germany, the Tyrol and the Peninsula. This was the beginning of popular nationalism in Europe, and Wordsworth knew it better than any other man in England.

His first group of political sonnets was written in or about the year 1802. Both in versification and prophetic character they were modelled on Milton. Wordsworth also saw in his mind ' a noble and puissant nation rousing herself like a strong man after sleep,' and he desired his countrymen to devote themselves to their mission with almost a Puritan's virtue. That such a national spirit, at home and on the continent, could be invoked against Napoleon, was Wordsworth's stirring apprehension. ' By the soul only, nations shall be great and free.'

This was his theme, not only in the sonnets, but in the *Tract on the Convention of Cintra.* In this lengthy pamphlet Wordsworth examined the failure of the British authorities in the Peninsula to take proper advantage of Wellesley's victory at Vimiero, and while from the military point of view he may have condemned them too severely, on the psychological and political issue he was right incontestably. The British forces, as he pointed out, had been sent to the Peninsula to encourage the Spanish and Portuguese patriots in their resistance to the French, yet in the Convention the British authorities had ignored and even scorned them. No doubt, from the point of view of the old-style British generals, the insurgents were an impossible lot. But Wordsworth would no more have permitted such an excuse than Byron would have allowed the disunities among the Greeks to have dissuaded him from Missolonghi. How could these ill-trained and ill-equipped rebels have made such a fight of it against the finest troops in Europe if they had not been impelled by moral heroism of the highest order? So Wordsworth argued.

> The power of armies is a visible thing,
> Formal, and circumscribed in time and place;
> But who the limits of that power shall trace
> Which a brave people into light can bring
> Or hide, at will,—for freedom combating?

So clear was Wordsworth's prophecy that he foresaw not only Napoleon's overthrow by the forces of nationalism but even the unification of Germany and Italy that were to come about half a century later.

Now that the tendencies of Nationalism have had time to work themselves out it is difficult to share the enthusiasm with which Wordsworth greeted their first arrival. One is tempted to question his assumptions and to examine his facts rather more closely. It is unfortunately not at all clear that Nationalism has been the all-permeating Liberal force that Wordsworth expected, and high-souled wars waged for it have had the habit of ending, not in free constitutions and social progress, but in reaction and dictatorships. The unification of Germany led to Prussianism, and to-day we are more conscious of Mussolini than Mazzini, of Pilsudski than Kosciusko. Even from the point of view of our own island, while George the Third may have been preferable to Napoleon (it is arguable), is not Wordsworth's grandiloquence excessive? The notion that the ' people ' of Great Britain were struggling for ' Freedom ' seems a little droll. Was it the Freedom that they were left to enjoy under Sidmouth and Castlereagh?

The better of these sonnets seem to spring from a real magnanimity. And yet the basis of political statement on which they rest is sometimes so weak that one is almost tempted to the dangerous doctrine that they should be read with no proper attention to their political context. Some of the less successful betray a sorry inflation. It is all very well for Wordsworth to tell us to admire the King of Sweden who ' work hath begun of fortitude, and piety and love,' but what language is this to describe an announcement by the half-mad and altogether disastrous Gustavus that he would press for the restoration of the Bourbons? It is surprising that even Wordsworth should have felt it to be notably pious.

In truth, Wordsworth rather easily allowed his tone in these poems to be more imposing than the situation would now seem to have warranted. And this led him to pomposity and a proud abasement that were equally unpleasant. His general debt to Milton has been noted, and there are some unflattering particular resemblances to the patriotic sentiments of the *Areopagitica.*

Milton observes that God reveals his truth, as his custom is, first to his Englishmen, and then laments that they have so often proved unworthy; and Wordsworth alternately informs his countrymen of their unique destiny, and upbraids them that they are too slothful to realise it. This is the invincible combination of pride and meekness that has so often led the Anglo-Saxon to inherit the earth. It has marked patriotic poetry since the first beginnings of our middle-class empire.

During the last war it was especially popular. While some of our divines were licking the temple dust in an effort to get God to beat the Germans, some of our professors were hunting up their Wordsworths and finding quite a new interest in his patriotic poetry. There were even publications on the subject. Perhaps the most regrettable was the chapter, ' The Lessons for the Present War of Wordsworth's Statesmanship,' in the book on *The Statesmanship of Wordsworth,* written in 1917 by Professor Dicey. This sort of writing normally comes from academic persons who have been searching for some spiritual authority to justify deeds which ordinarily they would feel to be abhorrent. Professor Dicey, assisted by his reading of Wordsworth, came to the edifying conclusion that although in a war waged for Liberty and Truth no one would wish to be carried away by mere desire for retaliation, yet ' we must also remember that it is our duty to do justice (and it may be very stern justice) in the way of punishment to Germany.' Looking back, one may agree that the ' punishment ' was very stern : one may perhaps doubt whether it was ' justice.'

Unfortunately, Wordsworth lends himself to such ' lessons.' His prejudices and his idealisms merge equally in self-righteousness, and in wartime that is what the public above all wants to be given. Both the liberal and the jingoistic streaks were in him early. The first group of sonnets contains ' Milton! thou shouldst be living at this hour! ' But it also has ' Inward within a hollow vale I stood,'—that survey of British patriots ending with the remark (it would be annoying only if it were less silly), ' France, 'tis strange, hath brought forth no such souls as we had then '; and the indecent academic heroics of ' Shout, for a mighty victory is won '—though, as a matter of fact, it was not won, but only anticipated by the poet in an uninspired moment. But on the whole, Wordsworth clearly entered the war as what might be broadly called a liberal, and it was under this inspiration that his best patriotic verse was written. He came out of the war as dull a poet of reaction as one can find anywhere. He began with ideals for making the war a crusade of regeneration; he ended it with blasphemous requests to the Deity to accept thanks for the settlement imposed upon Europe at Vienna.

As the war continued, Wordsworth became less intent upon his ideals and more engrossed with the passions of the moment. After all, the immediate business was winning the war. For a while, much to his sister's distress, he even became a volunteer himself (for home service) and one can be confident that if the French had ever got to Westmorland they would have found Wordsworth fighting with the foremost. The war saw an ever-narrowing conception of Liberty. At first, though he had primarily meant by it the struggle for national independence against rulers who might be imposed by foreigners, he had felt that the first-fruits of this struggle would be a general liberalising of society. This is of course the hope with which all liberals (I use the word in its general sense) set out when they would justify a war, but during its progress they devote more and more of their energies to the securing of victory, and by the time it has been won they never seem to be left in a position to ensure the carrying out of their original intentions. In a democracy it is the part of the liberal-minded to sanctify a war, of the tory-minded to wage it.

When a war has once been declared, an individual can support it or oppose it. But he must do one or the other; no middle course is possible. And if he supports it he must of necessity temporarily forgo his liberal principles and act like a tory; if he opposes it, though he is devoted to his country, he must seem like a traitor. The would-be liberal patriot is commonly one who has no deep-seated moral objection to war, but only a distaste for the illiberal measures that are necessary to win it. Such a man usually fastens on some idealistic element he can find in the struggle and by announcing this to the world tries to spiritualise the war for himself and his countrymen. As the war goes on the implicit impossibility of a middle position impresses itself upon his character and the process of winning the war irretrievably tarnishes his initial idealism.

This is what happened to Wordsworth, and the record of it is to be found in his patriotic poetry. When the war was over, his work was done, and all he had to do was to sit beside his cottage door and explain that ' it was a famous victory.' This he achieved to his apparent satisfaction, in a couple of odes and a handful of sonnets. For our present purpose there are two points of interest about the volume. In the Advertisement Wordsworth does notice the great distress that the war had occasioned, but believes that it will be transient (it lasted pretty well into the forties), and in any case he thinks it would be wrong to allow it to veil ' the splendour of this great moral triumph.' Secondly, Wordsworth says that these poems ' may be considered as a sequel to the Author's '' Sonnets Dedicated to Liberty '' '; which brings us forcibly up against the fact that by ' Liberty ' Wordsworth meant little more than freedom to choose one's own national dynasty. That was something, no doubt, but how limited a meaning for so large a word! Is it any wonder that Shelley, Hazlitt and the rest thought him an apostate? Of England in the year of misery 1814, when the ordinary people alike in the countryside and in the new industrial towns were more poverty-stricken and repressed than at any time for a hundred years before or since, Wordsworth could write :

> Hail to the crown by Freedom shaped—to gird
> An English sovereign's brow! and to the throne
> Whereon he sits! whose deep foundations lie
> In veneration and the people's love,
> Whose steps are equity, whose seat is law,
> Hail to the State of England! And conjoin
> With this a salutation as devout,
> Made to the spiritual fabric of her Church.

The sentiments were as spurious as the construction was faulty and the language stilted. Wordsworth had ceased to feel that generous political passion which had been the valid inspiration of his earlier sonnets. He had set out to liberalise the war, and he had ended by illiberalising himself. He had changed as his use of the word ' patriot ' had changed. When as a young man in France he had acknowledged himself a ' patriot,' his heart ' was all given to the people ' and ' his love was theirs.' Now when the word fell from his lips it was followed, not by ' the people,' but by Constitution, King and Church. He had commended the war to the spirit of his public and his own spirit had fallen its victim.

II.

There is less need to discuss in detail the parts played by Tennyson and Rupert Brooke in the wars of their times, for the typical elements in their response had already been shown in Wordsworth's response to the war with Napoleon. For forty years after that war England had had peace. By the end of that time she had forgotten what it felt like to be at war and many of her people were undeniably willing to refresh the national memory. The middle-classes were now completely in the ascendant in society, their civilisation was substantial and (to themselves) satisfactory. But it did lack glamour, and some even found it sordid. If another war should be declared there would without doubt be a large public disposed to welcome it and extremely eager for the attendant exploits and victories. A war, in short, was about due, and we easily drifted into one.

Of all our wars few can have had less justification than that in the Crimea. In origin (even by normal diplomatic standards) it was by no means 'inevitable,' its conduct was most unsatisfactory and it caused the greatest suffering. It came about chiefly because two men, Lord Palmerston and Stratford Canning, realised the potentialities of the situation and instinctively felt that the public at home was ready for their course of action. The original dispute between Russia and Turkey about the Holy Places in Palestine had been practically settled. The note sent from Vienna over the signature of the chief powers of Europe had been accepted by the Russians and would certainly have been accepted by the Turks had not Stratford Canning, who was British Ambassador at Constantinople, urged them that in its present form it was unacceptable. And as he amended it, it proved unacceptable to the Russians. Russia had already temporarily occupied two border provinces of the Turkish Empire, and Palmerston pressed vigorously for war with them. He was confident that the country was excited by the prospect, however shallow the pretext. So, in company with the parvenu French Emperor, the aspiring King of Sardinia, and Mohammedan Turkey, we went to war with the Christian Emperor of Russia over the custody of the Holy Places. Once we were in the war (however needless it may have been) the public wanted its heroics. Tennyson, who was Poet Laureate, was admirably fitted by his abilities and his shortcomings to oblige them. He did not hesitate.

It would be superfluous to try to add anything to Mr. Nicolson's general account of the way in which Tennyson's aspiration to be the Public Bard interfered with the flow of his poetry. Ever since he had associated with the Apostles at Cambridge he had been in danger, and he was doomed once he was appointed Laureate. In all things he endeavoured to express the Higher Thoughts of the Better People, and when the Crimean War came he was far too adequate a Laureate to remain silent. With his remarkable ignorance of the affairs and cultures of Europe, his bigoted insularity, his facile technique and his easy spiritual inflation, he was by far the most suitable literary personage to interpret the public's mood for it.

As a technician he has sometimes been compared with Virgil. He was not unlike him in wanting to be the bard of a prosaically successful empire. True, the eagles had got a little dingy He had only Queen Victoria for his Augustus, and London for his Imperial City. But at any rate the Russians were thoroughly adequate Barbarians and the Light Brigade a splendid equivalent of the Roman Legions. War was no sooner declared than Tennyson started.

At the time he was working at *Maud*. He had nearly finished it, but one cannot be quite sure how it would have ended had not the war opened and settled that for him. Posterity has thereby been left with one of the most surprisingly incongruous conclusions in the history of literature. After the poor neurotic hero has been torn and perplexed through two long Parts of the poem, there comes a Third Part (of merely five verse paragraphs) in which he suddenly discovers a tremendous interest in public affairs and all his troubles vanish! From this turgid ending we gather that all the fears of his little life have been swallowed up in the great wave of excitement caused by the war, which bears him exultingly onward. Tennyson is too skilled an artist to reveal his shallowness by being over-explicit, but the prosaic reader would assume that in a fine burst of enthusiasm his hero enlisted. Let us hope he did not think better of it when he reached the Crimea and discovered the realities of that great adventure.

This curious tail-piece contains all the stock ideas we have come to expect from the modern patriotic poet. The war is a great crusade against tyranny, and in it the ordinary man will forget the sordidness of his prosperous past.

> It lighten'd my despair
> When I thought that a war would arise in defence of the
>   right,
> That an iron tyranny now should bend or cease,
> The glory of manhood stand on his ancient height,
> Nor Britain's one sole God be the millionaire.

Tennyson's hero (it is a common symptom of war-fever) feels that as he is drawn into the Cause he loses his private afflictions and merges everything into the Higher Reality.

> It is time, O passionate heart and morbid eye,
> That old hysterical mock-disease should die.

But whether he lose his private perplexity or not, what a magnificent liberation of soul for his country!

> Let it go or stay, so I wake to the higher aims
> Of a land that has lost for a little her lust for gold,
> And her love of a peace that was full of wrongs and shames,
> Horrible, hateful, monstrous, not to be told;
> And hail once more to the banner of battle unroll'd!
> Tho' many a light shall darken, and many shall weep
> For those that are crushed in the clash of jarring claims,
> Yet God's just wrath shall be wreak'd on a giant liar.

Just about here Tennyson's technique began to desert him a little, as it so often does desert writers who try to harness their God to a faction. (Writers of ancient war poetry were at least more objective, and from their ample pantheon could reveal some gods as fighting on one side and some on the other). Tennyson goes on to his grandiloquent conclusion:

Let it flame or fade, and the war roll down like a wind,
We have proved we have hearts in a cause, we are noble
    still,
And myself have awaked, as it seems, to the better mind;
It is better to fight for the good, than to rail at the ill;
I have felt with my native land, I am one with my kind,
I embrace the purpose of God, and the doom assign'd.

The volume, *Maud and Other Poems*, appeared in 1855. Besides
the title piece it contained *The Charge of the Light Brigade, An
Ode on the Death of the Duke of Wellington*, and a few other
poems. The volume must have had some effect for in eleven
years it went through thirteen editions. And *The Light Brigade*,
which appeared originally in *The Examiner*, was reprinted and
sold everywhere as a pamphlet. And one may consider with it
another poem, *The War* (later known as *Riflemen Form*) which
appeared in the *Times* in May, 1859, and did much to stimulate
the Volunteer movement.[1]

---

[1]That the war passages in *Maud*, though a small part of the whole
poem, attracted attention, may be illustrated by a reference to
an *Anti-Maud* published in 1855 by ' A Poet of the People.' Almost
all of it attacks *Maud* for its jingoism. A couple of stanzas may
be quoted :

Who clamours for war? Is it one who is ready to fight?
Is it one who will grasp the sword, and rush on the foe
    with a shout?
Far from it;—he is one of a musing mind, who merely
    intends to write,
He sits at home by his own snug hearth, and hears the storm
    without.

I grieve that a noble soul should trudge on a beaten road,
And a voice that can move the heart—a vulgar war-whoop
    swell;
Hounding his brethren onwards, urging them on with a
    goad
To the smoking field of death, where the contestants close
    with a yell.

We have noticed how Wordsworth allowed his interest in a foreign war to diminish his zeal for reform. Tennyson is even more explicit.

> Let your reforms for a moment go,
>   Look to your butts and take good aims,
> Better a rotten borough or so,
>   Than a rotten fleet or a city in flames!
>   Form! Form! Riflemen form!
>   Ready, be ready, to meet the storm!
>   Riflemen, riflemen, riflemen form!

This is sad stuff. But, in spite of the fact that its rhythms have been dinned into our ears since schooldays, the same cannot quite be said of *The Charge of the Light Brigade*. Technically, at least, it is quite efficient popular verse. And even the most militant pacifist would not deny the heroism of its theme. The most quoted lines in it,

> Their's not to reason why,
> Their's but to do and die,

led Shaw (I believe) to say that the poem must be the greatest satire we have on the profession of soldier. But unfortunately satire and irony were far removed from Tennyson's thoughts. There seems, indeed, to have been an unusual popularity in Victorian times for this theme of ' Faithful unto Death.' People were especially moved by the spectacle of fidelity in the unreasoning creatures: in dogs, in children and in the lower orders of society. What might be called the Casabianca ' motif ' has seldom been so prevalent in literature and painting. But although one might well wish there had been more ' reasoning why,' especially on the part of the public, one can admit that the poem has certain merits. It is not sentimental, and it is not pompous. But even if one thought it splendid, one would have to say, echoing the French general, *C'est magnifique, mais ce n'est pas la guerre*.

Thus Tennyson and Wordsworth showed many similar qualities in their patriotic poetry. Wordsworth took a wider view (perhaps because he was a solitary, far from the madding crowd), and he certainly approached nearer to great poetry and was more truly liberal-minded in the early stages of his war than was Tennyson. But the predominent elements in their 'messages' are similar: that the war is a crusade, not a vulgar scramble, that the individual can lose in it the petty cares of peace, and that through it regeneration will come for both individual and nation. Rupert Brooke, who may be taken as the third illustration of modern war poetry, is not accorded the poetic rank of Tennyson and Wordsworth, but the mood of his war poetry is comparable to theirs, and one is ready to read him with greater respect for the perhaps not strictly logical reason that he at least carried his feeling to the farthest possible point of action.

III.

The wars of the latter half of the nineteenth century were small and distant from England, but that which began in August 1914, was at our very doorstep. And it would clearly need the whole resources of the nation for its successful prosecution. In mobilising opinion the British Government was very fortunate, particularly in the cry of ' poor little Belgium.' The steps that committed us to the war were taken before Germany invaded Belgium, but the invasion followed so quickly that the Government was actually able to make the pretence that we were entering the war because of the tearing up of ' the scrap of paper.' This was an immense advantage in appealing to the chivalrous instincts of the people. The late E. D. Morel said that Truth is the first casualty in every war, and this use of the invasion of Belgium was but one glaring instance of the way in which the British (and of course all the other) governments tricked the half-formed idealism of young men into ' the service of the country.' The result of this appeal may be read, rather pathetically now, in the verses written by the civilian soldiers of the early war-days. There are few claims now made for their poetic value, but they have their human value none the less, and show how men felt that their finest impulses were linked with the struggle. The forgotten Streeter's line, ' O Liberty, at thy command we challenge death! ' may typically express the feeling of most of them. In the later years there came reaction, and the exaltation of the poets of 1914 was succeeded by the bitterness of Sassoon and the realism of Robert Nichols. Rupert Brooke is the only one of the early war poets still generally read by the public. He did more than merely express the current mood of idealism : his expression of it was so influential that he helped to form and perpetuate it in others. And, as has often been said, his death set the seal on his reputation.

He was concerned with war more personally than were Wordsworth and Tennyson, and yet it must be said that in inspiration his war poems are curiously derivative. So much is this so, that one is forced to question their ultimate authenticity. They are unquestionably sincere at a certain level, but they seem to lack an achieved integrity of spirit. The most fitting criticism is undoubtedly that of Charles Sorley, another soldier-poet (I take it from Mr. Middleton Murry's essay, *The Lost Legions* in his *Aspects of Literature*) :

' He is far too obsessed with his own sacrifice. . . It was not that '' they '' gave up anything of that list he gives in one sonnet : but that the essence of these things had been endangered by circumstances over which he had no control, and he must fight to recapture them. He has clothed his attitude in fine words : but he has taken the sentimental attitude.'

If one examines these sonnets one finds that they were written in a way which would inevitably evoke the ' stock responses.' Their vogue was due to that, and to their author's technical ability. The first sonnet,

> Now God be thanked who has matched us with his hour
> And caught our youth and wakened us from sleeping

sounds that same note we heard in Tennyson and Wordsworth. The nation is to arouse itself from sloth and throw itself with God-given strength into the struggle. And Brooke finds a relief not unlike that of the hero of *Maud* in leaving ' all the little emptiness of love ' and abandoning himself to war enthusiasm. Again, in his third sonnet, there is the old quaint feeling that in peace there was something dishonourable, and that the war has somehow brought back ' Holiness ' (what a ghastly notion!) :

Honour has come back, as a king, to earth,
    And paid his subjects with a royal wage;
And Nobleness walks in our ways again;
    And we have come into our heritage.

It would have been interesting to have seen, if Brooke had lived, whether in 1917 he would have written as Sassoon did. By then most of the poets, except the stay-at-home ones, were disillusioned. But just as idealism in the other countries was ebbing out, there came a new and embarrassing flood of it from America. This was only natural—we had felt it earlier. But the fact that this mood and ours so badly synchronised was the psychological factor behind some of the surface friction that surprised those who looked for an entirely smooth alliance. It is said that when in 1917 Mr. Masefield told the graduating class of Yale University that war was ' damned dirty, damned dull, and damned disgusting ' there was an astonished silence and they did not know what to make of it.

If one looks back, then, at some of the typical war poetry of the last hundred years, one may make certain generalisations. The poetry that has been popular has been that which has told the public in accents of sincerity, if not of the completest intellectual integrity, that the war was a righteous war and one of God's own choosing. With the aid of any idealist elements they could find in the struggle, the poets have ' liberalised ' the war for the verse-reading public and for those influenced by the verse-readers. They have suggested that the peace preceding the war had been sordid, and that this war would be in the cause of Honour because it demanded sacrifices from those who had been prosperous previously. The services of the poets have been especially important in rallying the middle-classes : somehow the working-classes, though they may have responded to calls, have preserved a not uncritical sense of humour, and quite literally, have ' made less of a song about it.' In looking at the history of mankind one's final feeling may be disgust at our incompetence in permitting the continuence of war as an institution, but in reading the war poetry of the last century one is above all impressed by the way in which the surface stirring of generous impulses has assisted in the perpetration of barbarity.

H. L. ELVIN.

EXCURSION

I was thankful when we landed
For the quiet heave and dip of man-swung oars;
And those dry fish scales on the granite jetty;
And water nudging weeded bulwarks. These
Were an assurance that the sea still kept
Her first uncalendared tradition, changeless always,
And constant in the attitude of change. That day,
The garish seaport town, with August heavy on it,
For me held a faint root among the Heroes;
I hoped from their cold resurrected ashes
Some chance-stored spark might light a modern tinder,
And I was glad to find,
Among the men who loitered on the jetty,
Some who still spat and were not tied
To facts and figures. I knew well their tongues
Could raise a world of myth for sixpence,
And stole some comfort from this knowledge.
Lacquered telescopes, in situ on the promenade,
For less would quench the eye's strong lust for distance,
Groping for buoy and headland where the sun
Blurred out the edged horizon. I was glad
To lounge and drop all purpose like the trippers;
And with them be self-conscious in my ease—
Pay twopence for a seat where one might hear
Wagner emphasised upon the trumpet, or admire
Scarlet geraniums planted out in rows.
Somewhere I have read
That men released from prison do strange things;
But we, that day released, did nothing stranger
Than to pretend we always lived at ease
Among the gestures of this sea town : yet we knew
The same conditions clamped and bolted us.

The thin grey smoke haze on the skyline
Suspended sentence of return to us who served
The gilded gods of debt and balance.

*   *   *   *

I have often thought
Geranium's fierce colour held a key
To life; and glimpses might be caught
In seamen's eyes of some dim prophecy
Withheld. Such things, seen in a day
Of aimless crowds and cheap banality,
Have blinded with the sense of vision brought,
As sun seen at the end of a dark passage way.

C. H. PEACOCK.

COMMENTS AND REVIEWS

THE LITERARY RACKET.

things rank and gross in nature
Possess it merely. That it should come to this !

In discussing the state of reviewing with people of experience—reviewers, editors, publishers and authors—we were
commonly, when illustrative anecdote had begun to accumulate
into monotony, presented with the conclusion: ' But everybody
knows all about it. And anyway, there's nothing you can do.'
In a sense everybody does know. Yet if we could print (as for
sufficiently obvious reasons we cannot) some of the choicer of the
instances we collected, most of the readers of *Scrutiny* would
have a shock. For the fact is that the cultivated in general do
not realize how completely reviewing has ceased to have anything to do with criticism: honest and intelligent reviews still
occur, but the function of reviewing (the legitimate function) has
lapsed.

Even observing the discretion necessary to escape legal
revenge (the law of libel is not as an outraged sense of decency
would have it) we might yet surprise the reader with histories
and other data illustrating the value of advertising, the reach
and thoroughness of the Literary Racket, and the power and
vindictiveness of the gangs. But it would still be felt that, while
all this was no doubt representative of the classy Sunday papers,
the dailies and the more hearty weeklies, yet it had little bearing
on—well, on the only weekly (whichever it is one may have
chosen) that an intelligent person can read. And to bring the
bearing home would require a particularity that is obviously
precluded.

This is not to deny that there are honourable exceptions
(again particularity would be indiscreet). But it would be in any
case a mistake to stress exclusively racketeering and the grosser
forms of abuse. What is meant by saying that the function of
reviewing has lapsed may be best put in this way: though the

need for intelligent reviewing is greater than ever it was before, no intelligent critic can hope to find steady employment in the exercise of his qualifications.

Why this is so may be indicated by considering the problem that faces a conscientious literary editor. In the first place the problem is one of dealing with the sheer bulk of reading-matter that comes to the office for review. He would be a gifted person if he could decide offhand which of some scores of books are worth serious criticism. Moreover, even if he could, intrinsic value could not be the final criterion determining space and treatment: publishers are clients of the Advertising Manager, as the most conscientious editor can never be allowed to forget. To rescue him from this predicament—that is, to spirit away the obscene fact of its existence—there is to hand the fraternity of Higher Reviewers, themselves products and victims of the situation. Some of them may once have been potential critics. But they, like the editor, have livings to make, and in the process of making a living they have inevitably left behind what critical qualifications they may have had.

Nevertheless, they are distinguished critics and authorities, with pretensions to maintain and self-esteem to cherish. The inevitable outcome, as indicated in the first number of *Scrutiny,* is solidarity. See them fall upon the rash outsider who undertakes to remind the world what serious standards are. As for the traitor from within, anyone inclined that way does not need the comradely warning that revolt means extinction. But we will not, by instancing melodramatic cases of this kind, give them a disproportionate emphasis. Comradely feeling (and there is a great deal of it) has in general much pleasanter functions. There are those little dinners at the Berkeley, those cocktail parties, and so on, where authors and reviewers learn to ' get together.' Mere sense of decency makes unkind reviews or reviews in the wrong spirit impossible.

And so what might appear to be the problem facing the conscientious editor disappears. As for that pamphlet called *Have with you to Great Queen Street* which came out some time ago—well, pamphlets—or episodes—of that kind don't often come out.

But social pressure and the pressure of the Advertising

Manager are, after all, symptoms rather than causes. The radical fact is the advance of civilization. The supply of literature has become an industry subject to the same conditions as the supply of any other commodity. For many firms publishing is a business like the manufacture of 50/- suits, and the methods of Big Business are accordingly adopted. The market is raked for authors—for potential profit-makers—the wares are boosted by the usual commercial methods. The gigantic advance in output that makes good reviewing more than ever necessary has been its destruction—by asphyxiation in various forms.

Are we, then, beating the wind? Those who tell us so, tell us at the same time that these things are commonplace. They may be. But we do not believe that the greater number of clients of the ' higher journalism ' realize how preponderantly the reviewing they read is what it is—oil for the cogs of the publishing machine. To get this fully recognized by those capable of recognizing it has never been whole-heartedly attempted. It is worth attempting. And there is certainly somewhere a public— if it can be mobilized—that will support criticism—if it is offered.

THE WORDSWORTHS AND COLERIDGES

AN ESTIMATE OF WILLIAM WORDSWORTH, BY HIS CONTEMPORARIES, 1793-1822, by Elsie Smith, Ph.D. (Blackwell, 18/-).

DOROTHY WORDSWORTH : THE EARLY YEARS, by Catherine Macdonald Maclean (Chatto and Windus, 15/-).

UNPUBLISHED LETTERS OF SAMUEL TAYLOR COLERIDGE. Edited by Earl Leslie Griggs (Constable. Two vols. 37/6d.).

Those who attempt to gather the literature concerning the Wordsworths and Coleridges have equipped themselves from the beginning with capacious book-cases, but they will need more yet.

The three works now under notice are typical of the accessions that are always occurring. The ghost of Crabb Robinson, too, is not laid. ' What various manuscripts we meet ' in almost every general sale catalogue, proposing to industrious minds fresh studies in the Lake Poets and their little clan!

All three of the present publications are the results of research, but one is cast in a form concealing the processes of scholarship as much as possible: this is Miss Maclean's biography of Dorothy Wordsworth, which has the air of being everybody's reading, not limited to those who grow agitated over the printing of a letter without the inclusion of the postmark. The writer has traced out, through a circumstantial chronicle, an intimate portrait of a wonderful woman. It may be noted, in regard to the position of Dorothy Wordsworth among those who were so much indebted to her gift, that this book includes enough actual pictures of them, but no physical portrait of her. The method chosen by Miss Maclean for her general presentation, although it will attract some, must be troublesome to others. Perhaps there is a justifiable jealousy, touching a personality so delicately fine as that of Dorothy Wordsworth; as she took the trouble to record her own experiences so often, we are liable to be prejudiced against any adaptations of her own testament, however thoughtfully evolved. The description of presumed emotional apprehensions, like that which occupied so much of Miss Lowell's biography of Keats, is hazardous. ' Why the swift flame to end in darkness? Why the brief ecstasy of the blood to lead to a huddle of tortured days? Why the barter of a life for a strange, late flowering? Truly Life drove a cruel trade.' These reflections, these locutions are put before us as the thought of Dorothy Wordsworth when she passed the grave of Mrs. Ibbetson; but they do not quite harmonise with what we know of her way. Miss Maclean writes with fluent fancy, and with touches of rhapsody ('Gold dust of poetry rained from heaven upon them all '); her affection for Dorothy is the beauty of the book, which has disadvantages besides the main one of uncertain though picturesque paraphrase and conjecture—especially, the sequence of paragraphs without transitions, effective in a brief narrative but scarcely so in this long one.

Dr. Smith's compilation follows the chronological order of Wordsworth's publications, and affords us a view of opinions on his powers and performances until the time when—being fifty years old—he was no longer ' a young poet,' and ' of great promise.' These opinions are collected from the magazines and reviews of the time, from the letters of friends and acquaintances, from Crabb Robinson, and from one or two additional sources in prose and verse. The plan of campaign has been easily sufficient for the filling of some 400 pages; but I am inclined to think Dr. Smith has mainly overlooked the daily and weekly newspapers, and it is easy for anyone who has invaded those to forgive her. Still, as one may judge by the many bulging scrap-books of that period, the critical notices and correspondence and verses friendly or mischievous which appeared in the morning, evening and Sunday press had a great share in the formation of public taste in poetry. A writer in the *Times Literary Supplement* has already indicated the minor errors, misprints and so on, in Dr. Smith's pages; notwithstanding all which, it is useful to have a means of consulting Wordsworth's early reviewers without disturbing the old *Gentleman's Magazine, Analytical Review, Monthly Reviews* and other slumbering antiquities.

Among these new Romanticities, Professor Griggs's book is the grandee; it is, indeed, an important first edition of S. T. Coleridge. Almost forty years have passed since the other collection of Coleridge's letters, also in two lordly volumes, was produced; and E. H. Coleridge besides bringing off that feat left considerable preparations for what is now achieved. There is no describing the labours of Professor Griggs in a sentence or two, and as he intends to edit the whole of Coleridge's extant correspondence he does not wish for compliments at present on the range and particularity of his enquiries. Let us condole with him over his visit to Malta in search of his hero's official and unofficial papers there. They *were* there, until 1900, when one of those bonfires that men make every now and then for the torture of coming hero-worshippers was successfully organized. Selecting from what he has rescued in other places, Professor Griggs sets before us 400 letters of Coleridge, many of them very long and most of them rather longer than in a non-Coleridgean system of daily affairs they need have been. (Some of these relics are not entirely new to print, but the correct and complete versions amount to fresh discoveries.)

The letters of Coleridge are like everything else of his, a class apart, and they have the contrasted qualities which even his poetry-book has; now you think him a consummate ass, now nothing ' less than Archangel ruin'd,' and very often as wise a man of this world as ever breathed. The multitude of his interests and personal contacts alone makes such volumes as these bewildering. He had the privilege of opening his mind to a host of people remembered or forgotten now, but attracted to him and analysed by him with affectionate zeal. He is an egotist of the most thorough-paced kind, but egotism is on the whole nothing like vanity; it is the intense operation of a sleepless mind, which everything in experience sets going in a new cogitation,—Scott's poetry or Mrs. Rundle's ' *Cook-away Book*,' Newton's Assumptions or a bumble-bee in a fox-glove. One of the blessings of such editorship as that of Professor Griggs is that we are given our Coleridge unbowdlerized; for his impulsive violences of expression are as much part of his genius as his mildest cooings. Sometimes, however, he lost an opportunity, as thus: ' Some genius in a pamphlet entitled ' *Hypocrisy Unveiled* ' written against Mr. Wilson has pronounced poor Christabel '' the most obscene Poem in the English language ''—It seems that Hazlitt from pure malignity had spread about the Report that Geraldine was a Man in disguise. I saw an old book at Coleorton in which the Paradise Lost was described as an '' obscene Poem,'' so I am in good company.' The Coleridgean intonation of the word ' dear ' has always been a pleasant thing to his audience (as when ' dear ' Sara spilt the boiling milk on his foot); and here is another variant: ' Dear Mr. Estlin in speaking of me in a large company a few weeks ago said—'' His intellects are all gone, Sir! all his genius is lost, quite lost. He is a mere superstitious Calvinist, Sir! '' '

In a sense, we have already heard ' all about Coleridge,' the subtle-souled psychologist of Shelley's poem; we know the marvellous power, the magnificent torso, the mass of decaying spices, and other such classic definitions, and nothing can change the sense of a splendid failure implicit in his life. But there are passages in his history to elucidate and modify, questions of a medical importance to answer by reconsideration,—and countless instances of his poetical and practical faculties to add to those which have been enjoyed before. Here may be mentioned the

chief groups of letters included by Professor Griggs: to Byron, to
Derwent, Edward, George, Mrs. S. T. Coleridge, to the Morgans, to
Poole, to Sotheby the epic poet, to the other epic poet Southey,
to Daniel Stuart and to Josiah Wedgwood. And another little
group to Mr. Dunn, Chemist and Druggist, Highgate, discloses
Coleridge's occasional ' recourse to an Anodyne ' under Dr.
Gillman's very nose.

EDMUND BLUNDEN.

AND THE NOVEL ?

FOUR TIMES AND OUT ?

SARTORIS by William Faulkner (Chatto and Windus, 7/6d.)

Mr. Faulkner's *Sartoris* will make him a popular novelist.
It may, in fact, bring the Faulkner Club to an ignominious end
by making him a book-society choice. Mr. Gerald Gould, whose
proud immaculateness prevented his reading *The Sound and the
Fury*, can venture insides its covers without any fear of meeting
a Freudian bugaboo. It may even please him.

If one were feeling that way, one could suggest that the
story of the Sartoris family, and in particular of young Bayard's
tragedy, was evolved by crossing *Beau Geste* with *Death of a
Hero*. There is, aside from certain impressive episodes which were
bound to be sharply told since Faulkner is telling them, a noticeable effort to derive some meaning from the tale of a family whose
men fling their lives recklessly away while their women-folk with
a resigned impatience watch them die. But the comment does not
go beyond interjected notes on Bayard's inescapable doom and the
' blind fate ' which controlled the family fortune. Clearly Faulkner
never decided what this doom was.

In two earlier novels Faulkner invented a new style and
wisely or unconsciously limited himself to the kind of story which
demanded no other skills than those he possessed. Again here he
has augmented the technical resources of the novelist by showing
how unnecessary it is to tell a story covering several generations
by the linear method. *Sartoris* has an extraordinary depth because

events widely separated in time, but spiritually akin, are made to seem simultaneous. In this respect it is an achievement, for it puts to new uses the discoveries of Proust, Joyce and Virginia Woolf.

But Faulkner proposed to do more than write a saga in a new way. He not only attempts irony and the sinister, in which modes he is accomplished, but true tragedy as well. We are, that is, asked to believe that young Bayard is a tragic hero though he has not as much right to the dignity as Hotspur. The author of his being was rebuffed by the cold despair which kept everyone except his twin and idol from knowing his heart. It is impossible to have much sympathy for a skyrocket.

The novel was put to press too soon. There are bad repetitions, dissonances and absurd echoes, *e.g.* that sour reminiscence of Keats which closes the book, particularly unfortunate because of its association with (of all people) Horace Benbow. Faulkner, if he goes on at this rate, can easily lead the pack that help the *Saturday Evening Post* sell mouthwash to 50,000,000 Americans. He probably will. That way passed Robert W. Chambers—he, too, wrote a first novel—and Hergesheimer and others. Only the propagandists among American novelists, Dreiser, Sinclair, Dos Passos, are sufficiently self-willed not to succumb to the disease of mediocrity.

WILLARD THORP.

A SERIOUS ARTIST.

MANHATTAN TRANSFER by *John Dos Passos (Constable, 7/6d.).*

THE FORTY-SECOND PARALLEL by *John Dos Passos (Constable, 7/6d.).*

NINETEEN-NINETEEN by *John Dos Passos (Constable, 7/6d.).*

After *Manhattan Transfer* (1927) one remembered the name of John Dos Passos. After *The Forty-second Parallel* one looked eagerly forward to the succeeding members of the trilogy (for something of that order seemed to be promised) in the conviction that we had here a work demanding serious attention as no other appearing under the head of the novel during the past two or three years had done. *Nineteen-nineteen* is a challenge to justify the conviction.

The Forty-second Parallel established Mr. Dos Passos as an unusually serious artist—serious with the seriousness that expresses itself in the propagandist spirit. Unlike Mrs. Woolf, his antithesis, he cannot be interested in individuals without consciously relating them to the society and the civilization that make the individual life possible. Consequently, society and civilization being to-day what they are, his stress falls elsewhere than upon the individual life as such. In *Manhattan Transfer* his theme is New York, representing our ' megalopolitan ' civilization : ' The terrible thing about having New York go stale on you is that there's nowhere else. It's the top of the world. All we can do is to go round and round in a squirrel's cage.'

The undertaking involves a peculiar technical problem, one that none of the methods customarily associated with the novel will meet. No amount of enthusiasm for collective humanity will dispose of the fact that it is only in individuals that humanity lives, that only in the individual focus does consciousness function, that only individuals enjoy and suffer; and the problem is to suggest the multitudinous impersonality of the ant-heap through individual cases that, without much development, interest us as such. *Manhattan Transfer* represents a sufficient degree of success. It is of the essence of Mr. Dos Passos' method here—and of his vision of modern life—that of no one of his swirl of ' cases ' do we feel that it might profitably be developed into a separate novel; and yet we are interested enough. Here we have them in poignant individuality, a representative assortment of average men and women, engaged in the ' pursuit of happiness '—a pursuit sanctioned by the Constitution, but, of its very nature, and by the very conditions of the civilization to which they belong, vain. '' Darling, I'm so happy . . . . It's really going to be worth living now.'' Money, Success, Security, Love—in varied and ironical iteration we see the confident clutch : ' '' Elaine,'' he said shakily, '' life's really going to mean something to me now . . . . God, if you knew how empty life had been for so many years. I've been like a tin mechanical toy, all hollow inside.'' '

Manhattan Transfer ends with Jimmy Herf (the character to whom the author seems closest) walking, with an air of symbolic finality, out of New York. *The Forty-second Parallel* gives us the America into which he walks—a large undertaking, which calls for some modification of technique. The representative lives stand out more and are given less in episode-dialogue and more in consecutive narrative; narrative admirably managed in *tempo*, and varied dramatically in idiom with the chief actor. The ' Newsreels ' interspersed at intervals are a new device, their function being by means of newspaper-clippings and the like, in ironical medley, to establish the background of the contemporary public world. Moreover, also at intervals, there are lives, admirably compressed and stylized in what might be called prose-poems, of the makers, the heroes, the great men, the public figures, of American civilization. Thus Mr. Dos Passos seeks to provide something corresponding to the symbolic figures of a national epic or saga.

In general, for him, to be representative is to be unimpressive, and of his private characters only one is impressive and saga-like in his representativeness: J. Ward Moorhouse, ' public relations counsel.' It is significant. In him is embodied the power that, in the general disintegration, in the default of religion, art and traditional forms and sanctions, holds society together—the Power of the Word, or, let us say, Advertising. ' Clean cut young executive,' says J. Ward Moorhouse, looking at himself in the glass: the magician has reason to believe in the magic; it works for him. On this theme the author's art achieves some of its triumphs, and the aspect of modern civilization it exhibits is terrifying. ' We are handling this matter from the human interest angle . . . . pity and tears, you understand '—can a hundred D. H. Lawrences preserve even the idea of emotional sincerity against the unremitting, pervasive, masturbatory manipulations of ' scientific ' Publicity, and, what is the same thing, commercially supplied popular art?

' In America a fellow can get ahead. Birth don't matter, education don't matter. It's all getting ahead.' In the close of *The Forty-second Parallel* we see America welcoming an escape from this ' getting ahead,' a ' meaning ' with which to exorcise the void, in the War. *Nineteen-nineteen* gives us the War. The second part of the trilogy is decidedly less lively than the first. For one thing, the monotony of this world without religion, morality, art or culture is here, perhaps inevitably, emphasized. And this leads us to the more general question: What is lacking in the work as a whole (so far as we have it)?—why, in spite of its complete and rare seriousness, does it fall so decidedly short of being great?

For answer we have the state of civilization it celebrates. ' I guess all he needs is to go to work and get a sense of values,' says a character in *Manhattan Transfer,* exemplifying one of the author's best ironic effects. The comment on the prescription is the society portrayed: what kind of a sense of values can one acquire, what does a sense of values mean, in such an environment? The artistic shortcomings of Mr. Dos Passos' most ambitious work (which is not, like *Manhattan Transfer,* held together by the topographical limits of the setting) might thus be, not merely excused as inevitable, but extolled as propagandist virtues: they are necessary to a work that exhibits the decay of capitalistic society.

The argument, of course, would be specious. And the point in view might be made most effectively by reframing the question to run: What is lacking in the work as propaganda? This question is answered by asking what it is that Mr. Dos Passos offers us in the way of hope. The suggestion of hope, if it is one, that *Nineteen-nineteen* ends upon is revolution. Whether Mr. Dos Passos intends irony will, perhaps, be made plain in the last volume of the trilogy; but, as it is, the promise must appear as ironical as that upon which *The Forty-second Parallel* closed. Someone in *Nineteen-nineteen* says: ' it will take some huge wave of hope like a revolution to make me feel any self-respect ever again.' Such a wave of hope, in a world inhabited by Mr. Dos Passos' characters, would, it must seem, be of much the same order as the wave engendered by the outbreak of the War. His revolutionaries are as inadequate, as much ' tin mechanical toys, all hollow inside,' as his other persons. He plainly realizes this where they are intellectuals; where they are proletarians there is something embarrassingly like sentimentality in his attitude.

It may be that the concluding volume of the trilogy will show this last comment to be unfair in its implications. And perhaps comment on the inadequacy of individuals is discounted by Mr. Dos Passos' philosophy. Nevertheless a literary critic must venture the further judgment that the shortcomings of the work both as art and propaganda are related to a certain insufficiency in it when it is considered as an expression of personality (which on any theory a work of art must in some sense be). It is more than a superficial analogy when the technique is likened to that of the film. The author might be said to conceive his function as selective photography and ' montage.' That this method does not admit sufficiently of the presence of the artist's personal consciousness the device called ' The Camera Eye ' seems to recognize—it at any rate seems to do little else. What this judgment amounts to is that the work does not express an adequate realization of the issues it offers to deal with.

How far the defect is due to the method, and how far it lies in the consciousness behind the method, one cannot presume to determine. But Mr. Dos Passos, though he exhibits so overwhelmingly the results of disintegration and decay, shows nothing like an adequate awareness of—or concern for—what has been lost. Perhaps we have here the disability corresponding to the advantage he enjoys as an American. In America the Western process has gone furthest, and what has been lost is virtually forgotten. Certainly Mr. Dos Passos seems to share—it is a confirming sign—the attitude towards art and literature that so curiously qualifies the intelligence and penetration of Mr. Edmund Wilson's *Axel's Castle* (a book which only an American could have written). ' Art,' for the aspirant to ' culture ' in *The Forty-second Parallel,* is ' something ivory-white and very pure and noble and distant and sad.' The mind behind ' The Camera Eye ' seems to conceive of ' culture ' after much the same fashion in rejecting it: ' . . . . grow cold with culture like a cup of tea forgotten between an incenseburner and a volume of Oscar Wilde.'

What has disintegrated—this is the point—is not merely ' bourgeois ' or ' capitalist ' civilization; it is the organic community. Instead of the rural community and the town-community we have, almost universally, suburbanism (for the nature and significance of suburbanism see the article by Mr. W. L. Cuttle in *The Universities Review* for October, 1931). The organic community has virtually disappeared, and with it the only basis for a genuine national culture; so nearly disappeared that when one speaks of the old popular culture that existed in innumerable local variations people cannot grasp what one means. This is no place to try and explain. But let them re-read *The Pilgrim's Progress* and consider its significance, *Change in the Village, The Wheelwright's Shop*, and the other works of George Bourne, and, say, Cecil Torr's *Small Talk at Wreyland*, and then, for a commentary on the passing of the old order, go to *Middletown*. The education in reading offered, for instance, under the auspices of the W.E.A., is a substitute, and, as everyone who has lent a hand in it must at some time have realized, a substitute that can hardly begin to negotiate with the student's needs, and so must almost inevitably tend to a conception of Art as ' something ivory-white and very pure and distant and sad.' (It is relevant here to note that Mr. J. H. Fowler, in *The Art of Teaching English*, holds Ruskin to be ' the greatest writer of English prose that ever lived.')

The memory of the old order, the old ways of life, must be the chief hint for, the directing incitement towards, a new, if ever there is to be a new. It is the memory of a human normality or naturalness (one may recognise it as such without ignoring what has been gained in hygiene, public humanity and comfort). Whether, in a world of continually developing machine technique, a new order will ever be able to grow may seem doubtful. But without the faith that one might be achieved there can hardlly be hope in revolution. ' There'd be gaiety for the workers then, after the revolution,' says someone in *Manhattan Transfer*. And in *The Forty-second Parallel* we read of ' quiet men who wanted a house with a porch to putter around, and a fat wife to cook for them, a few drinks and cigars, and a garden to dig in.' This is all that Mr. Dos Passos suggests (as yet) concerning the way in which meaning is to be restored to the agonized vacuity that it is his distinction to convey so potently.

It seems to me that the more one sympathizes with his propagandist intention, the more should one be concerned to stress what is lacking in his presentment of it. To hope that, if the mechanics of civilization (so to speak) are perfected, the other problems (those which Mr. Dos Passos is mainly preoccupied with) will solve themselves, is vain: ' you know,' says someone in *Nineteen-nineteen*, 'the kind of feeling when everything you've wanted crumbles in your fingers as you grasp it.' Men and women might, of course, find happiness—or release from unhappiness—as perfect accessory machines. But that is hardly a hope for a propagandist to offer.

F. R. LEAVIS.

' THE BOOK SOCIETY RECOMMENDS. . . . '

It is important to know what is being read in fiction, and most of all what is being read at the book-society level—the level, that is, at which popular successes are believed to be Literature. ' Novel ' now covers so many non-comparable pieces of fiction that it is necessary to realise that gulfs exist between (a) the novel by a serious artist which succeeds (or does not) as a work of art, (b) the novel—*e.g. The Sound and the Fury, The Waves*—which is merely the work of a practised author doing technical stunts, (c) the novel which answers to the book-societies' conception of Literature, (d) the low-level best-seller. Class (c) is probably in most need of critical attention at the moment, since, for reasons I have suggested elsewhere, it looks like imposing on the educated public a spurious idea of what constitutes an important novel.

The *Rogues Herries* saga, *Broome Stages, The Good Companions,* have all been popular successes that have jerked their authors suddenly on to the level of ' classics,' and suggest some reflections upon the curious history of these authors. It seems to have been forgotten that Mr. Hugh Walpole commenced novelist as one of a younger group to whom Henry James gave respectful recognition in *Notes on Novelists;* that Miss Clemence Dane's early novels were thought worthy of serious criticism; and that Mr. Priestley, on the other hand, was an insignificant writer who justly received no attention at all. All three—stumbled upon?—no, arrived at, a popular formula which is the same formula, and now Mr. Louis Golding, upon whom the uncomfortable mantle of the late Israel Zangwill had fallen, and who had begun to work out his difficult destiny with several unsuccessful but not uninteresting novels, has elected to take the easier way. *Magnolia Street* is infinitely worse than any other novel he has written, but it is bad in a special way; any thoughtful reader of *The Good Companions* could have picked it out in advance for a Book Society choice. The characteristics of the novel of the Priestley genre are : meaty reading (value for money), defiant romanticism, a hearty intimacy with the reader, and a final warm note of rosy prophecy. Like his patrons, Mr. Golding will doubtless devote himself to turning out more popular successes, so that no one interested in the Novel need bother about him further. Here possibly is one answer, or part of one, to the question, What's wrong with the Novel?

Another meaty success of the same society's making is Pearl Buck's *The Good Earth*. Though it does not exist to be defended as a work of art, there seems to be a general feeling in critical circles that like *The Forsyte Saga* it is justified as a social document; just as that is said to give the enquiring foreigner a notion of the Victorian upper middle-class, so *The Good Earth* is supposed to give the occidental reader a veracious picture of Chinese culture and psychology. Anyone feeling a need to check this assumption should read Mr. Younghill Kang's review of *The Good Earth* in the *New Republic* (strange that no English periodical had the common sense to get an informed reviewer) and his longer article on the same subject in *The Symposium* for July of this year, where he registers a dignified disgust that ' *The Good Earth* has won its appreciation as a realistic novel, a true picture of the Chinese peasantry and a true rendition of Chinese psychology ' while being ' as false in its way as Cooper's dream-world of American Redskins.'

The top level of book-society choice is now the novel that calls out the critical vocabulary of Beauty—' a thing of beauty,' ' rare distinction,' ' exquisite,' ' enchanting loveliness,' the reviewers say. Mr. Ronald Fraser (whose *Rose Anstey* was backed by the late Book Guild) and Mr. Charles Morgan are characteristic recipients of these badges, though it would be unfair to Mr. Morgan to class *The Fountain* with *Rose Anstey* without adding that the latter is the grossest case of beauty-hunting. *The Fountain* is not gross, it is nothing wrapped up in veils of carefully composed sentences that have no emotional roots. Mr. Morgan (and the other novelists of this kind) for all their earnest determination to be literary might not be writing in an age that has witnessed the innovations of Joyce, Proust, Lawrence and

Mrs. Woolf. Quotations from *The Shropshire Lad*, Milton, *Adonais*, Plato and E. B. Browning appropriately usher in his sections; this is thin soil to plant a modern novel in, and the general effect, as might be expected, is much that of *The Testament of Beauty*. And as of Bridges's poem, it is a damaging consideration that its admirers are pretty sure to find ' unpleasant ' those modern works in which the sap flows—*The Forty-second Parallel*, for instance, and *Cakes and Ale*. Conviction that *The Fountain* is a beautiful piece of fiction precludes enjoyment of the sardonically critical spirit which gives life to *Cakes and Ale*, and alternatively, admiration of *The Fountain* comes easily to those who find ' modern ' novels distasteful. Hence the *Times Literary Supplement* declared that ' intensity of inspiration ' would be recognised as characterizing Mr. Morgan's previous novel by all those who, like the *Times Literary Supplement*, ' can still savour the classic tradition of English prose.' Incidentally, the novel of Beauty seems to have superseded the school of David Garnett, which is at least a point in its favour (oh that wit!).

By the way, it is painful to find Mr. Blunden (alas, Saul is also among the prophets) justifying his or his colleagues' choice of a very amateur story, *The Soldier and the Gentlewoman*, on the ground that it would have delighted Gibbon. Why Gibbon? We know that Gray's taste in fiction was lamentable, but what reason is there to assume that Gibbon would not have known better?

Q. D. Leavis.

AD IMAGINEM SUAM

THE ESSENTIAL SHAKESPEARE by J. Dover Wilson (Cambridge University Press, 3/6d.).

The habit of making fantasy Shakespeares is now discredited. So that Professor Dover Wilson does not pretend to any great seriousness in offering the Grafton portrait as an alternative to the Stratford bust. It is harmless speculation, for it does not touch the plays: no one was ever disturbed in reading *Lear* by a recollection of that pudding faced effigy. To relate four plays, including *Hamlet*, to the career of Essex is to make the fantasy much less airily irrelevant. It involves a manipulation of the evidence (*e.g.* a silence 1600-1603) and does not, without more proof, invite assent.

The Professor's style is breezy to the point of exuberance. Dowden's Four Periods are adopted, except that In the Depths becomes On the Heights—On the Razor Edge he calls it. Here ' The majestic peaks around him, Mount Othello, Mount Lear and the twin heights of Macbeth and his lady . . . keep him from slipping into the abyss of madness, brutality and despair that yawns beneath his tottering feet.' There is a note of hearty bluffness, transferred to Shakespeare (' this printing press was a new fangled invention ') which goes with Shakespeare's attractively virile vices, and with the Professor's taste for Rupert Brooke. *Measure for Measure* is compared with *The Waste Land*. It is also on the same page compared with *Point Counter Point*.

The Essential Shakespeare was obviously written for schools. It has already become popular there. It is easy to read: it contains much information, authoritative, doubtful and simply ' credible.' The scholar will sift for himself: the schoolboy will swallow the lot. Anyone who can respond to the passage quoted is unlikely to be capable of sufficient detachment to treat even the overt fantasy in the spirit in which it was written and it is only too probable that fifty per cent. of next year's School Certificate candidates will be firmly convinced that the Grafton portrait is the only true likeness of Shakespeare.   M.C.B.

THE ORATORS : AN ENGLISH STUDY by W. H. Auden (Faber and Faber, 6/-).

If *The Orators* is disappointing it is chiefly because one reads it as the successor to *Poems*. From the first book it was evident in the way in which he handled words, in his use of rhythm and imagery, that Mr. Auden was a poet of considerable technical ability; what he wrote was exciting, even when its significance was not clearly made out. One looked forward, therefore, to a work in which he would show a fuller control of his technique, in which his lyrical, merely poetic gifts, would be co-ordinated to a fuller purpose; but the most careful reading of *The Orators* fails to reveal such. One is faced, instead, by that obscurity to which his publishers, not without a certain smugness of inverted commas, draw our attention. The book, particularly in the opening prose section— the verse of the last, shows for the most part a falling off, a noticeable rhythmical weakening—is an interesting and moving experiment, which again emphasizes the fact that Auden's talent is specifically a poetic one (the distinction prose-poetry does not arise here), but it leaves the impression that it is as experiment rather than as achievement that it is remarkable. Or rather as a series of experiments, for the book has considerable technical variety. Throughout the first section one feels the influences—though they have been put to an exhilaratingly personal use—of Rimbaud and, more particularly, St. J. Perse, whose *Anabase* one would imagine Auden had been closely studying; just as in the last and perhaps most satisfactory of the Odes, there is a strong reminiscence of Emily Dickenson. Not that this supposition of influences, even if correct, is in itself in any way derogatory, but the fact that these two carefully stylized sections are divided by the naturalistically unorganized Journal of an Airman does give evidence of a lack of purposive organization which would account for one's disappointment.

It is probable that Auden had this criticism in mind when he was writing the opening sentences of the Journal: ' Organization,' he says, ' owes nothing to the surveyor. It is in no sense pre-arranged,' and though he does not state explicitly that this is intended as poetic theory, it would certainly seem to have an application to his method. And this impression is confirmed by the following phrases from a connected passage : ' while the fact that a state of tension seeks to relieve itself, seems to us perfectly obvious, *an orderly arrangement, the natural result of such an effort . . . .'* If this be intended as an account of the genesis of a poem (its similarity to the point of view of the *surréalistes* is striking) it would in large measure account for the obscurity of *The Orators,* for it amounts to proclaiming the absolute independence of the poetic impulse of any conscious intellectual direction. The poet's world, that is to say, is a system of arbitrary and private—Auden frequently insists upon privacy—values, to which the reader can only gain access by initiation. Failing that the poem must remain inchoate, to be enjoyed sporadically but not fully apprehended: but it should be emphasized that the resultant obscurity is different in kind and not merely in degree from the obscurity of *The Divine Comedy,* the ' great difficulty ' of which Auden comments on, ostensibly to an audience of school-boys, but with one eye also, perhaps, on his readers.

Douglas Garman.

MENCIUS ON THE MIND by I. A. Richards (Kegan Paul, International Library of Psychology, etc. Pp. xvi-132. Appendix Pp. 44. 10/6d.).

Dr. Richards continues in this book his study of the problems surrounding verbal communication. The first essential for accurate communication, one tends to suppose, is exact and unambiguous statement, but the central theme of this book is the necessity for flexible understanding and tolerant interpretation. Dr. Richards illustrates the principle in examining a passage of critical writing by Herbert Read, a passage whose meaning can be grasped from indirect clues although the wording will not stand ordinary critical inspection. Dr. Richards takes the keywords, Reasoning, Hypothesis, Fact, and Truth, and finds for these words senses that will render the whole passage self-consistent and acceptable in meaning. Reasoning for instance is to be taken ' *not* as inference from fixed explicit premises to a definite conclusion according to explicit rules; but as the placing of a number of observations in an intelligible order, a perceptible or rational structure.' The value of such a method of interpretation is unquestionable: it treats communication as a serious undertaking that demands co-operative effort, and it turns its back on the flippantly competitive pastime of terminological dispute. It is a method that most decent-minded people follow already, more or less wittingly. Dr. Richards' contention is that the time has come to make it explicit. He suggests the need for a dictionary of ' Multiple Definitions ' which should show the full range of meanings attached in Western and Eastern cultures to the more important terms in psychology, ethics, aesthetics, and so on. In illustration of the technique he himself gives multiple definitions of the terms Beautiful, Knowledge, Truth, and Order.

Dr. Richards seems to have left it to his readers' common sense to see that tolerance and flexibility of interpretation ought not to condone laxness of statement. I take it that future writers would, ideally, adhere to one sense for each term, and that the dictionary of multiple definitions would be used chiefly for the elucidation of earlier writers. The question is perhaps complicated by the fact that difficult thought is almost always uttered in poetic language where the control of understanding is not dependent on the narrow sense of the words, or in terminology invented *ad hoc* and seldom current beyond the writings of its originator. Explicit multiple definition would perhaps provide a bridge between the poetic and the scientific utterance of subtle intuitions. (One thinks of Trigant Burrow, whose efforts to communicate it would be instructive to compare and contrast with Blake's, since several of their intuitions seem to have been similar). But when the thought is fairly manageable, as it is in the passage by Herbert Read, it points to a serious defect in the writer if we have to resort to multiple definition before his words will make sense. Dr. Richards does not comment on the fault but he can hardly mean to condone it.

His attitude to communication becomes of peculiar importance when one culture is to be interpreted to another, and *Mencius on the Mind* consists largely in the attempt to translate and explain a few psychological passages from the Chinese thinker without distorting their meaning. Part of Dr. Richards' purpose is to draw attention to the intrinsic worth of Mencius' views, particularly on questions that modern writers regard as being on the borderline between psychology and ethics. It is largely because no such borderline existed for Mencius that his attitudes and assumptions are so attractive. But although Dr. Richards is extremely illuminating on Mencius' psychological conceptions, a large part of his purpose is to show that the task of interpretation is an almost impossible one. To stress the point he prints the passages in question in a very valuable Appendix, showing the Chinese characters and their literal translation. This Appendix gives a hint of the amount of ' smoothing ' that must have been done by some translators from the Chinese. But apart from the difficulties of language structure the commentator meets more fundamental obstacles in the form of peculiarities in Mencius' habits of thought and speech. And, as Dr. Richards shows, analysis of such characteristics in a remote culture may give us more insight into similar peculiarities in our own.

One of the most serious obstacles in the way of interpretation is Mencius' use of blanket terms, each covering what to us are several different meanings. ' *Ku*—with its senses of cause, reason, hold to, conviction, accepted of old, established, fact, datum, phenomenon—seems to stand for an idea which is none of these but out of which they may be developed through elaborated distinctions. Such a word as ' because ' in ordinary unreflective English has a somewhat similar width and vagueness of reference. Or ' grounds,' if we let its metaphor come to life, may give us something like its undifferentiated seeming simplicity.' One tool for tackling the difficulty is multiple definition. Not even multiple definition can succeed completely, however, for we cannot assume that Mencius intends *one* sense of a word in one place and a different sense in another: what he intends is a more primitive notion, inclusive and undifferentiated. It would not be accurate even to say that he intended a ' blend ' of our meanings. This difficulty Dr. Richards insists on throughout the book, but his success in revealing some markedly unfamiliar types of meaning shows that insistence on the difficulty is a way of partially solving it.

Formal praise of *Mencius on the Mind* should be unnecessary if these notes have suggested anything of its scope and its subtlety. The two aspects of the work—the technique of elucidation and the value of what is elucidated—are inseparable, and this of course adds to the difficulty of the book by making explicit, simple statements next to impossible. Part of the difficulty that many readers will experience is due to Dr. Richards' rather cryptic way of writing—a device perhaps for demanding competent reading. At times it seems almost as if he were trying to provide non-mathematical people with a development of thought as impressive and recondite as relativity. Thus he suggests that we should be unwise if we overlooked ' the possibility that the structure and functioning of the minds (including his own) that Mencius was discussing might differ from our hypothetical standard Western mind. . . Even though we refused to allow that differences between minds go very deep, we shall do well to ask ourselves just how we are estimating depth in this matter. And whether we are entitled (and if so, how) to take cognition, affection, conation, for example, for necessary co-ordinates in our comparisons as we take our three spatial co-ordinates in comparing boxes.' But the point is left too little developed to possess its full force even as speculation. The one example given, namely the possible absence of ' cognitive contemplation ' or ' autonomous cognitive interest ' among Chinese thinkers is of doubtful value, for it might be difficult to prove that such a mode of activity occurs even in Western minds. Further, although the absence of ' theoretical interest ' in Mencius is undeniable, this is surely very different from an absence of cognition. It is an error of tactics not to have argued this speculation more explicitly and more fully, for the suggestion, in spite of being revolutionary, is at present too nebulous to be stimulating.

A final quotation may indicate not only the Intention of the book but its Tone too, both of which will probably irritate those whom Dr. Richards means to irritate. ' Most studies of the processes of abstraction have been made as incidental steps in ambitious metaphysical undertakings. A more modest sense of where we are in our effort to comprise the universe in our thought would turn more attention upon our intellectual instruments. their historical development and their possible extensions.'

DENYS W. HARDING.

CHAUCER by G. K. Chesterton (Faber and Faber, 12/6d.).

This book avowedly makes no claim to specialism of any sort in the field of Chaucerian scholarship. It does not profess to reconsider the subject in the light of recent research—rushlight or gas may still serve. ' A man ' remarks Mr. Chesterton ' might learn more of the special spirit of Chaucer by looking at Daisies than by reading a good many annotations by Dons '—a characteristic gesture and suggestive of the method which he himself prefers to pursue, though it must not be supposed that he has never availed himself of the researches of dons in this book. The plain reader, however, requires more guidance than this to the understanding of Chaucer's sophisticated urbanity as it shows itself, for example, in the skilful pastiche of the Prologue to the *Legend of Good Women.*

Mr. Chesterton, as might be expected, is more interested in the historical aspects of his subject than in those which are more purely literary, but the general question of Chaucer's relation to his sources is forcibly handled. ' In that vanished world of community of thoughts and themes, a tale or a topic was in some sense set up . . . . to be told over and over again with variations by different storytellers . . . . One author did not so much rob as enrich the other.' This ' free trade in stories,' as W. P. Ker once called it, did not preclude spontaneity and sincerity on the part of the translator. The claim that Chaucer's translations were often ' more original than the originals ' is here supported by particular reference to the early translation known as the *A.B.C.*

The reader should be warned that Mr. Chesterton, like the Parson of the *Canterbury Tales,* is not always ' textual,' though, unlike the Parson, he does not submit his work to the correction of clerks. He writes from a full but unrefreshed memory which may confuse one poem or one speaker with another (*e.g. The House of Fame* with the Prologue to *L.G.W.,* or the words of the cock with the ironic comments of the Nun's Priest), or attribute the complimentary phrase ' my disciple and my poet ' to Gower instead of to Venus. Such lapses may easily be corrected if the reader does what Mr. Chesterton has failed to do and looks up the text. It is a more serious matter when the poet's personal opinions on political, religious or other questions are arbi-

trarily deduced from the speeches of his characters, from a
Boethian quotation, or from a direct translation like the Parson's
Tale. For the real purpose of this study is not the appreciation
of Chaucer's poetry but the more familiar and hazardous attempt
to reconstruct the opinions and character of the man from his
work. Mr. Chesterton has his own thesis and selects his evidence
to prove his point. It is one upon which, as he says, he cannot
be expected to be non-controversial. The superior sanity and
normality which he finds in Chaucer are apparently at once the
cause and the result of his being envisaged as 'the final fruit
and inheritor of the mediæval order.' He is thus made to sym-
bolise ' the Ages of Faith ' as contrasted with ' the Ages of Doubt
and Schism'; he is the text for a disquisition on the superiority
of the mediæval order with its balanced philosophy to the
unbalanced philosophies of the present:—' it is because we miss
the point of mediæval history that we make a mess of modern
politics.' From this standpoint Mr. Chesterton appears to invest
Chaucer with a kind of cosmic significance:—' he made a
national language; he came very near to making a nation ' (in
which he apparently collaborated with Joan of Arc). The claim
that he made the English language—by ' Frenchifying it enough
to make it English ' be it noted—is one which has long since
been refuted from the evidence of the language itself.

As always, Mr. Chesterton shows himself provocative and
stimulating even when most paradoxical. He is the last heir of
the euphuistic tradition and can ' hunt the letter ' or pun with
the best of them. To quote his own words: ' the very sense of
this is its nonsense; its aptitude is its ineptitude.' It has the
true Gilbertian ring.

H. M. R. MURRAY.

REMINISCENCES OF D. H. LAWRENCE.

Some who are most impatient of the traffic in personalities that
substitutes for interest in literature turn with eagerness to reminiscences of D. H. Lawrence. I have said elsewhere that he matters
because he was a great artist. But the case is not so simple as that
might suggest. His art bears a peculiarly close relation to the man—

' the man who suffered '—and that is its importance. If we find him great, the supreme importance of his books is perhaps that they assure us that he existed. Those of them which are most successful as art are in some ways saddening and depressing. The fact of personal existence of which they assure us is perhaps the most cheering and enlivening fact the modern world provides. Here was a man with the clairvoyance and honesty of genius whose whole living was an assertion of what the modern world has lost. It is plain from his books that he was not able to maintain steady confident possession of what he sought—wholeness in spontaneity; a human naturalness, inevitable, and more than humanly sanctioned; a sense, religious in potency, of life in continuity of communication with the deepest springs, giving fulfilment in living, ' meaning ' and a responsive relation with the cosmos. But it is equally plain that he didn't merely seek.

And it appears, too, that his best creative work was not fully representative of him. He himself—the personality behind the best stories—was a less equivocal incitement than these to the recovery of what has been lost. The man appears saner than the art. And how essentially sane are some of those works in the mixed mode—those lyric-expository prophetic extravaganzas, which, for all their preoccupation with the dark gods, are lit with sun. It was not, in any derogatory sense, an abnormal mind that wrote *Apocalypse*.

It may be that Lawrence is approached largely in a wrong spirit, but it is difficult to believe that his influence can be anything but wholesome, and it is exhilarating to think that in a world of suburbanism, book societies and Marie Stopes he imposed himself. Only those who suppose his message to be that of *The Conquest of Happiness* are likely to see in him the all-sufficing wisdom that will save us. But it is a suspect wisdom that dismisses him in fear or revulsion or contempt. That is why some who a good while ago formed the habit of taking the *Criterion* seriously, now, when they compare the obituary attention given to Harold Monro with that which was given to Lawrence, feel a kind of final depression.

*   *   *

Whether the book that was the occasion of this note and has been withdrawn was unjust as well as objectable-against one cannot presume to determine. Interesting personal reminiscences of D. H. Lawrence present a problem; they are bound to give offence somewhere. But whether or not D. H. Lawrence would have brought objections against *Son of Woman* was, for various reasons, a problem the author had no need to let worry him overmuch. We may be sure, however, that if Lawrence could make his comment now it would be worth listening to.

F.R.L.

PRIVATE PLEASURE

THE YEAR BOOK OF EDUCATION 1932. Edited by Lord Eustace Percy (Evans Brothers, 35/-).

THE TRIUMPH OF THE DALTON PLAN by C. W. Kimmins and Belle Rennie (Ivor Nicholson and Watson, 6/-).

REMINISCENCES OF A PUBLIC SCHOOLBOY by W. Nichols Marcy (Elkin Matthews, 6/-).

Here are three books—a bird's-eye view of the world of school—a puff of a teaching method—a defence of a way of living. Here you may learn that Monmouth demands a quarter of an hour longer for scripture than Cornwall, that Ernie Todd aged twelve prefers the Dalton plan because you can spend more time on the subjects in which you are weak, that louts who accuse prefects of immoral relations with fags are, unless they quickly apologise, justly and soundly thrashed. Data to support almost any contention. Ratepayer, well-fed, daring his wife to contradict, may thump the breakfast table, shout ' Disgraceful. They're playing ducks and drakes with our money. The nation can't afford it.' Folk-dancer, remembering a once-sore behind, thinks ' Ah, had the masters loved me, I should have expanded like a flower.' Old boy in club, having another, solemn as a clergyman declares ' You can't get away from it. A good school stamps a man.'

It is going on. It is going to be like this to-morrow. Atten-dance-officer will flit from slum to slum, educational agencies will be besieged by promising young men who have no inclination to business, examiners chuckle over a novel setting of the problem of Achilles and the Tortoise, fathers sell grand pianos or give up tobacco, that little Adrian or Derek may go to Marlborough or Stowe.

Like everything else in our civilization, the system we have made has become too much for us; we can't stop the boat and we can't get out into the cold sea. The snail is obeying its shell. All we can do is to become specialists. Just as the soldier devises new methods of gas attack, or the poet a new technique of verbal association, the teacher vigorously pursues the logic of his tiny department. ' How many pupils can I get? ' ' What is the optimum method for getting the greatest number of them through school certificate? ' No one can afford to stop and ask what is the bearing of his work on the rest of the world, its ultimate value. It's his job, his bread and butter. Should he stop for one moment, there's his ego dinning like a frightened woman ' But what's going to happen to me? You'll be sacked without a testimonial.'

Education, all smoothly say, is the production of useful citizens. But, good God, what on earth is a useful citizen just now? If you are a policeman or a cabinet minister, it's a person who won't give you any trouble. Education is a dope to allay irritation. If he is poor, now that you no longer want him very much on the land but in mass-production plants, better give him something to think about lest he sense the absurd inadequacy of the operations he is made to do, and start to smash. Better teach him enough to read the *News of the World*. Every worker shall attend an elementary school. If he's rich, your sort, then segre-gate him with the other young of your sort, let him year by year through his school-days feel all the excitement of a social climber, and make him so afraid of the opinions of your sort, that you may be sure he'll never do anything silly, like forgetting his class. Public school men will always lend each other money.

But there are some, who, though comfortably off, with no right to fear, have nightmares. ' Of course, the world is really alright,' they say, ' it's only the way I look at it. If I'd been differently brought up, if men had understood me, life would be the jolly thing it ought to be. Besides, even if there is anything wrong with the world, if I do try to do anything about it, I shouldn't make any difference: I should only lose my money. It's all so very diffy. Let's go and ask the children. Perhaps they will know. Now remember; no slapping. The most wonderful thing in the world is love.'

And off they go to live with the children, and splendid they are at it too. The children brighten up no end,—in their heads. Stupidity which is a natural defence against living beyond one's means collapses under the intense fire of their kindness. Girls of eleven paint like Picasso, boys of sixteen write pastiches of Joyce. Every child responds to the love smarm—for a bit. But emotionally it withers. Before a man wants to understand, he wants to command or obey instinctively, to live with others in a relation of power; but all power is anathema to the liberal. He hasn't any. He can only bully the spirit.

And so unconsciously the liberal becomes the secret service of the ruling class, its most powerful weapon against social revolution.

For the freedom they boast of is bogus, management by flattery, persuading people that your suggestions are really their own. Its power lies in the inexhaustible vanity of the human heart. Don't think that you can behave as you like in a liberal school—a little recalcitrance, yes that is amusing, but a will of your own! Make no mistake about that.

The public schools are at least better than that. They offer an intense social field, the satisfactory nature of which can be seen in the fact that, their members, like bees taken from a colony, when they leave it, spiritually die. They fail because they are only for the splendid people: they are economically parasitic. Those who leave them will not attempt to create a similar kind of society in the world because that would mean admitting the others, those who have frizzed hair, or eat peas with a knife.

But what can one do? Dearie, you can't do anything for the
children till you've done something for the grown-ups. You've
really got nothing to teach and you know it. When you have
repapered the walls perhaps you will be allowed to tell your
son how to hold the brush. In the meantime some of us will
go on teaching what we can for a sum which even in its modesty
we do not really deserve. Teaching will continue to be, not a
public duty, but a private indulgence.

                                                    W. H. AUDEN.

WORLD - LOSERS

1. THE DISCOVERY OF POETRY by P. H. B. Lyon.

2. POETRY AND THE ORDINARY READER by M. R. Ridley.

3. ABOUT ENGLISH POETRY by C. F. Bradby.

4. THE ART OF TEACHING ENGLISH by J. H. Fowler.

5. EXERCISES IN CRITICISM by David Shillan.

6. COMMON SENSE ABOUT POETRY by L. A. G. Strong.

' But aren't they at the Tennyson stage? ' said someone to a
schoolmaster who proposed to introduce an upper form to Mr.
Eliot's work. The background and attitude implied in this objection
sterilizes the teaching of English in schools as exemplified in such
books as the above—taken from dozens of their kind in the library
of an energetic specialist. The conceptions of poetry they authorise
are so pernicious that the intelligent product of such teaching is
likely to be permanently excluded from an interest in poetry : the
intelligent may graze for a time on a very limited and profitless
plot. They provide no critical armoury : though five of the authors
would reply by pointing to their laborious discussions of rhythm
in terms of musical notation and classical feet. They can do nothing
to check an ' increasing inattention,' for they are themselves part
and parcel of it.

Number 1 (which was hailed by a heavy review as one of the
most important contributions to English criticism since the war) is
the kind of book a Censor should suppress at once. ' '' Motorbuses

for town stop here," ' says Mr. Lyon, ' is not a poetical phrase, and
" The stars rush out, at one stride comes the dark " is definitely
poetry; but you would find it hard to say why.' It is not hard
to see what Mr. Lyon expects from poetry :—' We live there in
our dreams, and in our waking hours books and our own wandering thoughts are ever at hand to guide us there.' (My own thoughts
wander to p. 320 of Dr. Richards' *Practical Criticism.*) If these
quotations sound like something from *The Observer*, they do their
author no injustice; and Mr. Lyon's discovery of good poetry in
Messrs. Binyon and Gibson typifies the ineptitude of such mentors
as these in approaching the modern field.

Papers read before the English Association are incorporated
in Number 4, Number 2 consists of broadcast talks, while Number
3 avoids the usual tract of classical metres by referring the reader
to Professor Murray. Mr. Shillan manages in the same breath to
recommend Nos. 1 and 3 and to invoke Dr. Richards' books, but
disclaims any intention of offering a digest of his ideas. After
this it was hardly modest of him to answer the questions ' What is
a poem, what kind of an experience does it offer, what is rhythm? '
etc. Dilution is a fitter word for a process wherein are cited such
authorities as Miss Sitwell and the Archbishop of York. Thirty
unsigned poems are then presented for evaluation, with tuck-in
sheets revealing authorship and criticism, which invites us to
approve of the products among others of Canton, Wolfe, Longfellow and Meredith, while *modernique* at the tea-shop level is
represented by Miss Sitwell. So no surprise is occasioned by finding Donne reprimanded as farfetched and perverse.

Mr. Strong's book is not meant for schools, and its intentions
are less pretentious and its tone less nauseating than its companions. ' What the book does attempt is to suggest that, among
all activities of mind and body, none has a better claim on man's
attention; and to show how far common sense can take us towards
an understanding of poetry.' And it may justify its existence by
converting Plain Men into lovers of Pure Poetry; but it is unfitted
for general use in schools by the limitations and implications of
his second aim, together with such weaknesses as the recommendation of *Poems of To-day* and the devotion of a quarter of the
book to metres. It might be tried on the First Fifteen.

DENYS THOMPSON.

AMERICAN LIBERALS SEEKING A HOME

TRAGIC AMERICA by Theodore Dreiser (Constable, 10/-).

DEVIL TAKE THE HINDMOST by Edmund Wilson (Scribners, 10/6d.).

ONLY YESTERDAY by Frederick Lewis Allen (Harpers, 12/6d.).

Theodore Dreiser's *Tragic America* and Edmund Wilson's *Devil Take the Hindmost* are two interesting examples of the tendencies of critical liberalism in America. The liberal critics have acquired a new warrior in Mr. Dreiser. His novels, to be sure, showed an awareness of the extensive evils in American life, but he has not before made a factual attack upon them. *Tragic America* is an avalanche of facts; it has the size of an avalanche at least, if not the grandeur. The facts are imbedded in a paste of political-convention rhetoric, bristling with italics, Roman capitals and exclamation points, redundant and journalese. However sympathetic to his cause, one cannot avoid being annoyed by his method. But worse, one is continually led into suspicion of the facts themselves. Statement after statement is made without the mention of any authority; even such an important one as that in 1930 dividends increased $350,000,000 while wages fell $700,000,000 is offered without analysis or support. Who supplied these figures and must they be qualified in any way? Elsewhere one feels that a more careful presentation of the figures might not be so partial to Mr. Dreiser's case as he would wish. These suspicions of the layman are confirmed by such a reputable economist as Mr. Stuart Chase, who claims to have found nine errors of fact in one chapter. Some of the boulders in the avalanche turn out to be porous stuff, fly-weight.

The general theses of the book are unquestionably correct: that the wealth of the United States is being concentrated in the hands of a few people, that individuals, both as consumers and labourers, suffer abuses by the corporations, that the police, through a blind acceptance of the private enterprise ideal if not

actually through bribery, commit further outrages upon the
'small individual,' that religion has been corrupted and cheapened by adopting business methods, these general charges are
true. It is unfortunate that when Mr. Dreiser attempts to particularize he arouses honest prejudice. Being a Communist and a
novelist could he not consider with profit the case of John Dos
Passos?

It is impossible to say how Mr. Dreiser would thrive in the
Communist state. The charges he brings are largely economic
and Communism would mend them. Personal questions he does
not mention.

Mr. Wilson's criticism is less a torch-light attack with barrel
staves; it is conducted by day, carefully. *Devil Take the Hindmost* is a collection of Mr. Wilson's writings in the *New Republic*
during the past year; the first twenty-six are largely accounts of
the small man's struggle for existence in various parts of the
United States, the labourer, the clerk, the farmer. The book combines the journalistic virtue of empiricism with an imaginative
interpretation and coherence. In each article Mr. Wilson
sets the scene carefully, describing the town, or the building, or the room, the appearance and nature of the principal
characters, and giving what background information is necessary,
then proceeding to the event itself. A Communist march on
the New York City Hall, the life of workers in Detroit, a
short biography of Henry Ford, the struggles of miners and mine
unions in West Virginia, these are typical articles. There are
exceptions to the usual pattern, as the satire on Los Angeles in
semi-Joycean language. But for the most part the author remains
an impersonal observer and the writing a meticulous record. It
is so skilfully done, however, that he can afford to omit comment.
The conclusions are apparent. In the first place, one has a bird's-
eye view of America, each section described through a typical
spot, the beautiful as well as the ugly, and the economic and
social interests of its people are portrayed. One recognizes the
same evils that Mr. Dreiser assails, but visually rather than
through statistics. And one realises that what prevents their
correction is the disorganization of the two groups which have so
far been numerous enough to be potentially effective: labor and
the liberals or progressives. The Progressive Conference in

Washington showed that each man present had a different idea of what should be done; nothing was done. But labour, with a far more biting drive to action, is similarly incapacitated. Having proved itself futile the American Federation of Labor can no longer be looked to as a large national organization which from weight of numbers might bring reform. What remains are scattered Communist unions and in between them and the Federation in policy, local unions.

The last three chapters are the most significant. Here Mr. Wilson modifies his journalistic manner to permit himself more analysis and interpretation. The first of the three is ' The Best People '—the wealthy, the managers, the executives, those who feel themselves superior to the rest of the country. Their superiority, Mr. Wilson contends, comes almost entirely from possession of material goods. This is a thin basis. A ruling class, from which an honest feeling of superiority might be derived, they are not. ' Mr. X does not govern. He gets his orders from officials higher up, and they may get their orders from the bankers from whom they borrow. Yet neither bankers nor high officials constitute a governing class : they are merely people of all sorts of origins, capacities and ideals who come and go in lucrative positions. The system they belong to governs, but they are only individuals on the make. They take no collective responsibility and their power is not hereditary—so they have none of the special training which permanent power and responsibility requires and which may dignify and refine a strongly established owning class.'

The question of capitalism is two-fold; it is an economic theory and a way of life. If ' the best people ' could combine in such a manner as to remedy the economic ills their values would still remain to be questioned. This Mr. Wilson does from his own point of view in the next chapter, ' The Case of the Author.' While admitting his bourgeois background he claims never to have been satisfied with the values of the stock-broker class. He has tried various techniques, from Menckenian superiority to ' the liberal attitude that American capitalism was going to show a new wonder to the world,' but these were only compromises and unsatisfactory. Now he is a Communist.

One may save objections until reading the last chapter, when they become clearer: ' A Man in the Street,' an article of only a few lines. ' He is a tall man with square shoulders—looks able-bodied and self-dependent. A pure Nordic type, he has straight brows and long straight nose.' But h᾿ seems soiled, pale, bewildered, incongruous in the wealth of Fifty-eighth Street. From ' the best people ' Mr. Wilson is turning to him; he is the type of the proletariat; he is the norm of the hoped-for Communist order, its ideal. Would Mr. Wilson be satisfied with the culture this man will establish? Or is he taking a romantic view? That is what one suspects. Although doubtless true that economic evils would be eliminated and that living solely to make money would no longer be possible, granting that that would please Mr. Wilson greatly, yet is he not hoping to be more at peace with the new order than actually he will be? Is any mass movement greatly concerned with the sensitive values which concern such a man as Mr. Wilson? One feels that he might find himself on the outside looking in. Certainly when he announced his decision to join the Communist party one heard no cheers from their ranks.

Mr. Wilson and the rest of the critical liberals would reply that they were weary of minority individualism and an eclectic set of standards, that they wanted to be part of a coherent move-ment, in the flow of an inevitable social current, and that since they cannot remake or modify Marxism they are willing to accept it as it is. Mr. Wilson doubtless wished to imply a turning away from the old values when he described the man in the street, to whom he looks for the future and with whom he will march. It remains a strange picture; one thinks of Rousseau contemplating the Red Indian.

Only Yesterday is a journalistic account of what happened in the 1920's in the United States; it is a useful background to the other books under discussion. All the available material of the scandals of the Harding administration is collected for the first time. The revolt of the highbrows is treated in a cavalier fashion, doubt-less wisely. In the other chapters, such as those on dress, racket-eering, the Red scare, and the inflation period, one finds what one already knew neatly summarized.

DONALD CULVER.

ETHICAL RELATIVITY by Edward Westermarck (Kegan Paul, 12/6d.).

Prof. Westermarck is the best of possible guides to the moral emotions. His *History* left upon the reader an impression of peculiar richness: it was rich not only in information, but in sympathy, and it led the reader to sympathize. *Ethical Relativity* leaves a similar impression. Professor Westermarck still has much to say—this time rather about the use men have made of the data of ethics, than about the data themselves—and still knows how to arrange what he says. The old contrast rises to one's mind: how much more encouraging this book is than that, say, of Prof. Moore, with its *non possum* attitude. Prof. Westermarck not only declares that he can, but proves it.

But the contrast with Prof. Moore does not, this time, work so wholly in favour of Prof. Westermarck. Prof. Moore's attitude was extreme, and outraged common sense; but it was taken up at the dictates of metaphysical scruples, and Prof. Moore, whether or not a sound, is an acute metaphysician. There is some propriety about metaphysics dictating to ethics. Prof. Westermarck seems to make ethics dictate to metaphysics, and there is little propriety about that. Further, whatever he may be as a student of ethics, as a metaphysician he is hardly acute.

Consider his definition of objectivity, which we find on p. 3 of the text: ' The supposed objectivity of moral values . . . implies that they have a real existence apart from any reference to a human mind.' Is there any way in which this can be glossed so as to give the semblance of truth to the following statement, which we find on p. 4? ' If any one of the theories of normative ethics has been actually proved to be true, the objectivity of moral judgments has *eo ipso* been established as an indisputable fact.' I do not think so. An analogy, which seems always at the back of Prof. Westermarck's mind, occurs on p. 59: it is between the pain caused by a fire which burns us and the moral emotion roused by the actions of our fellows. It does not seem particularly fortunate. Of course the pain is not in the fire; but what of that? Does it give rise to concepts? If it does, are they merely ' subjective? ' Similar passages are not far to seek. The very title— though it may not be Prof. Westermarck's—savours of the correspondence columns of the *Times,* in which Einstein is invoked to ratify any and every solution of the problem of agriculture or of the Sunday cinemas.

Perhaps Prof. Westermarck, tired of finding metaphysics apparently on the side of his more obstinate opponents, wishes, once and for all, to drag it over to his side. He might have paused, reflecting that it is perhaps within the province of time to reveal that his opponents are not metaphysically so blameless, after all. The problem of the relation between ethics and metaphysics, though important, is not too pressing. With no greater metaphysical equipment than he possesses here, Westermarck succeeded, in the *History*, in performing work of immense value. This is not, of course, to say that had that equipment been different or greater the work might not have been more valuable still.

The importance of *Ethical Relativity* may be that it will compel a final distinction between what is and what is not of value in the *History*. That work is above all a mass of evidence, in the light of which it is impossible to deny some connection between the emotions and the moral concepts. But what that connection is is by no means so clear. It is not clear that when philosophers claim that the emotions follow instead of preceding the concepts they are, as Westermarck would have it, putting the cart before the horse. What are carts? and what are horses? What, above all, is priority? These are questions that demand close and technical discussion; discussion more technical, at any rate, that Prof. Westermarck is willing to give them in *Ethical Relativity*.

JAMES SMITH.

I LOST MY MEMORY : The case as the Patient saw it. Anonymous *(Faber and Faber, p. 306, 7/6d.).*

This is a popularly written account of a case of loss of memory and its psycho-therapeutic treatment without deep psycho-analysis. It provides a good close-up of this kind of treatment, with its methods of free-association and dream-recording, and it emphasises the laboriousness of the treatment for all concerned. An interesting feature is the introspective account of the difference between the patient's true memory of events when he regained it and the mere knowledge of them which he had previously been able to build up from other people's accounts. It is an easily read book and it should be useful in popular teaching—for instance in W.E.A. classes.

SELECTIONS FROM REMY DE GOURMONT.   Chosen and translated by Richard Aldington (Chatto and Windus, 3/6d.).

A popular selection from Remy de Gourmont has been for some time overdue in this country and the present volume forms a welcome addition to the *Phœnix Library*. It is unfortunate however that Mr. Aldington has tended to give undue space to those excerpts which illustrate his own views on sex, his own scepticism (*vide* introduction: ' So penetrated am I with the spirit of scepticism ' . . .), and his own bourgeois conceptions of liberty. The lapse of a quarter of a century has made some of the ' daring ' passages on love sound a little thin, and Gourmont's reaction to Socialism was somewhat naïve. The book contains plenty of stimulating material, but we could have done with less sex and more criticism.

SCRUTINY *is published by the Editors, 13 Leys Road, Cambridge, and printed by S. G. Marshall & Son, Round Church Street, Cambridge, England.*

Vol. I. No. 3.   December, 1932

SCRUTINY

A Quarterly Review

Edited by

L. C. KNIGHTS   DONALD CULVER
F. R. LEAVIS   DENYS THOMPSON

CONTENTS

EDITORIAL NOTE

WITH the publication of the next number *Scrutiny* will have completed its first year. It is plain by now that our confidence was justified. Indeed, we ought, in a sense, to apologise for not having had more, since the first number, though still in constant demand, has sold out, and many new readers have had to wait while the second number was reprinting: we are putting in a much larger order to the printer this time. We might call attention to the impressive amount of public notice we have had at home and abroad; but we are ourselves much more impressed by the letters we get, with new subscriptions, and from original subscribers, from all over the country and from America and elsewhere. These confirm us amply in our belief that there was more than a sufficient public consciously feeling the need of a review that should attempt the function of *Scrutiny*. We thank all those who have, by active propaganda, made our expansion of circulation possible, and we appeal for still more help of that kind, since there is still a large potential public that has not yet been reached, and we are without the ordinary resources of publicity.

We do not pretend to be satisfied with our performance up till now but we hope we have justified our Manifesto. We should like in especial to find more room for reviews, and, with the experience we have had and the connections we have established, we hope to be stronger in reviewing in the future.

And we have reason for hoping that the response to our efforts in the educational field will, in the coming year, show them not to have been altogether ineffective.

The main difficulty (since we have all to earn our livings and cannot afford to buy help) has been to get the necessary work done, editorial, secretarial and ' business.' The original editors, therefore, have formed with two other regular helpers an Editorial Board, one of the members of which signs the editorial beginning on the opposite page.

A subscription form will be found inside the back cover.

No payment is made for contributions.

American subscriptions may be sent to Sheldon Dick, Literary Agent, 33 West 42nd Street, New York.

All other communications should be addressed to : The Editors, 13 Leys Road, Cambridge, England.

'UNDER WHICH KING, BEZONIAN?'

IT would be very innocent of us to be surprised by the frequency with which we are asked to ' show our colours,' but the source of the command does sometimes surprise us. Indeed, this very formulation came first from Mr. George Santayana, and others whom we respect have repeated it, in substance, since. We should have thought that we had amply made out our case (if that were needed) for holding the assertion and application of serious standards in literary criticism to be an essential function, and one disastrously inoperative now.

Not that we suppose the service of this function to be the whole duty of man, or our own whole duty. The more seriously one is concerned for literary criticism the less possible does one find it to be concerned for that alone. *Scrutiny* has not, as a matter of fact, confined itself to literary criticism. But to identify *Scrutiny* with a social, economic or political creed or platform would be to compromise and impede its special function. This, in its bearing on the challenge now in view, has already been glossed by : ' the free play of intelligence on the underlying issues.' More, of course, needs saying. What is immediately in place is to insist that one does not necessarily take one's social and political responsibilities the less seriously because one is not quick to see salvation in a formula or in any simple creed. And it is unlikely that anyone actively and sympathetically interested in *Scrutiny* (whether as a reader or otherwise) will exhibit this kind of quickness. On the other hand, those of us who are particularly engrossed by the business of carrying on *Scrutiny* should perhaps resolve (though it seems unnecessary) to warn ourselves now and then against making the perception of the complexity of problems an excuse for complacent inattention : special duties are not ultimately served by neglect of the more general. But the special function of *Scrutiny* is an indispensable one, and there appears to be no danger of its being excessively attended to.

Supporters of *Scrutiny*, then, are, we suppose, of varying social, political and economic persuasions. But the function indicated would hardly have been fully realized if its bearing on such persuasions were left at this, no more immediate and particular than has yet been suggested. If there seems to be no reason why supporters of *Scrutiny* should not favour some kind of communism as the solution of the economic problem, it does not seem likely (there is no thought here of Mr. Middleton Murry) that they will be orthodox Marxists. The efficiency of the Marxist dialectic, indeed, makes it difficult to determine what precisely orthodoxy is (we do not find even Mr. Maurice Dobb, whom Mr. Eliot singles out for commendation, very lucid). But there can be no doubt that the dogma of the priority of economic conditions, however stated, means a complete disregard for—or, rather, a hostility towards—the function represented by *Scrutiny*.

Why the attitude expressed in the varying formula that makes ' culture ' (a term to be examined) derivative from the ' methods of production '—why this attitude must be regarded as calamitous Trotsky himself brings out in his *Literature and Revolution*. This book shows him to be a cultivated as well as an unusually intelligent man (which perhaps has something to do with his misfortune). But he too, unhappily, like all the Marxists, practises, with the familiar air of scientific rigour, the familiar vague, blanketing use of essential terms. He can refer, for instance, to the ' 2nd of August, 1914, when the maddened power of bourgeois culture let loose upon the world the blood and fire of an imperialistic war.' (p. 190). This, however, is perhaps a salute to orthodoxy. And it would not be surprising if he had thought it wise to distract attention, if possible, from such things as the following, which uses ' culture ' very differently, and is hardly orthodox : ' The proletariat is forced to take power before it has appropriated the fundamental elements of bourgeois culture; it is forced to overthrow bourgeois society by revolutionary violence, for the very reason that society does not allow it access to culture.' (p. 195). The aim of revolution, it appears, is to secure this accursed bourgeois culture for the proletariat. Or, rather, Trotsky knows that behind the word ' culture ' there is something that cannot be explained by the ' methods of production ' and that it would be disastrous to destroy as ' bourgeois.' To assert this

un-Marxian truth is the aim of his book. ' The proletariat,' he says
(p. 186), 'acquires power for the purpose of doing away with
class culture and to make way for human culture.' And he insists
that the necessary means to this consummation is to maintain
continuity. That is, he knows, and virtually says, that ' human
culture ' at present is something covered by ' bourgeois culture,'
the Marxian blanket.

But even Trotsky, although he can speak of the need to
' turn the concept of culture into the small change of individual
daily living ' and can say that ' to understand and perceive
truly not in a journalistic way but to feel to the bottom the
very section of time in which we live, one has to know the past
of mankind, its life, its work, its struggles, its hopes, . . . '
cannot (or may not) realize the delicate organic growth that
' human culture ' is. Otherwise he could not so cheerfully contemplate fifty years (p. 190) of revolutionary warfare, during
which everything must be subordinated to proletarian victory,
and assume, without argument, that the result will be a society
in which ' the dynamic development of culture will be incom-
parable with anything that went on in the past ' (p. 189). But
perhaps, and ' dynamic ' strongly suggests it, ' culture ' again
means something different.

Indeed, Trotsky at this point in the argument, like all the
Marxists, becomes indistinguishable from Mr. Wells. Neither of
them has faced the problem, though Trotsky, unlike Mr. Wells,
appears capable of seeing it if it is put. A Marxist intelligent
enough and well-enough educated to speak of a ' human culture '
that must, if it is to exist at all, carry on from what orthodoxy
dismisses as ' bourgeois culture,' can hardly have failed to
divine that, if he thought too much, not only his orthodoxy but
his optimism would be in danger. Nothing brings out more
strongly that orthodox Marxists (like most other publicists) use
the word ' culture ' uncomprehendingly than their failure even to
perceive the problem—the problem that their dogma concerning the
relation between culture and the ' methods of production ' confronts
them with in a particularly sharp form.

It confronts us all. For it is true that culture in the past
has borne a close relation to the ' methods of production.' A
culture expressing itself in a tradition of literature and art—such

a tradition as represents the finer consciousness of the race and provides the currency of finer living—can be in a healthy state only if this tradition is in living relation with a real culture, shared by the people at large. The point might be enforced by saying (there is no need to elaborate) that Shakespeare did not invent the language he used. And when England had a popular culture, the structure, the framework, of it was a stylization, so to speak, of economic necessities; based, it might fairly be said, on the ' methods of production ' was an art of living, involving codes, developed in ages of continuous experience, of relations between man and man, and man and the environment in its seasonal rhythm. This culture the progress of the nineteenth century destroyed, in country and in town; it destroyed (to repeat a phrase that has been used in *Scrutiny* before, and will be, no doubt, again) the organic community. And what survives of cultural tradition in any important sense survives in spite of the rapidly changing ' means of production.'

All this seems fairly obvious, and what should be equally obvious is the new status and importance of leisure. Leisure (however much or little there might be) mattered less when work was not, as it is now for so many, the antithesis of living. (See, *e.g.* George Bourne, *Change in the Village* pp. 200-216). Now, unless one is unusually lucky, one saves up living for after working hours, and for very few indeed can the bread-winning job give anything like a sense of fulfilment or be realized as in itself a significant part of a significant process. Marxists do not contemplate any reversal of this development; nor is enthusiasm for Five Year Plans, the sense of a noble cause, or romantic worship of mechanical efficiency, to be permanently the sanction of labour in itself unsatisfying. ' The Revolution,' writes A. L. Morton, a Marxist, in the October *Criterion*, ' neither creates nor is intended to create a new leisure class. It is intended rather to create a leisure community. . . .' The Marxist, then, who offers his Utopia as anything better than Mr. Wells's, must face the problem that we should all be facing. For any reasonable hope for civilization must assume that the beneficent potentialities of machine-technique will be realized, and there seems no reason to doubt that the material means of life might be assured to all at the cost of small labour to each.

The problem is suggested by Mr. Morton here: 'The state of poetry is largely dependent upon the connection of the leisure class with the productive powers. The connection must be close and vital, though that of the individual poet need not be, since he expresses less himself than his social environment. The great ages of poetry have been those in which the poetry-producing class was young and vigorous and was breaking through existing productive relationships. Conversely, a class without social functions tends to produce decadent poetry.' Without being uncritical of Mr. Morton's generalizations one may ask: What will ' social functions ' be in a leisure community—a community, that is, in which the ' productive process ' is so efficient as no longer to determine the ordering of life? Mr. Morton speaks of a ' leisure community integrally associated with the productive forces in a way in which no one class has ever been before '; but there is surely no particular virtue in being ' associated ' with productive forces so mechanically efficient that ' integrally,' here, seems to mean very little? No doubt when we are all leisured the special moral disadvantage of belonging to a leisure class will be gone, but ' social function,' it is plain, means so much more in the generalizations about culture and the productive process that it is inapplicable here, or, if applied, becomes a mere arbitrary counter. It is a comment on the Marxian dialectic that it can take a man in this way up to the problem and leave him unable to see it.

The problem faces us all, and not hypothetically, but practically and immediately. It is a more difficult one than Trotsky, that dangerously intelligent Marxist who has some inkling, suggests in his statement of it (p. 193): ' The main task of the proletarian intelligentsia in the immediate future is not the abstract formation of a new culture regardless of the absence of a base for it, but definite culture-bearing, that is, a systematic, planful, and, of course, critical imparting to the backward masses of the essential elements of the culture which already exists.' The problem is, rather, not merely to save these ' essential elements ' from a swift and final destruction in the process that makes Communism possible[1], but to develop them into an

---

[1]' Industrialization is desirable not for itself, but because Communism is only possible in an industrial community.' A. L.

autonomous culture, a culture independent of any economic, technical or social system as none has been before. Whether such a rootless culture (the metaphor will bear pondering, in view of the contrast between the postulated communist society—in constant ' dynamic ' development—and any that has produced a culture in the past) can be achieved and maintained may be doubtful. If it cannot, we have nothing better to hope for than a world of Mr. Wells's men like gods, and have rather to fear that the future has been forecast in California[2]. If it can, it will be by a concern for the tradition of human culture, here and now, intenser than Trotsky's (the Marxist excommunicate); a concerted and sustained effort to perpetuate it, in spite of the economic process, the triumphs of engineering and the Conquest of Happiness, as something with its own momentum and life, more and more autonomous and self-subsistent. And in its preoccupation with this effort *Scrutiny* does not find itself largely companied.

This plea, however, will not bring us off; we have no illusions. There is a choice; we must speak or die : Stalin or the King by Divine Right? And the Marxist dialectic, with its appearance of algebraic rigour, stern realism and contemptuous practicality, has great advantages—in dialectic—over those who are pusillanimous enough to let themselves be bothered by the duty and difficulty of using words precisely. The rigour, of course, is illusory, and, consequently, so are the realism and the practicality. ' In general,' says Mr. Edmund Wilson approvingly in the *New Statesman and Nation* for October 15th, ' it is surprising how promptly the writers are lining up in one or other of the camps, and how readily their antagonisms are developing.' When people

---

Morton. *The Criterion*, October, 1932. Cf. ' The essential point is that agriculture ought to be saved and revived because agriculture is the foundation for the Good Life in any society; it is in fact, the normal life. . . . And it is hardly too much to say that only in a primarily agricultural society, in which people have local attachments to their small domains and small communities, and remain, generation after generation, in the same place, is genuine patriotism possible. . .' T.S.E. *The Criterion*, October, 1931.

[2]See *Stardust in Hollywood*, by J. and C. Gordon.

line up so promptly one suspects, not only that the appeal of
the *chic* has something to do with it, but that the differences are
not of a kind that has much to do with thinking; and the ready
development of antagonisms among those whose differences are
inessential should surprise only the very innocent.

Trotsky's use of the term ' culture ' has already been noted.
It is part of what Mr. Wilson calls the ' Marxist technique '; he
himself speaks of the ' old bourgeois culture ' and the ' culture
of Marxism.' ' Bourgeois ' and ' class,' likewise, are primary
indispensables of the technique. Prince Mirsky, in his celebrated
essay in *Echanges* (December, 1931), dealing with ' la poésie
bourgeoise,' takes as ' le poète bourgeois ' Mr. T. S. Eliot. He
exhibits less acuteness—or (and very naturally) more orthodoxy—
than Trotsky, who would hardly have been naïve enough to
pronounce (though he does contradict himself, and is capable, he
also, of sentimentality) : ' La bourgeoisie est vide de valeurs,
toutes les valeurs vivantes sont du coté de la classe ouvrière.' The
' values ' of the working class (though, of course, one never
knows what definitions the Marxist, when challenged, will produce
from under the blanket) are inevitably those induced by the modern
environment—by ' capitalist ' civilization; essentially those, that
is, of the ' bourgeoisie ' and of most Marxists. Mr. Wilson (to
illustrate this last point), a critic intelligent enough at his best to
have written the best parts of *Axel's Castle,* was capable of resting
the structure of that book on the values of the ' man who does
things,' and, seeing that he had thus proclaimed himself a contemporary of Dr. John B. Watson, we ought not to have been
surprised when he came out as an admirer of Kipling and
innocently assumed that Lytton Strachey was a great writer.

Prince Mirsky, although, presumably, he does not enjoy Mr.
Wilson's advantage of having been born to the English language,
has over Mr. Wilson the advantage of living in London. He
would not, as Mr. Wilson has (see the *New Statesman and
Nation*), have solemnly endorsed the collocation of ' Dostoevsky,
Cervantes, Defoe and E. E. Cummings. . . .' And he may have
a good critical sensibility. But that is not proved by his exposition, intelligent and adroit as it is, of Mr. Eliot's poetry. What he
certainly shows is unusual skill in applying the ' Marxist technique,' and the way in which in explaining *The Waste Land* he

seizes on the 'structural symbols,' *l'Humide, le Sec et le Feu,* and overstresses their function, paying little attention to the essential organization, betrays the influence of the Marxian training. But the significantly betraying thing is the footnote : ' les lecteurs d'Edith Sitwell sont en grande partie les mêmes que ceux de Bertrand Russell dont les *Principles of Mathematics* sont l'évangile des logistes.' Mathematicians are often illiterate, and Bertrand Russell wrote *The Conquest of Happiness,* and Prince Mirsky might as aptly have said that the readers of Edith Sitwell are in great part the same as those of Ernest Hemingway.

The relevance of this further appeal to performance in literary criticism should not need urging. To be concerned, as *Scrutiny* is, for literary criticism is to be vigilant and scrupulous about the relation between words and the concrete. The inadequacies of Mr. Wilson and Prince Mirsky as literary critics are related to their shamelessly uncritical use of vague abstractions and verbal counters. What is this 'bourgeois culture ' that Mr. Eliot represents in company, one presumes, with Mr. Wells, Mr. Hugh Walpole, *Punch, Scrutiny,* Dr. Marie Stopes and the *Outline for Boys and Girls?* What are these ' classes,' the conflict between which a novelist must recognize ' before he can reach to the heart of any human situation '? (See *Literary Criticism and the Marxian Method* by Granville Hicks in *The Modern Quarterly* for Summer, 1932). The Marxist, of course, is pat with his answer : he will define class in terms of relation to the ' productive process.' The concept so defined—how usefully and how adequately to the facts this is not the place to discuss—will at any rate engage with its context. But when one comes to talk of ' bourgeois culture ' the context has changed, and only by virtue of the Marxist dogma and the Marxist dialectic is it possible to introduce the concept here and suppose one is saying anything. Class of the kind that can justify talk about ' class-culture ' has long been extinct.[1] (And, it might be added, when there was such ' class-culture ' it was much more than merely of the class). The

---

[1] Prince Mirsky refers to ' la classe où appartenait Donne '; but what has that ' bourgeoisie ' in common with that of the Victorian age or that of to-day?

process of civilization that produced, among other things, the Marxian dogma, and makes it plausible, has made the cultural difference between the ' classes ' inessential. The essential differences are indeed now definable in economic terms, and to aim at solving the problems of civilization in terms of the ' class war ' is to aim, whether wittingly or not, at completing the work of capitalism and its products, the cheap car, the wireless and the cinema. It is not for nothing that Trotsky's prose, when he contemplates the ' dynamic development of culture ' that will follow the triumph of Revolution, takes on a Wellsian exaltation (see *e.g.* pp. 188-9), and that, when he descends to anything approaching particularity, what he offers might have come from *Men Like Gods* (see p. 252). And the title of Prince Mirsky's essay, *T. S. Eliot et la Fin de la Poésie Bourgeoise,* should have been one word shorter.

The rigour of the Marxian dialectic, then, is illusory, and the brave choice enjoined upon us the reverse of courageous, if courage has anything to do with thinking. Must we therefore take the other alternative offered us: ' si le poète—l'idéologue—bourgeois veut opposer à la Révolution quelque chose de positif et de convaincant (de convaincant pour son propre esprit) il ne peut avoir de recours qu'à la résurrection de quelque revenant médiéval. . .'? Must we be Royalists and Anglo-Catholics? In the first place reasons have been advanced for doubting whether those who find Marxism convincing, for their own minds, are applying minds in any serious sense to the problems that face us and them. So if, while agreeing that the recovery of religious sanctions in some form seems necessary to the health of the world, we reply that they cannot be had for the wanting, the Marxist had better not start to think before he twits us with ineffectiveness. And as for Anglo-Catholicism and Royalism, those who may find these, *pour leurs propres esprits,* convincing do not convince us that they are taking up an effective attitude towards the problems. The impressive statement, in the abstract, of a coherent position is not enough. And the main reply to the gesture that bids us, if we respect ourselves, line up there, as the logical and courageous alternative, is not that *The Principles of Modern Heresy* and *The Outline of Royalism* have not yet, after all, been given us, but: ' Look at *The Criterion.'*

The Editor's spare—too spare—contributions almost always exhibit the uncommon phenomenon of real thinking turned upon the ' underlying issues,' though, in their bearing on concrete problems, they show no signs of coming any nearer than before to effective particularity. But we must not, under Marxian incitement, suggest unfair tests. The effective particularity we can fairly demand would involve maintaining in *The Criterion* high standards of thinking and of literary criticism. The point that it is necessary to make is, in view of our own enterprise, a delicate one, but only the more necessary for that. Let us suffer the retort when, and as much as, we may deserve it, and express now the general regret that the name of *The Criterion* has become so dismal an irony and that the Editor is so far from applying to his contributors the standards we have learnt from him.

The relevance of the point may be enforced by remarking the particular weakness of *The Criterion* for the dead, academic kind of abstract ' thinking,' especially when the ' thinker ' (incapable of literary criticism) stands in a general, abstract way for ' order,' ' intelligence ' and the other counters, all of which are worth less than nothing if not related scrupulously to the concrete.

The Marxist challenge, then, seems to us as heroic as Ancient Pistol's and to point to as real alternatives. And we do not suppose that, in *Scrutiny,* we, more than anyone else, have a solution to offer. But, looking round, we do think that, without presuming too much, we can, since there seems no danger of too great an intensity of concern for them, make it our function to insist on certain essential conditions of a solution. Nor, inadequate as our insistence may be, does it appear superfluous to insist that the essential problems should be faced.

Nothing more (if it lived up to this account) should be needed to justify *Scrutiny*. But if some more immediate engaging upon the world of practice would reassure, then we can point to it. We have a special educational interest, and the association of this with the bent already described is unprecedented and has already shown its strength.

F. R. Leavis.

FESTIVALS OF FIRE

' The solution of the problem of life is seen in the vanishing of this problem.'

I. ALLEGRO MODERATO E RUBATO[1]

Along the broad rides out from the elm-choirs
Oaks clump raggedly, gnarled and
Wrinkled as an old man's veined
Hand. We came down the rides, feigned terror
Fetlock deep in brown bracken dusted
With snow, seeking berries white and red. The
Holms are sprightlier, ape spring in age.

Untimely kisses were shelved when
Our argute voices vied amid the bramble
Brakes, the parasite was predestined
For four walls, but Sylvia, a shell
Of a girl in a vermilion coat with four
Buttons had moist warm hands. They
Sometimes wear scarlet on the Grands Boulevards.

Her brother did not wait for
Arteriosclerosis, or boggle at
The price of gin. In a ditch three
Dumdum bullets left a brainless jaw
On the Massachusetts coast: a token
For a law enraged at Caponë's

---

[1]This is Section I of a poem in four sections.

Bilk of income-tax returns. Pray
For him in all seasons, of Cotswold
Race, sundered beside the foaming
Shore, Brotachos, who came
Hither not for this. Let
Not the alien mould press heavy upon
Him since he is denied the gift
Of that asbestos cape wherein
Our rulers vainly fold themselves.

The fire came and will come, the red flower
Shaded in a fennel stalk, the refiner
That leaps in the dark.
The rebel bringer lighted
On the brief angles of the world, furled
Himself in his shadow and found fear
Behind him. Deftly he unloosed
The mechanic arts to men, trickeries
For prolongation of a bootless leisure, built
On a frame of tears. We are
Halted sharply in a wilderness
Of angled mirrors, and what man
Can bear to look upon the hinderparts
Of his own glory? There is a boom due
In the usury of self-exploitation:
Below the limen springs
A sunflower self, Walt Whitman ruminating
In a jazzed-up poster, smalltalk in
Headlines. Darkness
Calls for a sign, let us build a cosmos
Of signs, a sanguine cloud of metamorphoses.

Christmas comes but once a year:
And when it does it brings food
Coupons, Charity Balls, the leer
From the gutter, a full-throated
Shout in a sere avenue.
Then the three kings journeyed

Bringing a jargoon, brilliant
Cut, and a platinum
Set chrysoberyl from the Rue
Royale, fondants from Fortnum
And Mason's, from the druggists
Of the East mandragora.

The log crepitates and spits, unfolds
Mansions, caves in the fire, untenanted,
Unblazed by trumpeter. There
Amid the sawdust of former masteries
Juts out the awful abruptness of things,
Seen in a landslide or in the human
Body powdering confusedly away.

' The youngsters are giving a Yule
Play tomorrow afternoon
With programmes, oxen, Santa Claus
And so on drawn and coloured
By themselves. You'll come?
And, oh, please write your annual cheque
Out, Mr. Simpson, for the widows' fund. . . .'
' I shall never forget how his
Father looked when he perked
Open his puckered red eyes and
Caught the wind in his throat and coughed
And cried till he smiled from weariness. . . .'
' Bring out the '40 cognac, and, William
See that his nurse
Stops that damned brat's crying,
Our guests can hardly hear a note
That Whiteman's playing. . . .'
' Yes, darling, I have the latch-key
Safe. Expect me about one. There'll
Be no one around and, in any case,
I'll see you through. . . .'

' He's crying again. . . .'
His spinal ganglia have sensed

The sorrow of the world he could not
Save, neither for nor from himself. Time
Has slopped over the low
Embankments and left mud
On the academicians in the Tate. Memory
Smoulders like an abandoned hay-mow.

When we went down to the woods
Armoured cars stroked out
The anemones with a rattling cross
Fire; countermined, peonies
Shook their gory manes and
Rose with phantom faces like
Those in New York subways. Blood
Where are your Floridas, skulls
Where your Golgotha?

And they snarled at the fugue
As brittle counterpoint.

RONALD BOTTRALL.

SURREALISME

WHATEVER may be the contempt, the hate or the derision with which the surrealist group has been looked down upon, the future historian of our troubled times will perforce give it the attention it deserves. One must travel far back into the past to find a literary school whose activities have been so explosive, so versatile, and, one may venture, so fruitful. None was ever so ambitious, none has ever raised so many questions pertaining to the most sacred possibilities of the human mind, nor has been so magnificently borne to such a pitch of despair and pride. It is high time to assume in front of their doctrine and their works the critical attitude which has nearly always been refused to them. The task is not an easy one. To remain indifferent or impartial is, for the vast majority of people interested in literature or art (including critics), next to impossible. And then, the manifestations of the surrealist activity have been so many, so diverse, and sometimes, in seeming, so contradictory, that it is hard to be exhaustive and fair. The group itself has been split into schisms; by-schools have sprung up, violently antagonistic[1]; strayed sheep (if a surrealist may be called by so tame a name) have come back to the fold; dirt has been thrown by the most fervid disciples upon the leaders, and only a very few names of the beginning have remained unpolluted. Nevertheless, in spite of the confused and zig-zag evolution of the surrealist organism, one may attempt briefly to present the readers of *Scrutiny* with some information about its growth and significance. In any case, the importance and wide-spread (though not acknowledged) influence of the movement can no more be sheepishly concealed.

A few years before the war, in spite of some apparently formidable names, the situation in our letters had long since come to a deadlock. The famous ' *clarté française,*' the greatest title to glory the French bourgeoisie may boast of, which three centuries of a relentless exercise had brought to sterile perfection,

---

[1] *e.g. Le Grand Feu* or *Bifur,* the latter headed by G. Ribémont-Dessaignes, who left the main group in 1929 with many others.

could no longer grapple with a state of affairs which I emphatically refuse to call *modern,* but whose chief characteristic was its lack of complaisance—its unaptness, owing to its strange complexity and aggressive resilience, for being neatly sliced away and offered as food to any fastidious palate. Reason had dried up everything, and the divorce between ' art ' and ' life ' had never been so tragic, the more so since it was, as never before, to writers and artists of every description that an ever widening public looked up, as those from whom the serious solution ought to be asked. The novel was sterilizing itself in the deft hands of Anatole France, who may be considered as a kind of artful demi-god of letters, taking refuge in a smiling and dry scepticism—*à ne pas prendre au sérieux.* Poetry had pretty nearly come to ruin after the sickly efforts of symbolism, and the only true poets were those whose works were still either lost in the general indifference of an obtuse public, or derisively considered as unwarrantable idiocy. Philosophers have never enjoyed a great number of readers, and the name of Bergson alone stood as a serious challenge to that reason everybody yet adored, with however increasing diffidence. Social science may be said to have remained till recent years at the sentimental stage to which the eloquence of Jaurès had raised it, and only by the Russian experiment has it been brought to the logical conclusions a rigorously deductive mind is bound to reach sooner or later.

Then came the war and the unavoidable ' *trahison des clercs.*'

What confusion it brought about in the intellectual values there is no need to insist upon. A terrible onslaught was made on such tenets and *raisons de vivre* as had long remained secure in an atmosphere of peaceful comfort and satisfied debility of mind. How should art for art's sake, a humorous indifferentism, the Cornelian *mourir pour la patrie,* or such an inspiring motto as *Gott mit uns,* resist the demoralizing effects of so many months spent in mud and dirt, with the daily breakfast of a bellyful of horrors, under the inescapable threat of being blown to smithereens in the very act of, say, praying to God. Something was rotten—had been rotten for long in this world of ours—and the fine people who had had the mission of elevating mankind to this present state of civilisation might well be dubbed humbugs. Politics were humbug—philosophy was humbug—art was humbug—poetry . . . . well, poetry, let us see.

Anyhow, the reaction of the few who did not feel themselves obliged either to forbear any critical attitude, or to preach a hopeful campaign of revolt, was indeed what was to be expected from such men in such a predicament. Despair and hate, hemmed in by the impossibility of escaping the reasons for despair and hate, may produce a kind of hysterical and bitter revolt, far removed from the delightful scepticism of the happy; a revolt which will rage and rail at any prey offered to the mind. They will spit out their universal contempt, and find in this blasphemous revenge the only means of preserving the dignity of man. Negation and lacerating laughter directed against the most sacred ' *objets tabous* '— outrage for the sake of outrage—the utmost exertion of an unsparing destructive power.

Such were the ultimate ends of the ' *Mouvement Dada.*'

* * * *

The history of Dada remains to be written (and still will after this essay) even after the forthcoming book of M. G. Ribémont-Dessaignes who was one of the most active dadaists[1]. Suffice it to say here that Dada was born in Zurich, in 1916, the quaint fruit of the joint lucubrations of a now famous Rumanian poet, Tristan Tzara, an Alsatian, Hans Arp, and two Germans, Hugo Ball and Richard Huelsenbeck. A *bulletin dada* was issued and some manifestations of an as yet vague character were attempted. The dadaists soon realise the prodigious means of propaganda which scandal constitutes, and they will henceforward deliberately make of scandal their habitual weapon of destruction.

' . . . . *chaque page doit exploser, soit par le sérieux profond et lourd, le tourbillon, le vertige, le nouveau, l'éternel, par la blague écrasante, par l'enthousiasme des principes ou par la façon d'être imprimée. Voilà un monde chancelant qui fuit, fiancé aux grelots de la gamme infernale, voilà de l'autre coté : des hommes nouveaux. Rudes, bondissants, chevaucheurs de hoquets. . . .*'

[1]See: *La Nouvelle Revue Française,* June-July, 1931. Emile Bouvier's book: *Initiation à la littérature française d'aujourd'hui (La Renaissance du Livre)* provides some good historical information.

And, a few lines further, here is an attempt at self-definition:

' . . . . *abolition de la logique, danse des impuissants de la création : Dada; de toute hiérarchie et équation sociale installée pour les valeurs par nos valets : Dada; chaque objet, tous les objets, les sentiments et les obscurités, les apparitions et le choc précis des lignes parallèles sont des moyens pour le combat : Dada; abolition de la mémoire : Dada; abolition de l'archéologie : Dada; abolition des prophètes : Dada; abolition du futur : Dada; croyance absolue indiscutable dans chaque dieu produit de la spontanéité : Dada.*'[1]

This cynical frankness of the *Manifeste Dada 1918,* a strange mixture of nonsense and terrible seriousness, thus proclaims the absurdity of art among other things, the identity of contraries, and the absolute and tragical necessity of taking nothing for granted, except perhaps an irresistible need of genuine destruction. After the armistice, Dada emigrates to Paris. There it finds new allies in a group of similarly dissatisfied men, who are willing to wage the same war. They are the founders of *Littérature* (a mock title), a review curiously run by ancient cubists—Max Jacob, Apollinaire; painters—Derain, Picasso, Lhote; and even old symbolists—P. Valéry and A. Gide. But the active knot comprises new men like Picabia, André Breton, Louis Aragon, P. Morand, P. Eluard, B. Cendrars, Reverdy, J. Cocteau, G. Ribémont-Dessaignes, etc. All those who are really living, intellectually disgusted with the human or inhuman conditions brought about by the war or the after-war (still more, if that may be, spiritually repulsive) feel that there is something to be done, that a new start must be made. A certain amount of sacred enthusiasm urges them to a desperate attempt at universal renovation. But the necessity of pulling everything down must be made generally felt. The Dadaists fling themselves into enormous practical jokes played upon a curious, then horrified public. To the challenge: ' *Faites des gestes,*' they reply by scandalous manifestations, not unlike a frenzied students' rag, but compared to which the tricks of pre-war cubism or futurism were mere child's play. I draw again from the fore-quoted article of M. Ribémont-Dessaignes the following manifesto read by seven persons in front of a gaping audience:

---

[1] Quoted by G. Ribémont-Dessaignes.

' AU PUBLIC '

' *Avant de descendre parmi vous afin d'arracher vos dents
gâtées, vos oreilles gourmeuses, votre langue pleine de chancres,
Avant de briser vos os pourris,
D'ouvrir votre ventre cholérique, et d'en retirer à l'usage des
engrais pour l'agriculture votre foie trop gras, votre rate ignoble
et vos rognons à diabète,
Avant d'arracher votre vilain sexe incontinent et glaireux,
Avant d'éteindre ainsi votre appétit de beauté, d'extase, de
sucre, de philosophie, de poivre et de concombres métaphysiques,
mathématiques et poétiques,
Avant de vous désinfecter au vitriol et de vous rendre ainsi
propres et de vous ripoliner avec passion,
Avant tout cela,
Nous allons prendre un grand bain antiseptique,
Et nous vous avertissons :
C'est nous les assassins.*'

But the sacrilegous and blasphemous activities of the Dadaists
could not continue indefinitely. Absolute revolt is a metaphysical
concept which either must remain on the ideal plane or devour
itself. The Dadaists were speedily at a loss to imagine something
efficiently original and deadly, and they could not, as a group,
bring forth any positive assertion. In negation, *le difficile, c'est
de durer.* Dada bore in itself its own germ of destruction. Its
short and tormented existence, its practical failure, its inability to
produce were not, however, mere sterility. Dada marks a date
after which things possible before have become unreceivable. It
matters little if no work of genius remains after its passage. It
had been more of an ' *état d'esprit* ' than a school. Its principles
had helped to clear the ground more decisively than any
positive work. Its cruel irony had stripped ' literature ' of all false
pretension. Things had been brought back to a more human
ground. Humour and fantasy had been given again their true
importance in human affairs. Zest came again with the '*cocasse* '
and the unexpected. The sordidness of reality made way for a
new kind of marvellous, from which men had too long been led
astray. A young and vigorous sun shines at the horizon and the
air is bracing as if a new world were beginning. I cannot help

quoting the following reflections of A. Gide, given in *La Nouvelle Revue Française* in April, 1920:

'. . . . *Et ce ne serait vraiment pas la peine d'avoir combattu durant cinq ans, d'avoir tant de fois supporté la mort des autres et vu remettre tout en question, pour se rasseoir ensuite devant sa table à écrire et renouer le fil du vieux discours interrompu. Eh quoi! tandis qu'ont tant souffert nos champs, nos villages, nos cathédrals, notre verbe demeurerait invulnéré! Il importe que l'esprit ne reste pas en retard sur la matière : il a droit lui aussi, à de la ruine. Dada va s'en charger.'* . . . . ' *Déjà l'édifice de notre langage est trop ébranlé pour qu'il soit prudent pour la pensée d'y chercher encore un refuge, et devant que de rebâtir, il importe de jeter bas ce qui parait solide encore, ce qui fait mine de tenir debout. Les mots que conglomère encore l'artifice de la logique, il les faut disjoindre, isoler; les forcer de redéfiler devant des regards vierges, comme, après le déluge, un à un, les animaux sortis de l'arche dictionnaire, avant toute conjugaison. Et si, par quelque vieille commodité, typographique uniquement, on les met bout à bout sur quelque ligne, avoir soin de les disposer dans un désordre où ils n'aient aucune raison de se suivre—puisque c'est, avant tout, à l'anti-poétique raison qu'on en a. Et il importe également, peut-être même davantage . . . . de les dissocier de leur histoire, de leur passé qui les appesantit d'un faix mort. Chaque vocable-ilôt doit, dans la page, présenter des contours abrupts. Il sera posé ici (ou là tout aussi bien) comme un ton pur; et non loin vibreront d'autres tons purs, mais d'une absence de rapports telle qu'elle n'autorise aucune association de pensées. C'est ainsi que le mot sera délivré de tout sa signification précédente, enfin : et de l'évocation du passé.*

L'ennui pour chaque école, c'est cette possibilité de surenchère où le disciple, plus extrémiste que le maître, la compromet. Mais cette surenchère, vexatoire, on l'élude si l'on bondit d'un coup à l'extrême de sorte qu'il n'y a pas moyen d'aller au delà . . . . il s'agissait d'inventer ce que je n'ose appeler, une méthode, qui non seulement n'aidât point à la production, mais même rendit l'œuvre impossible.

Effectivement, le jour où le mot Dada fut trouvé, il ne resta plus rien à faire . . . Dans ce seul mot : Dada, ils auront d'un coup exprimé tout ce qu'ils avaient à dire en tant que groupe; et

*comme il n'y a pas moyen de trouver mieux dans l'absurde, il
faut bien à présent, ou piétiner sur place, comme les médiocres
continueront à faire, ou s'évader.'*

We have there, with the usual critical acumen of Gide, sketched
out the new poetical theory which might be elicited from the
dadaist agitation, and a true prophecy as regards its future. This
literary, or rather anti-literary doctrine, offers a wild appeal to
originality, and, at the same time, refuses to believe in the seriousness of any artistic creation. The enquiry: ' *Pourquoi écrivez-
vous ? '* involves a bitter mockery of all professional writers. On
the other hand, the dadaists have not gone deep enough into the
inmost needs of the human soul. A life of absolute revolt and fierce
individualism cannot be given as an aim to anybody. Only a few
people are able to live in accordance with such ' principles.' It
has been the privilege of men like Alfred Jarry, Rigault and
Jacques Vaché to throw themselves into a negation of society
amounting to suicide. But the others have found escape in altogether different activities (*J'écris des romans, je m'occupe, et
allez donc. .)*[1] or, after some years' meditation and struggle,
furthering their evolution without a denial of their primitive faith,
have raised a new citadel on the ruins of Dadaism. Such are the
Surrealists.

*　　*　　*　　*

The surrealist doctrine was evolved from the dadaist ' *état
d'esprit.'* The survivors of Dadaism are terribly in earnest. That
is their first and most illuminating characteristic. Their spiritual
attitude is no longer mere nihilism. They have come to the conclusion that self-murder is *not* a solution and they find life is
worth living. But it must be lived on entirely different grounds.
Surrealism is not only a literary school, but it has also its ethics,
its metaphysics. I think the first postulate of the surrealists is an
invincible belief in the dignity of man. They have become clearly
conscious of the reasons of revolt which had egged the dadaists
on to their extravagances. Man must stand out against all causes
of debasement which lurk around him. Not only does André
Breton say: ' *Je ne fais pas état des moments nuls de ma vie,'*

---

[1]Philipe Soupault, a renegade of Surrealism, now a journalist.

but the ideal would be to reduce those ' *moments nuls* ' to their minimum expression. In our present state of civilization the world teems with innumerable causes of debasement; *e.g.*, the social state, with its shameful agents of moral corruption, among which the conservative forces which crush down all the efforts of individual development, whether they be moral or material. First the idea of ' *patrie*,' with its accompaniment of historical remembrances and traditions, the pride derived therefrom, nationalism, the army, the police, and the hypocrisy of colonization: the surrealists ' vomit ' all that is considered as typically ' French.' Then religion of any kind and particularly the Christian, which represents for them the most hateful instrument of oppression in the hands of perverse *profiteurs*: they have no end of sarcasm against Jesus and his priests, one of their favourite jokes being to insult priests at every opportunity. Then the family, the tyranny of parents whose only aim seems to be to make of their children a perfect *succédané* of what they have themselves been, and to kill in the egg any attempt at a sincere realization of the self. Then, of course, all the social institutions, of whatever description, which help to keep the human being in moral and material servitude. Their programme of destruction reaches far and wide. They preach a total upheaval of the present conditions of life, and the title of their review is significant : it was first, *La Révolution Surréaliste* and then, still more obviously, *Le surréalisme au service de la Révolution*. No wonder that they should be drawn to sympathise with the Communist party. They have, however, long deferred their complete adhesion to the activities of the Communist organization, and the story of their relations with it would be very instructive. It would show that the surrealists are of one mind with the Communists as long as it is a matter of waging war again the civilization of the capitalist bourgeois. There is no other political creed to which they might turn. But they are more or less consciously afraid of the standardization of man which a Communistic civilization would bring. A surrealist in a Communistic state would still be a revolutionary. Their aim tends higher. They seek for man the possibility of enjoying life under all its forms. The notion of sin is unknown to them. They have such confidence in human nature that there is for them practically no law which man might not transgress. Or rather,

no law of the present time, for such law is always an outcome of the
vilest instincts of man regulated by the still viler reason. Yet,
they refuse to be called idealists: idealism dreads to look reality
in the face. Nor are they materialists: materialism is unable to
give its due to the life of the spirit. The ' *matérialisme dialec-
tique* ' of Hegel is, according to them, the only philosophical
position on which they can stand. It has been the basis of Marxism,
but it is more ambitious and leads farther. On this point,
the apprehension of the surrealist thought is a delicate matter, at
least for me.[1] Anyhow, Hegel is a God in the surrealist paradise.
Freud is another. But this is readily understood.

Indeed, the life of the unconscious is among the most
imperative preoccupations of the surrealists. From it they have
derived their literary doctrine. They believe it to be the most
sacred part of the human spirit. *There* are to be found the
deepest truths which alone deserve to be expressed through any
means man may have in his possession. Language is one of
those means, along with painting, design, sculpture, architecture,
the cinema, music, etc., all that is usually called art. But art
is not an end in itself (that would bring us back to the worst
days of ' art for art's sake.') Art is a means of expressing
a human condition, no matter what it be. Now a human
condition must, to be expressed as it really is, escape ' *une mise
en bouteille par la raison.*' Reason is antagonistic to the spirit.
It is constantly turned towards the useful, and mechanically
quenches any gratuitous impulse of the spirit: it has extended
its wasteful sway even into a field where above all it should have
remained a stranger. When the dadaists make their jolly
appeal to the absurd and the ' *cocasse,*' when they find beauty
in the proximity, on a surgeon's table, of a sewing-machine
and an umbrella, they anticipate the surrealists, but only
humorously. The thing is not to find beauty in such heterogeneous co-presence, but to have thought of actuating it. The
' *cocasse* ' of the dadaists becomes the ' *merveilleux* ' of the
surrealists. The association of thoughts or images must not be
led by the cold and dry tool of logical reason which itself works
under the control of all manner of pre-occupations foreign to

---

[1] See: *Le Second Manifeste du Surréalisme.*

the normal character of expression (shall I say that I want to kill my brother, shall I speak of this 'unnatural' impulse, and so on) but the mind must purge itself of its contents, just as a tank is emptied by the natural flow of the water under the pressure of the law of gravitation. This leads to the following definition of surrealism given in the *Premier manifeste du surréalisme* by A. Breton (Kra—1924): ' *Surréalisme : automatisme psychique pur, par lequel on se propose d'exprimer, soit verbalement, soit par écrit, soit de toute autre manière, le fonctionnement réel de la pensée. Dictée de la pensée, en l'absence de tout contrôle exercé par la raison, en dehors de toute pré-occupation esthétique ou morale.*' The process is also called: ' *écriture automatique.*' The result is a ' *texte surréaliste,*' the best example of which is given in *Champs Magnétiques (1921)*, jointly written by A. Breton and Philippe Soupault. By this process the mind is put in a state of absolute purity, of absolute liberty (as it should in the Freudian confession, though the confession is there '*dirigée*') and the pen writes whatever the hand directs it to write. The text thus obtained offers a strange succession of images, very often magnificent, but standing by themselves, or associated according to obscure laws, of which one cannot say that they reveal the inmost reality of the mind. Yet the surrealists believe it to be more than a mere experiment. They think they will thus reach a kind of superior reality *(surréalisme)*, expressed by new connections between words and images, out of which a new universe will shine out, absolutely untouched by the dirty hands of reason.— '*Qui est là? Oh : très bien: fâites entrer l'infini*': (Hegel). '*Le surréalisme repose sur la croyance à la réalité supérieure de certaines formes d'associations négligées jusqu'à lui, à la toute puissance du rêve, au jeu désintéressé de la pensée. Il tend à ruiner tous les autres mécanismes psychiques et à se substituer à eux dans la résolution des principaux problèmes de la vie.*' (*Manifeste du Surréalisme*, p. 46). It may be objected that it is impossible to reach this state of pure automatism, and that the most unexpected contingency may change the course of this inspiration. The surrealists will not gainsay it. They will only remark that hazard may be the least impure of contingencies and that this initial determinism once accepted, the mind may go its way. But they perfectly well realize that ' *de tristes imbecillités*

*écrites par des méthodes surréalistes n'en sont pas moins de tristes
imbécillités* ' (Aragon). The product of automatic writing will then
give the measure of the producing mind. What then? The
' infinite ' does not always enter.

It must be said that most surrealist texts thus written rarely
bring us this ' *collision flamboyante de mots rares* ' of which
J. Vaché spoke. And then, the method will soon turn into a
' *poncif* '—if it is only viewed from the standpoint of literature.
Even the precise notations of dreams have come short of our
expectation. So that some dissidents from surrealism have gone
back to another form of '*délire sacré* ' : that of Poe or Valéry,
who, instead of emptying the mind by an extreme disinterestedness, increase its power of creation by an extreme concentration
of attention.[1]

Anyhow, the aim assigned to artistic creation, or widely
speaking, to poetry, is twofold. First, it is an attempt to bring
back the marvellous into human life, and then to purify man
through it. ' *La force de la poésie purifiera tous les hommes.
Toutes les tours d'ivoires seront démolies, toutes les paroles seront
sacrées, et, ayant enfin bouleversé la réalité, l'homme n'aura plus
qu'à fermer les yeux pour que s'ouvrent les portes du merveilleux* '
(P. Eluard)[2]. Tristan Tzara, who after a retreat of many years
has now come back to surrealism, distinguishes between ' *la
poésie moyen d'expression* ' and '*la poésie activité de l'esprit.*'[3]
' *La poésie qui ne se distingue des romans que par sa forme
extérieure, la poésie qui exprime soit des idées, soit des sentiments, n'intéresse plus personne. Je lui oppose la poésie activité*

---

[1]See : *Les Cahiers du Sud, Dec., 1929,* R. de Renéville's article.
[2]'*La métaphore,*' says Lautréamont, '*rend beaucoup plus de
service aux aspirations humaines vers l'infini que ne s'efforcent
de se le figurer ceux qui sont imbus de préjugés* ' (quoted by
A. Breton—*N.R.F.* June, 1920)—one can understand the diffidence of Communism towards theories so strange. [3]'*Le Surréalisme au service de la Révolution* ' No. 4, Dec., 1931, Tristan
Tzara; article entitled ' *Essai sur la situation de la poésie* '
contains a good survey of the poets whom the surrealists have
some reason to make their own. It mainly covers the 19th century,
and in spite of some obscure statements is most illuminating.

de l'esprit.' What Dada wanted to ruin was ' *la poésie moyen d'expression,'* a product of a conscious activity of the mind. But ' *la poésie activité de l'esprit* ' should be the ultimate effort of man towards liberation. Dream, laziness, leisure should be organized in view of a Communist society where it is of highest necessity to provide for the increased need of enjoyment created by a new social organization. Thus would come true the famous sentence of Lautréamont: ' *La poésie doit être faite par tous. Non par un.'*

Thus poetry appears as a vaster enterprise than it has ever been. It far exceeds the capacity of the individual. The problem of language will however always stand in the way. New associations of words, of images, unthought-of metaphors, symbols fraught with all human experience, how far will all that be possible and efficient in the future surrealist poetry? Rimbaud and Lautréamont, who by turn, have been worshipped by the surrealists, have separately attempted the alluring undertaking. *Les Illuminations* and *Une Saison en Enfer* bear witness to the desperate energy which urged Rimbaud to translate the poetical activity of his mind into verbal expression. He could not find his salvation in the result and flung 'poetry-means of expression ' over the mill. Lautréamont is a still more deceptive case. After *Les Chants de Maldoror,* which is considered by the surrealists themselves as the typical work of their school, as the unequalled paragon never to be forgotten, he seems to have dismissed his raging, iconoclastic, wrath against God and humanity for a milder attitude involving, even, a belief in goodness.[1]

The poems which the surrealists have written, though they all bear the mark of a similar technique (unexpected and wild associations of images and words, ambiguity pushed to its farthest limits, elliptical turns amounting to obscurity) and deal with a subject-matter which is easily recognizable as theirs (dreams, love, death, despair, revolt, etc. . .)—not to speak of the tone (an exalted seriousness, a proud indifference towards the reader, as much as saying : ' here I am and you may be damned ')—

---

[1]See : *Les Chants de Maldoror* and *Poésies.* M. Léon Pierre-Quint has published a very good book on this strange poet : *Le Comte de Lautréamont et Dieu (Les Cahiers du Sud, 1929).*

yet are as personal as any poems ever written. I mean the distinctive personality of the poet shines of its own light. They ought to
be studied at greater length than I can afford, with the critical
methods applied to other poems. They would reveal great beauties
not unworthy of any ' golden treasury.' The fiery personality of
Aragon, for example, pushes him towards erotic themes, towards
the brutal expression of his hates or of his desires. His aggressive
lyricism challenges with an inexhaustible richness of vocabulary,
with a rude and sadistic power, all things ' sacred,' love
among others, and his last poem *Front Rouge* is a raving
appeal to revolution.[1] He is one of the rare surrealists credited
with a ' style.' A. Breton, colder, more ' intellectual,' is the
thinker, the theorist of the group. A true mystic of the surrealist
orthodoxy, cloudy in places, but unerring in his principles, he
wants to keep himself ' *absolument pur*,' and assumes the
rigidity of a Robespierre. He occasionally finds a penetrating
accent of sincerity, and even candour. His novel *Nadja* may have
repelled some readers, but I believe his heroine, ' a candidate to
madness who becomes mad,' is really a modern fairy, the fairy
of the street, who perceives without effort the most trivial
phenomena under the aspect of the marvellous. She transfigures
the sordid into poetry by an extreme ingenuity which reaches the
heart.[2]

P. Eluard,[3] at last, enjoys, even outside the surrealist group,
the fame of a great poet. It is useless to say he is only capable
of ' *marivaudage*.' Of course all his poems are not equally
beautiful. Some are thin, insignificant. But he has spoken of love
as nobody has done since Baudelaire. His language, extremely
pure and simple, offers an insinuating limpidity which it would

---

[1]The poem *Front Rouge* has exposed M. Aragon to legal indictment. It has been judged as ' *un appel au meurtre*.' M. Aragon,
having joined the Communist party and his attitude towards his
surrealist friends, who tried to help him out by means of a
petition, being judged dubious, has been violently expelled from
the surrealist group in spite of ten years of common efforts. See:
Misère de la Poésie (Les Editions Surréalistes, 1932). [2]A. Breton
is the author of the two *Manifestes du Surréalisme*. [3]See: *Capitale
de la Douleur, L'Amour la Poésie (N.R.F.)*, and *La Vie Immédiate*.

be absurd to call classical, yet which has something of the Racinian power of evocation. A miraculous unfolding of images, the tenuous perfection of the music and of the rhythm, the subdued tension of his despair, the rare quality of his sincerity, enable him to renew thus the old theme of presence in absence:

> *Ma présence n'est pas ici,*
> *Je suis habillé de moi-même. . .*

or again:

> *Le front aux vitres comme font les veilleurs de chagrin,*
> *Ciel dont j'ai dépassé la nuit*
> *Plaines toutes petites dans mes mains ouvertes*
> *Dans leur double horizon inerte indifférent*
> *Le front aux vitres comme font les veilleurs de chagrin*
> *Je te cherche par delà l'attente*
> *Par delà moi-même*
> *Et je ne sais plus tant je t'aime*
> *Lequel de nous deux est absent.*

A word should be said also of André Gaillard,[1] who though not officially a surrealist, cannot be separated from them. I would call him a modern Shelley, so aerial and sanguine were his escapes from this world. The short number of poems he leaves attest an ardent and free temperament which was the promise of great work.

*   *   *   *

It is time to conclude though much has been left out. Other names should be mentioned, like those of R. Desnos, René Crevel, Benjamin Peret, Daumal, J. Baron, Tanguy, A. Masson, S. Dali, L. Bunuel, whether they be poets, essayists, painters or producers.[2] But this essay is a mere modest introduction which everybody interested may easily follow up. The surrealist movement will find its critic later, I am sure. It is henceforward impossible to neglect such an activity which is the surest certainty we have in France at the present time that man is not altogether crushed by the evil powers of a collective resignation of the spirit.

---

[1]See: *Le Fond du Cœur* and *La Terre n'est à personne (Les*

One should not be frightened by the revolutionary trend of their agitation. They have taught us much; they are a magnificent illustration of the necessity of being conscious of all the possibilities of human nature. They are the artisans of a new spiritual progress, and whatever be the judgment of posterity upon their individual work, they will be remembered as fierce and imperious defenders of the dignity of man.

HENRI FLUCHERE.

NOTE.—I have made a few alterations of phrase in the above, which otherwise was written by M. Fluchère as it stands. I hope that I have not anywhere misrepresented his intention: there was no time to communicate with him.—F.R.L.

NOTE FROM M. FLUCHERE.—' Since the writing of this essay *This Quarter* has devoted a special number to Surrealism. I regret that the name of Aragon is only mentioned historically; otherwise the number may well be considered as an epitome of Surrealism.'—H.F.

Cahiers du Sud). The collected works of André Gaillard which have been refused by all the Parisian editors (this is characteristic) will be published this winter by *Les Cahiers du Sud,* Marseille. A. Gaillard died in 1929. [2]L. Bunuel is the producer of the two films: *Le Chien Andalou* and *L'Age d'Or*. The latter has been withdrawn from the screen after violent manifestations of a political character. The capitalistic order of things and the Church are the main targets of Bunuel's destructive lyricism. Some of the names quoted no longer belong to surrealism. Yet they have their place in its history.

CAR

I consider
               the time is short now.
Short is the distance. My car
Whether I step on the gas or glide softly
Will in the marked-off time attain its goal:
City by car to the ship and ship to the sea
Then from the ship to the city. . .

Everything that I am is in that coming:
Infinite time allows that coming to be.

So I consider it
                    easy, take your time;
Move as a man moves who'd pass out safely,
Move as a ladder swung between two cliffs,
Move as a careful captain who sees victory.

Move . . . but the general sits behind a desk,
Peers at his map through glasses, speaks to his runners,
Life is a game to him and his decision
Springs from no action!

Somewhere ahead of the mind's clear picture
Steps with a tragic laugh the soul and body
Out of the known world to the unknown darkness
Down, down, with a swift deed, defying
Death: for what is death, the choice certain?

So when I run I know the tape is broken,
So behind the wheel I thunder lightly,

So the airman covers his unknown seas,
So the spirit conceived the world and left it.

Given the will,
Given the choice. . .

THIS IS A WOMAN

This is a woman in the next room, moving
heavily on a bed
in the silence. Unseen she is living
and everything else seems dead.

Only a year back beside the river
I listened to the trees move
a little and then stop. And with a shiver
I thought of my love. . .

This is no particular woman. This is only
a woman on a bed.
She sleeps and does not dream. She is not lonely,
nor loves, nor hates. Nor is dead.
Only she moves. And in her motion
there is a power,
great since without use like the ocean
from hour to hour.

Hers not the hand for thread nor thimbles
nor even the duty of a wife.

. . .In the trees I no longer see symbols.
I see life.

SELDEN RODMAN.

MARVELL'S 'GARDEN'

THE chief point of the poem is to contrast and reconcile conscious and unconscious states, intuitive and intellectual modes of apprehension; and yet that distinction is never made, perhaps could not have been made; his thought is implied by his metaphors. There is something very Far-Eastern about this; I was reminded of it by Mr. Richard's discussion, in a recent *Psyche,* of a philosophical argument out of Mencius. The Oxford edition notes bring out a crucial double meaning (so this at least is not my own fancy) in the most analytical statement of the poem, about the Mind:—

> Annihilating all that's made
> To a green Thought in a green shade.

' Either '' reducing the whole material world to nothing material, i.e., to a green thought,'' or '' considering the material world as of no value compared to a green thought '' '; either contemplating everything or shutting everything out. This combines the idea of the conscious mind, including everything because understanding it, and that of the unconscious animal nature, including everything because in harmony with it. Evidently the object of such a fundamental contradiction (seen in the etymology: turning all *ad nihil, to* nothing, and *to* a thought) is to deny its reality; the point is not that these two are essentially different but that they must cease to be different so far as either is to be known. So far as he has achieved his state of ecstasy he combines them, he is ' neither conscious nor not conscious,' like the seventh Buddhist stage of enlightenment. (It is by implying something like this, I think, that the puns in Donne's *Extasie* too become more than a simple Freudian give-away). But once you accept this note you may as well apply it to the whole verse.

> Meanwhile the Mind, from pleasure less,
> Withdraws into its happiness;
> The Mind, that Ocean where each kind
> Does streight its own resemblance find;

Yet it creates, transcending these,
Far other Worlds, and other Seas;
Annihilating . . .

From pleasure less. Either ' from the lessening of pleasure '
—' we are quiet in the country, but our dullness gives a sober
and self-knowing happiness, more intellectual than that of the
overstimulated pleasures of the town ' or ' made less by this
pleasure '—' The pleasures of the country give a repose and
emotional release which make me feel less intellectual, make my
mind less worrying and introspective.' This is the same opposition; the ambiguity gives two meanings to pleasure, corresponding
to his Puritan ambivalence about it, and to the opposition between
pleasure and happiness. *Happiness,* again, names a conscious
state, and yet involves the idea of things falling right, happening
so, not being ordered by an anxiety of the conscious reason. (So
that as a rule it is a weak word; it is by seeming to look at
it hard and bring out its implications that the verse here makes
it act as a strong one).

This same doubt gives all their grandeur to the next lines.
The sea if calm reflects everything near it; the mind as knower
is a conscious mirror. Somewhere in the sea are sea-lions and
-horses and everything else, though they are different from land
ones; the unconsciousness is unplumbed and pathless, and there
is no instinct so strange among the beasts that it lacks its
fantastic echo in the mind. In the first version thoughts are
shadows, in the second (like the *green thought*) they are as solid
as what they image; and yet they still correspond to something
in the outer world, so that the poet's intuition is comparable to
pure knowledge. (Keats may have been quoting the sixth verse,
by the way, when he said that if he saw a sparrow on the path
he pecked about on the gravel). This metaphor may reflect
back so that *withdraws* means the tide going down; the *mind*
is *less* now, but will return, and it is now that one can see the
rock-pools. On the Freudian view of an Ocean, *withdraws*
would make this repose in nature a return to the womb; anyway
it may mean either ' withdraws into self-contemplation ' or
' withdraws altogether, into its mysterious processes of digestion.'
Streight may mean ' packed together,' in the microcosm, or
' at once '; the beasts see their reflection (perhaps the root

word of the metaphor) as soon as they look for it; the calm
of nature gives the poet an immediate self-knowledge. But we
have already had two entrancingly witty verses about the sublimation of sexual desire into a taste for Nature, and the *kinds* look
for their *resemblance,* in practice, out of a desire for *creation;*
in the mind, at this fertile time for the poet, they can do so
' at once,' being ' packed together.' This profound transition,
from the correspondences of thought with fact to those of thought
with thought, to *find* which is to be *creative,* leads on to the
next couplet, in which not only does the *mind transcend* the
world it mirrors, but a sea, by a similar transition, transcends
both land and sea too, which implies self-consciousness and all
the antinomies of philosophy. And it is true that the sea reflects
the *other worlds* of the stars. Yet even here the double meaning
is not lost; all land-beasts have their sea-beasts, but the sea also
has the kraken; in the depths as well as the transcendence of
the mind are things stranger than all the kinds of the world.

Green takes on great weight here, as Miss Sackville West
pointed out, because it has been a pet word of Marvell's before;
to list the uses before the satires may seem a trivial affectation
of scholarship, but at least shows how often he used the word.
In the Oxford text; pages 12, l. 23: 17, l. 18: 25, l. 11: 27, l. 4:
31, l. 27: 38, l. 3: 45, l. 3: 70, l. 376: 71, l. 390: 74, l. 510: 122,
l. 2. Less important, 15, l. 18: 30, l. 55: 42, l. 14: 69, l. 386: 74,
l. 484: 85, l. 82: 89, l. 94. It is connected here with grass, buds,
children, and an as yet virginal prospect of sexuality,[1] a power of
thought as yet only latent in sensibility, and the peasant stock
from which the great families emerge. The ' unfathomable '
grass both shows and makes a soil fertile; it is the humble,
permanent, undeveloped nature which sustains everything, and
to which everything must return; children are connected with
this both as buds, because of their contact with Nature (as in
Wordsworth), and unique fitness for Heaven (as in the Gospels).

> The tawny mowers enter next,
> Who seem like Israelites to be
> Walking on foot through a green sea

---

[1] cf. ' giving a green gown ' 16th century; ' having a bit of green '
20th century.

connects greenness with oceans and gives it a magical security;
though one must drown in it.

> And in the greenness of the grass
> Did see my hopes as in a glass

connects greenness with mirrors and the partial knowledge of
the mind. The complex of ideas he concentrates into this
passage, in fact, had been worked out separately already.

To nineteenth century taste the only really poetical verse of
the poem is the central fifth of the nine; I have been discussing
the sixth, whose dramatic position is an illustration of its very
penetrating theory. The first four are a crescendo of wit, on the
themes ' success or failure is not important, only the repose
that follows the exercise of one's powers ' and ' women, I am
pleased to say, are no longer interesting to me, because nature
is more beautiful.' One effect of the wit is to admit, and so
make charming, the impertinence of the second of these, which
indeed the first puts in its place; it is only for a time, and
after effort among human beings, that he can enjoy solitude.
The value of these moments made it fitting to pretend they
were eternal; and yet the lightness of his expression of their
sense of power is more intelligent, and so more convincing, than
Wordsworth's solemnity on the same theme, because it does not
forget the opposing forces.

> When we have run our Passions heat,
> Love hither makes his best retreat.
> The *Gods*, that mortal beauty chase,
> Still in a Tree did end their race.
> *Apollo* hunted *Daphne* so,
> Only that she might Laurel grow,
> And *Pan* did after *Syrinx* speed,
> Not as a Nymph, but for a Reed.

The energy and delight of the conceit has been sharpened or
keyed up here till it seems to burst and transform itself; it
dissolves in the next verse into the style of Keats. So his
observation of the garden might mount to an ecstasy which
disregarded it; he seems in this next verse to imitate the process
he has described, to enjoy in a receptive state the exhilaration

which an exercise of wit has achieved. But striking as the change
of style is, it is unfair to empty the verse of thought and treat
it as random description; what happens is that he steps back
from overt classical conceits to a rich and intuitive use of
Christian imagery. When people treat it as the one good ' bit '
of the poem one does not know whether they have recognised
that the Alpha and Omega of the verse are the Apple and the
Fall.

> What wond'rous Life is this I lead!
> Ripe Apples drop about my head;
> The Luscious Clusters of the Vine
> Upon my Mouth do crush their Wine;
> The Nectaren, and curious Peach,
> Into my hands themselves do reach;
> Stumbling on Melons, as I pass,
> Insnar'd with Flow'rs, I fall on Grass.

Melon, again, is the Greek for apple; ' all flesh is *grass*,' and
its own *flowers* here are the snakes in it that stopped Eurydice.
Mere grapes are at once the primitive and the innocent wine; the
nectar of Eden, and yet the blood of sacrifice. *Curious* could
mean ' rich and strange ' (nature), ' improved by care ' (art) or
' inquisitive ' (feeling towards me, since nature is a mirror, as
I do towards her). All these eatable beauties give themselves so
as to lose themselves, like a lover, with a forceful generosity;
like a lover they *ensnare* him. It is the triumph of his attempt
to impose a sexual interest upon nature; there need be no more
Puritanism in this use of sacrificial ideas than is already inherent
in the praise of solitude; and it is because his repose in the
orchard hints at such a variety of emotions that he is
contemplating *all that's made*. Sensibility here repeats what wit
said in the verse before; he tosses into the fantastic treasure-
chest of the poem's thought all the pathos and dignity that Milton
was to feel in his more celebrated Garden; and it is while this
is going on, we are told in the next verse, that the mind performs
its ambiguous and memorable *withdrawal*. For each of the three
central verses he gives a twist to the screw of the microscope
and is living in another world.

WILLIAM EMPSON.

ADVERTISING GOD

EVERY reader of *Scrutiny* should remember that he is a parasite—in the eyes at least of the authors of *Advertising and Selling* (edited by Noble T. Praigg—Pitman). To hear the ' admen ' talk, you might imagine that they were the lords of creation. And they are, in a sense. Advertising was once parasitic in dimensions as well as in function: but it has swollen so dropsically that its parent is dwarfed. A large part of the world won't work even inefficiently without lubrication by advertising, for (as a *Criterion* commentary said) ' the material prosperity of modern civilization depends upon inducing people to buy what they do not want, and to want what they should not buy. . . it seems a very flimsy structure. . . . '

This fact and its implications are apt to be forgotten. The neglect is not surprising. The channels for the diffusion of enlightened opinion are more tightly blocked in the case of advertising than in any other problem: periodicals can't be expected to bite the hand that feeds them. Far from it. The cruder dailies and the more luxurious weeklies are explicit in their direction to buy advertised goods (in one case, at the foot of every page), while there is often a subtler relation between the reading and publicity matter, *e.g.* in evoking and exploiting similar undesirable attitudes. The more solemn organs, whose predecessors used to cater for the intelligent, are unhelpful; one of the pseudosophical quarterlies even published a Defence of Advertising which paraded a string of the usual hack sophistries. Once upon a time there was a Select Committee which made very suitable recommendations on patent medicines and their advertisements. But they were never effected. And the latest committee, on ' skywriting,' seems to have been remarkably gullible; from the fat phrases of its Report we gather that though at first it was ' frankly apprehensive,' its fears were ' considerably allayed ' by the thought that this method of advertising was ' far more pleasant than many of the permanent forms.' It appears to think that ' skywriting ' should be fostered as a new ' industry.' This year one of the brighter weeklies reviewed advertising by means of a questionnaire. The more blatant fallacies were duly detected, but the sad significance of the answers is that those critics who excepted certain advertisements from their general condemnation of style chose for favourable notice those which do most damage, by debasing ideas and language and by promoting undesirable attitudes. Advertising's most hostile critics showed themselves gorged with the subtler baits.

Advertising and Selling consists of the speeches made by a hundred and fifty Advertising and Sales Executives at an International Convention held at Atlantic City. It offers a bird's-eye view of the advertising world, that is of the future to which we are Progressing. Anyone who believes that this country is putting up a sturdy resistance to 'Americanization' should read the account of how the British public was made 'raisin-conscious' (p. 322); or turn to p. 250, where we are told: 'This meeting of American and British advertising agents is one of those quiet, unassuming events, not uncommon in history, which give no outward sign of their real significance.' One outward sign is that the British speak the same idiom, emit the same noises, as the Americans. If England is less Americanized than America, it is in the discreditable sense that less resistance to the advance of civilization has been developed: no English university has produced a *Middletown*. This book provides useful hints of what to look for; there is much of the material necessary for producing an awareness that

>   the close
> Of our long progress is hinted by the crass
> Fogs creeping slow and darkly
> From out the middle west.

Fogs which are terrifying because they are so vast and impersonal. But a book like this provides a focus, a target. If it induces nausea and depression, it provides some incitement to resist; it is as if one were eavesdropping at a meeting of gangsters plotting one's murder. Certainly no gangster turning informer could provide more damning evidence. If the 'admen' were not so stupid (this book shows that they are uniformly illiterate), they would never have let the cat out of the bag like this.

Of the backward British manufacturer we are told: 'For

generations he has held the belief that quality production was his
first and only consideration.' And that advertising cheats the con-
sumer by lowering the quality of the goods is only one of the
many charges proved by Mr. Chase's books, especially *Your
Money's Worth (Cape, 8/6d.)*. But more pertinent here is its
achievement in debasing the currency of living—its effects on
language and ideas, art and religion. Where the business ethos has
ousted rival codes, the church has only survived by competing
with the same tactics, that is, by not competing at all. Organized
religion in the United States stands square with Big Business,
judging by the section devoted to advertising God, with such titles
as 'Applying Business Standards to Church Advertising,'
'Advertising the Bible,' and 'Spirituality in Church Advertising.'
Its fifty pages are pre-eminent in grossness. Churchmen and
'admen' use the same idiom. Where religion is 'sold,' when
'everyone likes to belong to a keen, alert, up-and-doing organization that is always on its toes,' God is worshipped as the
Biggest Business Man:

> 'Above all I would make my church advertising prayed-
> over advertising. I would no more expect to put out an
> announcement of any kind which had not been individually
> submitted to the Sales Manager in prayer, than I would expect
> to preach a sermon or lead a prayer meeting without so doing.'

Though in the United States business has subverted religion, the
religious attitudes are still useful to business, which canalizes them
for its own purposes. The religious sanction is crudely invoked:
'Next to God and religion, the utilities are the most important
thing in our lives'; and an invitation to use a certain elevator is
supported by a list of the 'Very Biggest Businesses,' 'every one
of which is headed by a religious man.' The more insidious
damage caused by advertisers is the same as that done by certain
novelists; by using emotional keywords, 'they call out the religious attitude to support an unworthy code.' 'Advertisement
writers,' I once heard Sir William Crawford say, 'should read
the Bible, Kipling, Stevenson and Burns, because they know how
to touch the human heart, and because they know how to use
words.' What this knowledge has done for the language may be
realized from *Prose of Persuasion,* a recent anthology of adver-

tising copy; and similar decay may be noted in many places, from politicians' speeches to schoolboy essays, which are liable to talk about the ' big things of life.' It must be insisted ' that what is taking place is not something that effects only the environment of culture, stops short, as it were at the periphery.' Crude or empty language is inseparable from crude or empty living; and even a slight study of the material available for a comparison of the style and careers of politicians supplies evidence for Mr. Pound's dictum: ' When . . . the application of word to thing goes rotten, *i.e.,* becomes slushy and inexact, or excessive or bloated, the whole machinery of social and of individual thought and order goes to pot.'

' It is more than a coincidence,' says an American on p. 210 of *Advertising and Selling,* ' that we lead the world in industrial advertising and journalism,' for it was in America first that there was ' no sharply drawn line between writing to entertain and writing to sell ' (p. 102). And it is no coincidence that novelists and journalists are often copywriters; they use the same language, *i.e.,* promote the same attitudes, the same ways of living and thinking. What happens to creative talent spent in copywriting may be seen from *Prose of Persuasion,* especially the introduction. The late Arnold Bennett would have made a very efficient copy-writer; his career is the type (increasingly exemplified) heralded by Mr. Dennis Bradley (Praigg, p. 74), who foresees ' the time— and that in the immediate future—when into the vortex of com-merce, because of the fundamental instinct to live, will be swept our great writers.' All Mr. Bradley's orotundities are valuable evidence. A generation which understands only the advertisers' use of language and sees no pictures but posters, has no ears and eyes for literature and art, and will make no protest when it is told (p. 311) that ' outdoor advertising, honestly and skilfully designed, belongs to the modern landscape quite as much as the trees and flowers belong to it.' If some of Mr. Bradley's rosy prophecies are realized, at least one looks odd in the light of subsequent slumps: ' Advertising is the new world force lustily breeding progress. It is the clarion note of business principle. It is the bugle call to prosperity,' etc., etc. It was certainly a con-tributing cause to the 1929 Wall Street crash.

Most of the ' undesirable attitudes ' referred to are covered by the idea of Progress, announced with a Rotarian note of unctuous hypocrisy. It warrants, for instance, the disgusting optimism which damns as a croaker any critic of the *status quo,* while it provides the authority for any infliction the advertisers may think fit—the Higher Standard of Living, for example—or in other words, the substitution for normal human activities of second-hand amusement and deleterious habits, increasing in number almost daily. ' Soap isn't bought any more to keep one's self clean, but to become beautiful.' A truism the slump should enforce is that peoples with the Highest Standard suffer most from depressions; by being in the rearguard of Progress, the ' backward nations ' are nearer a more satisfying human norm. But advertising ' will do for the backward nations the things it has done for America, in raising the standard of living, in quickening the flow of wealth among all classes. . . '[1] What it has done for America we know from *Middletown* and *Stardust in Hollywood;* and the process is not likely to be checked, even by political revolution—people conditioned by newspapers, films and the Higher Standard would not be more fulfilled than in the prosperity periods of capitalism. On p. 442 we read:

> ' Appeal to reason in your advertising and you appeal to about 4 per cent. of the human race. Appeal to instinct and you touch everyone from the Australian aborigine to the most highly developed product of twentieth-century civilization.'

The ' appeal to instinct ' has helped to reduce the victims of civilization to a plight which savages deplore; at this one dead

---

[1]Advertising mission work in Africa:—' EVENING DRESS FOR NEGROES—THEY LIKE THEIR CLOTHES FROM LONDON. African negroes prefer British evening clothes to any other garments.— This is what Mr. Lipos Tichin, a Greek by birth, whose home is in London, has to say about his trade in second-hand clothes with African negroes (reports Reuter).—If trade is moving slowly, he says a film is shown to the natives.—*They see white men parading in the very clothes which he is offering for sale. This rarely fails to clinch the business.*—Ivory, gold, diamonds and crocodile skins are given by the negroes for the clothes.'—From the *Evening Standard,* Monday, November 7th, 1932.

level, such victims are de-differentiated, to borrow the biologists' term, for as human beings they are losing faculties without compensation.

In this levelling-down process advertising (et cetera) has replaced education; it is significant that ' education ' is one of the words most frequently abused by the advertisers' lingo. ' To educate a great public to think a certain thing about a product. . . ,' and (an English specimen, from *The Brewers' Journal*) ' a campaign of sufficient magnitude to influence public opinion and educate the coming generation in the merits of the brewery product could be effectively taken.' And if we are ' to put our wave of progress in its proper place,' some kind of counter-education is necessary. Education (in the form of schools) is at the moment very busy mass-producing interchangeable little components for the industrial machine; public and elementary schools are at the same point on the conveyor belt. For the average public school boy only differs from the ' board ' school boy in that with his highly developed herd-instinct, his ready-made attitudes for the advertisers to play on, he is an easier victim of exploitation. Visitors to elementary schools note the dulness of the eldest pupils compared with the brightness and self-sufficiency of the infants; and the same contrast might be noted in other schools. In the interval they have been taught to write and spell, and their faculties over-taxed, until they are ejected, inarticulate and impercipient, and left to the mercies of the decreators. If the young must be taught the ABC, they should surely be taught something like Active Reading, to recognise a penny newspaper for what it is. And an Advertisement Defence period would do a great deal more for its pupils than the heading suggests at first; the saving of money would be the least benefit, for a full training in the subject would entail a knowledge of ' the difference between free and wasteful organization, between fullness and narrowness of life.' Some kind of training in critical reading would be useful in all subjects; economists might then be asked what they mean by ' human happiness,' when they say it is the goal of the ' economic process.' This book should have several uses, as a museum of fallacies and as a guide to the significance of advertising, in inducing a critical attitude to environment; for the concern of education should be to turn out 'misfits,' not spare parts.

DENYS THOMPSON.

WILL TRAINING COLLEGES BEAR SCRUTINY ?

THE defects of Training Colleges are so obvious to those (though, as we have to point out, not to all) who have passed through them that it is hard to realise that they are not equally obvious to Training College officials, the upper ranks of the educational hierarchy, or the world at large—as is clear from the increasing difficulty which ' untrained ' men and women find in obtaining posts in schools. Nevertheless, amongst the ' trained '—those at least who retain some critical independence after a systematic numbing of the faculties—the Training College has become a byword for futility, or worse. To mention it was, we found, to provoke outbursts of derision and indignation, the violence of which would surprise those who retain any illusions about the present system.

A digest of the information received in reply to a widely distributed questionnaire will suggest an answer to the query at the head of this article, and, perhaps, provoke a more complete investigation than we were able to carry out. The *Times Educational Supplement* or the *Journal of Education* will, perhaps, call attention to the problem more effectively.

Even in publishing these notes we shall incur animadversion and objection. We have not had replies from every Training College in England and Scotland; we have not discriminated sufficiently between elementary and post-graduate Training Colleges, between Training Colleges for men and those for women; we have not mentioned the one or two decent exceptions to the general rule; and so on. In short, we presume. Our reply is that we presume to make a start, since no one else seems likely to do so.

The problem of course cannot be isolated. The educational machine works in a round—School, University, Training College, School—and a study of the Training College in artificial isolation is only valuable if we remember that it gears on to the other two. The machine image comes naturally to mind, for the Training College, bent on justifying itself to the Board of Education,

like the school which adopts the business man's conception of
' efficiency ' (100% success in the School Certificate), is a
machine. So many compulsory lectures, so many notes assiduously taken, so many formulæ repeated on examination papers,
so many Diplomas and Certificates, and the ' efficient ' teacher
is produced. That at least is the impression gained from those
who have passed through the process, and come out duly marked
and labelled.

' The Training College day,' we are told, ' was characteristically a day of lectures; the electric bell rang every hour to
change lecture rooms, the classes filing along the corridors.' The
picture is symbolic. Compulsory attendance at lectures is the rule,
and in many colleges lectures take up the best part of a working
day, the subjects ranging from psychology and principles of
' method,' to hygiene, housecraft, and ' art.'[1] Many of them are
superfluous, though to cut even the most futile of them is a
serious offence. And the sense of frustration and of time wasted
is intensified by the methods adopted in the classroom. The
information imparted is dry, academic, often irrelevant and
normally suited to the intelligence of the lowest level of the
audience.

' My training was of very little use to me. I was forced
to attend lectures and take down notes verbatim on subjects
which I could have learnt more quickly by reading for myself.'

' We were supplied with numbers of pat little definitions,
pure, predigested examination matter meant to be noted,
underlined and learnt by heart.'

' No course took you sufficiently far to be of much use if
you had read or thought at all. Usually the lecturers got you
through the set books, expecting that you would not read them
if they did not read them with you.'

A lecturer who expected students to have read the text books,
merely using them as a basis for discussion in lectures, is com-
mented upon as an exception.

---

[1]' Ordinary courses compulsory for all students:—Principles of
Teaching, Hygiene, Physical Training, English, History or Mathe-
matics, Geography or Elementary Science.'—From a post-graduate
Training College.

Now compulsory attendance at lectures, even word by word dictation of notes to men and women who have taken an honours degree, might be suffered if there were any hope that, somehow, something valuable might emerge. Consider the student who is about to begin his thirty or forty years' teaching English in a school. He has, it may be presumed, some acquaintance with English literature. What he now requires is help in forming a technique, not for imparting knowledge, but for training the sensibility of his pupils. This the lecturers are quite unqualified to impart, and, if they were qualified, the majority of the students—thanks to their previous education—would probably not understand them. Only a few extracts are necessary to bring home the worse than waste that Training College ' English ' represents.

' Our English training was merely a continuation of a Grammar School course. We had eight or nine plays for study (particularly for ' context ' questions) and we did the history of the drama. Besides this we read on the development of the English language, and wrote essays. . . We spent our time reading the plays together, making the usual remarks on the characters, the plot, etc., writing the usual essays : '' Compare and contrast. . . '' just as we had done in the sixth form at school. We were thoroughly instructed and thoroughly uneducated.'

It was at this College that a student was ' particularly humiliated ' for daring to suggest that *John O' London's* was unnecessary in the common room.

This example comes from an ' elementary ' Training College where the problem is complicated because the students have not only to be trained as teachers, but to receive further instruction in their own subjects. But the situation is no better at those Colleges which exist to train graduates :

' The advanced English group did Shakespeare with the ordinary English group but were expected to '' read more widely.'' The criticism was of the How-many-children-had-Lady-Macbeth? type. Students were put on to *John O' London's* and Gerald Gould or Robert Lynd or whoever it was who did criticism for the *Daily Express*. The more intelligent of the lecturers had never heard of Eliot and only just heard of Lawrence. She asked to borrow my copies.'[1]

Finally there is evidence from a post-graduate Training College where intensive training in the teaching of English was reinforced by reference to Behaviourist psychology. Here the methods of teaching English are analysed with a great appearance of scientific rigour. Reading lessons, poetry lessons, composition lessons, are divided into sections and sub-sections, guaranteed to make any lesson fool-proof. (' Education is a matter of applying the correct stimuli to obtain the correct responses.') The lectures betray a complete ignorance of the mental processes involved in reading a poem. After analysis (so run the lecture notes) comes synthesis, in reading, repetition and ' telling the story of the poem.' Then, ' If the lines really mean anything they suggest a picture. Don't say, " What is the meaning of this line? " Say " What picture is there in this line? " (Similarly, after reading a chapter from *Treasure Island* the teacher is to tell the class to ' draw it for next day.') Poetry, it appears, is solely a matter of exciting visual imagery, and a lesson on *How They Brought the Good News from Ghent to Aix is* ' given reality ' by tracing a map of the journey.[2] Amongst all the paraphernalia for teaching every kind of English lesson there is not a hint that it is the teacher's business to ask his pupils ' What is the quality of the mind which created this poem? ' or to help them to find a criterion for discriminating the good and the bad. After this it is not surprising to hear of the ' lack of critical sensitiveness on the part of the lecturer, as shown by his choice for teaching purposes of poems by Squire, Drinkwater, Chesterton and Kipling—a choice which cannot be defended on the ground that it was for children and not for adults, since, he declared,

---

[1]Another says: ' When I told the English lecturer that I read Eliot and Pound, she replied that " Modernist poetry " was " dirty." ' [2]The teaching which results from such a system helps to explain why letters can appear in the *Times Literary Supplement* debating with vigour the route Falstaff took on his march to Shrewsbury.

"The choice is ideal if the poem is one that you (the teacher) like and one they (the children) like."[1]

This is a fitting place for a note on the usual training in 'Art' and the appreciation of music:

'My "advanced" subject was art. As far as I could see the aim was to turn out as many artists as possible in each class. There was no training in appreciation of pictures, textiles, pots and so on, nor any mention of museums, although all elementary school teachers have to take children on visits to museums and galleries. All the emphasis was on producing something with no standard in view beyond the Challenge Bookshop and Heal's. Much of the stuff that you were trained to produce was good, but it all had a sticky sentimental flavour.

'The lecturers were limited and kept to their own province. They had almost no knowledge of contemporary literature and probably still less of literature before the Brontës. I doubt if they ever read anything but fiction and a few essays to get extracts for lettering exercises for students. Even their own subject they knew narrowly although they were probably capable craftsmen (one exhibited two water colours in the Academy in 19—).'

This refers to one of the most famous of the London Training Colleges. And from an 'elementary' Training College we have:

'We obtained no musical education from this two years' course [given by a Doctor of Music.] We heard no good music either from him at the piano or from gramophone records. Singing a dozen or so songs and learning a few technical details comprised our course. . . . We were given a list of composers and their works to learn by heart, though most of them were still merely names to us and we had no opportunity of hearing them. At the beginning of each music lecture we had a short test to find out how many we could remember, *e.g.* Who wrote the *Messiah* ?—Handel, etc.'

---

[1] From another reply to the questionnaire: 'The lecturer in English was a specialist in Philology and Anglo-Saxon. . . . Phonetics were stressed to the exclusion of everything else.'

In such circumstances to talk of the training of sensibility seems ironic.

* * * *

After such an exposure of the inability of the Training Colleges to deal with a concrete problem it is useless to expect from them a coherent theory of the general function of education. In answer to the question ' Did any of your lecturers encourage you to consider the aims of education? ' one says: ' The lecturers were chiefly concerned with forcing people to get through the text books for the exams and being definite in their vague way. I suppose they included the aims of education in the History of Education, but I certainly don't remember discussions on the subject. It was too vague for them, I suppose.' And another : ' We were not encouraged to consider education broadly—nor anything else. To take notes of the work that the tutors had collected seemed to be all that was expected of us. At any rate that was all they left us time to do.' The wheels must be kept turning, no matter to what end. So there is no need to share the astonishment of one who, after describing a typical English course, said, ' And yet the tutor in this subject was well qualified and alive and interested in English.' Individual intelligence is not wanted in a machine-tender, nor can it be used when present.

There is no space to give in full the negative account which the Training Colleges, if scrutinized in detail, would be forced to yield. But before passing to the more important consideration of the type of men and women which the Training Colleges produce, it is necessary to mention two points on which a defence of the Training College system may be made; one, the ' school practice ' which is part of every course; the other, the general training in Psychology given at most Colleges.

Many would agree that the most valuable part of their train- ing was the experience of actual teaching for which the course provides an opportunity; the student has not to live down his blunders in a school which he will leave after a few weeks' teaching. But even under this head there are serious reservations to be made. Except in the case of those Colleges which send away their students for a term, to become virtually members of a school staff for that period, the conditions are artificial, and too much is

attempted in too short a time. ' The usual period of school practice
—two or three weeks—,' says a Training College lecturer, ' is
too short and artificial. It tends to be carefully stage-managed.'
' The school practice,' says another witness, ' was useful but dis-
jointed. One had no authority, yet since others were in the room
no disciplinary difficulties arose. The atmosphere was unnaturally
quiet and artificial.' And another: ' School practice wasn't much
use because you were never ultimately responsible for either the
work or discipline of the class. And the children knew you were a
student and indulged you.'[1]

In Psychology, McDougall seems to be the staple at most
Colleges, and even the more intelligent are not encouraged to ask
questions about, say, Freud, or even the more ' respectable '
Gestalt psychologists. The following extract gives a fairly favourable picture:

' " Psychology " consisted chiefly in McDougall illustrated
with students' stories of children they knew, as far as lectures
were concerned. But the list for private reading was fairly wide,
and bearing definitely on elementary school problems. It was
all rather rosy though. Considering the material they had to
work with the college authorities got a good deal done. But they
certainly didn't expect you to do much for yourself. Adler, Jung
and Freud were not considered. They were too controversial I
suppose. Certainly very few of the students were capable of

---

[1]There is of course another possibility. One witness writes: ' School
practice was practically of no value, because no free hand was
allowed to students. Nearly everything was determined for them
externally. Even when left alone, as they were for short intervals
only, they were subject to unexpected visitation in order to ensure
that they were working according to external time-table and
official Training College instructions. In addition the student
teacher inherited the methods of the class teacher, and any attempt
to change these was frequently the line of greatest resistance, *e.g.*
A student left alone with a class perfectly " disciplined," perhaps,
by a sadist was likely to be confronted with a vicious outbreak
as soon as the same class woke up to the change, and be cut
off from his future bread and butter as deficient in " class
control." '

sorting themselves out, let alone presuming to sort out other people. To have dealt with Adler, Jung or Freud would probably have done more harm than good. Even McDougall was Advanced to most of them. I should say that for the type of student that enters an elementary teachers' Training College the course was adequate, although a minority could have done with something better. The course certainly kept very close to elementary school problems in a limited way. It didn't produce psychiatrists and it didn't try to turn out amateurs.'

The impression that more ambitious psychological instruction cannot safely be encouraged is confirmed by the report of a student from a College which gives rigorous instruction on Behaviourist lines. A few extracts from his lecture note-book must suffice:

' Teaching may be defined as the art of giving or with-holding stimuli in order to produce or prevent certain reactions.'

Thus the problem of education can be reduced to a formula:

$$
\begin{array}{ll}
\text{' Environment} = \Sigma \ S & \text{Stimuli Situations.} \\
\text{Living} \qquad\ = \Sigma \ R & \text{Reactions. Adjustments.} \\
\left.\begin{array}{l}\text{Teaching} \\ \text{Learning}\end{array}\right\} \text{cycle} = S \longleftrightarrow R \ '
\end{array}
$$

' Whether a teacher or learner it's your job to link up certain Stimuli and certain Reactions.'

' Stimuli must be in an *invariable form,* the very words, otherwise you will not get exactly *that* Reaction.'

' A lesson is not taught until it has been learnt.'

And our informant adds: 'I seem to remember that the lecturer explicitly described the perfect teacher as a perfect automaton, mechanically working the correct Reactions by means of the correct Stimuli.'

After such crudities it is not surprising to learn that the lecturer repeated such aphorisms as, ' The state tends to embody the highest purposes of its best members,' and ' The aim of education is determined by the social ideas prevalent in a particular community at a given time. Sooner or later the schools conform to the dominant views of social progress,' reinforcing them by reference to the Cinema and the Newspapers as educative forces.

*   *   *   *

It is plain that the Training College system raises cultural problems of the first importance. This is no less plain if we turn from the details of technical training to the kind of men and women which the Training Colleges produce—for it did not need a psychologist to assure us that the products of this system (unless they are unusually resistive) can be easily recognised as ' types.' Such ' scientific ' classification is too obviously favoured by the system, a system the main object of which seems to be an arrested juvenility, an habituation to routine, and a meek acceptance of the *status quo*.

An objection—But why do they put up with it?—may be disposed of here. At the ' elementary ' Colleges they are caught too young, and at all there are obvious reasons for non-resistance. ' The staff wielded absolute power,' writes one witness, ' power over the future bread and butter of the students.' And another, a graduate with high honours in English, informs us that she submitted to attend lectures on Botany, black-board Drawing and elementary Arithmetic under the threat that to ' cut ' meant to forfeit her certificate. There is nothing for it but to submit—' The tutors have a great deal, in fact everything, to do with a student's final mark. . . . A high final mark and a good testimonial are a necessity (1) to pass the examination (2) to get a post in a decent school (3) to get a headship or make any progress later.' ' The staff maintained its dignity,' runs one report, ' by treating students as nonentities.' Minor matters gain significance from their context —' You had to wait ages outside the Vice-Principal's door and were treated with contempt by the office staff.' And another writes : ' There was as much distance between the staff and students as between the teachers and pupils at school '—which is also a comment on the school.

The mass of petty restrictions which constitute Training College rules are too well known to need much comment. Those who defend them will no doubt be ready with justifications on the grounds of expediency, economy and the like, but there is no real excuse. Perhaps in London Training Colleges composed of girls who are fresh from school some reason may be found for requiring students to be within doors by 6 o'clock (7 o'clock on Saturdays), but it is hard to see why the system of comparative freedom which obtains at the older universities should not work well enough elsewhere. And there is no excuse for the Training College, catering for men who are also taking a university course, which allows its students to be out after 10 o'clock only with special permission, which switches off its electric light at 10.30, and which condones the impropriety of a man's going out with a woman only when he has obtained permission from a member of the staff.

Compulsory attendance at lectures has already been mentioned, but the authorities are not content with that. Apparently no student can be trusted to work unless he or she is following the fixed routine of the place. Here is a specimen time-table from an ' elementary ' Training College:

Each morning—9 a.m. to 1 p.m. Lectures (with occasional periods of private study, for ¾ hour).

Two afternoons a week—2 to 5 p.m. Lectures.

Two afternoons a week—2 to 3.30 p.m. Lectures.

(Saturday and one other afternoon free in Junior year, Saturday and two other afternoons a week free in Senior year).

Every evening, 6.15 to 7.45 p.m. Private Study.
        8 to 9 p.m. Private Study.

During Private Study no talking or visiting is allowed.

After 9.45 p.m., no talking is allowed in the corridors.

10.15 p.m. Lights Out.[1]

---

[1]At this college—and others—not even the vacations are free. ' We were given a supply of work in each subject to be given in on the first day of the following term. . . . Mothers, brothers and sisters are employed to help in Handwork and Needlework, while the student crams in the written work, trying to get rid of the burden and spend one or two weeks at least without the thought of unfinished work.'

Lest it should be thought that this sort of thing is confined to Colleges for non-graduates we add extracts from two reports from Colleges containing university men and women:

' Students at the Training College lived a completely supervised boarding-school life, with set hours for " preparation," which was done in a large room, at desks, in silence. They slept in crowded dormitories and were never allowed out at night. . . In the University Hostels the sexes were separate and were not allowed to visit each other, though they met freely outside the Hostels, and were allowed to have three evenings a week out (two of these had to be at College Functions). . . . We were by no means overworked, although continually dashing from one lecture to another. Most of the students did nothing at all except attend lectures—no personal reading or study. One had time and opportunity for considerable reading in Psychology, but few took advantage of this. The students had no idea of studying for interest's sake, and worked solely with an eye on examination results.'

After this it is not surprising to learn that ' Games and dancing and dramatics were encouraged. They were the students' only interests, since their attitude to work was that of schoolchildren.'[1] Another, after stating that attendance at all lectures was compulsory, continues:

' You had to study every evening from seven till nine, or half past if you wanted. You couldn't leave the study till nine. In the summer you might work in your own room, but exams were near enough then to be an incentive, so they were safe. You were not allowed to go out with a man for a whole day— you had to come back to lunch or tea or supper. . . . A roll was called in study every evening and on Saturday mornings. You must bring an excuse if you were late. Lights Out was at nine forty-five. Prefects came and put out lights that were still burning at five to ten. There were innumerable rules of the same kind and bells ringing for all sorts of things.'

---

[1]From a Scottish Training College: ' Leisure amusements of students—bridge, " flicks," Saturday night " hops." '

It is hard to realize that immediately on leaving College—a cross between a barracks and a nursery—students, as adult men and women, take positions of authority demanding a mature control of the possibilities of living. But it is not hard to see why our schools are tenanted by nervous tyrants whose energies are centred in the problem of maintaining ' discipline.' ' The students,' says one lecturer, ' do not get enough time to think for themselves.' Training College life is a prolonged and hopeless childhood. We are not surprised to read in one report that ' Hostel heads gave permission for " dorm.-feeds " when people had birthdays. And there was a recognized " rag " on the Juniors during the first week of term when Hostel Heads conveniently went out as arranged with the senior student,' or that ' English teaching methods were all in the direction of A. A. Milne.'

As for the final product of such places, here are two extracts from reports :

> ' The students were generally of such low intelligence and so childish that in most cases excessive surveillance was necessary. The only time they resented it was when they'd caught a man and weren't able to stay out as late as they liked. They had no sense about cutting lectures—they only cut to go to the pictures with a man, never because the lecture was going to be no use to them. They were just ridiculous children trying to live like the School Friend stories and American College films. Naturally there were a few exceptions. . . . G.P. attachments were common. Sometimes they existed between two pretty girls who related their adventures with their men to each other and got the thrill twice over, who slept with each other, and usually walked about touching each other. Sometimes a sporty girl had a satellite who fagged for her and pushed her claims at college. There were few genuine friendships as far as I knew. People made friends because it was easier to hunt men in couples. Almost all of them worked hard keeping each other in the mood when they believed they were having the most wonderful time and it was all just like the " pictures." They were the most timid and mild set, absolutely herd-ridden, but they liked to think they were frightfully daring and gay. The men were on the whole boors. . . .'

' The highest decoration, the star and garter of the place, was called the ——— Prize, a passport to the " best " schools in Scotland. I had the fortune the other day to enter into conversation with last year's Prizeman, an English specialist. With the aggressive enthusiasm of the " born " teacher, which must have gained him his prize, he talked, in a Buchan accent, of two books belonging to the " In Search of Scotland " vogue, of Buchan's *Life of Scott*, and of J. C. Squire's Anthologies. These things he attempted to " put across " to me as of high value, and added that he had got one or two of them as his prize. I made no attempt to discuss, say, *The Waste Land, Ulysses*, or *To the Lighthouse* with him, because it would have been impossible.'

*   *   *   *

It should be obvious by now that the problem presented by the Training Colleges is only part of one still larger; it involves the whole educational system, and this, in its turn, cannot be considered apart from the general state of English culture at the present time. Elementary schools, secondary schools and universities must share in the responsibility for the bad state of affairs which we have outlined in this digest. And responsibility does not end with them. Behind the educational system stand the cinema, newspapers, book societies, and Big Business—the whole machinery of ' Democracy ' and standardization. So that the main charge against the Training Colleges is that they do nothing to check ' an increasing inattention,' nothing to foster such interests as their students may possess, nothing to encourage an adult sense of responsibility. Their students leave them perfectly fitted to their environment, perfectly unfitted for the work which they should do.

We may end with three extracts which raise the larger issues and which need no comment—the first from a lecturer at a Training College composed of graduates, the second and third from former students of an ' elementary ' and of a post-graduate Training College respectively :

' There are two big difficulties. In the first place their previous education has often killed any initiative. At the top of a secondary school they have been carefully crammed and allowed no leisure, at a university they have been assiduously over-lectured and have had little personal contact with their teachers. They come to be trained thinking that, if they attend some lectures, by some mysterious process they will be turned into teachers. The unreality and poverty of their subjects to them is glaring as soon as they are faced with the problem of adjusting them to children. They think of them as so much examinable matter. In the second place, as teaching is a highly subsidized and sheltered trade a proportion have no interest in or actively dislike their work. £3 a week as a teacher is better than £1 a week at something else—and there you are! A good teacher is the product of a good secondary school and college where he or she has had time to grow up, room to expand, to find out the things which are of interest, and has learnt how to read. The latter is terribly important—very few of my students can or will read for themselves.'

' It is no marvel that we were uninteresting, being eighteen years of age, having had no contact with ideas outside school life, having been stuffed with examination material for the past years and being stuffed still, not daring to go outside the syllabus fencing, not being encouraged to look round our work and connect it up with life, never being allowed to side-track into interesting points, for fear of losing time. . . . When I left the College I was still a school girl, awkward, ignorant on things outside my school subjects, and entirely undeveloped, but at the same time considered qualified to have sole charge of a class of young children.

' This may be due in part to the present methods used in Primary and Secondary Schools and continued in Training Colleges. The majority of students who leave a Secondary School at the age of seventeen or eighteen are like sponges—ready enough to sit and listen and soak up information but absolutely unable to set about working for themselves or even to go further on the knowledge that is given to them. One might blame the pupil for lacking in initiative, but it is odd that they are almost all lacking in the same way, that they are all so much alike. Perhaps it is not strange. . . . Once in the Junior School the scramble for results begins. There must be results for inspectors, good scholarship results. . . School vies against school, until the work becomes sheer grind for teacher and child. . . . Though this might be remedied in the High School it rarely is. . . . Full of information, but still without education, they arrive at College. Even here it is not too late and much might be done in two years that would be lasting. But it is easier to continue giving information, and so young teachers leave College with a Teacher's Certificate and little else. There has been no time for developing personality, no time for culture, not even time for general reading. It is difficult to know how to get rid of this circle; the examination system, I think, is largely responsible.'

' The chief flaw seems to be that the people who enter Training Colleges are so immature that they need treating as children if their parents' and the Board of Education's money is not to be wasted, i.e. if they are to be certified to earn their living under the present system. If a more careful selection of candidates were made there would be less than a quarter of the present number of students admitted. I doubt if these could supply the demand. But if the students were superior the majority of the lecturers couldn't satisfy the students' needs, or could do little more than they do now. And if the colleges could turn out better teachers the headmasters of the schools in which they teach are so unintelligent as a rule that the younger teacher is suspect and generally regarded as an enemy threatening the older teachers' standing, and prevented by established syllabuses from introducing anything new. And if he tries to introduce anything new as a by-product or tries to read anyone's poems instead of letting the children copy black-board notes about when he was born and died and how many children he had, he finds that the time allowed his subject in the year isn't enough for anything but the kind of treatment the other people give it. It's all such a vicious circle that it's difficult to see quite where to begin. I doubt if the Training Colleges are the starting point.'

*   *   *   *

Obviously to break it at one point would be an inadequate aim. But we must begin somewhere. And we intend, in subsequent numbers of *Scrutiny*, to attack at other points: an inquiry into the examination system is already in progress, and a consideration of the teaching of English will appear in our next number. Moreover *Scrutiny,* as we hardly need to remind our readers, directs itself in the exercise of its general function upon the cultural conditions that make the educational scandal possible.

But we do not want, in concluding, to leave the impression that, because the problem is so large and complex, it is useless to think of starting reforms in the Training Colleges. The criticism brought against them falls roughly under three main heads: (a) the inadequacies of the staffs; (b) the inadequacies and positive vices of the curricula; (c) the presence among the students of a large proportion of inferior material. It is no use, we know, to recommend wholesale ejection; but posts are continually being filled, and those who appoint to them must realize that, even more important than that the lecturer should be a trained specialist, is that he or she should be an intelligent and cultivated person. Negatively, one must insist that it is criminal to staff Training Colleges with refugees and *embusqués* from the outside educational world, school and university: the work is peculiarly responsible and exacting. As for (b), where lecturers are incompetent, it is useless to hope for positively good teaching; but we can insist that the actively vicious things should be eliminated—everywhere.

What these are has, as far as the disabling limits of space allowed, been indicated in this report. Training College authorities (or editors of educational journals) who would like greater particularity can have it for the asking: we shall be glad, from the mass of evidence at our disposal, to answer inquiries general or specially directed. (We should quite likely turn out to have evidence about the particular institution concerned). And we would, of course, gladly make positive suggestions regarding curricula, methods of work, teaching technique and books (preferably in some public reply, in order to economize the available time and energy: perhaps the *Times Educational Supplement* or the *Journal of Education* will provide an opportunity). As for (c), the present moment, when the educational market is heavily overstocked, is an especially good one for enforcing a higher standard for admission to Training Colleges. Not that we regard the presence of poor material as a valid excuse for the compulsory infantility so generally complained of. It is preposterous and disgraceful to treat university graduates as they are, the evidence shows, treated. You do not help young

men and women to maturity and responsibility by attempting to
break their spirit and destroy their self-respect. And even the very
immature are best helped to develop by treating them as men and
women rather than as children.

Our authority for talking like this? A mass of material, only
suggested above, from men and women who have recently passed
through Training Colleges or are teaching there, and discussion with
experienced and intelligent persons from all over the country.

L. C. KNIGHTS
(For the Editorial Board)

[*The Editors wish to thank all those who helped in making
the present survey. A scrutiny of the Examination System will
appear in an early issue, and they would be glad if all who have
experience of the system either as examiners or teachers and who
have criticism to offer would write to them.*]

FROM 'COOLSTONE PARK'
A NOVEL

' *There is no mass of sincerity in any one place. What there
is must be picked up patiently, a grain or two at a time;
and the season for it is after a storm, after the overflowing of banks, and bursting of mounds, and sweeping
away of landmarks.*'

W. S. *Landor.*

I REMEMBER vividly the drawing-room at Coolstone Park. I
remember the old French chairs with their eighteenth century
elegance; the wide bow windows which looked over the park
to the ridge of hills beyond; and the room itself, which seemed

always critical of its occupants. The chairs, which stood back to the wall, were the disciples of decorum: it was impossible to lounge or cross a leg in them. One felt that they imparted by their touch a moral code peculiarly their own; or perhaps they had .reached an agreement with the critical blue walls against which they stood as to what was right and wrong in society. The walls never quite approved of the pictures which were hung upon them, nor the curtains of the designs of the carpet. The stranger entering for the first time would not be aware of these things. He might even take a chair from the rank against the wall and lounge in it for some little time before he realized that such things were not done in the drawing-room of Coolstone Park. We who lived in the house never made any mistake like this. We knew, and had always known, that our attitude towards the house and its furniture must be one of perpetual apology. There were so many flanges to hold us on the rails of convention. The rails did the steering, and so the journey from our birth was predestined without our being conscious of the fact.

It is quite easy to compare the memory with an emery wheel which, while it makes a thing smaller with grinding, at the same time makes it brighter. I have found that the memory polishes certain incidents and scenes which have been impressed upon it. The focus becomes smaller; but the actual recollection more vivid. It is a case, I suppose, of imagination working in opposition to time.

The recollection of the Coolstone drawing-room which I retain most vividly is in the evening after the long, formal dinner when custom demanded that we should sit and read, or play chess. It was always the time of half-silence. All that we wanted to say was by then supposed to have been said. We were preparing, in the school sense of preparation, for the lessons and trials of the morrow. I see now that the unconsciousness of self was the only thing which could have made this life endurable to us. We should be thankful for this drug, which took from us all power of questioning.

* * * *

It was curious how sometimes, when I returned from a walk, the house, white and puritanical among its trees, came upon my senses with a paralyzing shock. It was due to my mind having shifted its impressions and thoughts into a new pattern and then suddenly reverting itself into the old. It was like a number of scattered iron filings swept together by a powerful magnet. I see now the absurdity of being so affected by four walls and a roof. But youth will always erect symbolism round itself.

As for the house, there was nothing really to distinguish it in appearance from dozens of its type. It was the product of the middle eighteenth century. It was a house built to serve people who had very definite notions as to how a house should serve them. Yet they had treated bricks and mortar with the condescension of their own polished culture—they had put them on an equality with themselves. Therefore the manner of the house was sceptical and urbane. The pillars each side of the front door were not only an ornament, but seemed to give moral support to the whole house. And the windows, generously square, were a perpetual reminder that the generation who built them were conscious that the secret of life lay in taking a wide view. The garden, too, was laid out on the principle that nature must submit herself to the same decorum as society. Everywhere nature had been tamed; she had been cut and shaped as one might work a piece of cheese. There were triangular blocks of trees and vistas cut like canals. Only in corners could nature be herself, and then only in a tamed, self-conscious way. It was like putting an obstreperous child into a room and saying, ' Now be as naughty as you like, but remember I am watching.'

In its generation the house and garden would have been pleasantly domestic. There would have been no doubt that they had been created for the convenience of a superior being. The relationship of master and servant (condescendingly treated) would always be apparent. But to us things were completely different. We were in the position of being under a servant who no longer knew her place. As always, the question of servant and master is settled by the validity of domination; and this validity postulates having something which someone else hasn't got. The house became master by having in bricks and mortar the property of outlasting the generation which created it.

My brother was the most typical product of Coolstone Park. By his seniority he had signed the warrant of his own life sentence.

He had been brought up with the express purpose of assuming responsibility at the works when my father retired. The very word *responsibility* suggests its own subtle dangers. When we say that a man or woman is fitted to takes responsibility we pay them an apparent compliment, but we know secretly that nothing of the kind is meant. We know that those who are best fitted to take responsibility are those who have not the power of creating it—the people whose thin, narrow lives are without imagination. They are often accepted in the world as pre-eminently good, an acceptance which carries with it its own suspicion. We do not question things we do not fear. It is the fate of these people to open charity bazaars.

* * * *

It is easy for me to summarize my recollections of Coolstone Park—the very act of putting them into compressed form brings them to me more vividly. It is easy to see my brother and sister in the light of our common circumstances; but as to that self of mine which showed then I am not so certain. I sometimes wonder if it was the self I know now. I think I must have been a kind of living mirror which reflected things without actually taking part in them. I have impressions which I cannot dove-tail into places where they should fit. I remember, for instance, seeing a woman dressed in black sitting at a desk in front of a high narrow window. The desk was made of satin wood with an olive-green inlay. The woman's face might be that of a relative, possibly an aunt—but the room . . . . I can in no way place that room: it was oval. I am quite sure I have never seen an oval room, but every time that image flutters across my mind the oval room returns, always oval. I suppose the explanation is the fact that the mind forms composite pictures, that it cross-breeds the emotions provoked by one thing with those provoked by another, so that the product is unrecognizable. I am prepared to believe that the oval room is nothing more than a white hat box associated in some way with the woman at the desk.

It is only in recalling small intimate details that my mind confuses itself. The main impressions and events are vivid; more so, perhaps, than they were when new because my memory has had time to shuffle its cards; it has put aside those of small value and turned up only the aces.

*   *   *   *

The number of our acquaintances at Coolstone Park was small. They were very much the usual type of person—the type which one can call a human being, but in politeness can go no further. They moved round us in a circle of teas, dinner parties, fêtes and all other such functions at which it is a social stigma to say what you mean. I find it so easy to be bitter about them now, and see their faults and trivialities with such microscopic plainness. But the fact that I lived among them so long without questioning their status, condemns me as much as them. There was one Mr. Walters who was typical of his herd. It was difficult to realize that he had not been born with a teacup in his hand; that he walked anywhere else except in gardens given over to charity bazaars. Yet I believe he realized that there was a grandeur lacking in his life, and that something should be done about it. He had therefore tried to get himself acquainted with the atmosphere of great men. He had read an immense number of books about the Duke of Wellington and collected anecdotes of his hero as one might collect butterflies. His mind was a case of stiffened, pin-set anecdotes which were ready for display on any occasion. I blush to think how my brother and I revered Mr. Walters, mistaking his banality for inherent genius.

My father was the centre of society for some little distance round the neighbourhood : the Coolstone works gave a substantial income in those days. It was a society which was not sure of itself and was consequently driven to take refuge behind a code of formality which insured safety. It was a difficult code for a beginner to learn, and mistakes were seldom forgiven. There were, of course, exceptions made if a person's income was found to be larger than first rumoured; but the Intelligence Department was accurate and knew its work. The code, when mastered, became second nature. I was never conscious (brought up as I was in the academy which formulated it) that I was using a code at all. But all my gestures, all I said, signalled that I was in league with those around me. Unconsciously I kept assuring them that I would say nothing serious, nothing which could surprise them into thought. I pledged myself to ask no questions which might be awkward to answer. I signed a treaty of complete acquiescence whose major clause bound me to accept everything in society at its surface value. And yet I had no knowledge of what I did, nor how far I had committed myself. This ignorance was the mutual safeguard of the circle. Anyone who questioned the conventions which were mutually accepted would have automatically disqualified himself from society. By taking thought he would have pricked his own bubble. I should like very much to know how a real, living, thinking person would have affected the circle; but the very act of thinking was incompatible with entry. It is as useless to wonder how air would mix with a vacuum.

Yet even these people must have been alive once. I should be most interested to know how the change came about; was it through fear of life, or a disgust of it? Was the process a slow petrification, or a sudden freezing? It is a thing impossible to discover. If I were to meet one of these people now and ask them the question which I should most like answered, what reply would they give? The sudden shock of such a question might force an answer; but I could not wait for it. I could not bear the reproach in their eyes; they would accuse me of being a traitor—one who had broken the treaty of acquiescence. And I should feel a certain amount of that moral discomfiture which is felt always, I think, when our own superiority shows itself in contrast to someone else; and yet we know it is not we, but mere chance, which has brought the superiority. In my case it was chance which released me from Coolstone Park, and at a time when I was still sensitive enough to get the rhythm of a new life. I shudder to think how near I was to becoming another Mr. Walters.

C. H. PEACOCK.

COMMENTS AND REVIEWS

ORDEAL BY VULGARITY

Many readers of *Scrutiny* who do not ordinarily see the *Daily Telegraph* have, no doubt, had Miss Rebecca West's now notorious fling of vulgar spite brought to their attention. 'Who *is* Rebecca West?' some of them will have asked. And it must be replied that, intrinsically insignificant as she is, the times are such that Mr. I. M. Parsons' very adequate ' placing ' of her in the *Spectator* was necessary. Jealous inferiority, however gross, snarling at un-ignorable and unsuppressible distinction, can now be taken as authority, and to have to take notice of it is an humiliation to which we are all exposed. It is, for instance, also necessary, per-haps, that we should repudiate all community between our attitude to Mr. Eliot and Miss West's. To criticize him as we have done is to acknowledge our enormous debt to him—a debt that we all in this age share, whether we will or not. If there is no Chinese Wall to keep out the barbarians that is certainly not his fault, but the fault (if one) of those of us who, capable of seeing the need, are not prepared to do our utmost in the building and the manning.

' CHUCK IT, SMITH ! '

This heading is not urbane. But it comes irresistibly as the appropriate comment on the genteel, belletristic futility of the essay by Mr. Logan Pearsall Smith that, announced as an ' outstanding feature,' filled most of the September *Life and Letters* and was puffed in two columns of the *New Statesman and Nation* by the Hon. Harold Nicolson. From Mr. Smith's elegant and prolix maunderings *On Reading Shakespeare* it is apparent that he, like most of the cultivated, is incapable of reading Shakespeare. It is the representative nature of his case that makes it worth con-sidering. What responsibility must be laid, positively, on education, and, negatively, on the virtual absence of even the beginnings of Shakespeare criticism, will be brought out by the reminder that Mr. Smith wrote that excellent little book *Words and Idioms,* and showed in it the kind of interest in language needed for the critical approach to Shakespeare : nothing but the author's name connects the two works.

In this essay on reading Shakespeare he has forgotten ' words and idioms.' As a result, he can tell us, without any perceptible embarrassment, that Scott ' was, at however great a distance, more like Shakespeare than any other writer '—in a sense a brave pronouncement, however you read it; the ambiguity cannot make the aplomb any less remarkable. Nor is the pronouncement made less remarkable by the concession that ' plays, unlike novels, demand close attention, a certain effort of the mind and of the imagination.' By dint, we must suppose, of such attention and such effort Mr. Smith arrives at the conclusion that '*Troilus and Cressida* . . . is, in spite of the splendid passages, a most unpleasant play.' There would be no point in quoting further : most of the ingredients of the essay had been more than ' twyes hoot and twyes cold ' before Mr. Smith set them simmering again, and it is interesting solely as evidence of what the cultivated public thinks it ought to get from Shakespeare—an easy sympathy with characters ' as real as life,' and a mild hypnosis induced by the ' magic ' of blank verse. Shakespeare is praised because he provides ' the illusion of reality,' because he creates characters ' independent of the work in which they appear. . . and when the curtain falls they go on living in our imaginations and remain as real to us as our familiar friends.'

For Mr. Smith it is all ' magic ' and ' miracle ' as it was already for the English mistresses in the best girls' schools who are now lending the treasured number to their most promising charges. Many essays will echo the intoxicated eloquence provoked in Mr. Smith by ' this draught of Shakespeare's brewing—the potent wine that came to fill at last the great jewelled cup of words he fashioned.'

But no one will find anywhere in Mr. Smith's essay any hint of the emotional and intellectual discipline that alone could justify the publication of yet more writing about Shakespeare.

The contemporary world needs no encouragement to suppose that Mr. Smith's kind of discourse represents an interest in literature; and it seems an occasion for those of us who care seriously for literature to dissociate ourselves, with some brutality if necessary, from those whose concern for Life and Letters means an elegant interest in *belles lettres*.

YE MERRIE BUSINESSE OF PEPPING UP YE CLASSICS.

Mr. Walpole's latest work, *The Waverley Pageant,* besides being an astute business proposition (' 350,000 words price 8/6d.,' ' not even the combined inventive power of H. G. Wells and Edgar Wallace can surpass that displayed in these amazing stories. . .') represents an attempt to revive not merely Scott's lost popularity but also his faded prestige by equipping him as far as possible to compete on an equal footing with modern best-sellers. The method, a selection of the so-called best passages arranged under such tempting headings as ' The Merrie Business of Writing Immortal Novels,' ' Heroes and Villains,' etc., is quite likely to make the book, as its publishers predict, ' a best-seller among best-sellers.' But Scott's reputation is no more likely to be improved by this new device of making him readable by magazine standards, than by the traditional practice of thrusting him in whole novels upon bored schoolchildren. If Scott is to survive not merely as a name in literary history or a rival to Edgar Wallace it will be because of certain qualities imperceptible in extracts, and primarily the quality, as far as possible eliminated by these extracts, that demonstrates Scott not to have been a contemporary of Kingsley or of Blackmore or of Mr. Walpole. Meanwhile the public Mr. Walpole has in mind will undoubtedly be won by the introductory information that Scott delighted in leg-pulling, was normal, healthy-minded, always half a boy, and above all a great gentleman. Mr. Walpole has in fact succeeded in recreating Scott in his own image; he would certainly not understand what is meant when we say that the good-fellow ticket was unknown in Scott's time.

It is Mr. Walpole's conception of the Novel, implicit in his selection and explicit in his introductions, that concerns us. He attributes the neglect of Scott to the fact that he did not choose to deal, like the modern idols, in ' unpleasantness ' and ' Ideas '; had he chosen, ' Mr. Joyce himself might have to bow the head.' After a great deal of this the essential function of the novelist is declared to be ' this hard business of creating a world for us, a world filled with people in whom we may believe. . . Among the creators in this kind Walter Scott is one of the greatest.' Useless to suggest to Mr. Walpole that nothing is easier than to ' create ' plausible characters; the Sunday newspapers every week praise brilliant first novels for doing it. Useless to assure him that no sensitive reader of Stendhal, Flaubert, Henry James, D. H. Lawrence, could accept Scott as a great novelist or even begin to discuss him as a serious writer; by his references to Proust and Joyce Mr. Walpole shows himself incapable of reading great novels with any profit. Useless also to tell Mr. Walpole that precisely what he admires in Scott, judging from his selections, is evidence for that: his ' best passages ' of Scott are mostly schoolboy heroic posturings—he has even included perhaps the worst example in this kind Scott ever wrote; and without the excuse of rescuing it from oblivion either, for the *Oxford Book of English Prose* had done that already (extract no. 326). And this deduction of Mr. Walpole's critical incompetence is confirmed by a volume of academic studies, *Sir Walter Scott To-Day* (edited by Prof. Grierson), where Mr. Walpole writing as an authority among authorities tells us how he has always cherished an admiration for *Lorna Doone* and other mushy historical novelettes.

The Waverley Pageant, besides suggesting an ominous precedent for publishers alive to the commercial possibilities of non-copyright classics, has a dedication (' For Virginia Woolf Who Does not Scorn Sir Walter ') which recalls and reinforces some painful impressions left by the Hogarth Letter Series. Mr. Walpole's *Letter to a Modern Novelist* in its unctuous heartiness and insolent complacency could arouse in the intelligent reader only one reaction : Who is Mr. Walpole to give advice to the young novelist, and what can the Hogarth Press be thinking of to take him by the hand? And that series generally suggests that Bloomsbury has anticipated Mr. Priestley's broadcast advice ' To a Highbrow ' to have a drink, be a man, and join the new order of broadbrows.

We should not care to have it thought that we have any personal feeling against Mr. Walpole. No. We do not grudge him the fruits of his labours : let him by all means have his commercial success, let him even have his ultimate knighthood (or baronetcy) for ' services to letters,' *but* for decency's sake let him keep his hands off Literature and let those whose duty is quite other refrain from abetting him.

D. H. LAWRENCE AND PROFESSOR IRVING BABBITT

THE LETTERS OF D. H. LAWRENCE. Edited and with an Introduction by Aldous Huxley (Heinemann, 21/-).

There are some writers a serious interest in whose work leads inevitably to a discussion of their personalities. Mr. Middleton Murry's offence lay not in supposing D. H. Lawrence's personality to be of the importance that justifies public discussion, but in discussing it as he did. In choosing to discuss Lawrence publicly he could have had no stronger endorsement than Mr. Eliot's, and to the importance of D. H. Lawrence there could, perhaps, be no stronger testimony than that Mr. Eliot applauded Mr. Murry's offence. And if, again, one is obliged to be more personal about Mr. Eliot than one would like, that is a testimony to *his* importance.

No one has (and had) dealt with Mr. Murry more appropriately than Mr. Eliot, and yet, of so highly characteristic a performance as *Son of Woman,* he could say (*The Criterion,* July, 1931): ' The victim and the sacrificial knife are perfectly adapted to each other.' However drastic the criticism that Lawrence, on the accessible evidence, might have seemed to deserve, he did not deserve that. And Mr. Eliot, though he could attest that ' Mr. Murry quotes with astonishing accuracy and justice,' had, by his own account, an imperfect acquaintance with the accessible evidence. The quotation of Mr. Murry's that he repeated, in order to endorse Mr. Murry's characteristic commentary, came from *Lady Chatterley's Lover,* ' one of the novels,' remarked Mr. Eliot, ' which I have not read '—the plea that *Lady Chatterley's Lover* was not accessible would, in more than one way, it is plain, not cover the case. Yet with a lack of caution very remarkable in Mr. Eliot he committed himself to a passionate moral condemnation of Lawrence. Of the passage that he knew only in Mr. Murry's context (a passage from a novel) he remarked: ' Such complacent egotism can come only from a very sick soul. . . .' He had already said of Lawrence's history that it was 'an appalling narrative of spiritual pride, nourished by

ignorance. . ,' and, to make the force of the condemnation quite
unmistakable, gone on : ' had he become a don at Cambridge his
ignorance might have had frightful consequences for himself and
for the world, " rotten and rotting others." ' Mr. Eliot should be
asking himself earnestly how he can make ' an amends ' more
adequate than the reference in *Thoughts After Lambeth* to
Lawrence along with Mr. James Joyce[1] as ' two extremely serious
and improving writers.'

The moral passion that overwhelmed the critic admits, perhaps, only of explanation, but for serious misunderstanding of
Lawrence there was every excuse. The novels and the other books
do in many ways—in their ' Old Moore's Almanacking,' as
Lawrence calls it (he had no humour, says Mr. Eliot), and their
intense and narrow preoccupation—suggest the fanatical eccentric.
And even the successful art (the judgment that Lawrence ' never
succeeded in making a work of art ' suggests that Mr. Eliot was
indeed content to take a great deal as read) is far from representing the man. Nevertheless, it should have been plain that
Lawrence had much more in common with Blake than with
Rousseau (the comparison that Mr. Eliot offered Mr. Murry).
In fact, Mr. Eliot might have found in an essay on Blake included
in a book called *The Sacred Wood* some admirably said things
that might have been said of Lawrence. At any rate, on the lowest
estimate of his importance, it should have been plain that Lawrence
was for *The Criterion* an opportunity and a test. How it actually
economized its obituary honours and distributed its generosity has
already been noted in *Scrutiny*.

For several years before the *Letters* came out one's sense
that Lawrence was greater than his writings had been steadily
growing, as the signs accumulated and understanding increased.

---

[1]How Lawrence would have taken this coupling is suggested by
the following (which is not necessarily fair as criticism) : ' I had a
copy of *Transition*, that Paris magazine—the Amer. number. My
God, what a clumsy *olla putrida* James Joyce is ! Nothing but old
fags and cabbage-stumps of quotations from the Bible and the rest,
stewed in the juice of deliberate, journalistic dirty-mindedness—
what old and hard-worked staleness, masquerading as the all-
new ! '

The *Letters* confirm that sense with a completeness that could not
have been anticipated, at any rate by those who did not know
him. The account of his history ' as a narrative of spiritual pride,
nourished by ignorance,' becomes ridiculous. It is true that from
the beginning he had a complete certitude of his genius: ' Tell
Arnold Bennett,' he writes in 1915, ' that all rules of construction
hold good only for novels which are copies of other novels. A
book which is not a copy of other books has its own construction,
and what he calls faults, he being an old imitator, I call characteristics. I shall repeat till I am grey—when they have as good
work to show, they may make their pronouncements *ex cathedra*.
Till then, let them learn decent respect.' And three years earlier
he had written: ' I think, do you know, that I have inside me
a sort of answer to the *want* of to-day: to the real, deep want of
the English people, not to just what they fancy they want.'
With such convictions we should expect to find some measure of
' complacent egotism.'

But of ' complacent egotism,' in eight hundred and fifty pages
of private correspondence, written, unquestionably, with no
thought but of the reader addressed, there is not the least sign,
and this remarkable fact should in itself suggest that the convictions were not altogether unjustified. And so far from appearing
' a very sick soul. . . totally incapable of intimacy,' Lawrence
shows himself normal, central and sane to the point of genius,
exquisitely but surely poised, and with a rare capacity for personal
relations. It is true that he writes to Mr. Middleton Murry: ' And
I very much dislike any attempt at intimacy like the one you
had with—— —— and others. When you start that, I only feel:
For God's sake let me get clear of him.' He also says: ' I'm sick
to death of people who are wrapped up in their own inner selves,
inner lives.' But such remarks, Mr. Eliot would agree, are not
evidence for his account of Lawrence. Lawrence, so far from being
the 'impossible' fanatic offered us, shows himself, under all kinds
of provocation, beautifully understanding, delicate and forbearing,
while never for a moment compromising his integrity. The intense
preoccupations of his novels, it is plain, express no narrowness in
the man, but rather a resolution to concentrate upon what seemed
to him the centre of the problem. But the problem was far from
being all of his life. ' They simply are,' he wrote, ' so eaten up

with caring. They are so busy caring about Fascism or Leagues
of Nations or whether France is right or whether Marriage is
threatened, that they never know where they are. They certainly
never live on the spot where they are.' Lawrence always lived
on the spot where he was. That was his genius.

Not that he was careless of the ' before and after.' His sense
of value, like his spiritual insight and his intelligence, was quick
and sure. The qualities that made him incapable of self-deception
made him the finest literary critic of his time. He had exquisite
spiritual manners, and was always grateful for help, but he
' placed ' Georgian poetry in 1913, and nothing could have
induced him to pretend that the Poetry Bookshop was an institution of European importance. We find him in 1913 giving Mr.
Edward Marsh, who found fault with his craftsmanhsip, Dr.
Richards's case (essentially that) against prosody, and remarking
to someone else that ' that *Golden Journey to Samarcand* only
took place on paper—no matter who went to Asia Minor.' And
how delicately he refuses to countenance Mr. Murry's estimate of
Katherine Mansfield! Arnold Bennett (' I hate his resignation ')
he calls ' a sort of pig in clover.' Mr. Wells—but one could extract
a small book of literary criticism from the *Letters*.

Lawrence, then, it turns out, offers a serious ' classicism ' a
severer test than could have been divined. ' What true education
should do— . . . ,' wrote Mr. Eliot, imagining the frightful
consequences of Lawrence's being a don at Cambridge, '—is
to develop a wise and large capacity for orthodoxy, to preserve
the individual from the solely centrifugal impulse of heresy, to
make him capable of judging for himself and at the same time
capable of judging and understanding the judgments of the
experience of the race.' That, in the abstract, is wisdom. But
much may happen between the abstract and the concrete. And
the degeneration, in practice, of such wisdom produces something
far more common in the academic world—an incomparably less
remote danger—than what Mr. Eliot fears in Lawrence : there is
a dry rot that anyone may find without much search, ' rotten and
rotting others.' A ' spiritual askesis,' ' a training of the emotions,'
tends very readily to get confused with something very different,
Professor Irving Babbitt's preoccupation with the ' inner check,'
and that is only a comparatively respectable form of something

that prevails in most institutions, academic and other. ' I only want to know people who have courage to live,' wrote Lawrence. And while he could say, ' More and more I admire the true classic dignity and responsibility,' he was moved to exclaim, ' This classiosity is bunkum, but still more cowardice.' Mr. Eliot once remarked how much better Bertrand Russell would have been for an education in the classics. Lawrence wrote in 1915 : ' What ails Russell is, in matter of life and emotion, the inexperience of youth. He is, vitally and emotionally, much too inexperienced in personal contact and conflict, for a man of his age and calibre. It isn't that life has been too much for him, but too little.' The difference in diagnosis is characteristic. The bent represented by Mr. Eliot's prescription, going with fear of Lawrence, would hardly tend to discourage ' classiosity.'

As Lawrence should have been a test, so now, as revealed in the *Letters* in something like his fulness, he offers us a test to apply. He was, as he says again and again, essentially religious. Mr. Eliot will point out the dangers of a religion that expresses itself in this way : ' What intimations of immortality have we, save our spontaneous wishes? God works in me (if I use the term God) as my desire.' But the notion that Lawrence was in any way Rousseauistic or romantic would not survive a reading of the *Letters*. ' Is there nothing beyond my fellow man? If not, then there is nothing beyond myself, beyond my throat, which may be cut, and my own purse, which may be slit; because *I* am the fellow-man of all the world, my neighbour is but myself in a mirror. So we toil in a circle of pure egoism.' Mr. Eliot himself never exposed Humanitarianism more effectively. And it is Lawrence's greatness that he convinces us of his actually believing in something ' beyond his fellow-men.' He alone cannot give us the religion for lack of which the human spirit withers, but the fact that he lived and was so is a highly valuable fact. And he helps those of us who, respecting intensely Mr. Eliot's mind and personality, have, though conscious of theological incapacity and lack of experience, attempted to follow his religious utterances, to define our attitude towards them.

Lawrence's preoccupation with sex was religious. Mr. Eliot's religious preoccupations involve an attitude towards sex. Writing on Lawrence in *La Nouvelle Revue Française* for May, 1927,

Mr. Eliot wrote: ' Quand ses personnages font l'amour . . . non seulement ils perdent toutes les aménités, raffinement et grâces que plusieurs siècles ont elaborés afin de rendre l'amour *supportable*,[1] mais ils semblent remonter le cours de l'évolution . . . jusqu'à quelque hideux accouplement de protoplasme.' Surely the rejection of Romantic Love, Love as the Absolute, does not necessarily lead one to *this?* We cannot help connecting the passage with such things as these in Mr. Eliot's introduction to *The Intimate Journals of Baudelaire,* and concluding that here too he speaks for himself: ' . . . the recognition of the reality of Sin is a New Life; and the possibility of damnation is itself so immense a relief in a world of electoral reform, plebiscites, sex reform and dress reform, that damnation itself is an immediate form of salvation—of salvation from the ennui of modern life, because it gives some significance to living ' . . . ' Having an imperfect, vague, romantic conception of Good, he was at least able to see that to conceive of the sexual act as evil is more dignified, less boring, than to think of it as the natural, " lifegiving," cheery automatism of the modern world. For Baudelaire, sexual operation is at least something not analogous to Kruschen salts.' Is this all there is to the dogma of Original Sin? Does belief in the supernatural depend on that sleight with the word ' natural '? Lawrence hated ' sex reform ' and ' cheery automatism ' at least as much as Mr. Eliot, but he did not turn against life, or find it necessary to run to damnation to escape ennui. ' I always labour at the same thing, to make the sex relation valid and precious, not shameful.'

All this is no doubt crude. It is not meant to suggest that Lawrence solved any problem for us, but to suggest why he, more than anyone else in our time, makes it possible to cherish some faith in the future of humanity. If the religious sense that he represents so magnificently cannot be generally recovered it is difficult to think with hope of the future forecast by Dr. Richards: ' Being, by hypothesis, able to become any kind of mind at will, the question, " What kind of mind shall I choose to be? " would turn into an experimental matter. . .' (*Practical Criticism,* p. 347). ' Thank God,' said Lawrence, ' I'm not free, any more

---

[1]*Not* Mr. Eliot's italics.

than a rooted tree is free.' While he said also, ' Unless from us the future takes place we are death only,' it was in the past that he was rooted. Indeed, in our time, when the gap in continuity is almost complete, he may be said to represent, concretely in his living person, the essential human tradition; to represent, in an age that has lost the sense of it, human normality, as only great genius could.

How different a phenomenon he is from the *Surréalisme* described in this number of *Scrutiny* by Monsieur Henri Fluchère does not need elaborating. Of that kind of revolt (however sincere) Lawrence says: ' they want to destroy every scrap of tradition and knowledge, which is silly.' This, again, is relevant: ' And yet affection and trust and even morality are not in themselves a swindle. One can't live without them.'

And those who, the plight of the world being what it is, are impatient of any preoccupation with other than economic issues, would do well to ponder this: ' Don't think of me as a raving, impractical, vain individual. *To be material at this juncture is hopeless, hopeless—or worse than impractical.'*

It remains to add that we are all heavily in Mr. Aldous Huxley's debt, and that the index, so necessary, is almost perfect.

F. R. LEAVIS.

A PROFESSIONAL ENEMY

THE DOOM OF YOUTH (Chatto and Windus, 10/6d.).

FILIBUSTERS IN BARBARY (Grayson, 12/6d.).

THE ENEMY OF THE STARS (Desmond Harmsworth, 10/6d.).

SNOOTY BARONET (Cassell, 7/6d.).

It is unfortunate that the first time one should be asked to write about Wyndham Lewis the occasion should be the publication of four books so much below the highest level of his achievement as these; for it means that, while adverse criticism will have the emphasis of immediacy, admiration will be tempered by retrospection. The common faults of three of them at least—*The*

Enemy of the Stars is a republication of one of his earliest works—
are a slapdash carelessness in the writing, too great a reliance upon
mere transcription of other people's views, and a proclivity to
follow, at the expense of the central argument or narrative, any
red herring that may cross his trail. In some measure these are
present in much of Lewis's work, but in the best noticeable only
as tendencies, to be passed over as the perhaps inevitable adjuncts
of a uniquely vigorous style and a mind more than usually well-
stored and enquiring. Here, however, since two of the books
are expressly designed for a wider public than his others have
enjoyed (see the Introduction to *Doom of Youth* and the dust-
jacket of *Filibusters*), one suspects Lewis of that contempt for
his readers which takes the form of refusal to exert himself.

And this immediately raises one of the most important
problems of contemporary culture : that of communication between
the intellectual advance-guard and the literate public. How is
a writer at one level of intelligence and culture to make contact
with an audience at a very much lower one? The Edwardian
solution (if we disregard that of the ' ivory tower ' which is after
all mainly an evasion) was to serve up a mixture of art and
edification, in which the jam was scarcely distinguishable from
the powder : the post-war answer has been to fall back upon the
glib classification of ' high-brow ' and ' low-brow.' But that
this side-stepping of the issue is unsatisfactory is clear from the
fact that the three men, Lawrence, Eliot and Lewis, who have
deservedly—though this is not at all to assign to them pre-
eminence as writers—become the literary ' leaders ' of to-day,
should all have felt the need of supporting their achievement
as artists with a background of social criticism. How satisfactory
their ideological structures have proved is another matter. Certainly Lawrence's attempt to build one is largely responsible for
his present unedifying apotheosis; Mr. Eliot's would seem to have
landed him temporarily in the backwater of Anglo-Catholicism;
and Mr. Lewis's we have now for a moment to consider.

It was Lewis's critical writings—*Tarr* received much less
recognition than it deserved—that announced his entrance into
the literary arena. Briefly they may be summed up as an attack
on the Bergsonian philosophy and the literature attributed to its
influence; an attack on pseudo-revolutionism; an attack on

liberalism and the resultant forms of democracy : and these three main lines were supported by a savage guerilla warfare on cliques, a number of individuals, and the mass-mind. The rotten state of Denmark was for him a matter, not for solitary brooding, but for savage invective and vigorous, if sometimes undiscriminating, criticism. Upon a scene that echoed with the gloomy *à quoi bon* of defeatism, a Waste Land where the despair of the inhabitants was too often a sentimental fashion, he arrived energetically and, what is more important, as fully equipped with the paraphernalia of modernism as anyone he attacked. It was the latter fact, combined with the pungency of his style, that gave his criticism its peculiar value. He was not condemning in the querulous tones of one to whom psycho-analysis and relativity are mere new-fangled bogeys, but in the robust voice of one who is authentically of his time. He cannot be brushed aside as an arm-chair critic : he is emphatically, and defiantly, post-war.

But unfortunately he has not been content for his activities to remain purely destructive—unfortunately because by his limitations (*e.g.* his unscrupulous use of evidence) as well as by his qualities, Lewis is admirably equipped as a destructive force; as, in fact, a professional Enemy. For such there is most certainly room; for one, that is, as he says in the *Doom of Youth,* ' taking Occidental disintegration for granted.' But the function of such an one should be, for its maximum effect, confined to commenting on, to directing, in a sense, and hastening that disintegration. It is no necessary part of his business to adumbrate more fully than by the implications of his criticism the future reintegration : and, indeed, any attempt to do so is simply to offer himself as a further object for destruction. It is the weakness of Lewis's case that he does not always forgo the temptation to do so; tentatively, in his criticism, by a somewhat platitudinous insistence on certain qualities; more overtly, in his satiric fictions, by the introduction and preferential treatment of characters embodying those qualities.

This tendency has been apparent in all his work, but its ill-effects are more readily noticeable in the books under review. He displays it blatantly when, in the *Doom of Youth,* he insists that he is writing ' from the stand-point of genius,' for by his insistence he emphasizes his central weakness—that he has two standards of judgment. His eye, so bitterly critical when it is turned upon the world at large, is blurred by a narcissistic film immediately it encounters the species *genius*. Yet just what he means by genius, what represents the positive principle in his desiderated scheme of things, Lewis has so far never adequately revealed; though Arghol—the protagonist in *The Enemy of the Stars*—is perhaps an attempt to do so. ' Men,' says this master-spirit, ' possess a repulsive deformity. It is generally referred to as " Myself." This is a disfiguring disease.' But though Arghol is thus expressing his creator's principal dilemma, the ' Not-self ' is a shadowy enough concept to put forward as the representative of human value.

Just how insubstantial, one discovers upon investigating Lewis's world of fiction, which is constantly disturbed by its introduction. Of this *Snooty Baronet* furnishes an example. At the outset, Snooty, who is narrating his own experiences, ' wishes to make clear at once that he occupies himself only with scientific research.' He compares his attitude towards his human specimens to that of Fabre towards his insects, claiming thereby for himself a disinterested extra-human view-point. That such a claim cannot, in point of fact, be substantiated goes, of course, without saying, but it may be entirely justifiable for the purposes of imaginative creation. But it will only be justified when—to continue the simile—the animal and insect worlds are kept distinct by the observer. There can be no substitution of the one set of values for the other. The imaginative reality of Lewis's scene, that is the point, depends entirely on the consistency of its unreality; directly an outsider is admitted who is unsusceptible to the laws which govern it, its validity is destroyed. But this mistake Lewis does not always avoid. Just as in his fiction he dulls the edge of the satire by playing off against his behaviourist puppets characters judged and approved by a human standard (Tarr and Pierpoint in his earlier novels, MacPhail in *Snooty Baronet*), so he detracts from the value of his criticism by a comparable confusion of values. When he does avoid the mistake—and there are several occasions in *Snooty Baronet* and *Filibusters*—he shows himself a master of brilliant and astringent comedy. But at such times his romantic hankering after the ' Not-self ' is forgotten; he is so completely absorbed into the scene, that his creatures act and live with his own abundant vitality.

DOUGLAS GARMAN.

DRYDEN REDIVIVUS

THE POETRY OF JOHN DRYDEN, by Mark Van Doren. Intro-
duction by Bonamy Dobrée (Gordon Fraser, The Minority Press,
Cambridge, 1931).

The re-issue of this book is well timed. When the first edition
appeared in 1920, and when Mr. Eliot wrote of it and of Dryden
in 1924, there seems to have been a narrower interest in Dryden
than now, to judge from defensive passages which then, no doubt,
were requisite enough. Mr. Van Doren argued that ' if there was
something fatuous about the opulence of the Augustans there is
something desperate about the simplicity of the moderns,' a plea
that has already dated, now that the later Georgian poets are
forsaking this simplicity for that opulence. Mr. Eliot in *Homage
to Dryden,* felt that ' for those who are genuinely insensible to
his genius (and these are probably the majority of living readers
of poetry)' there were perceptions lacking, a deficiency chiefly to be
ascribed to nineteenth century tradition. But during the last eight
years some advance at least seems to have been made towards
conditions in which Dryden is more acceptable and Mr. Eliot's
majority reducible. It is symptomatic that Mr. Davenport should
have expressed the drollery:

> Eliot, Rabelais, Dryden, Donne,
> Bless the bed that I lie on,

and though we might naturally expect to find, as we do, references
to Dryden in Mr. Richards' *Principles of Literary Criticism,* a
slightly earlier theorist might well have ignored him. Moreover,
when we see Mr. Richards alluding to his aesthetic system as
' this machine,' and recollect Dryden's insistence that *pictura* and
poesis shall have rules, we may detect a deeper sympathy between
the two ages. Practice assists us; for not only does Miss Sitwell
borrow from *Annus Mirabilis* ' in eastern quarries ripening precious
dew ' (a line not so grateful to Mr. Van Doren), but she uses
effectively the pauseless line with ' the quality of momentous
directness ' which Dryden, as Mr. Van Doren tells us, developed
from Cleveland. A younger poet, Mr. Julian Bell, has more
recently presumed ' with Dryden's couplet to engage the wild

philosophers '; but others also have returned to the heroic couplet: from Edgell Rickword to Jack Lindsay the changes are rung, some, it is true, in the mode of Pope; though Drydenic cadences can clearly be heard. The revival of Pope was staged in a more popular manner by Lytton Strachey and Miss Sitwell. No such ovation has yet been vouchsafed to Dryden; yet through our poets, and our more professionally academic critics, his credit is slowly rising—a gradual process the origin of which is remoter than immediately appears. In the nineteenth century Sir Edmund Gosse took Dryden's part with greater vigour but less minute scholarship than Mr. Van Doren has in the twentieth; while to Porfessors Ker and Verrall must be attributed much of the valuable and unobtrusive work which was accumulating beneath the surface poetic movements of ' simple bird song,' tree-and-nature-worship, and what not, against the eventual return to our etiolated aesthetic of a fresh conception of Dryden's magnificence and intellectual fire. During the last three years books on Dryden, as the catalogues bear witness, have multiplied, and may argue an increase both in the authors and readers so interested. Yet it is improbable that such a public is large or that Dryden will in our time appeal to more than the whole small educated class of this country; but that he should appeal to the whole would be much.

There is still ample room for Dryden literature; it was a happy thought to reprint Mr. Van Doren's book in England, where no other analysis, so full and well reasoned, is available. Yet misgivings, lulled in the lap of erudition, may occasionally arise when the writer's opinions are expressed; and statements which may be challenged do occur, this for example: ' no poet has talked at greater length about the passions, or about sublimity. Yet no great poet has managed to acquire a firmer reputation as a bungler in these departments.' The pith of the matter is surely that Dryden's Sublime was different from and less encumbered than ours; a simple grandeur, uncomplicated by Salvatoresque gloom, the darkness considered in Burke's essay, the wildness constructed by Macpherson on an Aristotelian basis, and other Baroque expansions that lie between us and the heroic dramas. Mr. Eliot who, I may venture, has an understanding of Dryden even more sympathetic than Mr. Van Doren's, warns us not to expect suggestiveness in Dryden's words; extend this *caveat* to his idea of the

Sublime, and it may occur to us that Dryden was not after
' suggestiveness ' at all, but after unshaded delineation, to which
colour, and not chiaroscuro, remains *lena sororis*. Those who
agree to this may also agree that some of Mr. Van Doren's ' False
Lights ' are incorrectly alleged to be false; not through a misconception, but through a diffidence about looking, for the nonce,
through neo-classic glasses. One cannot help noticing examples of
this hesitancy; indeed, the general tone of the book seems to be
not unlike that of a counsel for the defence who feels it his duty
to do his best for his client (and a most brilliant and learned best
it is), but feels little personal enthusiasm for his case, even though
he may not be actually sensible of his sympathy with the prosecution. ' His exterior too often glitters and leaves us cold '; ' he is
not a prober among mysteries; he is not exquisite ' : these and other
remarks suggest an under-current of nostalgia for the poetry whose
function is to ' warm ' and be mysterious,—but may not some
kinds of art be valued for successfully glittering, and leaving us
cold, which is their specific function? Nor does it again appear
to be by chance that Dryden's Fresnoyan theory of a generalised
and re-organised Nature should come up for discussion under the
' False Lights ' heading. While the nostalgic motive seems to speak
for itself, we may perhaps also assume another; one of caution,
prompted by the suspicion that unless Dryden is presented with
due concessions to the taste of an age not yet fully recovered from
the pseudo-Wordsworthianism of the early twentieth century, he
will not be welcomed at all. Since the first appearance of the book
the grounds for this fear, if it ever caused the author uneasiness,
have, I fully believe, lessened considerably.

SHERARD VINES.

*NEWS FROM THE MOUNTAIN, by Richard Church (Dent,
3/6d.).*

If the end of literary criticism be understanding, and its
method classification, the analysis of any piece of writing must
be in some degree useful; while that of productions which have
much of the aspect, but none of the essence, of literature cannot
fail to be of profit, if only as a personal discipline, tending to
make one's appreciation of accepted works more intense because

more conscious, and less indolently snobbish. Mr. Richard Church has provided some excellent material for an exercise of the second kind. *News from the Mountain* is one of the best examples of what might be called ' near-beer ' poetry that I have encountered.

Lack of space precludes any attempt here at an exhaustive investigation into the characteristics of Mr. Church's bogusness, but a pretty fair indication of them may be given by means of a few concrete examples. Let us take, to begin with, the eponymous item of this collection. The big news from the summit of this rather tiresomely symbolical eminence is that the author has come through various levels of experience to a state of contemplative impassibility, tinged with a slightly incongruous hysteria :—

Cruel as stars,
And passionless as moonlight, I look down
Upon the waves of that mercurial sea
Which lies in lazy grandeur on human earth,
Where all I was, and ever might be, sleeps,
Sleeps on beneath the drug of material air.
Now without mercy, I wake to solitude,
Lift up the silver trumpet of my madness
And blow defiance over the huddled world.

The earlier stages of the spiritual pilgrimage narrated in this poem are represented by the plains, the foothills, the coniferous belt, and the snow-line.

As a specimen of Mr. Church's middle style (his ' lighter ' efforts, as readers of his contributions to *Whips and Scorpions* may remember, are really too embarrassing) I have chosen a piece called ' Latter-day Euridice.' The poet has just taken leave of his beloved at, say, Tottenham Court Road Tube station : he watches her ' vanish down the escalator ' : he reflects :—

Who, in that mad, electric universe
Could think two lovers parted thus, their hearts
Aching with faith and the deep burden of joy?
But such were you and I, by circumstance
Doomed for some days to go our separate paths .   .   .

Ah! as motionless you vanish into hell,
Into the bright electric hell of underground
Where stood the slot-machines for sentinels
With lips of brass, ...
. . . . Farewell,
Modern Euridice! . . . .

As verse it would pass for a tolerable parody of Tennyson's
style in ' The Princess '—' And here we lit on Aunt Elizabeth.'
As a conception, as a fancy, it might well have been found jotted
down for future use in the commonplace book of any industrious
but not very inventive novelist. But, to a person who can enjoy
poetry, novelists often resemble a toastmaster reading aloud,
perhaps with admirable fluency and correctness of pronunciation,
from a book in a foreign language he cannot understand. Mr.
Church is like that. He seems never to have mastered intellectually
and spiritually the situations he depicts. Hence, even where verbal
clichés do not extrude, emotional platitudes still oppress. Readers
of *Scrutiny* who feel inclined to try the method of *Practical
Criticism* on their less sophisticated friends, might well make use
of *News from the Mountain* for that purpose.

GILBERT ARMITAGE.

PROLETARIAN CRITICISM

ZOLA, by Henri Barbusse (Dent, 10/6d.).

A distinction is necessary : when Barbusse is recreating the
life and times of Zola he is, in spite of a gratuitously irritating
technique, comparatively rational; it is only when, in the final
chapters, he discusses the general issues raised by Naturalism and
the Novel that he becomes preposterous. It is unfortunate that
even French communist eloquence when translated into English
should read like Marie Corelli in full cry, nor is this the fault of
the translators, since Barbusse's denunciation of modern ' bourgeois ' literature appears as purely emotive as her attacks on
Edwardian high-life. It is unfortunate too that a member of the
Clarté group should be unable to express himself in a general
way otherwise than in a frenzy of confused ejaculations. What
finally emerges from the trapeze exhibition (a dizzy flight from
assumption to assumption) that he calls ' logical perspectives ' is

an appeal to ' elaborate a solid and victorious proletarian literature which will set the red flag flying.' This is to be the culmination
of an evolutionary process by which the Novel has been moving
from the contemptible efforts of Stendhal in ' the confused realm
of Romanticism ' to Zola's ' partial scientific realism ' and will
be crowned with success if the novelist will but realise that only
' the law of the division of labour ' separates the artist from the
social campaigner and so abandon his ' fictitious element ' for
scientifically based propaganda. (M. Barbusse's style is infectious).

But what of the system of values by which Stendhal's work
is felt to be exquisitely valuable artistry and Zola's only clumsy
and now unreadable journalism? What are to be the values of
this victorious proletarian literature? Perhaps the standards of
proletarian criticism are most seizable in the judgment Barbusse
passes on the author of *War and Peace*: ' a very great writer
unfortunately sterilized by the mean crust of decrepit superstitious
adorations with which he encased his great heart.' After this he
assures us : ' My position here is solely that of literature, of the man
of letters. I am not making an artistic creed depend on a political
creed.' Well, well. Observing how sedulously our English Barbusses
push their claims to Lawrence as a proletarian artist—Lawrence
who so freely expressed his loathing of democracy and the
masses—one wondered why such a doubtful claim was not abandoned in favour of Bunyan, *Pilgrim's Progress* being the only
work of art in the language that results from a genuine popular
culture; one had of course overlooked the fact that Bunyan was
sterilized by a mean crust of decrepit superstitious adorations.

Q. D. LEAVIS.

---

*THE COMMON READER : SECOND SERIES, by Virginia
Woolf (Hogarth Press, 10/6d.).*

If of a critic we expect an adequate response to contemporary
writing and in his work on the past a constant reference forward
to the present, *The Common Reader : First Series* was a contribution to criticism and the *Second Series* is not. Mrs. Woolf's interest
in the past is not as helpful as it might be; an interest in amiable
eccentrics has become almost exclusive, and even Donne is
approached from this angle. The treatment accorded to him is

symptomatic : the verdict (from a highly respectful essay on Meredith) runs ' he will be read, one may guess, by fits and starts; he
will be forgotten and discovered and again discovered and forgotten
like Donne, and Peacock, and Gerard Hopkins.' There is nothing
here to give a sense of direction to a reader floundering in the annual
fourteen thousand book spate; a strenuous interest in modern
literature, one would have thought, could hardly have produced so
mild and incomplete a statement as ' It may be doubted if the
Bedfords and the Drurys and the Herberts were worse influences
than the libraries and newspaper proprietors who fill the office of
patron nowadays ' (*Donne after Three Centuries*).

Something seems to have happened to the author of *How it
Strikes a Contemporary* and the publisher of *Hunting the Highbrow*.
Perhaps it has become too unpleasant to be hunted; perhaps Mrs.
Woolf really does concur with the Common Reader whose sanction
she seeks—the wrapper unplausibly insists on ' unprofessional critic.'
And a revised account of that Common Reader is overdue. Is he
the religious book-of-the-week soaker? Or the man who Does as
He Likes? For what would Arnold have said to this : ' The only
advice, indeed, that one person can give another about reading
is to take no advice, to follow your own instincts, to use your own
reason, to come to your own conclusions.' This advice was given
to a school. As it embodies a heresy noisily preached by popular
authors with interests vested in giving the public what it wants
in absence of standards and authority, it comes strangely from
the critic who earlier deplored the want of ' a rule, a discipline,
which controlled the great republic of readers in a way which
is now unknown.'

This collection does not help the Common Reader to discriminate. But there are several good essays, on Sterne, George
Gissing and De Quincey; and that on Hardy's Novels is especially
welcome in the dearth of good criticism of this author. Many of
these essays are the product of misplaced creative talent, but Mrs.
Woolf does not attempt to write a novel about Hardy. Innocence,
not malice, is the reason for her critical misdirections; which are
thus more sinister, more dangerous, for the profiteers from the
Gre-eat Tradition of Ye English Novel acquire a valuable, because
disinterested, ally. Mrs. Woolf's interest in Scott is not on the
same footing as that of his centenary advertisers.

DENYS THOMPSON.

'LORD, WHAT WOULD THEY SAY . . . ?'

*VISIONS OF THE DAUGHTERS OF ALBION, by William
Blake. Full-colour facsimile (Dent, 15/-).*

The police, it is said, when Lawrence's paintings were being
seized, asked also for a warrant against one William Blake, a
fellow-exhibitor and -offender. And, though Blake died a hundred
years ago, it does strike one with fresh surprise, every time
one opens his works, that he should be prescribed by dons for
undergraduate study. For he is as lethal as Lawrence to the
smoke-room story—a terrifying cleanser; and to be so is, where
Restoration Comedy is applauded on the modern stage by conservative moralists of both sexes, the unforgivable immorality.
Nothing could bring home more strongly that the accepted classics,
though perused, are rarely read. Decorous scholars, maiden ladies
and Garden Suburb uplifters pore over the Prophetic Books to
piece together the meaning—

> Lord, what would they say
> Should their Catullus walk that way?

Their approach, of course, preserves Blake's meaning from
ever being surprised by them. And we may be sure that, if
academic studies survive fifty years hence, Lawrence will suffer
the same mummifying consecration. The meaning of the *Visions
of the Daughters of Albion,* the most lucid of the prophecies, is
plain enough—too explicit, in places, for quotation; this negative
formulation, from *A Song of Liberty,* comes as close as
will serve: 'Let the Priests of the Raven of Dawn no
longer, in deadly black, with hoarse note curse the sons of joy. . .
Nor pale religious letchery call that virginity that wishes but acts
not!' Yet even in the *Visions,* where there is so much poetry, one
sees what Lawrence meant by saying: 'Blake, too, was one of
those ghastly, obscene *knowers.*' Blake's inadequate art ('bad
art') betrays him to Urizen, who has a predominant hand in
the prophecies. That is, the analysis gets lost among abstractions,
and Blake, ultimately, among words. The grip and coherence of
Lawrence's most 'prophetic' work comes out in the contrast:
even *Women in Love* no longer looks like mere disaster. The

novel, one realizes, offered Lawrence far more appropriate methods for this kind of exploration than any Blake could hit on. But if Lawrence in this respect was favoured by the age one must not inadvertently appear to slight his superior genius: Lawrence was much the greater of the two.

Messrs. Dent, in these facsimile reproductions, are doing a great service. The colours, so far as one can judge without seeing the originals for comparison, are good. The enterprise deserves support.

F. R. LEAVIS.

MUSIC IN LONDON 1890-94, by Bernard Shaw (Constable, 3 Vols. 6/- each).

The future musical historian will be grateful to Mr. Shaw for leaving him such a complete and entertaining picture of a very important period in the history of English taste, and for once the reader of the present can agree with the historian in finding these volumes useful and interesting. For the first impression of a musician in reading these reviews of forty years ago can scarcely fail to be one of satisfaction. Dissatisfaction with present conditions will give place for a time to gratitude for what has been accomplished since that day. Music has won a position in the cultural life of the critical few that it did not enjoy in the nineteenth century.

The England of Shaw's reviews was still very much under the domination of heavy and pretentious German masters. The Latin genius had not yet managed to throw off the stiff rhythm of the classical harmonists, and the English cared too little for music to try to think for themselves. They went on pretending to be edified by lifeless imitations of Mendelssohn and Gounod, and Wagner was still something of a revolutionist to most of them, though he had been dead twenty years.

A change, however, was beginning, and Shaw was admirably fitted to help in forming a more intelligent public. To natural good taste in music he added a critical understanding and appreciation of the other arts; and this was just what music most needed at a time when it was a prey to suburban young ladies and professionals of little general culture. He indicates quite clearly his own limitations. History only interests him when it has a direct bearing on the present: he tells us that he always begins a history of music at the end and works slowly to the front. Nor does purely technical analysis interest him: ' It is perhaps natural that gentlemen who are incapable of criticism should fall back on parsing; but for my own part, I find it better to hold my tongue when I have nothing to say.' These limitations are assets, for they allow the free expression of sensibility unclouded by academic irrelevancies.

If Shaw had a blind spot, it was Brahms, though one is glad that he was never taken in by the Requiem and that he ' never could stand Brahms when he was serious.' Of course there is a good deal of Wagnerian propaganda in the perfect Wagnerite's reviews, but that does not prevent him from perceiving 'that Wagner was the end of the nineteenth-century, or Beethoven, school, instead of the beginning of the twentieth-century school; just as Mozart's most perfect music is the last word of the eighteenth century, and not the first word of the nineteenth.' On the other hand, ' Bach belongs, not to the past, but to the future—perhaps the near future.'

This clear perception of where advance would be made and with what inspiration the coming generation would be fed enabled Shaw to see the shallowness of many of the tricks of modernity. ' The rule for making music sound modern. . . is to write ordinary diatonic harmonies, and then go over with a pen and cross the t's as it were, by sharpening the fifths in the common chords.' It also enabled him to assess the true value of the new English school, whose appearance is the most significant fact of this period. He praised the 'absolute music' of Parry and Stanford ,but ridiculed their dull oratorios. Above all, he saw that their chief lack was good criticism. ' If you doubt that Eden is a masterpiece, ask Dr. Parry and Dr. Mackenzie, and they will applaud it to the skies. Surely Dr. Mackenzie's opinion is conclusive; for is he not the composer of Veni Creator, guaranteed as excellent music by Professor Stanford and Dr. Parry? You want to know who Dr. Parry is? Why the composer of Blest Pair of Sirens, as to whose merits you have only to consult Dr. Mackenzie and Professor Stanford.' Music is not the only art that suffers in this way, and it is well to have a critic as incorruptible as Shaw, and one whose sensibility so sturdily insists that ' there is nothing a genuine musician regards with more jealousy than an attempt to pass off the forms of music for music itself.'

BRUCE PATTISON.

READING ABOUT ART

AN INTRODUCTION TO THE LANGUAGE OF PAINTING AND DRAWING, by Arthur Pope : Vol. I, 1929; Vol. II, 1931 (Harvard University Press—Oxford, Humphrey Milford, 13/6d. each).

PRINCIPLES OF ART HISTORY, by Heïnrich Wölfflin (Bell, 16/-).

THE SUBSTANCE OF ARCHITECTURE, by A. S. G. Butler (Constable, 7/6d.).

The preface to Mr. Pope's series, An Introduction to the Language of Painting and Drawing, is a clear presentation of an important duty of the art critic. He aims, he says, to give a detailed analysis of the representational possibilities of painting and drawing, a ' rhetoric ' of these arts. It is to be of service to the layman, who since the nineteenth century has been the chief patron, and to the artist. Since the decay of the apprentice system of study (which coincides with the rise of popular patronage) the young artist has not been able to acquire that technical information which used to be his heritage from the master under whom he worked. The information was not as complete as that Mr. Pope supplies, but it was all that was necessary to do work in the prevailing artistic tradition. Since, however, there is to-day no tradition the partiality of the knowledge given by ' academies ' cannot be excused. This condition Mr. Pope hopes to remedy. His final remark is that a ' rational eclecticism ' is the inevitable course of modern art. This opinion one may accept or not, but denying it does not make understanding of the possibilities of art any less necessary—for artist, critic, or amateur.

The first volume of the series discusses colour, or more technically, tonal relations. The relations of colour are represented by a three-dimensional mathematical figure, which although a hard task to understand is a tremendous help in perceiving qualities and differences of paintings. The volume concludes with a short chapter on the palettes used by various schools and the sort of colour harmony which they employed. The second book takes up the different modes of drawing and painting, as for instance the possibilities of line, illustrated by Chinese, Renaissance and modern examples. The book is short and clear. Yet to appear are the third and fourth volumes, which will analyse design and the actual processes of drawing and painting.

Herr Wölfflin's *Principles of Art History* is a book which was published in German in 1915, and since then its ideas have found their way into most schools where art history is taken seriously. To the student it will sound familiar; for others it should be the best introduction to the problems of the history of style. The differences between western European art of the sixteenth century—architecture, painting, and sculpture—and that of the seveneenth century (the Baroque) are exhaustively analysed. Differences of race and individual personality are also brought out but are kept subordinate to the two larger categories. Herr Wölfflin does not attempt to estimate the worth of one period over the other but rather to show that such an attempt is impossible since the two are completely integrated and self-sufficient styles, each in itself. Further, the Baroque cannot be considered as a mere decay of classicism. Although growing out of classicism inevitably, it was at its height a homogeneous attitude. ' It is comprehensible that the conception of a unity of parts whose independence has been swamped in the total effect [the Baroque] could only succeed the system with independently developed parts [the sixteenth century classic], that to play with the hidden adherence to rule presupposes the stage of obvious adherence to rule.' The Quattrocento was a period of experiment, unsure of its ultimate intentions, bound by plane-composition and struggling to get free, while the artists of the sixteenth century knew that they wanted to compose in planes and hence used the discoveries of the previous century—for example, foreshortening and perspective—to strengthen their effects.

The greater part of the book is taken up with the analysis and comparison of the two great styles, by means of five opposing pairs of concepts. The method yields in the main convincing results. The analysis of Baroque art, however, tends in places to be vague and impressionistic, more than the treatment of the classic. One chapter contrasts the ' clearness ' of classic art with the ' unclearness ' of Baroque. That classic forms are clearly defined is incontestable, but to suppose that the Baroque was fundamentally interested in the half-seen and unclear for itself seems a misinterpretation; rather their interest in movement leads them to stress part of a form and suppress the rest as an inevitable technical device. Similarly there is throughout too much emphasis on the ' apparently adventitious ' in the Baroque; most examples of this can also be shown to be a device for producing the subtle movement which was most desired. The suggestion of movement and illimitable space as opposed to repose and limited space is the essential contrast, and this contrast is sometimes obscured by Herr Wölfflin's concern with secondary matters.

The discussion of the part played by colour is highly unsatisfactory, because vague. For a clear understanding it is always necessary to supply the more detailed analyses of Mr. Pope. It is the duty of the art critic first to speak as explicitly as possible of explicit things in a work of art—tone relations, design, use of line, and so forth; then if necessary he may make impressionistic generalizations. Thus the statement (as specific as Herr Wölfflin becomes about colour) : ' Uniform clearness of colour is replaced by partial clearness of colour. Colour is not there from the outset, finished at all points : it becomes.'—That is vague and inefficient; without precise explanation and illustration it is liable to be misleading.

The book also considers other developments from a classic to a Baroque style, such as occurred in French sculpture between the twelfth and fifteenth centuries. These are homonymous developments, similar in outline, but with different starting points and aims. The conclusion to be drawn by the historian of style is that ' the development—will only fulfil itself where the forms have passed from hand to hand long enough or, better expressed, where the imagination has occupied itself with form actively enough to make it yield up its Baroque possibilities.'

Mr. Pope's series of volumes, as an introduction to clear

seeing, and Herr Wölfflin's presentation of the problems of the history of style are important books. One can only indicate their contents and hope that readers may be lured.

It is doubtful if anyone would read far enough in Mr. Butler's *The Substance of Architecture* to justify a discussion of its fallacies and ambiguities. Obviously Mr. Butler's intentions were honest. but one objects to the results. To quote two sentences at random is enough : ' Beauty is æsthetic value in the appearance of objects. Though assumed to be subjective, the æsthetic value is due to a particular quality in the appearance of things which have always been considered beautiful.'

DONALD CULVER.

THE SALUTATION, by Sylvia Townsend Warner (Chatto and Windus, 7/6d.).

In *Lolly Willowes* this author's slender talent for handling the *conte* of David Garnett with persuasive *chic* produced a certain success, compromised only by the writer's occasional uncertainty as to the precise degree of seriousness to which she was committed. In this new volume of short stories she engages more earnestly, but on experiments where her special qualifications are useless. The sophisticated playfulness that gave distinction to *Lolly Willowes* is ineffective when Defoe and T. F. Powys, who rely on personal modes of feeling, are the models. Now the naïve expression of genuine feeling is not in Miss Warner's bag of literary tricks. So that in these stories, though each is based on a clever enough idea and worked out carefully to pattern, the sensitive reader finds only a sterile exercise, lacking the genuine poignancy always present in T. F. Powys even when, at his worst, he appears to be merely using a formula himself. Miss Warner, and this is true of the class of writer to which she belongs, is ineffective in proportion to her pretentions. This is shown by the title-story: it is pseudo-sensitive, the undertaking demanding a far deeper kind of sensibility than Miss Warner possesses. This is of course to apply serious standards; it hardly needs saying that *The Salutation* is far above circulating library level.

Q.D.L.

AN AMERICAN LEAD

THE EXPERIMENTAL COLLEGE, by Alexander Meiklejohn (Harper, $3).

It is to be feared that Dr. Meiklejohn's book will receive less attention in England than Dr. Flexner's (reviewed in the first number of *Scrutiny* by Dr. Willard Thorp). *Universities, American, English and German* offered rich nourishment to English complacency, and the critical comments on English universities, as, for instance, on the contrast between the Faculty System in intention (the Royal Commission's) and in effect, were put with a modest uninsistence that made it possible to ignore them. *The Experimental College,* on the other hand, should make the English reader blush. Can one imagine in any English university the kind of experiment sanctioned by the ' Faculty of Letters and Science in the University of Wisconsin,' and recorded by Dr. Meiklejohn? We are apt to forget, in groaning over the effects of the Harvard tradition in ' English ' as reported by admirers and sufferers, and chuckling over the Business Courses, the degrees in Short-story Writing and the dissertations on Dish-Washing so frankly exhibited by Dr. Flexner, that the American academic world is also distinguished from the British by a readiness and a capacity, in places, to examine fundamentals and attempt the most arduous and uncomfortable re-orientations: ' At very considerable cost in distraction and strain, the Advisers at least have been going through a lively process of liberal education,' says Dr. Meiklejohn characteristically.

The ' Advisers,' or directors of the experiment, asked themselves, not as a matter of theory that might be left comfortably in the abstract, but with the concrete problems of application immediately in view: what should be the aim of education at the university phase (which, they insist, must be considered in its place in the whole process)? Their short answer is, ' Intelligence.' The admirable way in which Dr. Meiklejohn expands and interprets the term by reference to ' the power of self-direction in the affairs of life,' understanding of the contemporary world and active appreciation of the ' human values ' cannot be done justice to in this short review. Indeed, the book came to hand too late to be adequately dealt with in this number; and yet it seems

too valuable, and too immediately relevant to the aims of *Scrutiny,*
to be put aside till next quarter. So the reader is recommended,
in the strongest terms, to correct by reading it the injustice it
inevitably suffers here.

The great service that *The Experimental College* performs is
not more a matter of sound conclusions established than of
criticism invited. It may seem ungracious, but it is really a compliment, to insist on the latter in this review. To come back, then,
to the term ' intelligence ': Dr. Meiklejohn would agree that the
force of it for the critic depends less on definitions and eluci-
dations than on the concrete interpretation that it receives in
practice. It must be said, then, that the conception of ' intelligence,' and consequently of ' education,' exhibited in *The
Experimental College* is inadequate. There is no room here to
state fairly how the plan of making the undergraduate in his first
two years study and contrast the two civilizations, Athenian and
American, actually developed. The fundamental misconception
that remained, apparently, unperceived, peeps from behind these
questions, proposed to the student without any hint of the
real nature of the problem that they cover (pp. 78-9) : ' How much
do you think you lost of the Greeks and the Elizabethans by the
fact that their writings are inevitably reflections of a way of life
different in many respects from ours? How much of your interest
and pleasure was derived from the characters and ideas represented? How much from the beauty and power of the ordering
and writing? How clearly can you distinguish those two kinds
of satisfaction? ' etc. But the students, it appears, are assumed
for the most part not to know Greek. (And even if they did——.)
The crudeness of the notion of ' reading ' (' We have two years
in which to train young men in the art of reading for intelligence ')
implied here has correlates more immediately disconcerting in such
things as this: ' When the freshmen were reading the Greek
dramas we urged them to read also Ibsen and O'Neill. . . .'
(p. 55). We cannot get out of relating this to the following entry
in Appendix IV (p. 385), under *Talks for the Period*: ' Tuesday,
February 10th, " A New ' House of Atreus,' " Mr. B.' What
kind of ' An Approach to Poetry ' can have been illustrated a
week earlier by the same Mr. B., and what kind of education in
reading can have been provided by Advisers who could innocently

accept the *Mourning Becomes Electra,* or anything else of Eugene O'Neill?

The reviewer will, perhaps, be pardoned if he refers back to what he wrote under the title of *The Literary Mind* in the first number of *Scrutiny;* what can be said here must be manifestly and frankly inadequate. There is room for little more than the bare insistence that the training of intelligence towards which Dr. Meiklejohn points without realizing it (' a well-trained intelligence is not primarily a set of remembered formulas, but a kind of intellectual sensitiveness, an ability to use one's eyes when a situation is presented, to use one's ears when it is described, to use one's mind when its nature or its interests are to be considered. . . ')—that this training of intelligence must be at the same time a training of sensibility. It is not merely that without an ability to read literature (that is, to see that Eugene O'Neill doesn't exist), and without a sense of the human tradition such as cannot be acquired apart from an education in literature, one cannot acquire the sense of ' human values ' desiderated. It is that, if one cannot see that it is impossible to read Aeschylus (in English or Greek) as one reads Shakespeare, then one cannot read Shakespeare in any serious sense; and if one cannot read Shakespeare, then one cannot think (with the kind of ' thinking,' at least, that I am sure Dr. Meiklejohn, if it were put to him, would agree to be implied in his undertaking).

The training of sensibility indicated gives that capacity for testing and controlling abstractions for lack of which so much apparently rigorous thinking produces nothing more than cerebral corrugations. Let Dr. Meiklejohn look, for instance, at the review of Professor Irving Babbitt that fills twenty-four pages in the *Hound and Horn* for October-December, 1932, and reflect on the waste (and worse, probably, if one considers Professor Babbitt's ' thirty years of influence ') represented both by the reviewer and his subject. All that energy, that earnestness, and that cerebration, and nothing at the end where it wasn't to begin with! Cannot Dr. Meiklejohn see the connection between this futility of abstractions and verbalisms and Professor Babbitt's admitted lack of interest in contemporary literature (that is, in any)?

The true tribute to Dr. Meiklejohn and his colleagues would be to suggest how the spirit, and, to a great extent, the technique, of the Experimental College, might be applied in a real training of intelligence, a real education, which should start from, and be always closely associated with, the training of sensibility in the literature of the student's own language (where alone it is possible). But this must wait till the next number of *Scrutiny*.

F. R. LEAVIS.

RESOLUTE OPTIMISM, PROFESSIONAL AND PROFESSORIAL

LEISURE IN THE MODERN WORLD, by C. Delisle Burns (Allen and Unwin, 8/6d.).

SUCCESSFUL LIVING IN THIS MACHINE AGE, by Edward A. Filene (Cape, 7/6d.).

The second book, by a successful American business-man (who is introduced and endorsed by Sir Francis Goodenough, C.B.E.), is to be recommended for study as an extremely efficient exposition of the philosophy that ' the greatest total profits can be obtained only if the masses can and do enjoy a higher and ever higher standard of living.' One admires the conviction that puts it forth in the year 1932. And hunger-marchers, in America and England, might be impatient with Mr. Filene if he tried to explain to them what had gone wrong. Yet there is probably a good deal to be said for Mr. Filene's book as a forecast of the future, and 'standard of living,' to do him justice, appears to be a more radical concept for him than ' profit.' Capitalism, in him, points unwittingly forward to a kind of communism: the reader will, perhaps, pray to be delivered from that kind.

Mr. Filene's book is a more respectable thing than that of Mr. Delisle Burns, who is without convictions, courage or excuse. He also points—also unwittingly—to the same kind of future as Mr. Filene. He is a liberal idealist, which means that he refuses steadily even to begin looking at the problem announced on the cover of his book. He busies himself with assuring everybody that everything in the modern world is developing for the best and that there are no problems. All that we ' superior persons ' are afraid of in modern uses of leisure—journalism, advertising, the cinema, the wireless, motoring—he sees to be ' protections for what is really valuable, precisely because they concentrate upon what is superficial. . .': there is more ' inner life,' he thinks, than ever before. What Mr. Burns means by ' inner life ' comes out in his invocations of Mr. Charles Morgan, Mr. G. K. Chesterton, Flecker and Sir James Barrie. The book cannot, however, be regarded as funny: the contents of it were delivered as talks in the educational programme of the B.B.C. And the *Times Literary Supplement* described its predecessor (essentially the same book) as ' Conspicuous for lucidity of thought, breadth of view and sanity of judgment.'

F.R.L.

THE HISTORY OF THE RUSSIAN REVOLUTION, Vol. I., by Leon Trotsky (Gollanez, 18/-).

Trotsky is eminently qualified to write the history of the Russian Revolution. For over thirty years he has studied and engineered revolutions; as a man of action he has been one of the most brilliant figures of our time; and his ability as a writer is plain to everybody. He sets out in this book to tell first of all what happened and how it happened, but more than that to make it clear from the very telling why it happened in this way and not in another. Every candid reader I think will admit Trotsky's success. To say so does not necessarily mean that we commit ourselves to his particular interpretation, though nothing short of an even more cogent interpretation is good enough reason for rejecting it at present. To be sure, very few of us can check his accuracy, and it is difficult to say how much is distorted. For the facts, he went to unpublished material, and to innumerable periodical publications, Newspapers and journals, memoirs, reports, etc. (they are indicated only very occasionally—the excuse : ' that they would only bother the reader ') and he also makes use of his own recollections, though never, he assures us, without checking them from

verified sources. Remembering his taste for self-glorification, his warfare with Stalin, and his definite political position, we may reasonably suspect some distortion, and no doubt many readers will object
that the whole account must be distorted because Trotsky has a
definite philosophy of history. In his introduction Trotsky maintains that there is no special pleading for his political position, and
that ' impartiality ' is not to be expected, or even desired, in
historical writing—to understand anything necessarily means to
understand it from some point of view. His own point of view is
unmistakable enough—he is a political engineer seeking to understand the forces which move society only in order to control them
and to make use of them in building up a socialist state. Personal
desires and prejudices are a handicap; they cloud the understanding
and reduce efficiency. They must be eliminated as far as possible
and objectivity must be the aim of the investigator. Trotsky's
success as a man of action was due in no small measure to his
capacity for such ' objective ' understanding of men and events.
He uses his theories as tools or instruments; they are subject to
modification and development in practice; and the test of their
value is their usefulness to him. In his History this objectivity is
valuable. Objectivity is rare among historians and particularly
rare among historians of contemporary affairs. If Trotsky has
succeeded in writing a work of first importance, as we believe he
has, it is not in spite of his theories, but because of them.

What is surprising about this Revolution is not so much that
it should happen in Russia (though orthodox Marxists found this
surprising) but that it should lead to the dictatorship of the proletariat. Popular risings in the past have inevitably failed. A
popular movement, said Marat, ' always lacks knowledge, skill,
means, weapons, leaders, and a definite plan of action; it remains
defenceless in the face of conspirators, of experience, adroitness, and
craft.' Now Miluikoff and Kerensky were not without experience,
adroitness and craft, and the Bolshevik leaders, handicapped by
doctrinaire theories, had handed the power over to them after
the February revolution. Why then does this popular rising succeed
where others failed? It had the army with it, of course, for the
army itself was composed of rebellious peasants and workers, and
so it had weapons, and no doubt the Russian proletariat was fairly
well educated, after years of hard training in political strikes. But

the masses went into action with no preconceived scheme for social reconstruction; they merely wanted to end the old régime. ' Only the guiding layers of a class have a political programme and even this still requires the test of events, and the approval of the masses.' Lenin and the Bolshevik party had been working out a political programme for over thirty years, and the industrial workers understood their Marxian idiom. Lenin's genius is to see what are the real problems arising out of the social crisis, to find solutions which stand the test of events, and, what is more, to expound his views with such clearness and force that the masses see what ought to be done next and are willing to do it.

It is ridiculous to suppose that dialectical materialism is nothing but fatalism. Trotsky makes Lenin's personal importance abundantly clear—no revolution can guide itself, and without Lenin to interpret events the revolutionary cause might very well have lost the day. But this is not to say that Lenin was wholly responsible for its success. He was not independent of the masses, but worked with them and articulated their needs.

Trotsky's exposition might be improved in only one particular. He tells us far too little of the growth and organization of the Bolshevik party in the thirty years or so of preparation and he seems to assume that we know all about the 1905 revolution, ' the full-dress rehearsal for 1917.' It would be interesting to know how Lenin built up his reputation while he was abroad, and just how much influence he had on the Bolsheviks who remained in Russia, and in turn how far the Bolsheviks at home influenced the proletariat.

Trotsky is at his best when he is analysing the situations which confronted the revolutionary leaders and when he is recreating the struggles between different leaders. He succeeds remarkably in his attempts to suggest the mood and temper of the masses, the swift changes of opinion, the doubt and bewilderment and the growing restiveness as they see their leaders betraying them to Miluikoff and Kerensky. He can describe street-fighting and mob-excitement with great vividness, and his skill in satirical portraiture is as remarkable as ever, e.g. his sketch of the Czar, his portraits of Kerensky and Miluikoff, or his bead-roll of unfortunates—the members of the Social Revolutionary party or the commanding generals when asked their opinion on whether the Czar should abdicate.

This first volume carries us to the June demonstration. The next will deal with events from July to October, 1917, and will contain two chapters on the famous *coup d'état,* and an exposition of the equally famous theory of Permanent Revolution. Trotsky himself plays a far greater part in the events of these months and it will be interesting to see how far he can remain objective about them.

His translator, Max Eastman, writes a short biographical introduction—hero-worship undisguised, and adds a number of notes which are not altogether necessary, though sometimes useful. He might have completed his first-aid outfit with a map of St. Petersburg.

W. A. EDWARDS.

INDUSTRY AND EDUCATION IN SOVIET RUSSIA, by J. G. Crowther (Heinemann, 7/6d.).

Here is a book neither especially informative nor provocative, and with too ambitious a title, but it raises almost fortuitously a point of interest. Mr. J. G. Crowther, who is evidently well versed in the ways of technical education in England, made in 1930 a round of visits to schools and colleges in Moscow and Leningrad, and the book is a compilation of his rough notes. The point that emerges is that technical education in Russia has acquired significantly a new status. That is of course as it should be. That theory grows out of practice and not the other way round is a crucial theorem for communism. (The point is elucidated in Bukharin's paper on the theory of ' Theory and Practice ' published by Kniga). And in the event, an observer familiar with the atmosphere in which technical education is undertaken in England seems not to have had time (for Mr. Crowther's visit was of a holiday brevity) to recover from the initial shock of discovering a country where technical education is the tap-root of the educational system instead of a remote and pallid fibre. He can do little but note in passing details of some of the interesting changes such as the payment of students, the close connection between schools and factories, and the fact that teaching becomes less a specialized function and more a part-time job.

Space is lacking to go deeply into the question. Suffice it to say that the book indicates an approach to communism which leads the enquirer, almost abruptly, to the crux. The relation of technical education to the more general educational questions is understood by communists in a special sense: and the form of that relation gives communist thought its character. Mr. Crowther has, perhaps unintentionally, set up a train of thought which is not banal and may be useful.

MONTAGU SLATER.

EUGENICS AND EVOLUTION

THE CAUSES OF EVOLUTION, by J. B. S. Haldane, F.R.S. (Longmans, 7/6d.).

America has just been the host for two International Congresses, the first a Congress of Eugenics and the second a Congress of Genetics. Eugenics is the study of Genetics as applied to man and it is obvious from a study of the papers read before the two meetings that the applied science has far outgrown her parent in her ideas. Perhaps it would be more accurate to say that the parent, as is often the case, cannot endorse the ideas of her offspring. Eugenics seeks to improve the human race by selective breeding, but as eugenists themselves have not yet decided what are the desirable characters to select for, any concerted plan for positive eugenics must necessarily hang fire. Evidently the traits which are desirable are, for the most part, not inherited in a simple way. They are, in addition, so many that a few controlled matings would not produce the super-race that the idealists have in mind.

A saying so true that it has almost become proverbial is that it takes three generations to found a family and three to founder it. I suppose the eugenist would say that no foundering would occur if the family matings were made with due regard to the germ plasms brought together. But so many of the desirable characters are recessive in their inheritance that in the masses of the people we have an almost unlimited supply of desirable hereditary characters which produce good individuals as the recessive genes come together. This is becoming more and more evident with the improvement of environment, in other words of opportunity, now less and less a matter of being born into the right family.

In the same way the masses of the people represent a great reservoir of undesirable recessive characters and the reproduction of individuals more or less pure for these factors is already being controlled by segregating them in asylums.

The geneticist sounds a note of warning by pointing out that genes or hereditary germ units do not, as was at one time believed, affect one part of the body only. They may manifest themselves in other ways than in the merely superficial characters by which they are detected. An instance is to be found in the fruit fly—the classic laboratory animal of the geneticist. In this insect certain genes, easily detected by their effect on eye colour and wing shape, when inherited separately, lessen the life span of the individual considerably. But if they are inherited together, the insect possessing them all has a normal life span. This illustration points out the danger of controlling matings with regard to individual traits until we know far more than we do at present of the physiological action of the genes we are selecting. The ideal race cannot be created tomorrow, and by injudicious experiment our last state may be worse than the first.

Professor J. B. S. Haldane takes a much longer view of life than the eugenist. Instead of dealing with a few generations he deals mathematically with generations of the order of 10^6 and with time of the order of 10^9 years. He begins with a discussion of what is meant by Darwinism. Briefly his thesis is that evolution is a fact but that the causes of evolution are unknown. Darwin's general theory is that evolution takes place because the undesirable specimens of a varying species are weeded out by failing to survive. The survivors then vary about the mean which they themselves establish. But this does not fit in very well with our present experimental knowledge. The mean in continuous variation is not as a rule affected by selection, at any rate not for more than a few generations, as ' pure lines ' with a relatively fixed mean become isolated. Natural selection does act on the products of evolution

but it cannot be regarded as the cause of evolution. It is a policeman removing the offenders rather than a moralist improving them.
Some animals, such as *Lingula,* a small shell fish, have
remained remarkably constant for four hundred million years. This
animal shows a small continuous evolution, while other animals
such as the mammals have proceeded by a series of jumps, some
of their genes becoming drastically altered from time to time.
Occasionally the number of genes is altered by rearrangement of
the germ plasm. Why some forms should be so stable and others
so unstable is unknown. The large discontinuous variation may
occasionally produce new forms which are fitted to the environment
and hence have a high survival value.

In the case of man, the subject of one of Darwin's ' special '
theories, evolution is proceeding along a peculiar channel. During
the last few years intermediate forms have been found in China and
elsewhere which, according to Professor Haldane, have puzzled the
most ardent opponents of the descent of man from the monkeys.
They cannot agree amongst themselves whether to class these
forms as apes or as men, so that they must form an admirable
' missing link.' Man shows a curious reversion to the childhood of
animals. He has a much longer relative period before reaching adult-
hood than any other animal and consequently a much longer period
of educability. The brain also has a larger ratio to body weight than
in any other animal—a condition similar to that found in the
embryos of other species. This, together with other characteristics
has led the scientist to speak of this type of evolution as fœtali-
sation. If evolution in the human race continues along these lines
we may find a further retardation of maturity and a persistence of
character now regarded as childish. This view suggests the possibility that the time available for reproduction of the individual
may become so short that the race of man may evolve itself to
extinction, a fate which in other ways has involved innumerable
species.

S. A. ASDELL.

THE MORAL JUDGMENT OF THE CHILD, by J. Piaget
*(Kegan Paul, International Library of Psychology, etc. Pp. x 418,
12/6d. net)*.

This admirable book presents a fully documented account of
the changes that occur with increasing age in children's modes of
evaluating and ordering their conduct. The data collected relate
to the ways in which children regard the rules of their games, to
their judgments on lying and stealing, and to their ideas of justice.
The standardized interviews, by means of which the information
was obtained, appear to have been excellently planned and carried
out, and to have avoided the danger of distorting the facts through
artificiality in the way they were elicited.

The two main stages of moral development which Piaget
distinguishes are: first, the acceptance of adult injunctions as
unquestionably valid and as deriving their cogency purely from
having been promulgated by adults; second, co-operation with
other children on an equal footing and consequent obedience to
certain injunctions because their necessity to group activity is
recognized. This gives a more critical attitude to rules, which,
nevertheless, are in practice obeyed more carefully than are the
younger children's magically sacred rules. Similarly with justice:
whereas in the early years anything done by an adult is just,
later on justice demands the recognition of equality among children
of the same age. As a result of this development the childish conception of punishment changes: what is at first expiation for
an infringement of the mystically powerful rule becomes (when
co-operation has been reached) a redressal of the social balance,
this having been disturbed by the individual aggression that is
being punished. In this way there emerges ' the rather shortsighted justice of those children who give back the mathematical
equivalent of the blows they have received.' This one might
suppose to be the final development of a system of judgments
founded entirely on the maintenance of equality in social relationships. Some other principle would appear necessary in order to
explain any further advance.

Piaget however is completely committed to the view that
all morality arises from the social interaction of equals. ' Morality
presupposes the existence of rules which transcend the individual,
and these rules could only develop through contact with other

people.' He is careful, however, to dissociate himself from Durkheim's views. Where Durkheim sees social constraint as the origin of morality Piaget sees it as a feature of childhood, one which must give place to social co-operation before true morality develops : ' the unilateral respect belonging to contstraint is not a stable system, and the equilibrium towards which it tends is no other than mutual respect.' His data show that this process does in fact take place, but the whole tenor of his interpretation is to the effect that social equilibrium is an end in itself and not simply an aid to individual development. The effect of this interpretation appears in the curious confusion of the following passage : ' The essence of experimental behaviour—whether scientific, technical, or moral—consists, not in a common belief, but in rules of mutual control. Everyone is free to bring in innovations, but only so far as he succeeds in making himself understood by others and in understanding them.' Here Piaget disregards the fact that one may introduce innovations into one's own conduct or beliefs as a purely individual experiment. If others disapprove of the innovation (whether they understand it or not) they may put a stop to it and even penalize the innovator. But the innovation remains an individual experiment, to be judged good or bad according as its final results sort well or badly with the innovator's individual standards. This is not to underestimate the importance of social relationships in guiding the individual and helping to establish his standards; it is instead to make the notion of morality more fundamental than anything that can arise solely from social interactions—to make it, in fact, continuous with the physiological co-ordination which prevents flexors and extensors from being excited simultaneously, and the psychological integration (still individual) which solves the conflict between the desire to eat one's cake and the desire to have it.

The interpretation one adopts is extremely important in determining one's attitude to punishment. Piaget, by regarding social equilibrium as an end in itself, provides no satifactory means for advancing beyond the notion of revenge. He notes that ' As respect for adult punishment gradually grows less, certain types of conduct develop which one cannot but class under the heading of retributive justice. . . The child feels more and more that it is fair that he should defend himself and to give back the blows he receives. . . . It is entirely a matter of reciprocity. So-and-so takes upon himself the right to give me a punch, he therefore gives me the right to do the same to him.' He goes on, ' It may be objected that such a morality will not take one very far, since the best adult consciences ask for something more than the practice of mere reciprocity.' But this something more he goes on to characterize as ' charity and the forgiving of injuries.' Nothing could show more clearly the hampering effect of valuing social equilibrium for itself. For the conception of forgiveness involves hardly any *conscious* advance on the simple morality of ' a blow for a blow '; one forgoes one's right to exact full retribution, but the right remains implicit. And the forgiving child (or adult), not exercising his right to revenge, yet still clinging to it, demands in compensation at least a sense of superiority. He preens himself on ' forgiveness ' when he achieves a rudimentary awareness of the fact that his social ' rights ' are, in certain situations, useless to him. The stage of development that this awareness initiates, that of taking reparation when possible but declining revenge, and of distinguishing between deterrent punishment and requital, must be regarded as due to the individual's advance beyond the simple concern for social equilibrium. He is at last holding his fellow creature at arm's length and deciding on the best course of action for himself, an individual, regardless of maintaining his social rights for their own sake.

To disagree with the central assumptions of this book is by no means to lose one's respect for it. Only when applied to the facts of later childhood does Piaget's thesis seem inadequate and unilluminating. For the early years of childhood it allows extremely convincing and often subtle conclusions, of great pedagogical significance, to be drawn from observations which are in themselves of extraordinary interest and value.

Denys W. Harding.

SELECTIONS FROM REMY DE GOURMONT (Phoenix Library, Chatto and Windus). The price of this book is 3/6d. *not* 7/6d. as announced in the first edition of the second number of *Scrutiny*.

PATTERN AND VARIATION IN POETRY, by Chard Powers Smith (Scribners, 15/-).

Nothing, probably, will stop this book from having, with a little luck, a great success: lecturers and teachers whose notion of criticism derives from Mr. Greening Lamborn's *Rudiments* will find in Mr. Smith what they were waiting for. Its catholic modernity (*cf.* ' Mr. Elliott's *Waste Land* . . . . rationalistic pseudo-poetry ') makes its academic futility the more seductive. It will be useless to assure most professional students of poetry that ' technique ' as Mr. Smith conceives it has little relation to the business of criticism. But one cannot repeat too often that the profitable analysis of ' technique ' can have no use for graphs or scansions and demands the active co-operation of a trained sensibility. Mr. Smith's sensibility has been ' trained ' into use-lessness.

THE OFFENCE, by Pierre Bost (Elkin, Mathews and Marrot, 7/6d.).

This novel won the Prix Interallié, and though not a great or even a remarkable novel is well worth reading if one must read novels to pass the time. Unlike the English equivalents it obviously proceeds from a mature and adult sensibility, from an intelligent and cultivated man of the world who is yet in no degree stale or uncritical of his environment. The scene is contemporary Paris— the worlds of the student, the journalist and the artist.

THE TWO THIEVES, by T. F. Powys (Chatto and Windus, 7/6d.).

Mr. T. F. Powy's position is now such that all those who are capable of realizing that he is that rare thing, an original artist, may be presumed to have already had his work brought to their notice. Our alternative is either to criticize this new book of three stories at length or merely to announce it. Having no room for the former, we rely on the latter to direct the attention of serious readers to *The Two Thieves*.

THE PRESS AND THE ORGANIZATION OF SOCIETY, by Norman Angell, mentioned in the first number of *Scrutiny* as out of print, is being reprinted immediately by the Minority Press (Cambridge) at 3/6d.

NOTES ON CONTRIBUTORS

S. A. ASDELL is a Professor at Cornell University.

WILLIAM EMPSON, author of *Seven Types of Ambiguity*, is Professor of English at Tokyo.

HENRI FLUCHERE is a member of the *Conseil de Rédaction* of *Les Cahiers du Sud* and is one of the foremost interpreters of contemporary English letters to France.

DOUGLAS GARMAN, one of the founders and editors of *The Calendar of Modern Letters*, has published criticism in *Scrutinies* and a book of poems, *The Jaded Hero*.

SELDEN RODMAN has recently published a volume of poems, *Mortal Triumph*, with Farrar and Rinehart.

DENYS THOMPSON is Senior English Master at Gresham's School, Holt. *Culture and Environment*, by him and F. R. Leavis (whose *How to Teach Reading : A Primer for Ezra Pound* is coming out immediately as a Minority Pamphlet) is being published by Chatto and Windus in January.

SHERARD VINES, whose latest book is *Return, Belphegor*, is Professor of English Literature at Hull.

SCRUTINY *is published by the Editors,* 13 *Leys Road, Cambridge, and printed by* S.G. Marshall & Son, *Round Church Street, Cambridge, England. Copyright U.S.A.*

Vol. I. No. 4.   March, 1933

SCRUTINY

A Quarterly Review

Edited by

L. C. KNIGHTS   DONALD CULVER
F. R. LEAVIS   DENYS THOMPSON

CONTENTS

APPEAL TO READERS

WE have to announce that we have arranged for the distribution of *Scrutiny* to be taken over by Messrs. Deighton, Bell and Co., Ltd., Trinity Street, Cambridge. It had been for some time becoming obvious that we could not go on carrying the whole burden of work ourselves. But the new arrangement inevitably involves further expense, and, since *Scrutiny* was only just paying its way (a remarkable enough achievement), it is plain that we must have more support if there is to be a confident future. So we appeal to subscribers to renew their subscriptions (they need have no fear of our defaulting); to readers, where they have not done so already, to subscribe ; and to all who think that *Scrutiny* performs an important function to do all the propaganda they can : our potential public is still much larger than the actual, as the steadily growing circulation indicates.

We have economized to the utmost : the rinds were thin enough anyway. So we are asking subscribers to pay postage in future, viz., 8d. extra a year, and correspondents who require answering to enclose stamps.

A subscription form will be found inside the back cover.

American subscriptions may be sent to Sheldon Dick, Literary Agent, 33 West 42nd Street, New York City.

Scrutiny may be bought at the NEW REPUBLIC BOOKSTORE, 419 West 21st Street, New York City.

Communications for the Editors should be addressed to them at 6 Chesterton Hall Crescent, Cambridge, England.

Subscriptions, orders and business communications should be addressed to Deighton, Bell & Co., Ltd., Trinity Street, Cambridge, England.

No payment is made for contributions.

RESTATEMENTS FOR CRITICS

CRITICAL attention is something to be grateful for, even when it is as pettish in animadversion as ' Ille Ego's ' review of *Scrutiny* in *The New English Weekly* for January 5th. This is not to be ungrateful for the generous notice that we have been so widely accorded: warm acknowledgments are due. Nor is it to flatter ' Ille Ego ' with the suggestion that his comments are very subtle or profound: his pettishness betrays itself, in the familiar ways, as one of the familiar manifestations of uneasily ambitious immaturity. But the misunderstandings he exhibits in naïve forms have, we know, from spoken criticism and from correspondence, a fairly representative quality, and we tender him thanks for the occasion he provides.

Scrutiny, he complains, refuses to be committed. Instead of giving honest and undivided allegiance to its true ' god,' T. S. Eliot, from whom it ' obviously derives ' (like most else in ' literary Cambridge these past ten years ') it goes whoring after D. H. Lawrence. Worse than that, it was conceived in sin, and it has from birth onwards denied its god: ' It has its origin in a desire not to be committed to Mr. Eliot,' or to any other god or prophet. ' It is very definitely not-committed. Indeed, its primary concern appears to be precisely that: to avoid being committed.'

To what, it might be asked, is ' Ille Ego ' committed? Anyway, ' very definitely,' to knowing the ante-natal history of *Scrutiny* and the ' reality' of Blake, D. H. Lawrence and T. S. Eliot. Under three of these heads, at least, we admit to being much less 'committed.' But the more naïve self-committals of ' Ille Ego ' may be left to themselves. When he is usefully representative is when he puts his fundamental incomprehension in so plausible a form as this: ' The distinction is suggested in the title. The *Criterion* judges; *Scrutiny* scrutinizes. Compared to judgment, scrutiny is a non-committal occupation.'

We stand self-condemned, then, by the modesty of our title, by our very lack of pretension. Yet title and pretension are not everything. Forbearing the inquiry whether *Scrutiny* has committed itself less often and less decisively than any other journal in particular judgments, let us ask what, where judgment is in question, the criterion is: what are the standards? The values of intelligence, tradition and orthodox Christianity? But judgment is not a matter of abstraction ; it involves particular immediate acts of choice, and these do not advance the business of judgment in any serious sense unless there has been a real and appropriate responsiveness to the thing offered. Without a free and delicate receptivity to fresh experience, whatever the criterion alleged, there is no judging, but merely negation. And this kind of negation, persisted in, with no matter what righteous design, produces in the end nullity: the ' criterion,' however once validated by experience, fades into impotent abstraction, the ' values ' it represents become empty husks. The safety sought in this way proves to be the safety of death.

Of course there is more to be said ; there is another side. It is not wisdom that stops at advocating the free play of individual sensibility. Indeed, the truly living sensibility cannot be content to be merely individual and merely free. One cannot suppose it either possible or desirable to go on ' experiencing ' as if there had been nothing before. And with the beginnings of maturity the problem of organization becomes one for serious effort ; taken seriously, it leads to a discipline and a training, emotional and intellectual, designed to ' preserve the individual from the solely centrifugal impulse of heresy, to make him capable of judging for himself, and at the same time capable of judging and understanding the judgments of the experience of the race.' But this is no matter of simple acceptance or conformity. It is part of our great debt to Mr. Eliot that he has made it so plain that there can be no easy way or simple solution. Of tradition he wrote : ' It cannot be inherited, and if you want it you must obtain it by great labour.' But it is just our criticism of *The Criterion* that so many of its writers are condemned by the spirit of this dictum. Judgment cannot be a matter of applying the accepted (or ' inherited ') standards, any more than thinking can be a matter of moving the recognized abstractions according to rule.

Again, in his essay on Massinger, Mr. Eliot wrote : ' What may be considered corrupt or decadent in the morals of Massinger is not an alteration or diminution in morals ; it is simply the disappearance of all the personal and real emotions which this morality supported and into which it introduced a kind of order. As soon as the emotions disappear the morality which it ordered appears hideous. Puritanism itself became repulsive only when it appeared as the survival of a restraint after the feelings which it restrained had gone.' The bearing of this upon (say) a grave and persistent lack, in a journal standing for order, intelligence and orthodoxy, of critical sensitiveness to contemporary literature— to literature and art in general—does not need elaborating, perhaps.

Our criticism, then, is no repudiation of our debt to Mr. Eliot (and *The Criterion*), but the reverse. Nor when we suggest that D. H. Lawrence should have been a test is it necessary, or intelligent, to conclude that we have transferred our allegiance to D. H. Lawrence. ' But to *use* Eliot to escape the reality of Lawrence,' pronounces ' Ille Ego,' ' and to use Lawrence to escape the reality of Eliot, is to insult both of them.'—To suggest that one should ' accept ' Mr. Eliot or D. H. Lawrence is to insult both of them, it might be retorted, by gross incomprehension, for, whatever the ' reality ' of either may be, it is certainly such that to contemplate ' accepting ' it is to repudiate it. The reality of Mr. Eliot in one sense is just what is in question. And to propose Lawrence as a test is not to suggest that Lawrence's reality is simple, a matter for allegiance, loyalty or acceptance. An intelligent, that is, a respectful, attitude towards him must necessarily be a discriminating one ; for though ' Ille Ego ' speaks of Lawrence's ' philosophy ' as something to be accepted or rejected, those who have read what Lawrence wrote know that he was inconsistent, and inconsistent in such ways that to think of systematizing him is to betray a complete obtuseness to his significance.

What Lawrence offers us is not a philosophy or an *œuvre*— a body of literary art—but an experience, or, to fall back on the French again, an *expérience*, for the sense of ' experiment ' is needed too. In him the human spirit explored, with unsurpassed courage, resource and endurance, the representative, the radical and central, problems of our time. Of course he went into danger-ous places, and laid himself open to reprehension as setting dangerous examples and inciting to dangerous experiments. But if he earned reprehension, we owe him gratitude for earning it.

More than one summing-up is possible, and it would be absurd to demand agreement with one's own ; the stress will fall here for some and there for others. But especially by those who stand for ' order ' should he have been recognized as a test : a refusal on their part to consider him seriously must appear a very bad sign indeed. And to take the easy recourse of dismissing him in a plausible, too plausible, bracket with Rousseau, or to use Mr. Murry against him, amounts to such a refusal. The reluc-tant conclusion is at last compelled that the insidious corruptions attendant upon ' classicism ' have not been sufficiently guarded against ; that ' order ' and 'tradition ' have ceased to be a living tension, a strenuous centrality, and have become something very different.

' Ille Ego ' complains that we desert ' at the point where Eliot becomes the orthodox Christian. That, as might have been expected, is too much for Cambridge.' But what *is* orthodox Christianity? (And is ' Ille Ego ' ' committed ' to it?). If it means the kind of rejection of life implicit in Mr. Eliot's attitude towards sex, then we do certainly dissociate ourselves at that point. Law-rence's preoccupation with sex seems to us much less fairly to be called ' obsession ' than Mr. Eliot's, and very much preferable. And we know that many who profess Christian sympathies share this view.

If we go on to say that it does not follow that we accept any Laurentian religion we shall, perhaps, not now be taunted with cowardly evasiveness. What, indeed, was Lawrence's religion? 'Curse the Strachey,' he wrote during the War, 'who asks for a new religion—the greedy dog. He wants another juicy bone for his soul, does he? Let him start to fulfil what religion we have.' To talk of the 'religious sense ' that he represents may sound weak, but it should not to those who have read the *Letters*. For many to-day the essential thing is to meet such a sense in the concrete, dominating (' I am a passionately religious man '), and unmistakably an expression of health, courage and vitality. And we meet it, we find, in Lawrence—in the Lawrence who has the right to exclaim as he does against ' glib irreverence,' because all his writing exhibits reverence as a fact, a fact of honesty, strength and sensitiveness ; the Lawrence who disturbs complacency about ' sex reform' so much more potently than Mr. Eliot.

This is not to pronounce against the ultimate necessity of theologies, creeds and rituals : it is probable that *Scrutiny* enjoys, and will enjoy, support from readers who profess and practise. But most, we imagine, who respond to Lawrence's ' one must speak for life and growth, amid all this mass of destruction and disintegration ' find the possibility of adhesion to any formal religion a remote one—as remote as a satisfying answer to the question, What does such adhesion mean in effect? Does, for instance, a declaration of ' faith in death ' mean a negative acquiescence in the drift of things here below, or, as it might, the opposite?

We have at any rate some notion of the test. And we know that, in such a time of disintegration as the present, formulæ, credos, abstractions are extremely evasive of unambiguous and effective meaning, and that, whatever else may be also necessary, no effort at integration can achieve anything real without a centre of real consensus—such a centre as is presupposed in the possibility of literary criticism and is tested in particular judgments. But ' tested ' does not say enough ; criticism, when it performs its function, not merely expresses and defines the ' contemporary sensibility '; it helps to form it. And the function of *Scrutiny*, as we conceive it, is (among other things) to help to persuade an effective ' contemporary sensibility ' into being—for that, rather, is what the critical function looks like when decay has gone so far.

The peculiar importance of literary criticism has by now been suggested : where there is a steady and responsible practice of criticism a ' centre of real consensus' will, even under present conditions, soon make itself felt. Out of agreement and disagreement with particular judgments of value a sense of relative value in the concrete will define itself, and, without this, no amount of talk about ' values' in the abstract is worth anything. And it is not merely a matter of literature (' It would appear that "literary appreciation" is an abstraction and pure poetry a phantom'— T. S. Eliot, *Selected Essays*, p. 257): there is hardly any need to illustrate the ways in which judgments of literary value involve extra-literary choices and decisions. It should at any rate be enough to suggest that those who differ philosophically and theologically—who differ about religious ' beliefs '—may agree that Mr. Eliot and D. H. Lawrence both (however one may ' place ' them relatively) demand serious attention, and that the supersession by Book Society standards of the standards that compel this judgment will, if not fiercely and publicly resisted, be a disaster for civilization.

Such consensus can, and must, test and justify itself in action. Above all there are, or we should determine that there shall be, immediate consequences in education: at any rate, the determination, resolutely pursued, would provoke real agreement and real differences. This (need it be said?) is not to show contempt for creed and theory, or to suggest that the function represented by, for example, *The Criterion*, is unnecessary. But what we propose does seem to us certainly necessary if creed is not to be merely debilitating and theory a relapse upon the wrong kind of abstraction, inert and unprofitable.

The Marxist, however, will still protest that (as one correspondent puts it) we are invoking education in order ' to escape the urge to political action.' It is of no use, it would seem, while he remains a Marxist, to reply that we do not offer education as an alternative. We cannot, it is true, look forward with any hope to bloody revolution, but we are not (again, need it be said?) politically indifferent. It seems appropriate here to speak in the first person. Let me say, then, that I agree with the Marxist to the extent of believing some form of economic communism to be inevitable and desirable, in the sense that it is to this that a power-economy of its very nature points, and only by a deliberate and intelligent working towards it can civilization be saved from disaster. (The question is, communism of what kind? Is the machine—or Power—to triumph or to be triumphed over, to be the dictator or the servant of human ends?)

When I add that I believe one cannot reasonably pretend to lay down what are the right immediate steps without consulting specialists, and that one of the functions of *Scrutiny* is to provide criteria, from the realm of general intelligence, for determining which specialists can be trusted, and how far, the Marxist will smile. I can only reply, by way of earnest, that a serious educational movement will inevitably, and, as far as I am concerned, explicitly, aim at fostering in schools and in education generally, an anti-acquisitive and anti-competitive moral bent, on the ground (there are others) that the inherited code is disastrously and obviously inappropriate to modern conditions.

But this is not said in any hope of conciliating the Marxist, for he it is who insists on the one thing, the one necessary preoccupation: to confess to a sense of complexities is to play the bourgeois game. Thus our correspondent complains: 'you refuse to admit that "art" and "culture" are among the chief instruments of oppression—a form of dope. Or if you recognize this . . . you are scornful at the idea that Eliot *and* Walpole, Wells, *Punch, Scrutiny,* Stopes and the *Outline for Boys and Girls* are all manifestations of bourgeois culture. I contend that they are—and Eliot seems to me as typical as *Punch,* but " at a different level of appeal" (or "sensitiveness" or "intelligence").' —Marxism is indeed, to adapt Lenin's adaptation[1] of the ' dope ' formula, the alcohol of the intellectual, warming and exalting, obliterating difficulties, and incapacitating for elementary discriminations. After the passage just quoted, one is not surprised to get a defence of Prince Mirsky's *' toutes les valeurs vivantes sont du coté de la classe ouvrière,'* for to include Mr. Eliot and *Punch* under ' bourgeois' is to empty the term ' value ' of all serious meaning.

It is true that one might call not only *Punch* and Mr. Walpole, but also Mr. Eliot and D. H. Lawrence ' products ' of capitalist civilization, in that the use made by these two last of their talents was determined by the environment into which they were born. But rejection, after all, is not the same as acceptance, and it is a bourgeois incapacity that cannot recognize the human values that Mr. Eliot and Lawrence, in their different ways, are asserting against the environment—very different ways, and if the

---

[1]See W. Gurian, *Bolshevism: Theory and Practice,* p. 223 (Sheed and Ward, 10/6d.). We have had regretfully, for lack of room, to exclude a review of this book, which is the more useful because its point-of-view (Catholic) is explicit.

values are different too, they are alike in being equally not gener-
ated in the modern economic process. Indeed, this is our criticism,
that in the matter of ' values ' the Marxist is too bourgeois, too much
the product of the material environment. It is impossible to believe
that he who is so obtuse to essential distinctions means anything
when he speaks of the ' culture ' that will supervene upon a politico-
economic revolution: the finer human values have, so far as his
sense of them goes, been left behind for good in capitalist Progress.

The simplifying dialectic itself works like a machine. ' You
are quite right,' says the correspondent already quoted, ' in stating
that '' the dogma of the priority of economic conditions means a
complete disregard for—or hostility towards—the functions represented by *Scrutiny*.'' Orthodox Marxists (*i.e.* Leninist Marxists)
would be hostile to *Scrutiny* . . . ,' and he goes on to stigmatize
as a ' *contre-sens* ' our talking of a culture that will have a
' momentum and life of its own' when we have admitted that ' the
economic process must profoundly affect existence.' Yet, by anyone
not trained in the Marxian dialectic, the nature of the complexity
is not hard to recognize. There seems no reason for repeating the
argument of *Under Which King, Bezonian?* that the dialectic
itself brings the Marxist to the point at which he must contemplate
a quite different relation between culture and the economic process
from that of the past. To put it simply, instead of dictating to the
mass of mankind their uses of time, the economic process will
free their time, in large measure, for uses dictated by inner human
nature, if there should be one capable of dictating.

But is there such a thing as ' inner human nature?' The
Marxian theory (and historical forecast) would seem to leave little
room for it, though implicitly postulating the need for a very potent
one, to take over when the Class-War ends and the economic process recedes into unobtrusiveness ; and that is why the Marxian
future looks so vacuous, Wellsian and bourgeois. That mechanical
efficiency should be a religion for Russia, and ever more ambitious
engineering a sufficient future, is, in the present phase, under-
standable and perhaps necessary. But, however badly civilization
may work, the West can imagine a ' technocratic ' or ' planned
economy ' America too easily to find it an inspiring vision ; a more
adequate incitement to devoted activity is needed, and needed at
once.

We assume an ' inner human nature,'[1] and our recognition that it may be profoundly affected by the ' economic process ' persuades us that it must rally, gather its resources and start training itself for its ultimate responsibility at once. A cogent way in which the human spirit can refute the Marxian theory and the bourgeois negative lies open in education. ' *L'éducation pourra tout,*' the correspondent referred to above credits us with believing : that, perhaps, is answered. ' *Scrutiny* will, no doubt, offer destructive analyses of education as it is—there are precedents enough—but the Scrutineers will effect no change.' If we do not make the obvious and modest response, that is not because we rate our own powers or importance high, but because we know that we speak (having the luck to be in a position to do so) for a formidable and growing body of conviction. Whether or not we are ' playing the capitalist game' should soon be apparent, for a serious effort in education involves the fostering of a critical attitude towards civilization as it is. Perhaps there will be no great public outcry when it is proposed to introduce into schools a training in resistance to publicity and in criticism of newspapers—for this is the least opposable way of presenting the start in a real modern education. Yet the inevitable implications, accompaniments and consequences of such a training hardly need illustrating.

The teaching profession is peculiarly in a position to do revolutionary things ; corporate spirit there can be unquestionably disinterested, and by a bold challenge there, perhaps the self-devotion of the intelligent may be more effectively enlisted than by an appeal to the Class-War.

F. R. LEAVIS.

---

[1]Some readers, of course, will demand more at this point, appealing to ' the judgments of the experience of the race.'

CULTURE AND LEISURE

M R. LEAVIS, in the last number of *Scrutiny*, issued a
challenge which will be, I think, very welcome to Marxists :
a challenge to reflect upon, and to restate, their attitude to
questions of the utmost importance. It is impossible for me to go
into the greater number of the issues raised in *Under Which King,
Bezonian ?* but I should like to offer a few reflections upon two of
them ; the conceptions of culture and of leisure.

Now first of all, I think Mr. Leavis is not quite correct in
thinking that Marxists regard culture as the outcome of the
' *methods* of production.' A more accurate phrase would be ' *mode*
of production,' that is, ' the totality of productive relations.' This
may seem a small, verbal point, but it really has some importance,
since it has led Mr. Leavis to conceive the connection as a rigidly
determined, mechanical one rather than a fluid, dialectical one.
Though secondary, the cultural level reached by a society at any
point becomes in its turn a factor helping to determine productive
relationships.

When we talk of ' bourgeois culture ' we refer to the sum of
the ideological superstructure characteristic of the present historical
period, in which the bourgeoisie is the ruling class. This includes
much that the Editors of *Scrutiny* would perhaps prefer to call lack
of culture. The novels of D. H. Lawrence and the methods of
salesmanship described in Mr. Denys Thompson's article *Advertising God* do not, indeed, seem to have much in common at first
sight. A little consideration will show, however, that neither could
have come into being save in an advanced industrial country and
in the 20th century. Both are perfectly natural products of the
capitalist system in the period of Imperialism.

There is here a possibility of an ambiguous use of the word
culture, and Trotsky seems to have used it indifferently in both
senses. Bourgeois culture, then, is the result of a historic process,
and cannot be accepted as uniformly valuable or rejected as

entirely valueless. The purpose of *Scrutiny* seems to be to combat the harmful elements of the bourgeois 'culture complex' and to preserve what is valuable. This is entirely praiseworthy: the only question we have to ask ourselves is: what are the most hopeful means towards this end?

Is is possible, on the one hand, to purge away those elements that we find objectionable? And on the other hand, may not the proletarian revolution, while sweeping away advertising and the gutter press, destroy also the delicate flower of 'culture' in the restricted sense of that word? This seems to be the opinion of Mr. Leavis, and, presumably, of the Editorial Board of *Scrutiny*.

Here Trotsky's misleading formulations have led to a misapprehension of the nature of the transition period between capitalism and communism. The main weakness of *Literature and Revolution* is precisely its undialectical approach to this. Trotsky seems, as it were, to see capitalism on one side of a ditch and communism on the other, with the necessity to jump over, 'bearing' just so much 'culture' as can be conveniently stowed away in one's pockets. Actually, the period of proletarian dictatorship is not a ditch but a bridge, a period in which the new is growing out of the old. It is a period in which much is destroyed, but far more is it a period of enormous construction. And just as the economic structure of Communist society will be built, and can only be built, on the basis of the achievements of earlier periods, so the cultural superstructure will begin with the most valuable elements of bourgeois culture. History proves that anything which is of cultural value, far from being a 'tender organic growth' possesses a quite amazing tenacity.

Among the things that will be accomplished during the proletarian dictatorship will be the education of the masses in the use of leisure, and a reorientation of outlook on the whole question of leisure and work. This will follow inevitably the growth of responsibility among the workers as members of a ruling class.

It is important here to understand just exactly what 'leisure' is. Clearly it is not merely the state of having nothing to do. No one would think of talking about leisure in connection with the unemployed. On the other hand the Editors of *Scrutiny* are obviously extremely busy people whose time is of considerable value. Yet they have sufficient leisure to undertake the production of a quarterly magazine. It seems to me that we must adopt a conception of leisure that is largely psychological. We cannot usefully speak of leisure except in the absence of all the anxieties and uncertainties that beset not merely the unemployed man but also the great majority of wage-earners. Nor can we speak of leisure until work is no longer the antithesis of living.

A leisure society, then, will not mean a society in which no one has any work to do. It will be a society in which drudgery is reduced to an absolute minimum, and in which for the most part the distinction between work and leisure has disappeared. And since men will not have to be relaxed in the intervals of toil, or doped into acquiescence in a system of organized exploitation, there will no longer be any place for the mass production novel or the tabloid press, and the arts will cease to be the preserve of a parasitic minority or of little groups of honest intellectuals attempting to order chaos with pitifully inadequate resources.

Here, and here only, is the ' organic community ' which Mr. Leavis and I are at one in desiring. This ' organic community ' disappeared not with the coming of industrialism, but, long before, with the coming of the State. (It still exists, or has existed within living memory, in obscure corners of Melanesia and elsewhere). I invite Mr. Leavis to think things over once again, to attempt to get behind that ' Marxian blanket ' (which isn't there nearly as often as he imagines), to consider the proportion of means and end, and to see whether the struggle to 'maintain the tradition of human culture ' can really be carried far on a basis of ignoring the struggle of classes with which it is inseparably connected. I feel that *Scrutiny* is far too valuable a weapon against the Philistines to be left permanently in the position of the two heroes who ' wept like anything to see such quantities of sand.'

A. L. MORTON.

NOTE.—Mr. Morton's communication arrived too late to be explicitly referred to in the editorial note dealing with Marxist criticism. It must be left to readers to judge whether Mr. Morton's points are adequately provided for in that note and elsewhere in *Scrutiny*. We need hardly say that we are grateful for such criticism as Mr. Morton's.

EVALUATIONS (I)

I. A. RICHARDS[1]

CONVERSATIONAL comments on Richards' work, favourable or unfavourable, seldom express opinions about his actual views; they seem more often than not to be reactions to the general tone of his writing. Nor can this aspect of his work be neglected in an attempt to formulate a more precise opinion: some peculiarity of tone, or some prevailing attitude, undoubtedly distinguishes him from most scientific and critical writers. It would be laborious to analyse this attitude in detail. As a handy label for it, the term 'amateur' (with some of its implications) will perhaps do. It is suggested for one thing by the slight acerbity with which so many 'professionals'—literary critics, psychologists, metaphysicians—dismiss him, together with the slight awe that he inspires in the virginally lay. But it has more important justification than this in two essential features of his work, namely in his insistence upon the significance for 'normal practical life' of his special interests, and in the buoyancy with which he rides over difficulties of detail by means of general principles.

Take, for instance, his basic hypotheses for criticism, and consider the difficulty and labour that would be involved in proving them. Only the spirit of the amateur could enable Richards to express them with as little inhibition as he does. 'The first point to be made is that poetic experiences are valuable (when they are) in the same way as any other experiences. They are to be judged by the same standards.' (*Science and Poetry*, p. 28). 'The greatest difference between the artist or poet and the ordinary person is found, as has often been pointed out, in the range, delicacy and freedom of the connections he is able to make between different elements of his experience.' (*Principles of Literary Criticism*,

---

[1]This is the first of a series of ' Evaluations ' which will be continued in future numbers of *Scrutiny*. There will also be a series of ' Revaluations '.

p. 181). 'The ways then in which the artist will differ from the average will as a rule presuppose an immense degree of similarity. They will be further developments of organizations already well advanced in the majority. His variations will be confined to the newest, the most plastic, the least fixed part of the mind, the parts for which reorganization is most easy.' (*Principles of Literary Criticism*, p. 196). ' It is in terms of attitudes, the resolution, inter-inanimation, and balancing of impulses . . . . that all the most valuable effects of poetry must be described.' (*Principles of Literary Criticism*, p. 113). Nor has his confidence waned with time. He is still ready to assert (see *The Criterion* of October, 1932) that the explanation of the difference between good and less good experiences 'is inevitably in terms of that order or disorder among "impulses" (or however else you care to describe the elementary processes on which consciousness depends) . . . .' Contrast the more 'professional' attitude towards similar problems. 'Personally I do not think the problem of ethical valuation [of different cultures] is hopeless, but it need not necessarily be undertaken in a purely sociological inquiry.' (M. Ginsberg in *Studies in Sociology*.) 'Moreover, in humanity as it exists at present it is not easy to decide that one physical type is better adapted than another, and, when it comes to deciding which emotional and intelligent types are better or worse, the situation becomes far too complicated to handle with any probability of success.' (T. H. Morgan in a paper in *The Foundations of Experimental Psychology*). These quotations, I think, fairly represent the attitude of qualified specialists when they refer to ethical questions: not hopeless but . . . . The contrast with Richards need not be stressed.

Three hypotheses, distinct although closely related, are expressed by Richards in the passages quoted. They are, roughly, (a) that art and the rest of human activity are continuous, not contrasting; (b) that art is the most valuable form of activity; and (c) that the value of any activity depends on the degree to which it allows of a balancing or ordering among one's impulses. It is the third which is fundamental and upon which the other two depend, and our attitude to his work in general must depend to a great extent upon the view we take of this account of value. The practical purpose of his account must not be overlooked: he is attempting to discover 'a defensible position for those who believe that the arts are of value,' and it is clear from the context that he intends primarily a position that can be defended against all those who regard art as something other than one of the practical affairs of life. He attempts in effect to meet the friendly and intelligent Philistine on his own ground. Hence his account of value is best regarded as a systematization based on certain assumptions which are not questioned by the people whom he has in mind. He assumes first that living activity is its own satisfaction and that any questioning of its 'value' is bogus questioning. Next he implies a conception of quantity in living activity and assumes that a further unquestionable satisfaction arises as one becomes *more* alive; he takes as the unit of living activity the satisfied impulse, so that the value of an activity or attitude can be measured, hypothetically, in terms of the number of impulses it satisfies. Further he adopts the view that in all living organisms there is an unquestionable effort after greater and greater differentiation and integration of experience.

The necessary limitations of such an account of value have to be recognized before its usefulness for particular purposes can be judged. It is clear that it cannot, even hypothetically, give us grounds for judgment when a difference of opinion rests on a fundamental constitutional difference between two people. Richards for instance condemns swindling and bullying because they lead to a thwarting of important social impulses: the implicit assumption is that the swindler and bully in question possess the 'normal' social impulses. If they do not, then they cannot be condemned on these lines. You might as well try to convince a tiger of its misfortune in not being a buffalo. The numerical treatment of impulses will not help here; it would be flat dogma to assert that the man without social needs must achieve a lower total output of satisfied 'impulses' than the man with them. And according to Richards it is the total number that matters, for the 'importance' of an impulse is only another term for the number of other impulses that depend upon it. It is difficult to suppose that the tiger, given equal strength and good health, satisfies fewer 'impulses' (fewer of 'the elementary processes on which consciousness depends') than the buffalo. This is only to point out that Richards' systematizing of value judgments cannot, even in theory, lead to agreement in evaluations unless the parties concerned have the same fundamental constitution. In point of fact Richards keeps his numerical conception in the background, and implies that greater ordering or integration will of itself lead to the satisfying of more impulses. 'At the other extreme are those fortunate people who have achieved an ordered life, whose systems have developed clearing-houses by which the varying claims of different impulses are adjusted. Their free untrammelled activity gains for them a maximum of varied satisfactions and involves a minimum of suppression and sacrifice.' (*Principles of Literary Criticism,* p. 53). Similarly in the much finer discussion of development in *Practical Criticism,* where he relates the sayings of Confucius on sincerity to modern biological views, it is the ordering alone that is insisted on. The implication here and throughout his work is that everyone begins with the same fundamental impulses, but that they and the secondary impulses dependent on them get muddled and disorganized, thwarting each other unnecessarily. He is profoundly convinced that the function of the arts is to bring back order. In the discussion of sincerity, moreover, he brings forward, perhaps not explicitly enough, the idea that art is not merely remedial (restoring an original order) but that it aids in positive development; aids, that is, the assumed effort of the living organism to become more finely differentiated in its parts and simultaneously more integrated. 'Being more at one within itself the mind thereby becomes more appropriately responsive to the outer world.' Fundamental difficulties confront anyone who attempts to grasp the full meaning of this integration and this appropriateness. But the essential feature of Richards' attitude to art is clear: he pins his faith to the possibility of its being shown to be a means of further progress along the lines of what we regard as biological advance. This is the essence of his defensible position for the arts. Its significance rests perhaps less on the usefulness of its contentions than on the fact that it was formulated by a writer who is genuinely sensitive to poetry, not by one with convictions of its uplift value, nor by a philosopher who felt that he 'ought' somehow to provide art with a pedestal in his exhibition of the universe.

The practical usefulness of Richards' account of value in convincing the plain man of the value of poetry or in helping us to reach agreement over disputed points is doubtful. After outlining the theory Richards writes (*Principles of Literary Criticism,* p. 51) 'We can now take our next step forward and inquire into the relative merits of different systematizations.' This step remains to be taken, unless it consisted in the brief discussion which follows, on the importance of the social virtues. In practice, of course, Richards is able to give us no more help in making these judgments than, for instance, T. H. Morgan offers, in the passage quoted. One might innocently suppose that we should judge a work of art by assessing the number of impulses it satisfied. It is needless to point out that Richards has nowhere done this, nor even pointed out what main impulses any one work of art has satisfied in him. It is of course quite clear that 'the impulse' will not serve in practice as a unit of measurement. Who can say what this smallest impulse is in terms of which the importance of the others must be expressed? There is obviously a vast gap between Richards' theory of value and any actual judgment one may make. To say that 'It is in terms of attitudes, the resolution, inter-inanimation, and balancing of impulses . . . . that all the most valuable effects of poetry must be described' is perhaps as true, and just as helpful, as to say that it is in terms of the combination and disintegration of molecules that all the effects of modern warfare must be described. Even the difference between a pleasing and an irritating variation of rhythm is 'a matter of the combination and resolution of impulses too subtle for our present means of investigation.' (*Principles of Literary Criticism*, p. 138). And in making up our minds about a poem 'We have to gather millions of fleeting semi-independent impulses into a momentary structure of fabulous complexity, whose core or germ only is given us in the words.' (*Practical Criticism*, p. 317). And if his account of the basis of valuable experience has little practical significance for literary judgments, as a means of judging other arts it is more remote still. The greater part of his chapters on painting, sculpture, and music, must be regarded as something very close to psychological eyewash; he hardly makes the gesture of applying his main theory to these subjects. We have to conclude that this attempt to provide a conception (of a balance of impulses) which will establish continuity between the everyday standards of a civilization advanced enough to condemn the bully and swindler and the standards of its art critics, fails through the remoteness and elusiveness of the common denominator chosen—the impulse.

This conclusion does not affect the significance of Richards' profound conviction of the value of poetry and his belief that

SCRUTINY

this value is of the same kind as that implicitly recognized by the civilized Philistine. The significance lies in the fact that such a writer should have felt the need to meet the outside world of common sense and science on its own ground and justify his position by current standards. It is one sign of the uneasiness that those with special qualifications in the arts are experiencing. They cannot now confidently remain specialists, secure in the knowledge of fulfilling a recognized function. They have to become amateurs, looking at the matter from the point of view of the majority and attempting to prove that their function does exist before they can attack their own more specialized problems. This consideration may account for the kind of use to which Richards puts psychology. In the first place it is a means of shaking the complacency of practical people, who are more uneasy at the hints of psycho-analysts than they are at the gibes or fury of artists. 'Human conditions and possibilities have altered more in a hundred years than they had in the previous ten thousand, and the next fifty may overwhelm us, unless we can devise a more adaptable morality. The view that what we need in this tempestuous turmoil of change is a Rock to shelter under or to cling to, rather than an efficient aeroplane in which to ride it, is comprehensible but mistaken.' (*Principles of Literary Criticism,* p. 57). Secondly, psychology as Richards uses it seems to help him in repudiating the pseudo-mystical monopolists of æsthetic theory whose ideas do more harm than good to his demand for the recognition of poetry as a practical assistance in living. It seems to confer authority on such a statement as '. . . the experience of "seeing stars" after a bang on the nose is just as "unique" as any act of musical appreciation and shares any exalted quality which such uniqueness may be supposed to confer.' (*Principles of Literary Criticism,* p. 171). On the other hand, the work of psychologists on æsthetics has not been of the kind he has any use for; it has usually implied other standards than his in its approach to works of art, and it has done nothing to show the practical value of such art as it has dealt with. Hence his care to dissociate himself from the professional psychologists. 'Such more complex objects as have been examined have yielded very uncertain results, for reasons which anyone who has ever *both* looked at a picture or read a poem *and* been inside a psychological laboratory or conversed with a representative psychologist will understand.' (*Principles of*

Literary Criticism, p. 8). And rather than be committed to existing psychological methods he draws still further on the already heavily mortgaged future of neurology. Musical effects, for instance, '. . . . belong to a branch of psychology for which we have as yet no methods of investigation. It seems likely that we shall have to wait a long while, and that very great advances must first be made in neurology before these problems can profitably be attacked.' (*Principles of Literary Criticism*, p. 170). But there is a marked change of tone in *Practical Criticism*. After reiterating his dissatisfaction with much of the psychological work on æsthetics he goes on, 'The general reader, whose ideas as to the methods and endeavours of psychologists derive more from the popularisers of Freud or from the Behaviourists than from students of Stout or Ward, needs perhaps some assurance that it is possible to combine an interest and faith in psychological inquiries with a due appreciation of the complexity of poetry. Yet a psychologist who belongs to this main body is perhaps the last person in the world to underrate this complexity.' (*Practical Criticism*, p. 322). Again, speaking of the harm done by the cruder psychologies, ' But the remedy of putting the clock back is impracticable. Inquiry cannot be stopped now. The only possible course is to hasten, so far as we can, the development of a psychology which will ignore none of the facts and yet demolish none of the values that human experience has shown to be necessary. An account of poetry will be a pivotal point in such a psychology.' His attitude here seems to be one of willingness to leave professional psychology to make its contribution to the problem in its own way, whereas the tendency before was to short-circuit psychological methods by dogmatizing about the essentials of the conclusions they must reach. The change may perhaps be related to the fact that in *Practical Criticism* Richards has a much more demonstrable function that he had in the earlier work. For one thing he can offer his work as a contribution to academic psychology: '. . . . to find something to investigate that is accessible and detachable is one of the chief difficulties of psychology. I believe the chief merit of the experiment here made is that it gives us this.' (*Practical Criticism*, p. 10). Further he offers his work as a contribution to education, and is able to show that even by existing educational standards such work as he has done here has an important and undeniable function. ' This, then, may be made a positive recommendation, that an inquiry into language . . . . be recognized as a vital branch of research, and treated no longer as the peculiar province of the whimsical amateur.' (*Practical Criticism*, p. 337).

It is undoubtedly in dealing with problems of communication that Richards comes most closely to grips with his material and least shows the characteristics of the amateur. But to say this ought not to suggest that his work falls into two isolated compartments, one concerned with evaluation and the other with communication, and that they can be appraised separately. It is in fact through a consideration of his theory of value and its limitations that the importance of his work on communication can best be seen.

The conclusion that his account of value gives a basis for agreement only when 'normality' (or identical abnormality) is assumed, might seem to leave us no defence against an endless variety of critical opinions, each justified by an appeal to a fundamental constitutional peculiarity in the critic. Since innate differences do of course exist, we must perhaps admit that in the end we shall have to recognize distinguishable ' types ' of critical opinion founded on psycho-physiological differences in the critics, and irreconcilable. But this is too remote a consideration to give 'type' psychologists any excuse for extending their literary labelling. It is still possible to show that differences of opinion in literary matters frequently arise from errors of approach which even those who make them can be brought to recognize. With people who assert that they know what they like the one hope is to demonstrate to them that in point of fact they *don't,* that according to standards they themselves recognize elsewhere their judgment here is mistaken. As these inconsistencies are faced and abandoned, the possibility of agreement with other people grows greater. We cannot tell how far this principle may be pushed, but undoubtedly we have a very long way to go before innate psycho-physiological differences are the sole cause of disagreement between us. The most important part of Richards' work consists in extending the possibility of agreement. From one point of view it is work on problems of communication; from another it offers us exercise in attaining self-consistency in literary judgments, and remotely approaching the 'self-completion' that Richards sees as the ultimate form of valuable experience.

In this part of his work there are so many distinct contributions—close, fully-illustrated discussions of actual instances—that little general comment is in place. Many of them offer a starting point for further investigation; sometimes there seems a possibility of fresh preliminary discussion, where, as for instance in his treatment of intellectual truth in poetry and of rhythm, Richards does not seem free from ambiguities and shifts of ground; all draw attention to serious possibilities of mis-reading and mis-judging, and all go towards stressing the same main theme, that the adequate reading of poetry is a discipline and not a relaxation.

The relation between the two aspects of his work is well set out by Richards himself. 'The whole apparatus of critical rules and principles is a means to the attainment of finer, more precise, more discriminating communication. There is, it is true, a valuation side to criticism. When we have solved, completely, the communication problem, when we have got, perfectly, the experience, *the mental condition* relevant to the poem, we have still to judge it, still to decide upon its worth. But the later question nearly always settles itself; or rather, our own inmost nature and the nature of the world in which we live decide it for us. Our prime endeavour must be to get the relevant mental condition and then see what happens. If we cannot then decide whether it is good or bad, it is doubtful whether any principles, however refined and subtle, can help us much. Without the capacity to get the experience they cannot help us at all. This is still clearer if we consider the use of critical maxims in teaching. Value cannot be demonstrated except through the communication of what is valuable.' The difficulty of demonstrating the rightness of an opinion even on these lines ought not to be under-rated; over the Longfellow poem, for instance, it seems only to have been a drawn battle between Richards and the protocols. But a reliance on improved methods of reading as the most hopeful way of reaching agreement in literary judgments undoubtedly grows out of Richards' practice more naturally than does his explicit theory of value. The suspicion is left, however, that in making practical judgments he is assuming more principles of evaluation than one would expect from the passage just quoted. One weakness of Yeats' transcendental poetry, for instance, is 'a deliberate reversal of the natural relations of thought and feeling. . . .'

(*Science and Poetry*, p. 74). His charge against Lawrence is rather similar. But *natural relations* . . . Lawrence might have detected a principle of criticism here. The fact is that principles of evaluation remain a necessity for the practising critic even when interpretation and understanding have been carried to their hypothetical limit. How large is the highest common factor in human natures, and how far it can be formulated into agreed ethical principles, are questions that will not be answered in the near future. Yet guesses have to be made; 'To set up as a critic is to set up as a judge of values.' This is a fact that receives less prominence in Richards' later work than it did in his earlier, and it is not surprising to find Father D'Arcy reminding him (in *The Criterion,* January, 1933) that we have to set out 'both to understand the meaning of others *and* the truth of what they say.'

The importance of Richards' work on communication is unfortunately obscured for many people by their annoyance at a too frequent outcropping of the amateur spirit. This shows itself particularly as a romantic inflation of the significance of the topic, in the form of dark hints at the extent of our ignorance and the cataclysm that awaits us as The Theory of Interpretation is pushed further. Exploitation of the Tremendous Idea makes a peculiarly strong appeal to one side of the amateur: for one thing, every professional immediately has the ground cut from under his feet. No matter what a man's standing, and no matter how impressive the substance of his views, you can still regard him from an unassailable vantage-ground if only you happen to observe that he isn't capable of understanding what's said to him. This, according to Richards (in *The Criterion,* October, 1932), is the weak place in the armour of Max Eastman, T. S. Eliot, and Irving Babbitt. They are all 'untrained in the technique of interpretation . . . this is not their fault since the proper training has not yet been provided . . . you must *understand* before you argue . . . When the right training has been provided, our three champions here will be seen to be each journeying through and battling with his own set of mirages.' So much for Irving Babbitt, T. S. Eliot, and Max Eastman. The earlier work too occasionally betrays this anxiety to cut the ground from under the feet of those who might otherwise seem qualified to express an opinion: 'neither the professional psychologist whose interest in poetry is frequently not intense, nor the man of letters, who as a rule has no adequate ideas of the mind as a whole, has been equipped for the investigation [into the nature of poetry]. Both a passionate knowledge of poetry and a capacity for dispassionate psychological analysis are required if it is to be satisfactorily prosecuted.

It will be best to begin by . . .' (*Science and Poetry*, p. 9). It is probably, too, as an aspect of the amateur that we must interpret the curiously romantic tone that sometimes appears in Richards' writing. *Science and Poetry*, for example, leaves a strong impression of a thrilled responsiveness to the difficulties and hazards of 'the contemporary situation,' and also of some failure to get at grips with any definite problems that concern people. The latter is a serious failing here, for it prevents him from clinching his argument that poetry is of supreme value as a means of re-orientation. The nearest he comes to specifying more closely 'the contemporary situation' of which one may be 'agonizingly aware' is in his discussion of the neutrality of nature and the impossibility of beliefs. But the former is surely not a concern of fundamental importance to most informed people nowadays, though in some moods they may feel chilled by it. And the impossibility of beliefs—except in some quite limited sense—seems itself to be impossible. Certainly T. S. Eliot has repudiated Richards' suggestion that *The Waste Land* is without beliefs ; but apart from this repudiation it is impossible to see how any living activity can go on without beliefs in some sense, and we must suppose that Richards is speaking only of a special sort of belief. Indeed he seems only to mean that most people have ceased to believe in the possibility of supernatural sanctions or aids. If this is all, the excitement apparent in his tone seems naïve. ' It is very probable that the Hindenburg line to which the defence of our traditions retired as a result of the onslaughts of the last century will be blown up in the near future. If this should happen a mental chaos such as man has never experienced may be expected.' (*Science and Poetry*, p. 82). 'Consider the probable effects upon love poetry in the near future of the kind of inquiry into basic human constitution exemplified by psycho-analysis.' These are very bourgeois bogies. Their worst feature is the way they play into the hands of the would-be emancipated, those whom L. H. Myers has described in *Prince Jali* : ' they depended basically upon a solid, shockable world of decorum and common sense. They had to believe that a great ox-like eye was fixed upon them in horror.'

These defects of tone in Richards' writing cannot be passed over. In the first place they tend to attract the least desirable kind of audience, though the astringency and discipline of Richards' best work should be a sufficient safeguard against this. A more serious consideration is that they offer a needless obstacle to an appreciation by better readers of Richards' real significance. To sum up this significance one may indicate the two points of view from which Richards sees poetry: he sees it both as the practised reader who has acquired his standards of culture imperceptibly, and as the plain man of common sense and faith in science who needs *convincing,* without a gradual process of education, that poetry might be of some importance to him. A large part of Richards' work can be regarded as an attempt to find common ground for these two points of view; to find a set of standards recognized by the second man which will lead logically to the position of the first. He sets to work in two ways; first by an explicit theory of value, second by showing up the kind of mistakes that are likely to lead to an under-estimation of poetry. The second method really consists in making explicit, and at the same time telescoping, the steps which those who adequately value poetry must at some time have taken, normally without having analysed them. This second method is obviously of enormous value to people already prepared to take poetry seriously; it may well divert university students, for instance, from their otherwise almost inevitable progress towards the point from which they regard ' the time when they read poetry ' with slightly more wistful feelings than they have for ' the time when they played Red Indians.' But whether Richards' methods would be effective in convincing the intelligent and friendly Philistine is another matter. It may be that his work fulfills its purpose by giving those who already value poetry a new assurance that their concern for it is a development, and not a distortion, of 'ordinary practical living.' If this is one of its functions it bears witness to the growing need of those with minority views to justify themselves at the bar of the main community. The main community may not be convinced; perhaps the fundamental need is that the minority should be.

D. W. HARDING.

HISTORY AND THE
MARXIAN METHOD

THE writings of the modern Marxists contain explanations which should at least open our minds to the consideration of the Marxian view of history. We need not fear the word 'materialist,' for we are now told that 'materialist' only means 'matter-of-fact'; for us at least, as will be seen later, it need signify nothing more than the modern scientific method in historical study. We understand—for it is satisfactorily explained—that the Marxist is no 'crude economic determinist'; the Marxian thesis does not rule out the influence of individuals or the power of ideas. An interpretation of history which purports to belong to the same intellectual world as 'the linguistic criticism of Mr. Ogden, the æsthetic criticism of Mr. Richards and the methods of the new psychology' is a thing which the most jaded historian would desire to consider afresh; and the worst of Philistines must wish to weigh a theory which claims to be appropriate to our capitalistic age. That variations in means of production are the starting-point of historical change; that what Marx calls 'production-relations' are factors in history which are in a special sense inescapable; that historical change is a dialectical process, the contradiction of thesis and antithesis setting up a movement which results in a new synthesis; and that deep at the bottom of our history there is really the immemorial class-struggle—these are propositions less strange but more intriguing, now, than in former days; for they do not drop into our minds without raising an echo, without stirring at least half a sympathy. So we may be more open to the consideration of the Marxian view of history, as it is embodied in the famous Marxian formulation of the historical process—the doctrine that, within an existing order of society, the discrepant interests of two economic classes provide a contradiction and provoke a struggle, which leads to the formation of a new order, where the same thing happens again. It may be useful to analyse this attempt to state the historical process by means of a formula, regarding it, as we are asked to regard it, namely as a 'clue' or an 'approach' to history ; and seeking to discover its virtues and to find whether it exposes the habitual fallacies of our own history; which, for the purposes of this argument, we may consent to call 'bourgeois' history. Then we may discuss the dangers of the Marxian system, particularly when it is taken as an 'interpretation' in a wider sense of the word; and this will concern its possible aspect as a 'verdict' upon history. And, to prevent ourselves from imagining that we are considering Marxism in its wider sense, and all that Marxism means— to avoid the misconception that we are examining the Marxian view in any sense save as an historical interpretation and an historical method—it would be useful for us to state the problem we are discussing in something like the following terms: what is the value of the Marxian view to a historian who is himself a bourgeois and who, philosophically, is not a materialist ; and who—if we may concede this for the sake of argument—is a conservative in politics?

In the first place, the Marxian formula is supposed to be the 'type' of what we call the historical process, and it maintains that there is such a thing as an historical process, complicating all the purposes of men. Its antithesis in this sense is what the Marxists call the 'individualist' theory of history, the view that history is what it appears on the surface, a human drama, Cromwell fighting Charles I, Fox fighting Pitt, and Gladstone fighting Disraeli. On the individualist view one man achieves his purpose, though it may not be till after he is dead; and so we must thank Martin Luther for our religious liberty, and Charles James Fox for the Reform Bill—emphasising the agency of individuals in the story of mankind. The Marxists do not deny that individuals are at work throughout the course of history; or that, as in the case of Lenin, an individual may succeed in a great purpose; but they emphasise the view that this work of individuals is complicated by interactions which are taking place in history, and they see an historical process of which human beings are the more or less conscious agents. Their whole idiom, when they are writing history, is less closely related than ours to the technique of biography.

In the second place, the Marxian formula puts before our eyes a certain pattern, and prepares us to examine historical change as though it were taking place in accordance with this pattern. We are told to look for a contradiction—a conflict between thesis and antithesis—and we are to expect, not that either of these will entirely gain a victory over the other, but that the conflict will be resolved by the establishment of a synthesis. History proceeds to something new by reason of contradictions which have arisen in the old order. And change is not the result of accomplished purpose so much as the product of a clash of wills. The antithesis to Marxism at this stage of the argument is the kind of history which hankers after some logical development, and sees men moving step by step towards some expanding purpose, freedom broadening down from precedent to precedent. It is the contrast between these views that Dobb is stating when he says that we ought to think of history 'not as logically continuous but as a dialectical process.' Some people, for example, assume that Protestantism logically 'led to' individualism. Some people see the continuity so directly that they say the Reformation 'led to' the French Revolution. On the Marxian formula we should tend to enquire whether the rise of Martin Luther did not set up a contradiction within the old order of Europe, and whether it was not the clash of authorities, the feud of Protestant and Catholic, which issued in the secular state and a new order that neither party had intended. When we say that 'feudalism declined' we are speaking, again, in simple, unilinear terms; the Marxist would arrive at the real complexity sooner, for he would ask what contradiction was set up within the feudal society to produce interaction and ultimately change. At the same time he does not deny the possibility of such a thing as logical development—he admits that it can take place in ideas and he only forbids us to transfer to the whole realm of general history the process which may take place in the simplified realm of the 'history of ideas.' Also the Marxist does not deny that, perhaps even below everything, there is a development in history—a development in modes of production, for example, in the transition from nomadic society to the capitalistic world.

In the third place, the Marxian formula provides us with a point of view from which we survey history—it is a formula of

internal reaction within a given society. That is to say, we are told
that in a social order a contradiction will arise and will produce a
clash, and this clash will end in the emergence of a new order, where
the same process starts over again. The Marxists take the whole of
society as the unit of study; and the balance of the story is affected
by this. We are given the history of a people, not the history of a
government. I think that if we honestly search our minds we must
confess that, for the most part, the history we learn and read is the
history of governments and governmental matters, and it is from
these that we are accustomed to take our centre, or to make our
approach to history. We do not confine ourselves now, it is true,
merely to the record of courts, battles and kings, but some of us
seem to imagine that we are telling the story of the people when
we are only giving the history of parliament or the analysis of
governmental institutions. And often when we talk of the people
we only mean the people who politically counted, or when we
do remember the whole society we really regard it from the angle
of government. I am not certain that we realise the full content
of the words: 'the history of the English people,' or that we
remember how little the history of England that we possess in
our minds really corresponds with the genuine fulness of the
concept. And though in our economic history it is true that we
study the manor and the craft-guilds, we do not always realise
how soon we turn back to the question of governmental action,
and how much in dealing with society we start at the top of the
pyramid, working downwards and always looking downwards;
and it is not without significance, if we are arguing with the
Marxists, that even at this point it is economic history that is
in question.

But the real advantage of the Marxian view of history, as
the study of internal reaction within a society, is most apparent
in the new solidity which it has given to what is called 'social
history.' For, if this branch of our study is in disrepute with us,
that is because our social history generally has something anæmic
about it. In the October number of the journal *History*, Sir
Charles Firth criticises Macaulay's famous chapter on the state of
England in 1685. There is a curious deficiency in this chapter
when it is regarded as a piece of social history, and we might
define the fault by stating that Macaulay only wrote the social

history that was preliminary to his political narrative; it is social history from the point of view of a political historian—social history regarded chiefly as background. Some time ago Mr. Rowse reviewed in the *New Criterion* the historical method involved in Professor G. N. Clark's book on the *Seventeenth Century*. He hailed the work as an illustration of what is meant by the Marxian point of view—the analysis of a whole society in every sphere of life, activity and thought—but he seems to think that Professor Clark would have been more consistent with himself and more successful in his undertaking, if he had avowedly adopted the Marxian principle and kept its terms in mind. The weakness of the book—the certain disappointment that it gives—does lie in the fact that it tends to be a series of separate sketches of finance, military organization, religion, philosophy, etc.—and often these sketches are really collections of illustrative data and curious information—when we might have had a deeper structural analysis, a closer study of the inter-relations between the various departments of life. Professor Clark rightly repudiates the view that all things in the 17th century can be regarded 'as mere phases of one common spirit of the age,' and rightly repudiates that interpretation of history which says that 'the economic life of man . . . . explains all the rest of his life.' In particular he does not attempt to explain everything in the 17th century by reference to the economic conditions of the 17th century itself— which would have represented the most childish of the perversions of the Marxian view which we are considering. It still remains true that the 17th century can be regarded structurally and not as a series of separate compartments, and that this conception of it depends upon the pre-disposition of the historian. It is not an accident that historical education, even in this university, is most lacking in the treatment of the inter-relations between the various phases of life; though the Marxists are unjust when they say that we keep our history in separate compartments purely to prevent the discovery of the importance of economic factors in other spheres. It is not a mere accident that bourgeois history fails most of all in what we may call 'social' or even 'general' history, producing trivialities, surface-descriptions, and illustrative tit-bits, or providing an introductory chapter that is like the setting of a piece of scenery. Whatever may be the faults of Pokrowsky's

History of Russia—and I am certainly not competent to pass judgment on the work in its actual execution—there is no doubt that the author had in his mind a Russian people, not a government; and there is something impressive in his conception of history as the profound structural analysis of a society.

Fourthly, the Marxian formula is couched in economic terms, and this raises the question of its aspect as an economic interpretation of history. It is important to bear in mind the conditions under which we are (at the moment) discussing the Marxian view of history; particularly as this is a point which the modern exponents of the theory have realized and have taken pains to stress. The Marxian formula defines a method, provides a clue for a person who wishes to construct a survey of general history, or to discuss some historical problem or to start a line of enquiry; it does not exist to answer questions which can only be answered by historical research. It is the definition of the predisposition which we should bring when we come to the study of history, and neither this nor any other interpretation of its kind can validly provide us with anything more. This point has been greatly stressed by modern exponents of the theory. In other words, where we should in any case act upon one assumption or another, the Marxian formula prescribes a way of approach; it tells us which end of the stick to pick up. We may ascribe the downfall of Spain to the personality or the policy of Philip II, saying, as so many writers say, in parenthesis, that at the same time there were economic difficulties which were out of his control. I think one could find many writers on Spanish history who have made this interpretation the basis of the very architecture of their story, even when the interpretation is contradicted by the things they themselves say, but say only in parenthesis. With the Marxian method it is simply a question of the order in which these things present themselves in our minds. This method would lead us first to enquire whether the discovery of the New World did not present Spain with problems that the economic knowledge of the time was incapable of meeting; but if he found this to be true, it would not prevent the Marxist from saying that the situation was aggravated by the personality or the policy of a man like Philip II. The Marxian method is not a denial of the influence of ideas upon history; it does not prevent us from believing that ideas influence economic facts and even modes of production; it allows us to believe that ideas can influence one another or even make their own logical development; and the extent to which these things are true can only be discovered at any given point by actual historical research. But it does affect the structure of our history whether we begin by seeing the action of a man like Philip II upon the world, and then noting in parenthesis that he himself however was conditioned by a historical situation; or whether we start with an examination of the world he lived in, beginning with the economic conditions and rising if we like to the highest range of abstract ideas, and then see Philip II, greatly conditioned by all this, but acting, so to speak, only on the margin of it. The Marxian interpretation which we are considering is an economic interpretation only in a restricted sense of the words: it claims that there is a fallacy in an attempt to estimate the influence of Protestantism on the economic world, if first of all we have not examined the influence of the surrounding world and of economic conditions upon the development of Protestantism itself. It is not at all a denial of the fact that Protestantism and its religious ideas had an influence in history.

Taking another aspect of the question of the economic interpretation, and speaking for the moment very roughly and by way of crude analogy, we can say that for the Marxist economic history has acquired a special emphasis—it has been given the privileged position which political history has generally had with us. The Marxist puts economic history at the bottom, and, roughly speaking, lays everything else on the top of it, till he rises to the realm of ideas; while we put political history at the top and range everything else below it, reaching ultimately even down to the economic stratum in our turn. This, I think, is particularly our habit when we are dealing with general surveys of modern history. And, whereas, to the bourgeois historian, political history seems sometimes to be the sum of all history, the State is regarded as an all-inclusive end, and politics are at the top of everything—with the result that social history, as we have seen, is a sort of adjunct or background to political history—the Marxist does not need to make such a pretentious valuation, he does not need to say that economics are the most important things in life; he has only to show that, to the historian, the economic element sits somehow at the bottom, and that it is taken first because there is a sense in which it comes first. He only has to show that it sets the conditions in the last resort, that it is always reached in the last analysis, and that we shall do well to work until we come to it, even if what we are studying is a religious revival or a political programme or a moral disintegration in society. It is in sympathy with this view—though it is not a necessary corollary of the Marxian method—that the Marxist should analyse modern imperialism, for example, in terms of economics; whereas we are accustomed to an analysis in terms of politics. And Marxian history blossoms out into these economic diagnoses, whereas whig history flowers into its most typical product in what we call political science. And if any of us should believe that this political science has the chief part in forming a discrepancy between our mentality and the contemporary situation, so helping to prevent us from even realizing the issues in the right categories of thought, we might agree that this economic approach to history—even in what might be called its by-products—will better help us to construct a mentality that can squarely set itself to the lines of the modern world. If we do not believe this, it does not matter, for it concerns the by-products of history, not the essence of the Marxian method.

But the real antithesis to Marxism at this stage is the view that on the last analysis ideas do not merely condition but actually determine the course of history; and this view—however much it has been qualified and overlaid—is still the clue to a great deal of the bourgeois system. Rowse very justly quotes the statement from Lord Acton's Inaugural Lecture: 'It is our function to keep in view and to command the movement of ideas which are not the effect but the cause of public events.' In a sense the Marxist stresses the fact that we use history to explain ideas, while the bourgeois has tended to bring in ideas and use them in order to explain history. Pokrowsky, the Marxian historian of Russia, has ridiculed those people who ascribe the decline of tribal society to a decline of tribal ideas or a mysterious dissolving of the 'sense of kinship.' We have all ceased, I believe, to attribute the decay of feudalism to the decline of 'the feudal idea.' But, though we abandon the cruder forms of this heresy, the temptation does lie in the structure of our bourgeois system, and there is no telling to this day what the wisest of historians will not attribute to the Protestant idea. And sometimes the extreme form of our heresy is reached when we personify what we call the 'spirit of the age' and make it a special agency in the process of historical change. To the Marxist ideas are concrete facts of history, just as mechanical inventions are; in a sense they are the product of history before they can be the cause of anything. To the Marxist, who, in this respect, is only to be regarded as the matter-of-fact historian, man seems to rise out of nature, the struggle for existence apparently precedes the quest of the 'good life,' history begins where anthropology leaves off, and civilization does emerge as a sort of superstructure, reared last of all. And if God is at the back of everything, still the historian cannot say so; and if transcendental ideas are behind the rumblings of nature or the tides of human life, still they do not come within reach of historical evidence; and though the materialist explanation of the universe may not be a full explanation, or really an explanation at all, still it is the only kind of historical explanation which our apparatus enables us to give. Concerning man himself it may be said that the historian can never reach the essence of him ; for the historian can only study him in his external relations, his overt acts, his interplay with environment.

Fifthly, taken in its totality, the Marxian formula gives us a statement of the historical process when reduced to its lowest terms. It tells us, in one respect, where we must begin if we wish to construct a scheme or a survey of history. In another sense it tells us what we shall find conditioning historical change in the last analysis. But, from the moment when this formula is brought to the actual facts of history, we shall watch the historical process for ever complicating itself; for the formula is only a synthesis of the really primary statements that can be made about history. Plekhanov uses an interesting analogy to warn us against the common fallacy of regarding the economic element as a sort of highest common factor, when in reality it is related rather to the problem of reducing history to its lowest terms.

' If, for instance,' he says, ' the dance performed by Australian Blackfellows is a reproduction of the activities of the same tribesmen when engaged in collecting roots, we know where we are . . . . But a knowledge of the economic life of France in the 18th century will not explain to us the origin of the minuet.'

When the Marxist says that thought itself is conditioned by the development of means of production, he claims no more than that you will have no metaphysics, no experimental science, no rationalistic outlook, before the means of production have reached a certain level, have facilitated division of labour, have complicated the social structure, and have made possible certain kinds of technique. Napoleon said: 'The nature of weapons decides the composition of armies, the theatres of war, marches, positions of camps, orders of battle, and the situation and construction of fortresses.' It has been pointed out that, before Columbus could discover America, ship-building and technical apparatus had to reach the necessary stage to permit of trans-Atlantic voyages. We need not go anything like so far as Mrs. Virginia Woolf who seems to think that £500 a year and 'a room of one's own' are necessary antecedents to the production of good literature. But such statements are comments on the historical process; they are seminal in that they start appropriate lines of enquiry; and they are wise for they remind us that we are living on the earth. I think that they are calculated to encourage a certain form of historical-mindedness.

The Marxist, therefore, would define bourgeois history as that which tends to fall into the individualist heresy, while overlooking the importance of what we call the historical process; that which tends to slip into the mistake of regarding historical change as logically continuous, when this change ought to be viewed rather as a dialectical process; that which tends to see ideas determining change in the last analysis, rather than to assume that in the last resort economic factors are the conditioning element; and that which tends to take the government rather than the whole society as its centre, and to lay stress on political history while it fails to produce any profound social history. I do not think we can deny that the Marxist has put his fingers on the fundamental fallacies of that history which the average Englishman holds in his head. He has seized upon many of the heresies which we tend to unlearn as we become more highly-trained. He has diagnosed the very evils which bourgeois historians often deplore in their own history, particularly the evils which conservative historians often see in whig history. When one person argues that in the Renaissance we are dealing with only a handful of privileged people—that the majority of Italians, for example, were super-stitiously religious at that very time; when another person criticises the common view that the 18th century was the 'age of reason,' these people are only pulling us towards the position of the Marxists, who demand that we study the whole society as a unit, and condemn us for keeping our eyes upon a privileged class. When people attack the common habit of 'tracing ideas back into history'—watching the Reformation grow through Abelard, Wycliff, Erasmus and the Renaissance, or working towards the League of Nations through the Crusades, the Grand Design and the Holy Alliance—they are joining hands with the Marxists in a protest against one form of the heresy that history is a logical development, or they are attacking the bourgeois assumption that history can be regarded as the story of ideas. Those people who desire that the history of England should not be studied in this university in a number of separate compartments, but desire at the same time that it should not degenerate into a vague and spine-less non-technical 'social' history,—these most of all, perhaps, are really hankering after the structural virtues of Marxian history. And with them we might associate those people who feel dissatis-fied with the general study of modern European history, on the ground that it too easily falls into dry lines of political or diplo-matic story, instead of seeking the structural analysis of society and the relations between movements of thought and various spheres of life. Our economic studies are drawing us in the same direction, and while Plekhanov warns the Marxists that, after all, economic causes do not explain everything in history, our own scientific historians are often showing how, after all, some economic factor which we had ignored comes in to correct a bourgeois assumption. And sometimes it is we ourselves who fall into the heresy that Puritanism is merely the result of the growth of capitalism. But rather than admit the truth that exists in the Marxian interpretation of history, we prefer to go on living with a discrepancy in our minds; our real outlook has greatly changed while our historical theory seems determined not to catch up; and so we slip back, carelessly and unconsciously, into old fallacies that we had forsworn, and we are content very often to start by picking up, still, the wrong end of the stick. There may indeed be some point in the thesis which I think represents the argument of Mr. Rowse, that some of us would gain consistency with our-selves, and the history we conceive of would achieve new depth and solidity, if we consented to go the one step further and confess that, in this aspect, the Marxian theory is right.

The Marxian formula, as it is presented by its apostles at the present day, does represent the direction in which our bourgeois history is moving—though neither we nor the Marxists like to admit the fact. Also I think that this is seen most clearly in that kind of history which has a more conservative bearing; and the extreme antithesis to the Marxian method is rather what we usually know as 'whig history.' But if we resist the Marxian method there can be no doubt that the Marxists are much to blame, and if we have misunderstood and slandered the method— as some of its modern expositors assert—there can be no doubt that Marxists themselves have misunderstood it too and have been the cause of our misapprehension. For we cannot be blamed if we judge this method by its actual results when it is put into application by its own apostles, and the greatest argument against the Marxian view is the kind of history Marxists often write, and more particularly the kind of statements they often make about history. It is possible so to emphasise the historical process that we overlook the importance of the 'individual' altogether. It is possible to make the economic interpretation a too direct transla-tion of all history into terms of economics. It is possible to mini-mise the influence or deny the self-development of ideas, and to come to startlingly crude conclusions concerning the relations between culture and economic conditions. Indeed one could almost say that the Marxian method is very dangerous if one is really a Marxist in the complete sense of the word; its perils are only counteracted if one is bourgeois and perhaps a trifle conserva-tive; for there is no doubt that the tendency to see too directly the connections between culture and the economic situation, is a danger which is greatly heightened if one happens also to be an aggressive philosophical materialist, if one wants to believe that economic factors fully explain the emergence of human thought, and if one regards the Marxian interpretation of history as a weapon to be used in the cause of socialist revolution. Prejudices, passions, assumptions and interests are all pulling the same way, inviting the Marxian historian to an over-simplification of his own method, an over-emphasis of the truth that is in it. The dogmatic character of his creed encourages him to turn into dogmas or dead formulæ the hints and clues which are the virtues of his system if they are treated with flexibility. So the best historical method in the world—talking now not of methods in research, which remain the same, but of methods of approach and organization—is the monopoly of the party which, more than any other, is regarded as 'unhistorical.'

But the real objections to the Marxian over-emphasis are reached when the system is regarded not as an approach to history, but as a 'verdict' on the whole course of history. This takes place when the view of history as a dialectical process, a process that moves through contradictions, is translated into the general pronouncement that all history is the story of the class-struggle. Supposing we take the whole of society as our unit and seek a formula that shall be a statement of internal reaction within that society, supposing then that we look for a contradiction within that society, remembering that we are stating the formula in economic terms, then it is true that we have discovered a sort of minimum formula, epitomizing the historical process, but it is also true that, taken in the round, our formula is a description of an economic cleavage in society. This may mean that deep at the seat of human history there is always—though perhaps unconscious—a tension between economic classes. And the Marxist seems to claim that this tension has a primary importance, that it is a conditioning element which in the last analysis is in some way inescapable. Perhaps we shall not understand the Reformation in any given geographical region until we know what in that region the relations between economic classes were. Perhaps it is right that when we come to the study of history we should look for this fundamental cleavage in society and make it the beginning of our story. In other words the formula may be defensible when regarded purely as a clue, or an approach to history. But Marx himself is responsible for the further leap to what we may regard as the grand conclusion—the transportation of this original assumption to the dignity of a 'lesson' or 'verdict' of history. He is responsible for the pronouncement that all history is really the story of the class-war.

Further, the Marxist, in his protest against our partiality for the ruling classes, may merely invert our history and have eyes only for what he regards as the depressed classes, whom he may represent as the victims of exploiters and may find it easy to equate with the whole society—forgetting that, to the historian, rich and poor alike are part victims and part agents in the whole historical process. Without this complete reversal, which produces a particular organization of our sympathies and interests, we might adopt the Marxian view of history—even the view that all history is a class-struggle—and still be open at the end of our studies to take one side or the other in present-day disputes. Bourgeois history by a similar process can be conservative as well as whig, and admits of those who uphold authority as well as those who are advocates of liberty. Whatever may be the advantages of the Marxian approach to history, it must remain fundamentally true that our hopes for the future will depend on our philosophy and our values, and all our prophecies for the future will depend primarily on our diagnosis of the state of the world to-day. We could not consent to follow the Marxist in this example of over-emphasis; or to accept any corollary to his theory which may put historical study at the service of one party. And in fact there is no reason why the Marxian view of history, as it is described above and as it is defended by its present-day exponents, should not assist the development of a conservatism more enlightened by being freed from traditional historical forms.

The general view that history is the story of the class-struggle may not be more pleasing than the view that it is the story of ideas; but we must not forget that many people see history as the conflict between liberty and authority, and perhaps a Catholic might regard it as the fight between the Church and the World. It would need a cold abstraction, a great refinement of the mind, to think of the course of history and see no issue at all. Those who conceive their own present in terms of issues such as these, will not find it easy to avoid carrying the pattern and the ideas back into their history; and whether their aspiration is the class-less state, the reign of freedom, the victory of the Church, or the triumph of the League of Nations, historians will hardly realize the subtle ways in which they may slip into propaganda. Any of these theses, crudely held, may produce mere vulgar simplifications of history; but a scientific historian, though believing them profoundly, would produce a history in which they were qualified and greatly overlaid. And sometimes we do not recognize the propaganda unless it is propaganda with which we disagree. Marxian, Bourgeois and Catholic interpretations—taking now the word interpretation in its wider and more popular sense—occupy in this respect positions which, if not equal, are at any rate analogous; they construe the past in terms of the present as they conceive it, and they carry into history the issues and obsessions of their own contemporary world. But if it is allowable or unavoidable that men should see the past with the eyes of the present, then at least there is ground for asserting that the contemporary world from which we take our start should be really ours and really contemporary, not a world that was contemporary with our grandfathers; and perhaps we might realize some danger to our minds if it should transpire that we were accepting and handing down a sort of traditional historian's present—starting where old history-books had started, instead of reconsidering the situation again. It is here that the Marxian system makes a further claim against bourgeois history—that it does not start from an old 'present' made traditional by the continuity of historical studies over a long period, but writes history over again with reference to the living world of to-day.

There is a view of history which I believe we must hold whether we are Marxists or not, but which I think will help us to place the Marxian interpretation, as we are now considering it, in its proper light. The view that I mean is expressed by the thesis that the process of learning history is always the process of unlearning the history that we knew before; and that an interpretation of history is a thing which we start with and then proceed forever in a certain sense to unlearn. Every step of historical understanding is therefore a process of self-revision; and at the lowest we have to eliminate the thousand fallacies which assume that the past is like the present-day. Taking one point of view we may roughly say that we study the Renaissance by first learning that there was one; after this it may be brought to our minds that in reality there was no such thing as a Renaissance at all; finally we may see that in spite of everything there was one, but not in the way we had first imagined—and so we go on forever finding friction with the concepts we have hitherto held. The habit of these constant reshufflings gives our minds that elasticity which is the first condition of historical-mindedness. And in this way the history we learn at school comes to upset a childhood's legend; and this school-history, so thoroughly bourgeois, we somewhat qualify and partly unlearn at the university. Only, with the majority of us at any rate, it must be said that we never quite unlearn.

Now it is the fault of much of our criticism of the Marxists that we tend to compare the Marxian interpretation with scientific history in the most refined sense of the words, when in reality we ought to compare it with the bourgeois interpretation from which we take our start. For us as for them scientific history only lies at the end of the road—it is the reward of a long chastening, it is the drastiq re-visualization of the formulæ with which we began. We ought to bear in mind that, at the end of the long process of self-revision, the Marxian historian, who, we may be sure, will still carry on the work of research, will have overlaid his original thesis with a thousand complications in detail; just as a whig historian can go on tacking and compromising till he is recognizable as a whig no more. Bourgeois historians, having qualified their theses, seem sometimes almost to have learned something from the Marxists; and similarly the Marxists, when they write their history, make what we might imagine to be concessions to our point of view. And at their highest, Marxist and Whig will end by laying out very much the same piece of detailed history on a given subject—though they will speak in different terminology and move in a different order of ideas. It would be wrong to imagine that it is only the bourgeois system that can refine itself into what we call scientific history. For in the end both Marxist and Bourgeois must learn that the interpretation which they regarded as the verdict of history was itself neither more nor less than an assumption which they brought to their study of history; they must learn that in our interpretation of history we begin under the tyranny of our own present.

But if it should be argued that it does not matter with what interpretation of history we choose to begin—since an interpretation is a thing to be unlearned and scientific history resolves everything into detail—there are three answers to this objection, three reasons why, so long as history is widely taught, the interpretation which we choose to adopt is a matter of general importance. Firstly, though there is no question of denouncing scientific history as a pretence or as a piece of bourgeois artifice, this history does become incredibly bourgeois the moment it is abridged. Every text-book bears the evidence that when we abridge we do this work on a certain pattern and in a certain order of ideas; we are making assumptions and evaluations when we are choosing even what to take as the landmarks in the story. Secondly, there is the argument which Dobb employs—an argument to which I do not know the answer—that the scientific historian never really escapes from his traditional assumptions, though the point may not greatly matter within a piece of microscopic research. In other words we may qualify our bourgeois interpretation, but, however much we qualify, we never really abandon it. Finally there is the fact that in any event we do not all become scientific historians; we do not all get to the end of that process of unlearning our bourgeois legend; and perhaps the scientific historian is only scientific within the detail of some restricted field. So some of us are left in mid-air with what the Marxist would call archaic ideologies that do not satisfy our minds. Ideas which have long been out-moded may be tucked within the folds of our history, lurking in our text-book terminology and combining to direct the organization of our scheme. If it is true that we cast our history in old forms—after traditional valuations—then when we do return to the world of the present it will be with a discrepancy in our minds; and without knowing what is the matter with us we shall be at cross-purposes with the world—trying to formulate our own present in terms which are in no ways commensurate with it. If it is true that we come to history as though the 19th century were still our present, and if it is true that the Marxist takes his start from a later present and a less traditional analysis of it, then the Marxian theories under discussion may provide the very rejuvenation of history. And, though there is no subject on which we ought to move with greater humility of mind, we should be wrong to overlook the truth that if history may or must be allowed to have reference to the present, then, in so far as issues change and events demand a new shaping of our minds, each generation must re-write, or at least mentally reorganize, history for itself.

H. BUTTERFIELD.

NOTES ON COMEDY

I

LABOUR-SAVING devices are common in criticism. Like the goods advertized in women's journals they do the work, or appear to do it, leaving the mind free for the more narcotic forms of enjoyment. Generalizations and formulæ are devices of this kind. It is as easy and unprofitable to discuss the 'essence' of the tragic and the comic modes as it is to conduct investigations in æsthetics which end with the discovery of Significant Form.

Comedy has provided a happy hunting ground for the generalizers. It is almost impossible to read a particular comedy without the interference of critical presuppositions derived from one or other of those who have sought to define Comedy in the abstract. In the first place, we all know that Comedy makes us laugh. 'Tragedy and comedy bear the same relation to one another as earnestness and mirth. Both these states of mind bear the stamp of our common nature but earnestness belongs more to the moral, and mirth to the sensual side. . . The essence of the comic is mirth.' Put in this form the error is sufficiently obvious, but it lurks behind most of our generalizations about the nature of the Comic and the function of Comedy. Meredith's hypergelasts are enemies of the Comic spirit, but his ideal audience all laugh, in their polite drawing-room way. 'The test of true Comedy,' he says, 'is that it shall awaken thoughtful laughter.'

Once an invariable connection between Comedy and laughter is assumed we are not likely to make any observations that will be useful as criticism. We have only to find the formula that will explain laughter and we know the 'secret' of Jonson and Rabelais, Chaucer and Fielding, Jane Austen and Joyce. 'Men have been wise in very different modes; but they have always laughed the same way.' So if we are looking for a simple explanation we can refer to 'a sudden glory,' 'incongruity,' 'the mechanical encrusted on the living,' 'tendency wit,' or any of the other half dozen solutions of the problem of laughter,[1] none of which however will help us to become better, because more responsive, readers of Molière. There is evidence on the other hand that reading capacity is diminished by reliance upon any one of them. But it is time to clear away this particular obstruction. A neglected passage of *Timber* reads: ' Nor is the moving of laughter always the end of Comedy . . . This is truly leaping from the Stage, to the Tumbrell again, reducing all wit to the original Dungcart.' Comedy is essentially a serious activity.

After this particularly vulgar error the most common is that Comedy is a Social Corrective, comic laughter a medicine administered to Society to cure its aberrations from the norm of Good Sense. Meredith's celebrated essay, in which this theory is embedded, has been a misfortune for criticism. It has won eminence as a classic without even the merit of containing a sharply-defined falsehood. The style is that of an inaugural lecture in a school of *belles lettres*. The idle pose is betrayed by the key-words—' high fellowship,' ' the smile finely tempered,' ' unrivalled politeness,' ' a citizen of the selecter world,'—and the theory emerges obscurely from the affected prose. ' The comic poet is in the narrow field, or enclosed square, of the society he depicts ';— a commonplace as true of any representational art as it is of Comedy—' and he addresses the still narrower enclosure of men's intellects,'—the implication is false ; there is emotion in Jonson and Molière—' with reference to the operation of the social world upon their characters.' With the aid of what has gone before we can make out the meaning. Comedy is 'the firstborn of com-mon-sense.' 'It springs to vindicate reason, common-sense, right-ness and justice,' and this Sir Galahad of the arts springs to attack whenever men 'wax out of proportion, overblown, affected, pre-tentious, bombastical, hypocritical, pedantic ; whenever it sees them self-deceived or hood-winked, given to run riot in idolatries . . . planning shortsightedly, plotting dementedly.' There is nothing that can be said of such a theory except that it is of no use whatever in elucidating particular comedies and in forming

---

[1]*The Nature of Laughter* by J. C. Gregory shows the variety of responses that may be covered by laughter, the one constant factor being a ' relief-feeling.'

precise judgments. But it has the ill effect of providing the illusion
that we know all that is necessary about a comedy when we know
very little. ' The Comic Idea enclosed in a comedy makes it more
generally perceptible and portable, which is an advantage.'
Exactly ; there is no need to distinguish between the comedy of
Tom Jones and *The Secret Agent* when we have this Comic Idea
to carry around with us.

In Meredith's Essay we hear much of ' the mind hovering
above congregated men and women ' and we learn that the author
was in love with Millamant, but if we look for particular judgments we find : ' the comic of Jonson is a scholar's excogitation
of the comic . . . Shakespeare is a well-spring of characters which
are saturated with the comic spirit . . . they are of this world,
but they are of the world enlarged to our embrace by imagination,
and by great poetic imagination. They are, as it were, . . . creatures
of the woods and wilds . . . Jacques, Falstaff and his regiment,
the varied troop of Clowns, Malvolio, Sir Hugh Evans and Fluellen
—marvellous Welshmen !—Benedick and Beatrice, Dogberry and
the rest, are subjects of a special study in the poetically comic.'
None of which helps us at all in understanding *Volpone* or
Henry IV. We are not surprised when we find : ' O for a breath
of Aristophanes, Rabelais, Voltaire, Cervantes, Fielding, Molière !'
as though these diverse writers had the same literary problems
or solved them in the same way.

Profitless generalizations are more frequent in criticism of
Comedy than in criticism of other forms of literature. Since we
continue to speak of the Comic Spirit after we have ceased to speak
of the spirit of tragedy or the essence of the epic that bogus entity
may be held responsible. ' It has the sage's brows, and the sunny
malice of a faun lurks at the corners of the half-closed lips drawn
in an idle wariness of half tension.

Meredith's Essay serves as a warning that Essays on Comedy
are necessarily barren exercises. The point is brought home if
we consider how profitless it would be to compare one of Blake's
Songs of Experience with a poem of Hopkins as Manifestations
of the Lyric Impulse. As in all criticism the only generalizations
which may be useful are those, usually short, based on sensitive
experience of literature, containing, as it were, the distilled
essence of experience, capable of unfolding their meaning in

particular application, and those which suggest how the mind works in certain classes of experience. Of the latter kind one of the most fruitful occurs on p. 209 of *Principles of Literary Criticism*. ' Besides the experiences which result from the building up of connected attitudes, there are those produced by the breaking down of some attitude which is a clog and a bar to other activities.' The breaking down of undesirable attitudes is normally part of the total response to a Comedy.[1] But to say this is to admit that all the work remains to be done in each particular case. We have to determine exactly how this breaking down is effected, exactly what attitude is broken down, and what takes its place.

Apply Dr. Richards' remark, with the necessary qualifications in each case, to *Volpone* and *Le Misanthrope,* and it is apparent how divergent the effects and methods of comedy may be. Jonson is concerned to create the mood which is the object of contemplation.[2] He works by selection, distortion and concentration, so that the attitude created by the interaction of Volpone, Corvino, Corbaccio and the rest finally, as it were, blows itself up by internal pressure. The method is cumulative.

> Good morning to the day; and next, my gold!
> Open the shrine, that I may see my saint.
> Hail the world's soul, and mine!

The exaggeration reaches a climax in the attempted seduction of Celia:

> See here, a rope of pearl; and each more orient
> Than the brave Ægyptian queen caroused:
> Dissolve and drink them. See, a carbuncle,
> May put out both the eyes of our St. Mark;
> A diamond would have bought Lollia Paulina,
> When she came in like star-light, hid with jewels.

---

[1] If this is accepted we see the connexion between comedy and satire, wit, and irony. The possible connexion with laughter springing from a 'relief situation' is also apparent. [2] It is perhaps unnecessary to say that the best critical approach to Jonson is by way of Mr. T. S. Eliot's short essay in *The Sacred Wood*.

The world thus created, already undermined by the obscene songs and antics of the Dwarf, the Eunuch and the Hermaphrodite, is demolished by the plots and counterplots of the final scenes. But the catastrophe is not mechanical: it represents on the plane of action the dissolution that is inherent in the swelling speeches of Volpone and Mosca:

> I fear I shall begin to grow in love
> With my dear self, and my most prosperous parts,
> They do so spring and burgeon ; I can feel
> A whimsy in my blood: I know not how,
> Success hath made me wanton.

In *Volpone* the cathartic effect is relevant solely to the conditions of the play. Molière, on the other hand, is more directly satiric, drawing more directly upon the actual world for the attitudes which he refines and demolishes. The play is a pattern of varied satiric effects. How it works may be best discovered by comparing it with a direct satire such as the *Epistle to Arbuthnot*. The pitch and tempo of Pope's poem vary but the tone is fairly consistent. In *Le Misanthrope* on the other hand the tone varies not only from character to character, but also within the limits of a single speech, of a few lines ; and the speed with which the point of view shifts and the tone changes sets free the activity which breaks down the impeding attitudes. This is to confine our attention merely to one aspect of the play, but no criticism can be relevant which does not consider the peculiar mental agility required to follow the changes of this kind. Unlike *Volpone* the effects are repetitive (in kind, they are obviously not all the same) and a close examination of the tone and intention of each line in the first scene is the best way of discovering how the play as a whole should be read. Even to discover the points at which the author might be identified with the speaker is instructive.

It is obvious that the Social Corrective theory not only precludes discussion of a comedy in terms of the effects we have described but prevents those who accept it from even realizing that such discussion is possible. Its vicious inadequacy should be no less plain even if we admit, for the moment, that the function of comedy is 'critical.' Malvolio, Sir Tunbelly Clumsy, Squire Western may be considered simply as failures judged by some social norm, but in

many comedies the ' criticism ' is directed not only at the man who
fails to live up to standard but also at the standard by which his
failure is judged. In Shirley's *Love in a Maze* Sir Gervase Simple,
reproached that he is dumb in the presence of his mistress, replies,
' I cannot help it: I was a gentleman, thou knowest, but t'other
day. I have yet but a few compliments: within a while I shall
get more impudence, and then have at her.' Here the object of
criticism is not only the simpleton who has no court manners but
also the courtiers, acquaintance with whom he hopes will fill him
with unmannerly boldness. The method of two-edged satire may
be studied in some of the effects of Rabelais and Cervantes. It is
of particular importance in a consideration of literature in relation
to the social environment. Chapman's *The Widow's Tears* may
serve as an example. Part of the play is concerned with a wife,
who, after expressing her horror of second marriages, yields to
the first stranger who makes love to her on the, supposed, death
of her husband, the stranger being her husband in disguise. The
critics have seen here a satire on the frailty of woman, speaking
of the ' almost brutal cynicism ' of the play. But the satire is
directed not only at such frailty but at the contemporary attitude
towards widowhood. ' He that hath her,' said Overbury of a
remarried widow, ' is but lord of a filthy purchase,' and a minor
moralist writes with approval of widows who have lived alone as
they ought: ' Their rooms bore the habit of mourning ; funeral
lamps were ever burning ; no musical strain to delight the ear,
no object of state to surprise the eye. True sorrow had there his
mansion ; nor could they affect any other discourse than what to
their husbands' actions held most relation.' The effect of the play
is to cast doubts on the reasonableness of such an attitude. The
speech in praise of the horn at the end of *All Fools* may be considered in relation to 17th century marriage customs and cuckoldry.
But the method is relevant when we are discussing plays, etc.,
as social documents rather than as literature independent of temporary conditions for their effect.

' Social Satire ' is too vague and general to be of any use for
the purpose of criticism. It needs to be defined in each instance
in terms of the mental processes involved. The greatness of any
comedy can only be determined by the inclusiveness, the coherence
and stability of the resultant attitude ; to define its method is the

work of detailed and particular analysis, and abstract theories of
Comedy can at best only amuse. An examination of *Henry IV*
will help to make this plain.

II

Henry IV does not fit easily into any of the critical schemata,
though 'incongruity' has served the critics in good stead. But at
any rate since the time of Morgann, Falstaff has received a degree
of sympathetic attention (how we love the fat rascal!) that distorts
Shakespeare's intention in writing the two plays. We regard them
as a sandwich—so much dry bread to be bitten through before
we come to the meaty Falstaff, although we try to believe that
'the heroic and serious part is not inferior to the comic and
farcical.' Actually each play is a unity, sub-plot and main plot
co-operating to express the vision which is projected into the form
of the play. And this vision, like that of all the great writers of
comedy, is pre-eminently serious. It is symptomatic that Hazlitt,
defending Shakespeare's tragedies against the comedies, says,
'He was greatest in what was greatest; and his *forte* was not
trifling.'

The first speech of the King deserves careful attention. The
brittle verse suggests the precarious poise of the usurper:

> So shaken as we are, so wan with care,
> Find we a time for frighted peace to pant,
> And breathe short-winded accents of new broils
> To be commenced in stronds afar remote.

The violence of the negative which follows suggests its opposite:

> No more the thirsty entrance of this soil
> Shall daub her lips with her own children's blood:
> No more shall trenching war channel her fields,
> Nor bruise her flowerets with the armed hoofs
> Of hostile paces.

'Thirsty' contains the implication that the earth is eager for
more blood; and when the prophecy of peace ends with the
lisping line 'Shall now, in mutual well-beseeming ranks' we do

not need a previous knowledge of the plot or of history to realize that Henry is actually describing what is to come. The account of the proposed crusade is satiric:

> But this our purpose is a twelvemonth old, . . .
> Therefore we meet not now.

Throughout we are never allowed to forget that Henry is a usurper. We are given four separate accounts of how he gained the throne—by Hotspur (I. iii. 160-186), by Henry himself (III. ii. 39-84), by Hotspur again (IV. iii. 52-92), and by Worcester (V. i. 32-71). He gained it by 'murd'rous subornation,' by hypocrisy, his 'seeming brow of justice,' by 'violation of all faith and troth.' Words expressing underhand dealing occur even in the King's account to his son:

> And then I stole all courtesy from Heaven,
> And dress'd myself in such humility
> That I did pluck allegiance from men's hearts.

There is irony is the couplet that concludes the play:

> And since this business *so fair* is done,
> Let us not leave till all *our own* be won.

The rebels of course are no better. The hilarious scene in which the plot is hatched (I. iii. 187-302) does not engage much sympathy for the plotters, who later squabble over the expected booty like any long-staff sixpenny strikers. Their cause does not bear prying into by 'the eye of reason' (IV. i. 69-72), and Worcester, for his own purposes, conceals 'the liberal kind offer of the King' (V. ii. 1-25). But this is relatively unimportant, there is no need to take sides and 'like Hotspur somewhat better than the Prince because he is unfortunate.' The satire is general, directed against statecraft and warfare. Hotspur is the chief representative of chivalry, and we have only to read his speeches to understand Shakespeare's attitude towards 'honour'; there is no need to turn to Falstaff's famous soliloquy. The description of the Mortimer-Glendower fight has just that degree of exaggeration that is necessary for not too obvious burlesque, though oddly enough it has been used to show that Hotspur 'has the imagination of a poet.'

But if the image of the Severn—

> Who then, affrighted with their bloody looks,
> Ran fearfully among the trembling reeds,
> And hid his crisp head in the hollow bank—

is not sufficient indication the rhyme announces the burlesque intention :

> He did confound the best part of an hour
> In changing hardiment with great Glendower.

There is the same exaggeration in later speeches of Worcester and Hotspur ; Hotspur's ' huffing part '—' By Heaven methinks it were an easy leap '—did not need Beaumont's satire. In the battle scene the heroics of ' Now, Esperance ! Percy ! and set on,' the chivalric embrace and flourish of trumpets are immediately followed by the exposure of a military dodge for the preservation of the King's life. ' The King hath many marching in his coats.'—' Another King ! they grow like Hydra's heads.'

The reverberations of the sub-plot also help to determine our attitude towards the main action. The conspiracy of the Percys is sandwiched between the preparation for the Gadshill plot and counter-plot and its execution. Poins has ' lost much honour' that he did not see the ' action ' of the Prince with the drawers. When we see the Court we remember Falstaff's jointstool throne and his account of Henry's hanging lip. Hotspur's pride in himself and his associates (' Is there not my father, my uncle and myself?') is parodied by Gadshill : ' I am joined with no foot land-rakers, no long-staff sixpenny strikers . . . but with nobility and tranquility, burgomasters and great oneyers.' The nobles, like the roarers, prey on the commonwealth, ' for they ride up and down on her and make her their boots.'

The Falstaff attitude is therefore in solution, as it were, throughout the play, even when he is not on the stage ; but it takes explicit form in the person and speeches of Sir John. We see an heroic legend in process of growth in the account of his fight with the men in buckram. The satire in the description of his ragged regiment is pointed by a special emphasis on military terms—' soldiers,' ' captain,' ' lieutenant,' 'ancients, corporals . . . gentlemen of companies.' His realism easily reduces Honour to 'a mere scutcheon.' Prince Henry's duel with Hotspur is accompanied by the mockery of the Douglas-Falstaff fight, which ends with the dead and the counterfeit dead lying side by side. If we can rid ourselves of our realistic illusions and their accompanying moral qualms we realize how appropriate it is that Falstaff should rise to stab Hotspur's body and carry him off as his luggage on his back.

The satire on warfare, the Falstaff attitude, implies an axis of reference, which is of course found in the gross and vigorous life of the body. We find throughout the play a peculiar insistence on imagery deriving from the body, on descriptions of death in its more gruesome forms, on stabbing, cutting, bruising and the like. We expect to find references to blood and death in a play dealing with civil war, but such references in *Henry IV* are of a kind not found in a war play such as *Henry V*. In the first scene we hear of the earth ' daubing her lips with her own children's blood.' War is 'trenching,' it ' channels' the fields and ' bruises ' the flowers. ' The edge of war' is ' like an ill-sheathed knife' which ' cuts his master.' Civil war is an ' intestinal shock,' and battles are ' butchery.' We learn that the defeated Scots lay ' balk'd in their own blood,' and that ' beastly shameless transformation ' was done by the Welsh upon the corpses of Mortimer's soldiers. Later Hotspur mentions the smell of ' a slovenly unhandsome corpse,' and we hear of Mortimer's ' mouthed wounds.' So throughout the play. The dead Blunt lies ' grinning,' Hotspur's face is ' mangled,' and Falstaff lies by him 'in blood.' Falstaff's ' honour' soliloquy insists on surgery, on broken legs and arms.

To all this Falstaff, a walking symbol, is of course opposed. ' To shed my dear blood drop by drop i' the dust ' for the sake of honour appears an imbecile ambition. Falstaff will ' fight no longer than he sees reason.' His philosophy is summed up when he has escaped Douglas by counterfeiting death : ' S'blood! 'twas time to counterfeit, or that hot termagant Scot had paid me scot and lot too. Counterfeit? I lie, I am no counterfeit : to die is to be a counterfeit ; for he is but the counterfeit of a man who hath not the life of a man ; but to counterfeit dying, when a man thereby liveth, is to be no counterfeit, but the true and perfect image of life indeed.' The same thought is implicit in the honour soliloquy.

Once the play is read as a whole the satire on war and
policy is apparent. It is useful to compare the first part of *Henry
IV* with *King John* in estimating the development of Shakespeare's
dramatic power. *King John* turns on a single pivotal point—the
Bastard's speech on Commodity, but the whole of the later play
is impregnated with satire which crystallises in Falstaff. Now satire
implies a standard, and in *Henry IV* the validity of the standard
itself is questioned ; hence the peculiar coherence and universality
of the play. 'Honour' and 'state-craft' are set in opposition to
the natural life of the body, but the chief body of the play is,
explicitly, 'a bolting-hutch of beastliness.'—'A pox on this gout!
or a gout on this pox, I should say.' Other speeches reinforce the
age and disease theme which, it has not been observed, is a significant part of the Falstaff theme. Hotspur pictures the earth as an
'old beldam'

> pinch'd and vex'd
> By the imprisoning of unruly wind
> Within her womb.

Again, he says

> The time of life is short ;
> To spend that shortness basely were too long,
> If life did ride upon a dial's point,
> Still ending at the arrival of an hour.

The last two lines imply that no 'if' is necessary ; life does 'ride
upon a dial's point,' and Hotspur's final speech takes up the theme
of transitoriness :

> But thought's the slave of life, and life time's fool :
> And time, that takes survey of all the world,
> Must have a stop.

There is no need to emphasise the disease aspect of Falstaff (Bar-
dolph's bad liver is not merely funny). He 'owes God a death.'
He and his regiment are 'mortal men.' It is important to realize
however that when Falstaff feigns death he is meant to appear
actually as dead in the eyes of the audience ; at least the idea of
death is meant to be emphasized in connection with the Falstaff-

idea at this point. No answer is required to the Prince's rhetorical question,

> What! old acquaintance! could not all this flesh
> Keep in a little life? Poor Jack, farewell!

The stability of our attitude after a successful reading of the first part of *Henry IV* is due to the fact that the breaking-down process referred to above is not simple but complex ; one set of impulses is released for the expression of the Falstaff-outlook ; but a set of opposite complementary impulses is also brought into play, producing an effect analogous to that caused by the presence of comedy in *King Lear*[1] (compare the use of irony in *Madame Bovary*). *Lear* is secure against ironical assault because of the irony it contains ; *Henry IV* will bear the most serious ethical scrutiny because in it the serious is a fundamental part of the comic effect of the play.[2]

This summary treatment of a play which demands further elucidation on the lines suggested is, I think, sufficient to illustrate the main points of the notes on comedy which precede it. No theory of comedy can explain the play ; no theory of comedy will help us to read it more adequately. Only a morbid pedantry would be blind to the function of laughter in comedy, but concentration upon laughter leads to a double error : the dilettante critic falls before the hallucination of the Comic Spirit, the more scientifically-minded persuade themselves that the jokes collected by Bergson and Freud have something to do with the practice of literary criticism.

L. C. KNIGHTS.

---

[1] See the admirable essay on 'Lear and the Comedy of the Grotesque' in *The Wheel of Fire* by G. Wilson Knight. [2] The second part of *Henry IV* is no less interesting, though less successful, I think, as a play. No one has yet pointed out that drunkenness, lechery and senile depravity (in II, iv for example) are *not* treated by Shakespeare with 'goodnatured tolerance.' Shakespeare's attitude towards his characters in *2 Henry IV* at times approaches the attitude of Mr. Eliot towards Doris, Wauchope, etc., in *Sweeney Agonistes*. Northumberland's monody on death (I, i) needs to be studied in order to understand the tone of the play.

ENGLISH WORK IN THE PUBLIC SCHOOL

I N this essay I have found is necessary to make various assumptions that could be supported by arguments, but chiefly only of the wearisome statistical kind ; in so far as the result interests readers, presumably they will be either connected with teaching English, or with Public Schools and would be familiar with much that I put forward if I dealt with any matter in detail, so that I begin with the tabulation of certain principles, trusting the reader to excuse an apparent dogmatism that is merely due to the desire to avoid needless expansion.

(1) The general object of education, domestic or scholastic, is to promote the growth of an intelligence, free to apply itself to the maximum of problems.

(2) The chief enemy of intelligence is the repressed complex in which feelings, denied a natural outlet, and unrecognized, force the whole man to act in terms of a part. Instinct recognizes likenesses ; intelligence discriminates, and is creative, whereas instinct is reproductive.

(3) The subjects of instruction in a school are educational vehicles only. The master's concern is to discover a technique that will both instruct and educate. Life is the only subject of education.

(4) A Public School is a reservation for adolescent boys, where they can live by adolescent standards.

(5) Critical standards are the object of English studies. This is the intellectual counterpart of (1), which includes behaviour.

The purpose of this essay is to consider how the peculiarities of the Public School affect English work in the above sense, and it will be obvious at once that the close relation between (1) and (5) means that one is really discussing much more than a subject in the curriculum, for only the mind free of inhibitions is capable of objective criticism.

The peculiar principle of the Public School, that boys and masters live in it, produces various results ; it is an expensive, and therefore socially restricted world, but balances this defect by its freedom from parochialism; the boys gain by meeting others from all over the country, and indeed from all over the world, and the staff by the absence of a governing body of local magnates. It promotes closer relations between boys and masters than a day-school, the master standing in *loco parentis* to the boy and the two being thrown together in various activities out of school.

So far the peculiarities are, on balance, good, and offer the master opportunities for useful work, but there is a very serious drawback to consider.

The boy has to live his whole life in the school, and the school is responsible to his parents for his safety and to the community for his conduct, throughout the term, day and night. The legal responsibility of the school is very vaguely defined and the consequences of even a single escapade or accident may be extremely serious for the school once the matter receives publicity. It is a real difficulty and deserves sympathetic consideration ; it is not surprising that a Headmaster should have remarked to me about this, ' I want to know what any given boy is doing at any given moment,' for it is quite certain that juries expect this of head-masters. But, educationally, the consequences are serious, for this has led to the canalization of activities out of school and therewith to a mental attitude towards all activity that is narrow, formal and sterile.

The old methods were simple ; boys were locked up for a large part of the time and bullied into some kind of order for the rest. The violent alternations of licence and submission that resulted gave us the picturesque mutinies, sometimes only quelled by soldiers, that have now passed away. Organized games provided the remedy, of course, and in view of the great improvement in school life no one can dispute their value. The civilization of school life was the first necessity for it to become educationally good ; prefects and games did much to achieve it. What is not generally realized, however, about games is this : boys have always enjoyed and taken plenty of vigorous exercise, organized or not, and the real value to the school's system was not that the boys were play-ing games, but that they were occupied, under control. The transmutation of this system into a moral code of things ' done,' or ' not done,' is easy.

Finally, there is the effect of residence in a school upon the master. The boy is passing through a natural homosexual phase of development ; the environment for the master is not natural. It is inherently probable that the master will be regressive—a frozen adolescent seeking his natural milieu, the bosom of his Alma Mater or her substitute. He prefers the respectful and un-discriminating affection of the boy to the risk of meeting a woman on equal terms. It is not, of course, always so, but it is very frequently so, and since such a regression implies the acceptance of a fantasy world, it is not surprising that the whole outlook should become unreal ; it does—the school seems more important than the world, because it is the shelter of an essentially timorous nature.

I cannot forbear to illustrate unreality of this sort by quoting from a critique of my first article in *Scrutiny ;* it is culled from the *Journal of Education*. I had devoted a few lines in a long article to the importance of a boy's sex-education and drew a criticism, reeking with sex, indeed noticing little else, in which the writer said, ' The form-master or house-master is not the right person to deal with puberty ; it should be left to the school doctor, or, better, the family doctor. Untold harm may be done by inex-perienced hands ; a watch should be mended by a watchmaker.' The exquisite logic of the analogy, which would imply either that puberty is a breakdown of the machine or that only doctors ' make' sexual apparatus, or indeed what else absurd, can pass as mere stupidity. The timid childishness of it is what really calls for notice ; one can quite understand a boy's uneasiness at the phenomena of puberty, but an adult should not regard sex as disease. After all, country yokels and even primitive tribesmen manage to instruct their sons sufficiently, decently, and effectively. Shall an educated man be incapable of doing so? Must he run to Nurse?

The conjunction of a system securing discipline by wasting time with masters who habitually evade responsibility is sinister, and it is not surprising that there should be a general lack of critical standards among the men teaching English, the vast majority of whom believe in poetry as an anodyne to serious thought, and hold that *The Lady of Shallott, Innisfree,* and similar works are the height of poetry ; this self-regarding, self-pitying kind of romanticism is to creative thought as masturbation is to procreation ; but it is implicit, in every school book on the subject I know, that it is the true poetic. The results are to be seen in anthologies of school verse, for one of the natural consequences of a boy's fear to enter the school is a fantasy life on paper, and if a master, himself regressive, encourages the idea, it does much to prevent the boy from psychological growth.

Until the time when some headmaster ensures that his masters are not merely adults manqués and has the courage to build his curriculum on realities, it may be asked, what can be done with English?

In the first place, the English master can observe the boy's mind, and especially that of the ' misfit,' and can apply real standards to his poetry. Probably the ultimate result will be thoughtful prose, for if I can define a man's poetry as what he makes of life, that is the most that all but a very few will want to write. The ' misfit ' may be too big or too little for his place, and in the overwhelming majority of instances the school-poet is merely inadequate to being a schoolboy, because of a family fixation ; his poetry is compensatory fantasy, and its imagery and themes, usually pretty naïve, reveal its nature. Tactful handling of it can lead to a re-association of ideas that will help the boy considerably : such work, however, requires great patience and takes up a lot of time, and more can be done by a general policy of constructive criticism.

There are no doubt many ways of setting about the business, but I conceive that the first essential is that the boys shall know that the master is not afraid of the truth ; if he can be scared or put out by, say, a sexual idea he cannot hope to do much, for he will never give boys the confidence to overcome their childish fears if his evasions show his own. For this reason he may gain by submitting himself to analysis, so that he can be sure of himself in any circumstances ; self-analysis is seldom adequate in view of his probable psychology, and is likely to miss serious important sore spots.

Given self-control, however learned, the first object in teaching would seem to be to establish clear distinctions between feeling and thinking, and between the emotional and logical meanings of words. There are many interesting ways of doing this, such as rewriting a neutral police description to give a favourable or un-favourable impression of a man's appearance, rewriting a war-time account of a German defeat for German consumption, and so on ; in each case the structure must not be altered and the object is to distinguish between synonyms emotionally. Passages of verse can be rewritten, the emotionally coloured words being replaced by colourless ones, and similar exercises suggest themselves, their purpose being the clear presentation of the difference between objective and subjective statement.

Such a system, pursued further, might do no more than establish a self-contained logical machine that the boy would not apply to his business of living ; mathematics can produce this kind of abstract logicality and it can be consistent with, and indeed balanced by, a complete lack of practicality. The danger of this is easily avoided once realized, and the material has none of the abstract quality of that used in mathematical work.

From this elementary stage one can progress to criticism of poetry fairly easily by way of studying a cruder form of emotional statement that the boy is not afraid to criticize—advertisements. These cover the whole emotional range and lead very naturally to discussion of intelligence and its obstacles ; the magazine story, designed for the same public as the advertisements, takes the process a step further, and brings one to the whole crux of the matter, the difference between poetry of escape and creative poetry.

Such is a very rough outline of a progressive course that aims at facilitating psychological growth and building confidence in the boy's own power to criticize ; I need not trouble readers with the details. Clearly it would be equally usable in a day-school, but there are special points about its use in a boarding school that deserve attention.

The first is that the great weakness of the Public School is the number of boys who are ' frozen ' soon after arrival ; that is, they are so anxious to ' do the right thing ' and to escape isolation by conformity that they grow a hard protective shell modelled on their view at that time of what a Public Schoolboy is—and within that mould they stay. It is really a problem of loneliness, quite different from the normal problem of the day-boy alternat-ing between two lives. Work of this kind shows the boy that he can criticize and have standards of his own ; I am convinced of the general psychological value of such work when directed consciously to the conquest of an inferiority complex.

In the second place, various aspects of life are absent from the life of a Public School, and the artificiality of its conditions needs to be related consciously to actuality. The best way is the serious consideration of poetry, which endeavours to explain life.

But nothing could be worse than to adopt the attitude of the regressive person who values poetry as an escape from reality ; in his uncritical acceptance of sound instead of sense ('As some to Church repair, Not for the doctrine, but the music there'), if he does inspire a love of poetry he has merely taught sensuality— he might as well extol whiskey, swearing, or any other form of relieving sensual stresses. And by the examples of regressive poetry that he gives he is helping to fix the boy to the past instead of using his imagination to look forward; there is all the difference between dreaming and seeing a vision. I presume that it would be a work of supererogation to explain what I mean by the difference between regressive and aggressive imagination. Any student of the emotional use of language, whether in the body of literature or in the dreams of neurotics, knows it. The boy, too, can know it, and can very easily recognize the difference between what he feels and what he thinks ; and a careful system designed to assist him to that knowledge will not only enable him to criticize poetry, but to live sanely and intelligently.

The poetry of remote Edens, fruitless flowers, and embowered Ladies of Shallott will not lose its value altogether, for he will consider what manner of man it expresses. There may be less verse written at schools, but poetry will stand a better chance of recognition.

The whole gist of the matter was expressed by Shakespeare when he spoke of imagination as ' bodying forth the forms of things unknown.' The imagination of the fearful ' bodies forth ' the Unknown that they dare not face, a cycle of unresolved hesitations between desire and fear ; the aggressive imagination leaps forward to the future, confident, although it cannot know exactly what it holds in store, and expresses the whole, integrated man.

Are we to inculcate both as poetic?

MARTIN CRUSOE.

WORDSWORTH AND PROFESSOR BABBITT

FOR a long time we have been aware of a curious anomaly in Professor Babbitt's criticism, and his latest book *On Being Creative*, written, as the publisher's announcement tells us, ' in lighter vein,' has only increased our dismay. Briefly, Mr. Babbitt takes his stand as a humanist and insists on the validity of the Aristotelian dictum that the end is more important than the means ; yet in spite of this, he succeeds in writing in a style so highly emotive and provocative that the reader and Mr. Babbitt himself not only find it difficult to preserve a calm critical balance, but confuse ends and means continually, losing sight of the former in exasperation whenever one of Mr. Babbitt's aprioristic contentions is at stake. For instance it is typical of Mr. Babbitt's whole outlook that in his disdain for meddling psychology (his exclusion of the meddling psyche is at least as irrational as Wordsworth's of the ' meddling intellect,') his only consideration of so obvious an end as ' response ' to a work of art should limit itself to the barest allusions to the Aristotelian ' katharsis ' without explanation or application beyond telling us on one occasion that a certain interpretation of the term is wrong.

However, there is no need here to reveal all the fallacies in Mr. Babbitt's arguments ; I wish rather to correct his reading of Wordsworth, although in his Wordsworth essay he should, if anywhere, be on firm ground. Mr. Babbitt begins by arguing against the genetic method, of which, he says, the biographical approach is part. He incriminates Professors Harper and Legouis for ' unearthing' the ' choice morsel ' of the Annette Vallon episode, and particularly the latter for having allowed Annette to affect his ' enjoyment of one of the best sonnets in English ("It is a beauteous evening, calm and free ")' because Wordsworth meant it ' not for his sister Dorothy as had hitherto been supposed, but for his natural daughter Caroline.' One may remark that any pompous complacency we may discover in the sonnet after our knowledge of Annette, may have been hidden only by the previous bad reading given to anthology pieces and by a sentimental response induced by just as irrelevant preconceptions moral or even—for mention of Dorothy seems to destroy Mr. Babbitt's argument at once—biographical. We must agree with Mr. Babbitt that biography is in any case secondary, but in dealing with Wordsworth he has not realized the issues which have always been at stake between the two types of Wordsworthian—the differences of interpretation given to his work from Shelley onwards—which make Annette of great value if only for purposes of argument. Professor Babbitt's own analysis indeed of the difference between Wordsworth's earlier and later poetry never goes deeper than such terms as 'poetically felicitious,' 'poetic inevitability,' etc., so that he avoids any consideration of an implicit meaning and is thus lead to the absurdity of concluding that 'criticism of life' is synonymous with systematic philosophy, and that Arnold's appreciation— although Arnold attempted to hide the fact—was the same as Leslie Stephen's. For consideration of Wordsworth's repudiation of his early life, the effect on his poetry, and the bearing which Annette has upon the question, making his attitude and the psychological effect of France more comprehensible, and showing Shelley's view of Wordsworth as 'a kind of moral eunuch' to be much more plausible than the Wordsworthians', I would refer the reader unacquainted with the problem to Clutton-Brock's essay 'The Problem of Wordsworth' and to the relevant chapter in *Shelley: the Man and the Poet*. I do not suggest Mr. Read's book because Professor Babbitt has dismissed him in the essay. Clutton-Brock's view, though not very different, is not open to Mr. Babbitt's particular objections, although it is only fair to say that I think many people, at all events students of Kretschmer, would be able to agree provisionally with Mr. Read's view, even as represented by Mr. Babbitt, and see no validity in the latter's objection, made, as it is, without realization of the issues involved.

In spite of Mr. Babbitt's ability to cite the most astonishing range of authors and critics, the actual quality of that reading is not, I think, very high. His statement of the social problem is sometimes just, but his analysis of literature is often so superficial— he can criticize Rousseau, Blake, Wordsworth, Keats, *The Dynasts, Ulysses,* and Surrealism as if ultimately the difference between any responses they demand were negligible—that we may

E

well question his ultimate conclusions as to the connection between literature and society. For one thing, in spite of citing M. Benda, he does not consider whether the ' clerks ' were responsible or not for the state of affairs which made ' the great betrayal ' possible— he sees no need to make any division in the ' reading public ' which has presented a greater and greater problem from Coleridge on- wards ; we are thus led to assume, what obviously Mr. Babbitt himself assumes, that *Ulysses* effects in the reader the same kind of reaction to life as any best-seller.

But I will return to my own re-reading of the Wordsworth poems which Mr. Babbitt criticises:

> ' Perhaps no poet,' Mr. Babbitt says, ' ever saw life less dramatically than Wordsworth. The sonnet on London seen from Westminster Bridge is not only successful, it is splendidly success- ful. At the same time there is a certain element of paradox in treating a great city as a still life.'

Here again if Professor Babbitt had only troubled to analyse his reasons for liking the sonnet he would have discovered it was ' splendidly successful' *because* of the paradox, not, as he implies, *in spite* of it. Actually a more subtle thing than paradox—which we are apt to think of as something clever in a merely distracting way—this quality in Wordsworth has a power of suggesting by an implied contrast. ' Perhaps no poet ever saw life less dramatically than Wordsworth,' we admit, but it so happens that Mr. Babbitt has hit upon the most dramatic quality Wordsworth possessed: the power of seizing upon a moment of calm when action is vividly anticipated or remembered. The emphasis upon time and stillness in the Westminster Bridge sonnet is so exaggerated that, in our very attempt to preserve it in our imagination, the moment is lost and becomes unrealizable, and the city wakes into activity in our imagination. This was Mr. Babbitt's response, but he has been too astonished to realize it was the normal one—for the quality is sufficiently common in Wordsworth for us to assume it is inten- tional. For example in *To a Skylark* most effect depends upon the lines

> Thy nest which thou canst drop into at will,
> Those quivering wings composed, that music still.

where the moment of calm is chosen to suggest—this time in

recollection—the song and flight of the bird. An actual description of that song and flight must have been a failure, just as an actual description of the city's awakening activity would have suggested far less than the Westminster Bridge sonnet succeeds in giving us by an exaggerated denial of that activity. At times the most undramatic events appear to Wordsworth in almost a dramatic light: even 'the unimaginable touch of Time' (in the last line of the sonnet on 'Mutability') which 'The tower sublime of yesterday' could not sustain, becomes, by the very denial in the word 'unimaginable,' almost perceptible, almost felt dramatically by the reader. It is the same 'element of paradox' which Mr. Babbitt refers to ; but if paradox, it is of a peculiarly sublime kind. If this power we have described is not in itself dramatic, it at least supplies a sense of that moment when past experience can be most vividly seen in perspective and summed up in a word or phrase— a sense no dramatist can dispense with.

Some of Mr. Babbitt's humanist conclusions are supported by the very arguments and methods he attacks. For example he disparages psychology as it exists at present: 'On the pretext of being fully experimental the psychologist has come to be almost entirely concerned with the subrational and animal sides of human nature,' and later in the book he derides Taine's well-known remark 'sleep, madness, delirium, somnambulism, hallucination, offer a much more profitable field of experiment for the psychology of the individual than the normal state.' Thus the psychologist, lurking beneath this 'pretext of being fully experimental,' is really, according to Mr. Babbitt, conspiring in the insidious decentralizing attack on civilization of which the signs are to be found in every Romanticist from Rousseau onwards. We have already said that Mr. Babbitt is confident in his ability to reject his 'psyche' altogether ; the will, for him, is all sufficient. But more critical humanists may be unwilling to leave disregarded a part of their nature whose power is unknown, and may see in Psychology a means of exploring and controlling what Mr. Babbitt leaves uncontrolled. After all we must remind Mr. Babbitt that the end is more important than means and the psychologists' general plea for a greater co-ordination must increase the power of the will. Dr. Havelock Ellis' insistence on personal moral responsibility in the final volume of *Studies in the Psychology of Sex* is distinctly humanistic, we may remark, as are also the conclusions he reaches with regard to normal and subnormal states of mind in *The World of Dreams*. This last-mentioned book, too, contains a consideration of paramnesia which, if applied as criticism to the Romanticists (particularly Wordsworth), becomes exceedingly interesting—and from the humanist point of view. As far as we know, this application has never been fully developed although M. Cazamian has suggested the approach.[1]

As soon as it is stated it must be obvious that Wordsworth was subject to (a) agoraphobia and (b) certain disturbances of memory whose implications are easier to realize as soon as we accept the term 'paramnesia' and the psychologist's account of its symptoms. Wordsworth's description of himself as a child, 'many times while going to school I grasped at a wall or a tree to recall myself from this abyss of idealism to reality,' shows the early stages of what, as Mr. Babbitt says, developed into the typically Romantic capacity for wonder, which, in Wordsworth, sometimes invested an ordinary sight with 'visionary dreariness.' Let us state this differently and say that Wordsworth's account of himself as a boy shows that he was liable to extreme states of dizziness, peculiarly associated with open spaces, cliffs, lonely moors and so forth, so that we are justified in assuming that the condition was agoraphobia and definitely subnormal—the more so since the vivid revelationary nature of his experiences on these occasions was often associated with vague fear:

> I heard among the solitary hills
> Low breathings coming after me, and sounds
> Of undistinguishable motion, steps
> Almost as silent as the turf they trod.

And the famous passage which describes the frightening appearance of the mountain peak, while he was out rowing on the lake, occurs at once to one's mind. Particularly typical are those occasions when the expanse of sky is mentioned, not as something merely seen, but felt (that is, we have here an allusion to

[1] Legouis and Cazamian *History of English Literature* Bk. V, ch. i, in the English translation in one vol. p. 1030 and footnote.

the ' sixth sense ' Mr. Babbitt deplores), and felt as something oppressive or at least rather unearthly :

> While on the perilous ridge I hung alone
> With what strange utterance did the loud dry wind
> Blow through my ear ! *The sky seemed not a sky*
> *Of Earth,* and with what motion moved the clouds.

and, much more remarkable :

> . . . . then the calm
> And dead still water lay upon my mind
> Even with the weight of pleasure ; and *the sky,*
> Never before so beautiful, *sank down*
> *Into my heart and held me like a dream.*

His theory of spontaneity prevented Wordsworth from discovering that this state was subnormal, in spite of its vague reminiscence of dream states. On the contrary, he felt at times that his experiences were not subrational but fully superrational. The transition from the merely surrealist—using the word for the moment like Mr. Babbitt as a term of abuse—to the superrational is clearly seen in the following :

> . . . . the whole body of the man did seem
> Like one whom I had met with in a dream ;
> Or like a man from some far region sent
> To give me human strength, by apt admonishment.

Where the implication would be obvious, even if there were no mention of God in the last stanza of the poem. The most interesting development of such a feeling is to be found, perhaps, in *Stepping Westward*, and there are so many similar passages among his best-known poetry that it would be easy to continue citing examples.

The mood is that discussed in the essay on Wordsworth in *Oxford Lectures on Poetry.* Bradley, it will be remembered, remarked that Wordsworth's trance-like visionary state often takes the form of a kind of desiderium to pass arbitrary boundaries and limits. Here it will appear at once that we are back

again at Babbitt and his hatred of the primitivists who fuse themselves into infinity or 'Unendlichkeit.' For Wordsworth this
fusion had the fascination of danger.

These visionary experiences have this in common: they put
a high value on a state avowedly similar to the half-waking, half-
sleeping state when dream and reality seem one, and when
memory is seizing haphazardly events from our conscious life
and those from our unconscious, and blending them without any
sense of time. In this hypnogogic state the mind makes no selection: there is no will, merely 'spontaneity'; the most casual
impression, retained only in the depth of the subconscious, may
be given great prominence. There is no focus, only the loosest
association. When one is waking from a dream, moreover, the
scenes, however fantastic, are accepted as normal, and, however
trivial seem important ; it is thus the lowest, most discursive part
of the brain which presents to the higher perceptions what they,
devoid of will, must placidly accept.

Almost the same thing occurs in cases of paramnesia, or false
recollection. According to Mr. Havelock Ellis, the impression of
a scene is received through the usual channels of sense ; but, if
the mind is not alert, the unconscious mind receives the impression
first ; while the same impression, reaching the conscious perception later, creates an illusion of familiarity and revelational significance. It is precisely as if we dreamt of a scene and awoke to
find it unexpectedly before our waking eyes. Then the reason,
working amid material uncontrolled by the will—'spontaneous,'
in fact—finally hits upon some explanation typically similar to
conclusions reached in dream or hypnogogic states in that time
is ignored. Since the paramnesiac state of mind is so similar to
that of dreaming, it is scarcely surprising that a common explanation of its phenomena presumes some previous dream experience.
Another explanation is that the person has visited the scene before
and forgotten all about it ; another that in sleep his spirit has
travelled where he himself has not been, and another that he has
visited the place in some previous existence. Whether an explanation is attempted or not, the experience is often one of startling
vividness, but even this is sub- not supernormal. The hyperæsthesia
involves no selection so that there is no justification for the belief
that what is perceived is of the slightest real importance. In its

lack of voluntary control, the state is definitely pathological and is reconcilable to the affinity felt by the extreme Romanticist for the idiot and madman.

The Romanticist reluctance to interfere with mental processes acted in this instance upon Wordsworth's slight agoraphobia and made these occasions when

> . . . Bodily eyes
> Were utterly forgotten, and what I saw
> Appeared like something in myself, a dream,
> A prospect in the mind . . .

and when there was a lack of any voluntary attention, fairly frequent. To ascribe Wordsworth's ' visionary power ' to paramnesia, which seems inevitable after the foregoing account, and to recognize this paramnesia as a definite subnormality, is to comprehend even those ' blank misgivings of a creature moving about in worlds not realized ' about which Wordsworth himself seems to be rather dubious, even while raising ' songs of thanks and praise ' for them. Paramnesia, moreover, with its common presumption of a previous existence, will account for the Pythagorean argument of the Immortality Ode as a whole.

The Romanticists often stumbled upon something valuable by their very lack of focus, just as a person who ceases to concentrate or who is even on the point of falling asleep, sometimes remembers something he has been trying vainly to recall for hours. This can hardly persuade anyone, however, that a preference for dreaming over waking will serve adequately for a general principle in life, and the fact that the psychologist emphasizes the subnormality of such inattention cannot be forgotten.

Several more of Wordsworth's recognized characteristics would immediately confirm our approach, and seem obviously explicable to abnormal psychology. Wordsworth's peculiar insistence on the sense of sight which often takes the place of all the other senses for him, supplying—with typical confusion (*vide The New Laokoon* passim)—what they would normally supply, finds simple analogy in the process of falling asleep, when, we are told, the sense of sight persists longest, and in the fact that the pictorial is by far the most vivid aspect of dreams. Mr. Havelock Ellis also supplies evidence in support of the view that paramnesia is particularly liable to occur in intellectual workers at the end of a tiring day. This may conceivably give added significance to the 'sensations sweet' Wordsworth specifically mentions as occurring in 'hours of weariness,' and it may also explain why Wordsworth wanted to include 'lassitudes' among various things whose modifying influence would appear to be much more obviously explicable as bearing

> . . . a needful part, in making up
> The calm existence that is mine when I
> Am worthy of myself.

It is rather necessary to insist upon this point: that a subnormal state similar to Wordsworth's is as liable to occur to the hard worker as to him who indulges in the Romantic sin of spiritual sloth. It is a real danger to the humanist who believes in the omnipotence of the will: the subconscious has this power of retaliation. It is precisely like the refusal of the mind to produce a forgotten word—when inattention *for the moment* may be of use. We have italicised the proviso since it suggests the possibility of blending the conscious and the subconscious but with the definite intention of keeping the conscious dominant. Mr. Babbitt would have us ignore the subconscious ; but something has been done by the psychologists, and more can be done by individuals, to explore their subconsciouses, increase the conscious side of their minds, and thus, by better co-ordination, increase the sphere of the will also.

Too much reliance on 'spontaneity' may indeed be one danger ; so much we may grant. But if the humanists go to the other extreme and ignore the subconscious entirely, humanism will undermine itself precisely as the tired intellect falls prone to subnormal illusion. There is so much uncritical abandonment that the more popular approach to the humanist standard can just as easily be a Romantic one—an extreme and unquestioning acceptance of outward rule as a universal panacea, to the exclusion of any thought of the individual will and effort Mr. Babbitt himself insists on. Mr. Babbitt's opponents are Romanticists, but it would not be surprising if his followers were Romanticists too—for he can be as easily misunderstood as Aristotle was in the Renaissance, and his 'standards' will not be as easily distinguishable from standardizations, when passed on to other hands. In the preface to *The New Laokoon*, many years ago, he defined his position more carefully and separated himself from the extremists, but now he has lost his poise. I think he deserves any misinterpretation he gets, his first-hand criticism is too careless, and the bare ability to see that there is something radically wrong with the way Western civilization approaches life is not enough.

We have said that one of the humanist dangers is that of being affected by the subconscious without knowing it, and thus losing proper co-ordination. Professor Babbitt has so played into our hands that he will have to admit this point: While reading *On Being Creative* for the first time I myself experienced the illusion of having seen the page before. But my first suspicion that I was suffering from paramnesia gave way to recognition of Arnold's argument at the beginning of *Essays in Criticism*. Mr. Babbitt was producing the plea for the right of the critic to be called 'creative,' challenging the ascendancy of inferior 'original' or 'creative' writing over the best criticism, and doing so in similar language to Arnold's, reproducing Arnold's argument stage by stage, and even offering one of the same examples—asking whether Johnson had done better in writing *Irene* or *Lives of the Poets*. There was no acknowledgment, so it was Mr. Babbitt who had been nodding, not I ; for this essay of Arnold's, *The Function of Criticism at the Present Time*, must have attracted Mr. Babbitt's continual and particular attention, yet at the time of writing he must have been ignorant of the subconscious roots of his ideas. With reference to certain French critics Mr. Babbitt makes the following remark, which seems to be true of himself also, and likely to be even truer of his followers:

'Rousseau would, as a matter of fact, have the right to say (in the words of Emerson's Brahma) of many of those who profess to be reacting from him: "When me they fly, I am the wings."'

ROY MORRELL.

COMMENTS AND REVIEWS

MR. PUNCH'S POLITICAL SUPPLEMENTS.

Mr. Leonard Woolf's useful pamphlet, *Hunting the Highbrow* (Hogarth Press) needs bringing up to date ; for the facetious denigration of art and the snarls of the vulgar (when discomforted) are now common in journals with a higher conventional reputation that the *Daily Express*. It is not enough, for instance, to dismiss *Punch* as merely dull and reactionary. Reactionary it always was, after its first twenty years ; from its support of the pro-slavery South to its behaviour in the war, when (as the introduction to the recent *Punch* anthology informs us) it ' never served its country better than . . . between the years 1914 and 1918,' *i.e.* by heightening the country's fighting temper and by assiduously pumping the stimulus of indignation, horror and hatred into the public mind (See Lord Ponsonby's *Falsehood in Wartime*, Allen and Unwin, 2/6d.). But the younger *Punch* evinced a genuine comedic attitude and represented a social poise ; there might then be applied to it the now meaningless comparison with Aristophanes. *Punch* to-day exemplifies a modern tendency—the capitalizing of complacency, ignorance and irresponsibility by the complacent, ignorant and irresponsible. Its humour, for instance, is frequently ' anti-highbrow '; my three copies yield two gibes at Epstein, and two cartoons depreciating artists. The best analysis of the attitude comes from the *New Statesman* of March 28th, 1931, in a valuable essay, *The Artist and the Gentleman*; it is reprinted in *Fleet Street,* a recent anthology of journalism, which is otherwise only useful for laboratory purposes. ' How inferior are the conceptions of " gentleman " and " artist " in daily use may be perfectly seen from Mr. A. P. Herbert's *Tantivy Towers,* in which we have both reduced to their lowest common measure as mere egoists, and this is exactly how they appear to-day in the eyes of the majority of readers of *Punch*, which caters so cleverly for this emotionally uneducated public.'

This *Punch* anthology (compiled by Guy Boas, Macmillan) is a document of some anthropological interest, for it conveniently delineates the ideal reader of *Punch*. He is evidently a cat-, dog-, child- and mule-lover, who has derived from his public school those qualities which the silk-stocking makers desiderate when they advertise for representatives—' Public school type preferred '—in short, a gentleman of the type described by Mr. Turner, ' a half-wit who gapes at the mention of philosophy or music or poetry, who thinks it bad form even to take cricket seriously, as the Australians, for example, take it, and who grumbled at the Germans attempting to win the war by gas when he was only attempting to win it by guns and bayonets.' The humour is below the level of adult response, consisting largely of adolescent verbalisms and circumlocutions, like the advertisements for bottled salt-and-beef. At least two of the items are repeated in a slightly varied form, for the kinds of appeal made run to type as the stock response is constantly tapped. And the emotional plane on which *Punch* works was beautifully illustrated by this Observation from a Sunday puff: ' *Punch* has never forgotten that a comic poet should first of all ·be a poet. There are some lines of authentic loveliness among the jests of this anthology . . . (which) . . . remind one that *Punch* is an organ of taste and not just a receptacle for jokes.' The synthetic efforts at seriousness are even more betraying than the humour ; those verses, instinct with nobility and strongly tainted with Kipling, indicate that *Punch* humour is the complement of a certain vicious type of the patriotic-domestic sentimentality. Some who accept this account may object that it is not worth mentioning here ; but it seems necessary because *Punch* is a formative influence—a case might be made out for its exclusion from educational establishments. And they will agree that the spread of the *Punch* attitude to respectable journals is a sinister development.

It is not easy now to realize that in the 19th century we had a responsible press. Governments consulted the best papers, and the provincial sheets copied them, so that enlightened opinion radiated downward and outward ; it is said that in the nineties the working man followed politics as he now pursues sport and manhunting. The diffusion of ' the best that is known and thought in the world ' was not impossible, as it seems to-day, now that ' the free play of the mind upon every subject which it touches ' is hard to seek in the press. *Fiction and the Reading Public* recorded the growth of ' a whole *Punch* literature,' and consonant with it we have a journalism exhibiting the same ' anti-highbrow ' animus. We all know those weekly essays by the modern Lambs, whose lowbrow propaganda for their flocks is excelled in subtlety only by the genteel tobacco and tailoring advertisements, for copy- and essay-writer inculcate the same ethos ; and in criticism one form of the attitude is the clever depreciation of established figures (*e.g.* D. H. Lawrence) who did not ask leave to be great. A specimen passage, approvingly quoted in a Sunday paper : ' It must be a pure act of faith for anybody to believe that human beings are the better for having access either to Nature or to the arts.' That some of these papers print responsible comments on politics does not relieve their total anæmia ; politics are not an autotelic activity, and by neglecting the ends without which politics are so much ludo, the enlightened section of our press seems merely to be playing football with its own head.

If to particularize one mentions the *New Statesman,* it is because one would like to pay a personal debt to it, for its influence in forming a critical habit. It has been and (more likely than any other) may yet be, a valuable journal ; and one still accords it a pious but unconfident recommendation. Except as evidence, and for teaching in school what criticism isn't, its literary side is negligible : the latest intelligent review of poetry was in the funeral number of the *Nation,* February 21st, 1931, though an adequate placing of a best-selling novelist occurs about every six months, ten years too late. With monotonous regularity it is taken in by book-club currency ; and one fears, at times, that it is catering for, and hence forming, the kind of taste so adequately described in the essay already quoted from its pages. It is significant that Mr. Wodehouse's publisher finds it a worthwhile paper to advertise in, and that there recently appeared an advertisement from a *Punch* reader who wished to exchange papers with a reader of the *New Statesman.* Except for ' Critic's ' column, topical articles of value are so rare (on patent medicines about a year ago, and more recently on a revivalist movement) as to be individually memorable ; normally they are far below the level of the *New Republic*, which has of course more space for such contributions, as it does not insult its readers with puzzles, weekly essays, sports reports or motoring columns. (And if it did print a motoring column, it would be one that would really help a prospective purchaser—the *New Republic* is associated with Consumers' Research). Except for occasional lapses into sentimentality against British imperialism, the *New Republic* is an exemplar of what a journal of opinion should be ; it provides instruction how to resist civilization. (See ' A Middleman of Ideas ' in *Scrutiny* No. 1). Its journalistic ' debunking ' is excellent—pertinent, and not merely bright—and its literary criticism deserves the name ; it is never fooled by the substitute literature (Wilder, Wells, Hemingway and the saga-makers) for which English reviewers fall so gullibly. Nor does it strain after a spurious vitality by putting its personality across at get-together dinners for puzzle-solvers, to establish a flank-rubbing *camaraderie*—a process known to sales executives as ' The Speciality Appeal to Instinct,' or ' The Personal Touch in Advertising.' About the *Manchester Guardian* one would make the same comments and regrets as for the *New Statesman*, it too yields specimens of the higher Beachcombing.

The function of ' pulling out a few more stops in that powerful but at present narrow-toned organ, the modern Englishman ' was never more needed, and a critical journal which took its responsibilities seriously would command respect and possibly circulation. As it is, the innocent are corrupted and the wrong stops pulled out, and ' our more elegant weeklies ' will soon be no more than political supplements to *Punch*.

DENYS THOMPSON.

TRAINING COLLEGES: REPERCUSSIONS

The scrutiny of Training Colleges published in our December issue produced a large number of letters to the Editors, but has not, so far, provoked the more complete investigation we innocently hoped for, or, indeed, any comment at all from any of the educational journals. Significantly, it is reported that at a meeting of Principals where the article was discussed, it was decided that there was no need to read it since ' outside ' criticism could not possibly have any bearings on their particular problems. But the letters which we have received—almost all from lecturers in Training Colleges—would show, if they could be printed in full, that our case against the normal Training College system was completely justified.

Objections can be summarised under two heads: (a) that we did not know what we were talking about, and (b) that lecturers were doing their best and that it was rather ungentlemanly to mention the unavoidable defects of the present system. As for (a), a single quotation must suffice: ' I have no evidence that your questionnaire reached this college, and I cannot refrain from letting you know of the complete agreement with your criticisms of all of my colleagues who have seen the article.' We may say, for the benefit of those who complained that our survey was not ' scientifically conducted,' that the extract is representative.

We are tempted to go on quoting from the letters of those who confirm our case in detail and who comment on other aspects of the educational system, but we must reserve the mass of fresh material received, the fresh problems raised, to be dealt with in later numbers of *Scrutiny*. The objections under (b) do not seem to need an answer.[1]

Meanwhile, what is to be done? ' Bad as things are,' writes a correspondent (a university lecturer), ' I hope you will not be

---

[1] We have to acknowledge a report on ' Professional Courses in the Training of Teachers' by Miss Margaret Phillips (*British Journal of Educational Psychology*, November, 1931, February, 1932) sent us by the author. Much of the evidence confirms our own ; but the credit side of the Training College account is given in terms too general to be impressive. As evidence for the statement that ' For many women the Psychology course is the most important

persuaded to turn criticism too quickly into practical suggestions for immediate reforms without basic discussions ; authorities, if at all affected, would just patch up the old machine and jog on for another decade or two.' And we agree that our first business is to obtain full explicit recognition of the situation as what it is, and to provide a clearing-house of ideas for those who are engaged in solving practical problems in schools, training colleges and elsewhere. As for the performance of this latter function, we should like to remind our readers that we are painfully cramped for space, and that our public is mixed, so that we are likely to be driven sometimes to what many will find unsatisfactory compromises : there are special problems that could be dealt with adequately only by (say) detailed illustration of technique, where-as, some immediate recognition of the particular problem being desirable, we can allow the expositor only a few pages in which to throw out some provocation to debate.

Moreover, as other correspondents remind us, we are committed to something more than has just been suggested. Many of the questions that we admit to having invited—regarding method, technique, and so on—can be answered with any show of adequacy only by providing books. As a note in the review pages announces, a start has been made.

We may add that already more than a nucleus of an informal educational association has developed.

A Scrutiny of Examinations is going forward, and we shall be grateful for help.

L. C. KNIGHTS.

---

part of their training' we are given such things as the following answer to a questionnaire: 'Psychology gives me a feeling of peace with the world. . . As life and living are matters of tremendous importance I feel that the course of psychology was tremendously important and valuable.'

SELECTED ESSAYS, by T. S. Eliot (Faber and Faber, 12/6d. net).

This substantial and comely volume contains the greater part of Mr. Eliot's influential criticism. There is about half of *The Sacred Wood*, the three essays from the crucial *Homage to Dryden* pamphlet and the Dante study entire. The additions on the literary side include essays on Middleton, Heywood, Tourneur and Ford; two excellent studies of Senecan influence on Elizabethan drama, a rather discouraged dialogue on Dramatic Poetry and an essay on Baudelaire.

The novelty in the essays on the dramatists and on Baudelaire is the appearance of Mr. Eliot as an appreciator of moral essences. In this encroachment on the domain of such verbose critics as Mr. Murry and Mr. Fausset, he is not, of course, trying to put across an individual conception of morality ; tradition governs this as much as it does taste. Mr. Eliot's tradition of morality is the most respectable of all, and when he says that ' the essence of the tragedy of *Macbeth* is the habituation to crime,' one could do nothing but assent if it were not that the italics show that he is not referring to the man but to the play. Again, he tells us, ' in poetry, in dramatic technique, *The Changeling* is inferior to the best plays of Webster. But in the moral essence of tragedy, it is safe to say that in this play Middleton is surpassed by one Elizabethan alone, and that is Shakespeare.' But even if that is a safe thing to say, the way of saying it is not free from danger. For after subtracting the poetry and the dramatic technique what is there left by which the moral essence may be apprehended? Again, in the essay on Baudelaire he writes: ' In his verse, he is now less a model to be imitated or a source to be drained than a reminder of the duty, the consecrated task, of sincerity.' But is our sensation of the poet's sincerity anything more than one of the reactions attendant on the poem's successful communication? Is anything really clarified by talking of a technical as if it were a moral achievement? It seems a pity that an essay that at the outset affirms the importance of Baudelaire's prose works should not have given some consideration to *L'Art Romantique* and *Curiosités æsthétiques,* which illuminate Baudelaire's poetic much more than the diaries do. The ' revelations ' in the *Journaux Intimes,* written later than the majority of the poems, are perhaps rather specious intellectualizations, the violent efforts of a man to whom convictions of that sort were a novelty, to create a 'strong personality' for himself; their forthrightness is deceptive, I think. But Mr. Eliot 'hazards' an illuminating conjecture when he suggests 'that the care for perfection of form, among some of the romantic poets of the 19th century, was an effort to support, or to conceal from view, an inner disorder.' And he goes on to say: 'Now the true claim of Baudelaire as an artist is not that he found a superficial form, but that he was searching for a form of life.' I quote this, firstly because it is a good saying in itself, and also because the form of expression is comparatively new in Mr. Eliot's work. As it stands it is paradoxical. Not quite so paradoxical as Mr. G. K. Chesterton methodically is, but surprisingly near it. It marks a cleavage between Mr. Eliot's earlier and later criticism. It oversteps the conscious limitations of his earlier method. It must be every ambitious critic's aim to resolve the dichotomy between life and art; and every superficial critic does it constantly with negligent ease. Whether Mr. Eliot has the philosophical stamina, as he certainly has the poetic sensitiveness, for such a task, remains to be seen.

The latter part of this volume is mainly occupied by essays on attitudes rather than works and here Mr. Eliot is heavily engaged with the Martin Marprelates of to-day and yesterday, some of them within the Church, like Viscount Brentford, and some outside it. The outsiders, are, in general, those who believe that art, culture, reason, science, the inner-light or what-not, may constitute efficient substitutes for organized religion. Arnold, Pater, Aldous Huxley, Bertrand Russell, Middleton Murry and some American humanists who loom more sinisterly in Mr. Eliot's consciousness than seems necessary over here, provide a variety of scapegoats. His diagnosis of the disease that must ensure the ultimate instability of all such eclectic systems, built up from 'the best that has been thought and done in the world' is devastatingly acute. The antidote is provided in *Thoughts after Lambeth*.

This volume leaves us then, except for tentative branchings-out, as far as literature is concerned much where we were after the publication of *Dante*. One should not, perhaps, grumble at that; but the impression given by this heterogeneous mass is not so profound as that given by the slim volumes that found their way into the world more quietly. The essays on general subjects dilute that impression, for Mr. Eliot is not outstanding as a ' thinker ' as he is as a literary critic. His thinking is adequate to his own emotional needs, as a good poet's always is, but it has not much extra-personal validity. One may contrast the peroration of *Thoughts after Lambeth :*

> ' The World is trying the experiment of attempting to form a civilized but non-Christian mentality. The experiment will fail ; but we must be very patient in awaiting its collapse ; meanwhile redeeming the time ; so that the Faith may be preserved alive through the dark ages before us ; to renew and rebuild civilization, and save the World from suicide,'

with Berdiaeff's lucid and virile exposition of a similar conviction in his *Un Nouveau Moyen Age.*

I must try and say briefly why Mr. Eliot's earlier work seems to me more valuable than his later, or it may seem that I under-rate it just because its conclusions are unsympathetic to me. The intelligence displayed in the later essays might be matched by several of his contemporaries ; the literary sensibility of the earlier essays is not matched by any of them. ' Literary sensibility ' is a horrible phrase and it does not sound a very impressive faculty, but when one considers how very few people there are actually capable of responding to poetry or word-order generally without prompting from its prestige, or message, or because the objects named evoke a pleasant response, perhaps the possession of this gift may be appreciated at its proper value. It is only the beginning, of course, but its absence vitiates the other critical faculties. Sometimes, when it is present, there is an absence of the co-ordinating faculty and thus the response is deprived of any significance beyond that of a pleasurable sensation. It was the presence of these faculties in unison which differentiated Mr. Eliot's earlier criticism from the ' appreciative ' convention in vogue at the time. The method at which he aimed, and which he practised with such delicate skill is perhaps best described by a quotation he used from Remy de Gourmont—*ériger en lois ses impressions personnelles.* If Mr.

Eliot has for the time being gone outside literature, the loss is very much to literature ; no doubt there is a compensation some- where. But literature, in spite of wireless and cinema, is still the life-blood of the time ; we are not sots or sadists by accident and one should not be too fatalistic about the approaching dark ages. If literary criticism is not one of the means Mr. Eliot envisages of redeeming the time, nothing can obscure the value of his example. As our writings are, so are our feelings, and the finer the discrimination as to the value of those writings, the better chance there is of not being ashamed of being a human being.

EDGELL RICKWORD.

FORM IN MODERN POETRY, by Herbert Read; ESSAYS IN ORDER, No. II (Sheed and Ward, 2/6d.).

Probably I am the last person who should review Mr. Read's book : I mean that I seem to myself to distrust instinctively his conclusions, his methods, his sponsors, even his vocabulary. And the reasons for such a perfect distrust cannot be more than hinted at in a review. I shall of course do what hinting I can : but I hope no one will assume that I imagine I have done even the least portion of what is necessary.

To take an example : Mr. Read, in a ' direct statement on the nature of poetry,' quotes Signor Leone Vivante, who says, ' In the poetic period not only the attribute, but every word, every moment of thought, gathers up, renews the whole. The subject is recalled in its concept in every word of the proposition . . . . myriads of *nexus*—resemblances, accords, unities *ex principio*— form themselves. . . . On the other hand, constructive thought loses the *nexus* or necessities of principle proper to thought in its integral originality ; if we except the *nexus* belonging to formal logic. . . . In other words, in constructive thought *nexus of inherence* are comparatively prevalent, in poetic thought *nexus of essence.*' These are not Mr. Read's words, but he approves of them ; and I think they are very important for his essay. They are at any rate typical, not only of Signor Vivante's procedure, but of his own, and are worth examination here. They appear

to say, not only that the succession of words in poetry is in some
way more ' inevitable ' than their succession in prose—it would
hardly be worth while to say this—but also that this greater
inevitability is produced in a certain way. If they make this way
clear, then they are certainly very important, and a vexed question
is solved. Do they make it clear? We must ask ourselves how
strictly they are to be interpreted. The verbs ' renew,' ' gather
up,' for example—do they mean what they appear to mean,
namely ' summarize,' or merely ' keep alive in the memory of
the reader?' If the latter, they suggest more than they actually
mean ; the statement, moreover, loses whatever importance it
might have had. For any word, functioning not as a vocable but
as the member of a period—whether this period be of poetry or
of prose—has complicated references before and after : in the mind
of the attentive reader does not exist apart from the period in
which it is set, and easily becomes its symbol. If this is what
the verbs mean, Signor Vivante and Mr. Read are not pointing to
any difference between poetry and prose. On the other hand, if
the verbs mean ' sum up ' or ' summarize,' is the statement true?
It seems to me obviously false. Or rather, it seems to me obviously
false that every word in a poetic period sums up its predecessors ;
that any such word does so, seems to me very probably false.
I cannot persuade myself that ' incarnadine,' in a passage from
Macbeth quoted by Mr. Read as a specimen of poetry, ' sums
up '—that is, ' renews ' or ' gathers up' in any way significant
here—the matter by which it is introduced. It seems to me, of
course, closely connected with that matter ; but that is what no
one has ever doubted and what no one is concerned to deny.

So much to excuse my distrust of Mr. Read's vocabulary. But
the passage I quoted serves another purpose. Signor Vivante
distinguishes between logical *nexus* and those of essence. Perhaps
in his book he glosses these terms ; Mr. Read however, who equally
with him draws advantage from them, does not. They are metaphysical terms; but in an Essay in Order we expect and demand
metaphysics. Metaphysics alone can provide a basis for order.
Yet it is just Mr. Read's metaphysical references which are of
the vaguest. He does not explain how he would recommend the
distinction between logical and essential *nexus* to those who, from
Aristotle downwards, have held that essence is the source of

demonstration. Nor, enveloping himself in a variegated cloud of witnesses—Croce, Freud, Santayana, Roback, Coleridge—does he inquire into that which alone can give their statements significance. He approaches the psycho-analysts with an appearance of caution: ' As a literary critic,' he says, ' that is, as a scientist in my own field, I insist on maintaining my territorial rights when I enter into treaty with another science. I accept just as much as seems relevant to my purpose, and I reject anything that conflicts with my own special sensibility.' That is, on matters on which he is expert he is not to be led by the nose. But is this caution enough? It is on these matters that nose-leading is least to be feared. The credentials of the psycho-analysts are not, to put it mildly, above suspicion: to enter into treaty with them without prolonged investigation is not an orderly proceeding.

From the psycho-analysts Mr. Read seeks support for a distinction he draws between character and personality. Character is a fixed disposition to act in a certain way ; personality on the other hand, being responsive and sensitive, is ' essentially mobile.' It resembles, I imagine, prime matter or *nous,* which is potentially all things. Poetry is produced by the personality in an integral intuitive act ; and a poem is subject to none but its own laws. This is Mr. Read's grand conclusion: adumbrated already in his opening pages, by a distinction between ' form organic,' possessed by a work of art ' with its own inherent laws,' and ' form abstract,' which is organic form ' stabilized and repeated as a pattern.' Organic form implies the fusing of structure and content ' in a vital unity '; form abstract the adaptation of ' content to a predetermined structure.' These doctrines are not new ; and of the soundness of their psychological basis I am not competent to judge. But, in spite of their comparative antiquity, they seem to me to have a very unfortunate consequence for criticism. Unless I am much mistaken, the distinction between abstract and organic form, drawn as Mr. Read draws it, is thoroughgoing nominalism. Nominalism is the death of science, or rather, prevents its birth. To say that each poem has its own laws is to say that poetry, and therefore criticism, has none ; just as to endow each member of a community with sovereign rights is to establish, not order, but anarchy. Mr. Read demands that, as a critic, he shall be acknowledged as a scientist: I do not see how, according to his doctrines, he can be ; nor does a close reading of the later portions of his essay convince me that he is.

I said above that the words I quoted from Signor Vivante were typical of Mr. Read's procedure. Perhaps that is now clear. Signor Vivante disposed of the problem of the relations between the words of a poem by locating the poem in any single word ; Mr. Read locates the whole of poetry in any single poem. He disposes of problems such as those of tradition by saying that any genuine poem is thereby modern. The procedure is a claim to solve problems by causing them to vanish ; and has as its principle the complete neglect of the analytic moment of knowledge in favour of the synthetic. There can be no doubt that it is reprehensible. A scientist above all can afford no Wordsworthian reluctance to dissect. Ruthless dissection would provide him, if with nothing more, with some scattered truths. Mere contemplation of a unity can of itself provide no one with anything—at least under normal circumstances. It reduces the critic from the rank of an articulate being to that of one who murmurs *O Altitudo !*

JAMES SMITH.

LEVIATHAN HOOKED

THE SHAKESPEAREAN TEMPEST, by G. Wilson Knight (Oxford, 12/6d.).

This volume is the third of a trilogy and provides the documentation for a thesis implicit in the earlier books. Mr. Knight believes that the structure of Shakespeare's plays may be best seen through a study of their imagery, and that this reveals the fundamental categories of the Shakespearean schema to be Tempests and Music. Polarity is established between these two, and a number of subsidiary images group themselves about the one and the other. A coherent approach to the whole of Shakespeare's work is thereby attained. Mr. Knight has in short provided Shakespeare with a philosophy which, while wholly idealist in its tendency, is strictly dualist in its organization.

It is much easier to detect a structural correspondence to this curious arrangement in the style of Mr. Knight than in that of the

Plays. It is generally admitted, from Dryden onward, that it is characteristic of Shakespeare's genius to be rich, dishevelled, allotropic. Grammatical ambiguities, and verbal complexities, all the more obvious features of Shakespeare's style, confirm the judgment.

It is only by reducing poetry to imagery that Mr. Knight succeeds in erecting a schema: he ends by declaring that the Hecate scenes in *Macbeth* are 'The one stone necessary to complete the mosaic of our pattern' and that Theseus of Athens is 'a Christ-like figure.'

Mr. Knight's collection of references is both thorough and interesting, but in his desire to amass evidence he is inclined to ignore the context and the question of relative emphasis. For example, he says, apropos of Falstaff in *The Merry Wives,* 'The imagery is in the usual tradition. Mistress Page is compared by him to rich India merchandise ". . . she bears the purse too: she is a region in Guinea, all gold! . . ."' But Falstaff is only making love for the replenishment of his purse (as he explicitly states in the passage Mr. Knight has represented by some dots) so that this image is hardly on a par with 'Her bed is India: there she lies, a pearl.' Moreover, it is isolated in the play, and therefore cannot have the cumulative weight of the jewel images in *Troilus and Cressida.*

Mr. Knight has endeavoured to find a constant reference to tempests and music throughout Shakespeare's work. It is well known in Shakespearean criticism that he who seeks shall find: but the citation of the imagery of storm in *The Comedy of Errors* and *The Taming of the Shrew* only weakens the very admirable case that Mr. Knight puts concerning its importance in *Lear.*

The book is, in short, eccentric. There are some sensible remarks on the futilities of unenlightened scholarship in the Introduction, but they are countered by such statements as 'It is possible that a work of art is not intellectual in the ordinary sense, and demands a special intuition which transcends all reasoning; 'Poetry is a mystery. . . A man may be divinely inspired when writing poetry.' There have been hints of this attitude before: It is rather a melancholy spectacle to see one who so neatly exposes the Rationalist point of view swallowed up by that great Boyg of which Croce acts as a useful incarnation. It is precisely because

Mr. Knight abandons criticism for adoration that he can seriously contemplate *Titus Andronicus* as a unit in the same pattern as *Lear*.

Mr. Knight's method of approach is very fruitful for the major tragedies, the later plays and some of the histories, but hardly for the comedies. There is also great risk in considering imagery apart from movement and rhythm. Mr. Knight's balance and judgment are not equal to his genuine enthusiasm and his acute sensibility.

M. C. BRADBROOK.

OXFORD POETRY 1932. Edited by Richard Goodman (Basil Blackwell, 3/6d.).

Oxford Poetry 1932 is dedicated to Wystan Auden, Cecil Day Lewis, and Stephen Spender. But, with certain exceptions, the poems of which it is composed appear to be almost entirely uninfluenced by any modes of feeling or developments of technique more ' modern ' than those displayed in Mr. Edward Marsh's long-defunct ' Georgian ' anthologies. The problems resolved or stated in many of these verses, and the attitudes conveyed by them to the reader, seem to have little or no connection with contemporary interests. The pleasantly retrospective mood, however, evoked by a perusal of almost any volume of *Oxford Poetry,* reminds one by reference to one's own more or less distant undergraduate days of the superb timelessness of Oxford ; and when one reflects that two, at any rate, of the poets to whom the volume is dedicated were themselves contributors to one of its not very senior predecessors, one cannot fail to realize that the poets one is criticizing are remote only in place and not in time, and that the Oxford poet of 1932 may well be quite an important modern poet of 1935 or so. In a word there is something about the public school and university education (of which incidentally about nine-tenths of the better poets of recent years are products) which tends to induce a delayed maturity : a phenomenon which gives rise to the expectation, abundantly justified in one or two fairly recent instances, that quite an inconspicuous grain of talent discovered in *Oxford Poetry,* may possibly bring forth really considerable fruits of achievement within a remarkably short space of time.

It must not be supposed from the foregoing remarks that I wish to imply either that *Oxford Poetry 1932* is by any means without present interest, or that all or any of the contributors to it are necessarily destined for the highest poetical honours within the next few years. As to spotting winners, I refuse to be drawn into any such futile and invidious attempt. As to positive achievement, my own personal preference goes to the work of K. N. Cameron, who seems to possess a very respectable talent for writing verse and for making intelligent use of good contemporary models—capacities which more than any others justify optimism as to a young poet's future, since sophistication and subtlety of feeling, in the nature of things, develop later, and may well be assisted by the possession of technical ability.

The Editor, Richard Goodman, is another who stands out for having evidently been affected by contemporary influences—in his case the *New Signatures* group, if one may so call it. At present he is not infrequently a trifle naïve, *e.g.*

> 'Leapers out of earth, they marched erect like steel,
> their arms were pistons
> their strength was the lovely strength of steel.
> Where the spirit leaned out to sing, their eyes were stars. . .'

But he has undoubted vitality, which one hopes will keep him from the pathic nirvana of sentimental communism, where many others, besides Mr. Middleton Murry, seem destined to find an asylum from the perplexities of the age.

GILBERT ARMITAGE.

WYNDHAM LEWIS, A DISCURSIVE EXPOSITION, by Hugh Gordon Porteus (Desmond Harmsworth, 8/6d.).

Mr. Porteus is a disciple. The worship of Wyndham Lewis is his (inferior?) religion ; and one must not expect a devotee to be too critical of his divinity. He finds adequate praise difficult. Mr. Lewis's satire is better than Dryden's : his style as good as Shakespeare's (p. 118). ' I claim,' he says, ' for Lewis, purely on the strength of his *vision*, a place in art beside the greatest masters of all time.' One can't say fairer than that.

But though criticism of Mr. Lewis is too much to expect from the ecstatic Mr. Porteus, we may test his standard of values, perhaps, by his remarks about less divine persons. For example :

Dr. I. A. Richards, with tremendous ingenuity and patience, is attempting to reduce art to a set of scientific formulæ.' Joyce has ' no central vision and a very limited field of invention.' These two remarks are, I think, sufficient to show the quality of Mr. Porteus's sensibility.

Lewis's admirers usually admit that the master is careless. But, say they, how much he *knows*. His carelessness doesn't really matter. Mr. Garman in the last number of *Scrutiny* implies that ' slap-dash carelessness . . . mere transcription of other people's views, . . . and a proclivity to follow . . . any red herring ' are ' inevitable adjuncts of a uniquely vigorous style and a mind more than usually well-stocked and inquiring.' It may be said that ' any red herring ' in Lewis's work, is far more frequent than ' any fresh egg '; and such eggs as there are are mostly foreign—imported from M. Julien Benda.

That Lewis is well-informed and intelligent is obvious ; but the exaggerated contemporary estimate of him seems to rest on two things—the amount he has written, and his own self-advertisement. The Enemy is simply impresario for Wyndham Lewis ; and like most impresarios, he exaggerates. Lewis, like Shaw, Wells and the Sitwells, sells his wares. Unlike the Sitwells, he really has something for sale, but it would be absurd to take him at his own valuation. He is a symptom, not a leader of the age. For like all successful ad-men he has come to believe quite uncritically in what he sells : he has become his own inferior religion : he worships (as Mr. Garman notes) Tarr and Pierpoint—a fact which seems to me to invalidate much of his criticism.

Mr. Porteus bases his estimate mainly on Lewis's style and his satire.

The first he says is visual, imagist, the product of the Painter's Eye. Here I think he may be right ; for it seems possible that this explains the strange sterility of Lewis's style. Great emotive writing uses a fusion of many things—vision, sound, rhythm, meaning, etc. To use one of these things in isolation is to limit the possibilities of adequate communication. Mr. Porteus himself notes that it is necessary to regard Lewis's style as a translation into the visual. But this is a defect, not, as he supposes, a virtue. It is a misuse, or an inadequate use of language.

Lewis's satire seems largely self-indulgence. It reminds one of Halifax's dictum :—' Anger, like drink, giveth rise to a great deal of unmannerly wit.' I read recently of a German tailor, who, annoyed with his employer, had the latter's portrait tattooed on his behind. He exhibited it, to the delight of his friends, and the discomfiture of his enemy. Mr. Lewis's activity, in the *Apes of God*, and many of his other works, seems to me to be exactly analogous to the tailor's and just as valuable ; though he is scarcely the tailor's equal in precision and economy of technique.

T. R. BARNES.

NOTES ON LITERATURE AS A CAREER

A FACE IN CANDLELIGHT, by J. C. Squire (Heinemann, 5/-).

YOUNGER POETS OF TO-DAY. Selected by J. C. Squire (Secker, 6/-).

Mr. J. C. Squire, born in 1884, was educated at Blundell's and Cambridge. In 1907 appeared his first publication, a penny pamphlet named *Socialism and Art*. His first book, *Poems and Baudelaire Flowers*, came out in 1909 (it includes an eulogy ' To the Continental Socialists.') In 1912 he published a biography and his first parodies. In 1913, after *The Three Hills* (poems) and a second book of parodies he was appointed literary editor of the

New Statesman, the new Socialist weekly. Poems, parodies, critical studies succeed until in 1919 Mr. Squire founded the *London Mercury*. He has since been principal reviewer of the *Observer*, founder of a literary cricket club, Chairman of the English Association, introducer of books and editor of anthologies. He is now a chief reviewer for the *Sunday Times* and *Daily Telegraph* and he has just organized a Defence Committee for buildings which keen critics (not Sir Reginald Bloomfield) declare poor work by an architect seldom above mediocre.

Mr. Squire's poems down to his new book have been marked by ineptitudes of imagery, commonplace themes, language of romanticist fashion, and absence of rhythmical individuality. Lacrimæ rerum, contrast of human transience and material permanence, thoughts beyond thought, yearning for far land or fair woman, etc., always recur. His poems are proper to a man without critical power and having no more creative ability than is needed for the vulgar craft of parody or writing tales of ' if-consequence.' In ' Pastoral ' (1909) Mr. Squire looks gravely past his love's smile to her ' inner mouth and throat '

> Where like water-anenomes
> Pink mounds and tendrils float
> In silky salivan seas.

' At Night ' (1913) describes him sitting at the window ' smoking and alive ':

> Wind in the branches swells and breaks
> Like ocean on a beach
> Deep in the sky and my heart there wakes
> A thought I cannot reach.

' The World: 1918 ' (from *American Poems*, 1923) finds him there still:

> How curious and lovely and terrible is the world!
> I sit alone at midnight working here
> With ink and notebook and a glass of beer.[1]

---

[1] All Mr. Squire's volumes provide innumerable case-matter. The Augustan selection (Benn, 6d.) is the briefest guide to his mature deficiencies.

From 1923 Mr. Squire published no books of poems until *A Face in Candlelight*. The old faults sprout in it once more. In ' The Return of the Muse ' the dead fragments of his dreams rise up ' miraculously whole,' aureoled, and walk with linkèd hands on the green strands of bright crystalline streams and fly finally into the light on rainbow wings where they find loud harping ' And a sound as of a celestial choir that sings.' In ' John Donne To His Mistress ' Donne talks of kissing ' The red limp langorous mouth, the yielding lips apart.' See also ' The Woods in November ' (La Belle Dame motif), ' Winter Midnight ' (Death rather than hopeless sorrow), ' They Learn in Suffering ' (' You have forced my heart to red eruption now '), ' A Face in Candlelight ' (all the world's queans in a modern woman). Critical opinions include :

No other poet can give us the same grave pictorial beauty of the poem which gives its title to the book, alive and mysterious as a portrait by Giorgione—*Sunday Times*.

One welcomes his return to poetry in this book of deep feeling, eloquence and wit—Robert Lynd.

Mr. Squire must really see to it that we do not go another five years without poetry from him—T. Earle Welby *(Week-End Review)*.

We cannot guess if these poems are a valediction, nor can we well believe it. But in that mode they have the ' lacrimæ rerum,' and their mortality touches the mind—*Observer*.

The *New Statesman* gave an unsigned review, as careful to be neither critical nor contemptuous as to praise, but not too highly.

Mr. Squire's *London Mercury* was to ' represent no generation and no clique.' In 1923 its editor reviewed 'The Waste Land' :

. . . Conceivably what is attempted here is a faithful transcript, after Mr. Joyce's obscurer manner, of the poet's wandering thoughts when in a state of erudite depression. A grunt would serve equally well. . . If I were to write a similar poem about this poem the first line from another work which would stray into the medley, would be Mr. Chesterton's emphatic refrain ' Will someone take me to a pub? '

In 1926 he reviewed Eliot's *Poems 1909-1925* :

. . . Usually he is obscure, so inconsequent that the kindest things one can suppose is that he is experimenting with automatic writing. Why on earth he bothers to write at all it is difficult to conceive : Why, since he must write, he writes page after page from which no human being could derive any more meaning (much less edification or pleasure) than if they were written in Double-Dutch (which parts of them possibly are) is to me beyond conjecture. . .

In 1927 Mr. Squire edited a *Cambridge Book of Lesser Poets*. In it he gives a nod of encouragement to Hopkins by including his ' Heaven-Haven.'

Mr. Squire's new anthology does not quarrel with his judgments, though he has been able to find for it no poems so worthless as his own. Its best comes from Cecil Day Lewis. The remainder is dull rubbish, born of every sentimental or simple attitude in a medley of writers, Blunden, Roy Campbell, Sylvia Lynd, Sassoon, Shanks, Sitwell, Wolfe, Huxley and others.

Reading it through will not weaken the belief these notes may give to any undergraduate after a career, that a milligramme of talent, much self-confidence, and a left-wing ' allegiance ' can lead to quick advancement in the higher literary gangdom.

GEOFFREY GRIGSON.

MORE LAWRENCE

ETRUSCAN PLACES, by D. H. Lawrence (Secker, 15/-).

THE LOVELY LADY, by D. H. Lawrence (Secker, 7/6d.).

THE SAVAGE PILGRIMAGE, by Catherine Carswell (Secker, 7/6d.).

REMINISCENCES OF D. H. LAWRENCE, by J. Middleton Murry (Cape, 7/6d.).

THE EARLY LIFE OF D. H. LAWRENCE, by Ada Lawrence and Stuart Gelder (Secker, 7/6d.).

The latest—the last?—collection of Lawrence's stories will be valued mainly for the sake of *The Man Who Loved Islands*, which appeared first in *The Dial*. *Etruscan Places*, though not an exciting book, bears interestingly on the question, How much of romantic illusion was there in Lawrence's preoccupation with primitive peoples of the present and the past? How far did he really deceive himself in the quest that kept him wandering about the world, from Italy to Australia, from Australia to Mexico, and on? Some measure of self-deception there undoubtedly was in the hope that expressed itself in each fresh setting-out. But it was never for long, if ever, a radical self-deception—the crude hope of picking up (for he certainly believed a casting-back to be necessary) the lost continuity here, or there, in this or that primitive people. The *Letters* make it unmistakably plain (what should in any case have been gathered from the work) that he knew well enough what he was doing.

His migrations were a technique for inner exploration. And so when he says of the Etruscans, ' It is as if the current of some strong different life swept through them, different from our shallow current to-day: as if they drew their vitality from different depths that we are denied,' we do not inquire very anxiously whether he was right about them or not. What matters is that, in his exposition and commentary, he proves once again so plainly that he himself has access to ' different depths that we are denied.'

Of the three books about Lawrence it must be said that two of them, whatever regrets and qualms they may give us, are seen in contrast to the third to justify publication, though they quarrel: the justification, it may be added, does not, and could not, lie in any settling of the immediately personal issues. If the third has any justification, it is not one that can concern the reviewer: from his point of view it is a vulgar piece of book-making, dealing in such impertinent and worthless facts as that Strelley Farm is really such-and-such, and so on: it must make a number of personal identifications possible locally.

F. R. LEAVIS.

*BENTHAM'S THEORY OF FICTIONS. Edited, with an Intro-
duction, by C. K. Ogden (Kegan Paul, 12/6d.).*

J. S. Mill, in his essay on Coleridge, pointed to Bentham and
Coleridge as the two men who in the early 19th century divided
the field of serious speculation. 'Whoever could master the principles and combine the methods of both would possess the entire
English philosophy of his age . . . every Englishman of the present
day is either a Benthamite or a Coleridgean.' Mill's words still
hold true—though, nowadays, it is the similarity of the main
preoccupations of both rather than the opposition of their conclusions which will hold the startled attention of a careful student.
Coleridge writes in the autumn of 1800 to Humphrey Davy: ' I
have been *thinking* vigorously during my illness, so that I cannot
say that the long, long wakeful nights have been all lost to me.
The subject of my meditations has been the relations of thoughts
to things'; to Goodwin: ' I wish you to write a book on the
power of words, and the process by which the human feelings form
affinities with them. In short, I wish you to philosophize Horne
Tooke's system, and to solve the great questions, whether there
be reason to hold that an action bearing all the semblance of
predesigning consciousness may yet be simply organic, and
whether a series of such actions are possible? And close on the
heels of this question would follow, Is Logic the *Essence* of
thinking? In other words, Is *Thinking* impossible without arbitrary
signs? And how far is the word arbitrary a misnomer? Are not
words, etc., parts of and germinations of the plant? And what is
the law of their growth? In something of the sort I would
endeavour to destroy the old antithesis of Words and Things;
elevating, as it were, Words into Things and living things too.'
At the end of his life he gave his unpublished Opus Maximum the
title: ' The Power and Use of Words.'

Compare Bentham, 1775: ' What we are continually talking
of, merely from our having been continually talking of it, we
imagine we understand; so close a union has habit connected
between words and things, that we take one for the other.' Or

'*Instrument No. 1*, Division of entities into real and fictitious; or say, division of noun substantives into names of real entities, and names of fictitious entities:

' By the division and distinction thus brought to view, great is the light thrown upon the whole field of logic, and thereby over the whole field of art and science, more especially the psychical and thence the ethical and moral branch of science.

' It is for the want of a clear conception of this distinction that many an empty name is considered as the representation of a corresponding reality ; in a word, that mere fictions are in abundance regarded as realities.'

The history of modern philosophy sufficiently establishes that the starting points of great thinkers are of more importance to subsequent thinking than their conclusions. The similarity therefore of the preoccupations shown in Coleridge's only recently published letters and notes (Snyder, *Coleridge on Logic and Learning ;* Griggs, *Unpublished Letters*) and in Bentham's more than sixty-year-long cogitations—now for the first time made conveniently available and set in due perspective by Mr. Ogden—is extremely remarkable. The two have already—through their conclusions, which are more easily put into currency—exerted an influence second to that of no other English thinkers. The time has come when their common choice of Language as the key problem of philosophy, and their complementary initial analyses will have an even greater influence on the course of thinking.

That Bentham, contrary to the ordinary opinion of him (conveniently displayed by Mr. Oakeshott in a recent number of *Scrutiny*) was a highly original, persistent, penetrating and careful thinker, as remarkable for his linguistic investigations as even for his political, social and legal reforms, Mr. Ogden, in this selection and exposition of his methodical writings, clearly makes out. This claim is an immense one, but the evidence is here for those who will read Bentham, who are aware of the paucity of useful work hitherto done in this field and who can appreciate the difficulty of the problems he is concerned with. He is not at first easy reading. In his old age he deliberately devised a style of exposition which to the unaccustomed eye will seem singularly heavy and labored. Read on, fall into the admirably calculated *tempo* of Bentham's thinking, master the pattern and learn when to expect the word which requires deliberation ; and the effect is quite different. Mr. Ogden is not going too far in remarking that Bentham's style comes to have a charm as well as the merits of clarity and precision.

Some parts of Bentham's treatment will be more easily accepted to-day than they would have been ten years ago. His definition of Logic, for example. Latterly a definition given by Charles Saunders Pierce has won wide acceptance among logicians for the promise of enlargement and freedom it offers ; it was a favourite quotation of the late F. P. Ramsey : ' Logic is the Ethics of thinking, in the sense in which Ethics is the bringing to bear of self-control for the purpose of realizing our desires.' Compare Bentham : ' Logic is the art which has for its object or end in view, the giving to the best advantage, direction to the human mind, and thence to the human frame, in its pursuit of any object or purpose to the attainment of which it is capable of being applied' (p. lxv). But this type of definition, as Bentham remarks, can be traced back to Aristotle : Bentham's singularity is in his perception of the defects of this art and his determination to perfect it. ' Should there be any person to whom the ideas thus hazarded present themselves as having a substantial footing, in the nature of *things*, on the one hand, and the nature of *language* on the other—it will probably be admitted that a demand exists for an entirely new system of *Logic*, in which shall be comprehended a *Theory of language, considered in the most general view.'*

The ideas thus hazarded comprised the Theory of Fictions, an important part of which was a development of ' the discoveries, half-concealed or left unperfected' of Horne Tooke. ' Almost all names employed in speaking of the phenomena of the mind are names of fictitious entities. In speaking of any *pneumatic* (or say *immaterial* or *spiritual*) object, no name has ever been employed that had not first been employed as the name of some material (or say *corporeal*) one. Lamentable have been the confusion and darkness produced by taking the names of *fictitious* for the names of *real* entities.' (We may compare M. Arsène Darmesteter, ' In none of the languages it is possible for us to study is there an abstract word which, if its etymology is known, is not resolvable into a concrete word.') ' Of these fictitious entities,' Bentham continues, ' many will be found of which, they being, each of them, a *genus generalissimum*, the names are consequently incapable of receiving what is commonly understood by a definition, viz. a definition *per genus et differentiam*. But, from their not being susceptible of *this* species of exposition, they do not the less stand in need of *that* species of exposition of which they are susceptible.'

The provision of this species of exposition was Bentham's most original positive contribution. For fictions (and these for Bentham included the entities for which most psychological words are used as well as those for which such words as *right, power, obligation* are used) ' the nature of the case affords but one resource; and that is . . . paraphrasis '—by Archetypation and Phraseoplerosis. ' By the word paraphrasis may be designated that sort of exposition which may be afforded by transmuting into a proposition, having for its subject some real entity, a proposition which has not for its subject any other than a fictitious entity.' Archetypation is the taking of ' some real action or state of things' as the original of the metaphor (dead or living) from which the fiction arises. Phraseoplerosis is the filling in of the parallel between them (p. 86). Some of the assumptions Bentham uses in his exposition will seem questionable to a modern reader—his use of images for example. But Bentham is often most startling where he seems most naïve. ' To a considerable extent Archetypation—*i.e.*, the origin of the psychological in some physical idea—is often, in a manner, lost; its physical marks being more or less obliterated by the frequency of its use on psychological ground, while it is little, if at all, in use on the original ground. Such psychological expressions, of which, as above, the physical origin is lost, are the most commodious for psychological use.' The implication is that such expressions are void.

The assumptions taken and the inferences drawn by Bentham are often so extreme that they may divert attention from the more important aspect of his work as methodology. Mr. Ogden's very skilful expository introduction does much to guard against this danger. (A recently published development of Bentham's theory of metaphor, Professor Scott Buchanan's *Symbolic Distance*, Psyche Miniatures, is of great assistance also). While bringing the many scattered portions of Bentham's work on Fictions into perspective, the inventor of Basic English—towards which Bentham supplied an important hint—contrives, without straining interpretation, to indicate the immense field into which his suggestions lead. A singular sympathy with Bentham enables him to portray, vividly though economically, the relevant personal aspects of this extraordinary figure. My extracts may make the book seem suitable only for the earnest students of meaning. But those who read of Bentham's early adventures with Ghosts (there is a charming portrait of him at Oxford at the age of 12½) or of the sad case of Mr. Beardmore will not fail to benefit from a lightening of their spirits.

I. A. RICHARDS.

GENTLEMAN VERSUS PLAYER

THOUGHTS AND ADVENTURES, by the Rt. Hon. Winston S. Churchill, M.P. (Thornton Butterworth, 12/6d.).

The English are a feminine race, the perfect spies and intriguers, with an illimitable capacity for not letting the right hand know what the left hand is doing, and behaving so genuinely in their self-created legend of themselves as the straight-forward no-nonsense, stupid male that at first others are taken in. Afterwards they are not so sure ; indeed to-day it would be difficult to find anyone in Europe, Africa, Asia or America who is. Mr. Churchill has never really been trusted by the English because he is always letting the cat out of the bag. Honest Mr. Baldwin is the ideal figure for the English fascist government, the professional posing as the amateur ; Mr. Churchill is the genuine article.

The amateur is always interested primarily in himself, in his ideas and deeds as a father in the career of his sons, as extensions of his own personality, hence his love of publicity. The professional, interested only in his job, knows that if you are to realize your wishes, the less other people know about them, the better.

No one reading this book or indeed any by Mr. Churchill can credit him with having thought long or deeply about anything, but he is equally ready to write on any subject, the Quantum

Theory, Cézanne, or the Old Testament, and except for the title you will not be able to tell which is which:

1. We may imagine a great ship of war steaming forward into battle. On the bridge there are only lay figures in splendid uniforms making gestures by clockwork and uttering gramophone speeches. The Engineer has taken charge of the vessel and, through the vessel, of the Fleet. He does not see a tithe of what is going on. How can he, locked in his engine-room far beneath the water-line and the armoured deck? He has stoked up all his boilers, he has screwed down all the safety-valves; he has jammed the rudder amidships. He utters nothing but the wild command, 'Full speed ahead.'

2. No, we must take the loss with the gain. On the uplands there are no fine peaks. We must do without them while we stay there. Of course we could always if we wished go down again into the plains and valleys out of which we have climbed. We may even wander thither unwittingly. We may slide there. We may be pushed there. There are still many powerful nations dwelling at these lower levels—some contentedly—some even proudly. They often declare that life in the valleys is preferable. There is, they say, more variety, more beauty, more grace, more dignity—more true health and fertility than upon the arid highlands. They say this middle situation is better suited to human nature. The arts flourish there, and science need not be absent. Moreover it is pleasing to look back over the plains and morasses through which our path has lain in the past, and remember in tradition the great years of pilgrimage. Then they point to the frowning crag casting its majestic shadow in the evening light; and ask whether we have anything like that up there. We certainly have not.

3. But it is in the use and withholding of their reserves that the great commanders have generally excelled. After all, when once the last reserve has been thrown in, the commander's part is played. If that does not win the battle, he has nothing else to give. The event must be left to luck and to the fighting troops. But these last, in the absence of high direction, are apt to get into sad confusion, all mixed together in a nasty mess, without order or plan —and consequently without effect. Mere masses count no more.

The largest brush, the brightest colours cannot even make an impression. The battlefield becomes a sea of mud mercifully veiled by the fog of war. It is evident there has been a serious defeat. Even though the General plunges in himself and emerges bespattered, as he sometimes does, he will not retrieve the day.

I shall be surprised if the reader is able to detect that the first of these concerns Ludendorf, the second Democracy, the last the technique of painting.

Like all amateurs Mr. Churchill is a hero-worshipper ; first the pater, then the rest (can Lord Lloyd be the latest?) He has had the amateur's luck sometimes to have seen the wood where the professionals saw only the trees ; he was one of the first in England to realize the weakness of *laissez-faire* and the necessity for State-planning but lacked the necessary patience and self-effacement to go further, the self-knowledge and moral courage to forgo the psychological satisfactions of home sweet home. Hence the sniffing round the dictators. He wants to have his cake and eat it. To enquire into the genuine nature of the State, to base his actions as the professional must upon a reasoned and deeply-felt philosophy, for that he has neither interest nor leisure : it was politics for him for the sake of the ride.

With the result that over Russia he exhibits all the hysteria of the invalid or of the unforgivably insulted ; to discover that your coachman has not only thought of your schemes already, but is putting them into practice with a thoroughness and attention to detail of which you are incapable, must be galling, but Mr. Churchill might make some pretence at rationalizing this annoyance. He appears to know no more about communism than our left boot. Nor was it wise to touch on anthropology if this is the best you can do :

'The story of the human race is War. Except for brief and precarious interludes, there has never been peace in the world ; and before history began, murderous strife was universal and unending. But up to the present time the means of destruction at the disposal of man have not kept pace with his ferocity. Reciprocal extermination was impossible in the Stone Age. One cannot do much with a clumsy club. Besides, men were so scarce and hid so well that they were hard to find.

They fled so fast that they were hard to catch. Human legs could only cover a certain distance each day. With the best will in the world to destroy his species, each man was restricted to a very limited area of activity. It was impossible to make any effectve progress on these lines. Meanwhile one had to live and hunt and sleep. So on the balance the life-forces kept a steady lead over the forces of death, and gradually tribes, villages, and governments were evolved.'

No, Mr. Churchill cannot candidly be said to know anything, but he has his talent. He could have been, and indeed, to a certain extent he is, a great writer. His huge comic history of the war is in our opinion the best of all the war books. He has at times an extraordinary verbal sense, *e.g.* when describing the scene just before the German March offensive he says ' It was an hour of intolerable majesty and *crisis*' or again at the meeting of Clemenceau and Foch in the volume before us, ' But, thank God, at that moment the greatest Frenchmen of this *awful* age were supreme, and were friends.' Indeed the whole article (' A day with Clemenceau ') in which this paragraph occurs is Churchill at his very best.

We are unable to imagine any propaganda against Imperialist war more deadly than this account of senile homicidal maniacs :

As we reached the road a shell burst among a group of led horses at no great distance. The group was scattered. A wounded and riderless horse came in a staggering trot along the road towards us. The poor animal was streaming with blood. The Tiger, aged seventy-four, advanced towards it and with great quickness seized its bridle, bringing it to a standstill. The blood accumulated in a pool upon the road. The French General expostulated with him, and he turned reluctantly towards his car. As he did so, he gave me a sidelong glance and observed in an undertone, ' *Quel moment délicieux !* '

The old humbug can write. The contrast between artists and their creations is frequently startling, but we have never felt a more extraordinary one than this; to turn from the utterly humourless face which confronts us on the frontispiece to the savage vivid farce of the pages which follow.

W. H. AUDEN.

SCRUTINY OF CINEMA, by William Hunter (Wishart, 5/-).

The mass of professional film criticism to-day is so beneath contempt that even the most elementary endeavour to discuss the cinema from any serious angle must be welcomed. What is needed more than anything is a set of Aristotelian canons such as Béla Balázs attempted brilliantly for the silent film in *Der sichtbare Mensch.* There is nothing of the kind yet in English although the raw materials given by Mr. Hunter in this pamphlet suggest that he is seriously enough interested to attempt the task one day. His scrutiny consists of 28 pages of notebook jottings on some 25 films by Eisenstein, Pudovkin, Chaplin, Pabst, Clair, Feyder, Ruttmann, Lang and Bunuel, with a short introduction, and an appendix on the sound film. There are many things of interest, chiefly a distinction between technique and creative contribution, and a really serious examination of the problem of rhythm. The art of the cinema is declared to be in its infancy. Compared with the other arts it is ' of quite minor significance,' though certain directors, Pudovkin and Eisenstein, ' from a departmental view are both Titans,' and Eisenstein ' perhaps one day will stand in the same relation to the cinema as the pioneer Uccello stands to painting.' There is firm insistence that a film is best as ' an individual experience successfully communicated.' There are excellent disposals of films of predominantly technical interest, or mere statements of ' a simple psychological case in complex images,' of films with too crude didactic prejudices, of films in which there is mainly ' transmutation of phrases into images.' In the set analyses where Mr. Hunter is clearly occupied with unrelated expositions he is at his best.

For so short a pamphlet there is far too much beating about the bush, too great a setting up and knocking down of the familiar Aunt Sallies, Galsworthy, Priestley, Academic art, the Censor and middle-class morality. This might be taken for granted with the enlightened audience obviously addressed in a serious scrutiny, and in exchange more explained for a cultivated but technically uninstructed public. The growing habit of solemnly quoting from the holy writ of Richards seems little more than a basket of kittens displayed at a difficult transition in a film to evoke uncritical ecstasy.

The chief objection to the pamphlet is a lack of order and organization in much admirable material, and an evasion of important issues. A writer is rebuked for speaking of 'that something indefinable which is Pudovkin.' 'Surely,' says Mr. Hunter, 'it is the business of the critic, if he is to have any justifiable reason for existence, to define, or at least to attempt to define, that something indefinable,' but Mr. Hunter uses the word 'film,' sometimes in italics, without a hint of explanation. Of Ruttmann's 'excellent film *Berlin*' he says, 'Its technique is excellent, it is a *film*,' and Pudovkin's '*The End of St. Petersburg* is, I think, the finest complete film that the cinema has up to date produced. It is not necessary to discuss its technical qualities, nor its methods.' But surely, on Mr. Hunter's own showing, it *is* necessary. There is also a strange under-estimation of Eisenstein's contribution to the theory and practice of *montage*. It is untrue to say that Eisenstein 'remains too obsessed with the mathematical, metrical aspect of *montage*,' or 'does not seem to be sufficiently aware of the many complicated aspects of rhythm.' Eisenstein is never tired of pointing out that metrical *montage* is merely the most elementary of forms, and in his remarkable set of lectures to the Film Society some few years ago, and also his scattered articles, he analyses the increasingly complicated series of metrical, rhythmical, tonic and over-tonic *montage*, culminating in the ideological *montage* which would justify him in filming Karl Marx's *Das Kapital*. The religious procession in *The General Line* which Mr. Hunter praises as 'an extremely brilliant example of rhythmical cutting' employs all four methods in almost symphonic elaboration.

If Mr. Hunter proposes to write a serious and rounded scrutiny, he would do well to set in order some of the basic problems. The peculiar contribution of the cinema as an art, its relation to literature (his analysis of Feyder's *Thérèse Raquin* from this angle is excellent), the problem of the scenario (several have been published in full or in fragment), the problem of the document (the relation between the sacred dances as used in *Storm over Asia* and as shown 'uncut' in a recent documentary film), the problem of impersonality (his note on 'the directorial aside' is suggestive), the function of prejudice and propaganda, the relation between image content and image sequence, the problem of directorial style, even the problem of the audience from the ' physiological-psychological' angle, as well as an historico-technical analysis of films such as *Warning Shadows, Woman of Paris, Marriage Circle, Doctor Caligari, Earth, The Blue Express, New Babylon, The Ghost that never returned, Fragment of an Empire,* and *Secrets of the Soul.* It may be objected that I am trying to tell Mr. Hunter how to write his book. Well, I am. That is partly what a review is for. What is clear, however, is that his samples justify me in giving him a large order.

J. ISAACS.

THE PRESS AND THE ORGANIZATION OF SOCIETY, by Norman Angell (The Minority Press, 3/6d.).

There are thinkers more tidy and writers more clear and excitative than Sir Norman Angell, but this booklet of his, first published in 1922, has a value which unfortunately seems permanent. It will be worth constant reissue until intelligent morality recovers some power in the world. Morality shares in none of the principles of modern journalism which Sir Norman Angell truly sets down. Newspapers must be *entertaining* (there is one ' entertainment' for the *Times* public as much as another for the *Express*. Cf. *Times* third leaders or Mr. Chamberlain's recent letter on wagtails). That is the first duty. Newspapers therefore must foster the l.c.m. of attitudes and emotions and prejudices of the mediocre in every social layer ; and they cannot tell the full truth (in as far as a daily judgment on affairs can be ' true') if the truth is unpleasant. Apart from the power of advertisers on policy (exaggerated ; the advertiser is more anxious over circulation than over views) and the possibility of bribery in certain instances (rare in this country ; not from ' British morality,' but from the size of newspaper undertakings), moral values are kicked into Fleet Street gutters by the existence of each newspaper as a vast capitalistic enterprise, depending on selling itself as widely as possible and greedy for profits.

In its bones, that is Sir Norman Angell's unanswerable case. Every journalist is not a rogue ; but every journalist is a half-marionette jerked by the newspaper industry (which is nine-tenths a rogue).

State censorship, State monopoly of newsgiving, greater statutory power to interfere with press liberty cannot be justified by any (problematic) moral improvement. They would, for example, ossify into permanence present institutions by killing criticism and attack. What is Sir Norman's solution? None. No solution exists, unless miraculous means could be thought out for setting up, universally, high standards of value.[1] Palliatives? Sir Norman suggests two: making journalism a chartered profession with a professional code of honour and a status equal to that of law and medicine ; creating a State Press, managed by a ' journalistic judiciary ' pledged to impartial presentation of the news, independent of the Government of the day and fashioned much as the B.B.C. Other papers, etc., would continue.

On these it may be observed (apart from discussion of efficacy) that at present a journalistic code or a closed profession are not widely demanded by journalists, that the Institute of Journalists recently elected the Editor of the *News of the World* its president for a second term, that there is no realization (even among the generality of intelligent men of principle) of the extent of the present damage and danger, that the establishment of a State Press would be triumphantly fought by every paper in the country (cf. the attitude of the Press to the establishment of the *Listener*), that only a dictator (who would probably prefer suppression) or a parliamentary majority of a very different kind from any (Socialist or Conservative) in prospect could break such opposition or show any desire even for such a reform.

GEOFFREY GRIGSON.

---

[1]Of cinema attendance at Oxford : ' Does Hollywood languish unavailingly before the massed allurement of Theology, Law, Medicine, Literæ Humaniores, Modern History, English Language and Literature, Medieval, Modern and Oriental Languages, Physical and Biological Sciences, Philosophy, Politics, and Economics ; the Parks, the Union, the Isis, and the " George "? Hollywood does not.' Roger Dataller, *A Pitman Looks at Oxford.*

SNOBBERY WITH VIOLENCE, by Count Potocki of Montalk
(Wishart, 1/-).

Snobbery With Violence is an account of the author's experiences in Wormwood Scrubs prison, whither he was consigned for
six months by Sir Ernest Wild for the technical publication, by
submission to a printer, of some manuscript verses, alleged by the
prosecution, and found by the jury, to be ' obscene.' Some of the
incidents related in this pamphlet are not unentertaining, but what
is more interesting to the general public is the legal nature of the
crime for which this unfortunate writer was awarded a considerable
spell of imprisonment, for a first offence without the option of a
fine (the sentence has, I believe, been criticized in some quarters
as erring on the side of severity), and which almost any practitioner
of letters, in the present unsatisfactory state of the law on the
subject, might find himself convicted of, though innocent of any
intention of transgressing the strictest canons of civic virtue. The
power of the courts to punish the publication of an obscene libel—
that is the communication, if only to a single person, not being a
spouse, of any obscene, but not necessarily defamatory, document—
is derived not from any legislative enactment, but from an authority
assumed by the Star Chamber, and, on the dissolution of that
tribunal, successfully claimed by the Court of King's Bench, to be
the *custos morum* of His Majesty's subjects.

The legal definition of ' obscenity,' by which judges are guided
in cases of this kind, is nearly as unsatisfactory as the legal conception of what constitutes ' publication.' This definition, the author
of which was Chief Justice Cockburn, is as follows : ' The test of
obscenity I think is this, whether the tendency of the matter charged
as obscene is to deprave and corrupt those who are open to such
immoral influences and into whose hands such a publication may
fall.' What meaning should be attached to the words ' deprave '
and ' corrupt,' how the tendency of a given publication to produce
such effects is to be gauged, and what kind of persons are ' open
to such immoral influences ' belong to that esoteric class of knowledge that is locked within the breast of the judiciary, and to which
the layman has no opportunity of access, except as a result of
a deliberate or accidental infringement of its provisions. In other
words, the position with regard to obscenity is this: the ordinary
man has no means of knowing what he may or may not say in

writing, but if he makes a mistake, God help him ! That, quite apart from the outrageous and barbaric conduct of the authorities in connection with the works of Joyce and Lawrence, to mention only two notorious instances, is why a good many sane and respectable people are not altogether satisfied with our present law of obscene libel.

GILBERT ARMITAGE.

INVITATION TO POETRY, by G. Baseden Butt (Howe, 3/6d.).

THE ADVENTURE OF POETRY, by Frank Kendon (Black, 2/6d.).

ENGLISH PROSE, by John Brophy (Black, 2/6d.).

Hundreds of such unwholesome pretty booklets are continually being produced ; the identical stale and sickly mixture (tinned milk and water) noted in *Scrutiny* No. 2 is inexcusably served up again. The *Invitation to Adventure* which begins with Milne ends inevitably with the Discovery of C. E. Montague and Walpole, and these guides will infallibly be recommended by the Junior Book Club—for the literary racketeers, like the brewers, believe in catching them young. The only excuse for reiterating their futility here is to remind the responsible how completely the most important part of education is in the hands of the uneducated, energetically fixing children for life at emotional adolescence ; and how useless the assistance well-intentioned people like Mr. Brophy receive from their environment. As his last chapter indicates, his book would have been useful if he had had anything of a literary education.

D.T.

THE GESTALT THEORY, by Bruno Petermann (Kegan Paul, International Library, 15/- net).

Not a book that need be read by everyone interested in psychology. But it ought certainly to be read by anyone who finds himself making explanatory use of gestalt notions or taking them as a framework for his thinking. A full technical exposition of the theory is followed by a close critical examination, ending in a rejection of the gestalt psychologists' fundamental claims. A concluding section demonstrates the concealed 'metaphysical allegiances' to which the theory is committed, and through which, according to Petermann, it is rendered finally untenable. It is a laborious book to read, partly on account of its thorough treatment of technical matters, but largely because of the needless unwieldiness of its language.

THE CHILDREN WE TEACH, by Susan Isaacs *(University of London Press, 3/6d. net).*

A book whose excellences may not be recognized by those for whom it is intended. It is based on articles that appeared in *The Teachers' World.* In simple conversational language it offers teachers, especially those in primary schools, indications of the most recent psychological (but not psycho-analytic) investigations of childhood, and brief summaries of the more familiar work. Besides tending to induce general enlightenment in one's dealings with children is has the merit of keeping reasonably close to real situations and frequently offering practical suggestions. But its easy presentation of the subject, highly simplified yet not patronizing, may well deceive those who have 'done psychology' in their training college into supposing that nothing new has been said.   D.W.H.

ANNOUNCEMENT

CULTURE AND ENVIRONMENT: THE TRAINING OF CRITICAL AWARENESS, by F. R. Leavis and Denys Thompson *(Chatto and Windus, 3/6d.).*

HOW TO TEACH READING, by F. R. Leavis *(Minority Press; agent, Heffer, Cambridge, 2/6d.).*

HOW MANY CHILDREN HAD LADY MACBETH? An Essay in the Theory and Practice of Shakespeare Criticism, by L. C. Knights *(Minority Press, 2/6d.).*

Since these books are meant to be part of the undertaking represented by *Scrutiny* we merely announce them.

NOTES ON CONTRIBUTORS

GILBERT ARMITAGE, author of *Banned in England* (Wishart) is reading for the bar.

W. H. AUDEN's latest book is *The Orators: An English Study* (Faber).

T. R. BARNES is teaching English.

H. BUTTERFIELD is a Fellow of Peterhouse and the author of *The Peace Tactics of Napoleon* and *The Whig Interpretation of History*.

GEOFFREY GRIGSON, London correspondent of the *Yorkshire Post*, is Editor of *New Verse*.

D. W. HARDING is at the Institute of Industrial Psychology.

J. ISAACS lectures in English at King's College, London. He edited with W. Rose *Contemporary Movements in European Literature* (Routledge).

ROY MORRELL is English Lector at Helsingfors.

A. L. MORTON is familiar to readers of *The Criterion*.

EDGELL RICKWORD was one of the Editors of *The Calendar of Modern Letters*, and has published criticism in *Scrutinies* (Wishart) and also a book of poems, *Invocations to Angels*.

JAMES SMITH is also known to readers of *The Criterion*.

*SCRUTINY is published by the Editors,
6 Chesterton Hall Crescent, Cambridge;
distributed by Deighton, Bell & Co., Ltd.,
Trinity Street, Cambridge; and printed by
S.G.Marshall & Son, Round Church Street,
Cambridge, England.*